A Symphony of Silence

An Enlightened Vision

George A. Ellis

Library of Congress Cataloging-in-Publication Data

Ellis, George Anthony

A Symphony of Silence: An Enlightened Vision

ISBN: 1477459286
ISBN 13: 9781477459287
Library of Congress Control Number: 2012908735
CreateSpace, North Charleston, SC

Cover Design by FosterCovers.com

Dedicated To His Holiness Maharishi Mahesh Yogi

"*What* we have been saying from the beginning of the movement has been unbelievable but it has come to be believed. We have been impossible right from the beginning and we must continue to be impossible because we are raising a voice against suffering which has been considered to be the nature of life. It is our joy to be considered impossible—and it is our greater joy to make the impossible a living reality."

— His Holiness Maharishi Mahesh Yogi

Contents

Foreword

By Arthur John Anderson

DISCREETLY TUCKED AWAY in an indistinct corner of the universe, hidden somewhere amidst the glittering spangle of countless stars within equally countless strata of swirling galaxies, a tiny planet silently spins and orbits in serene obscurity. And, yet, because of this inconspicuous and unassuming planet, the entire universe rejoices. For those of us living on this planet, a long awaited awakening has occurred. We are witnessing the springtime of a new epoch. Powerful currents of knowledge, at first but a trickle, are now coursing through the many diverse rivers of humanity, breaking apart and washing away hard chunks of ignorance from winter's long siege. This thawing of ignorance and the concomitant onset of an Age of Enlightenment gained momentum more than fifty years ago when a holy man from the Himalayas, Maharishi Mahesh Yogi, emerged from silence and, responding to the need of the time, offered the world a simple technique to help restore balance and wholeness to life.

What happened next is what this book is about. It is a brilliant compilation of intimate discussions, interviews, and essays by people who lived when Maharishi lived, most of whom knew him personally, many of whom worked with him closely often on a daily basis, and all of whom grew generously in spirit and love because of him.

The contributors to this book offer an array of beautiful stories, sparkling with insight and experience, that reveal different facets of Maharishi and of his TM movement—which, as he said, is "meant to move." They write not of what they have heard from others, but of what they have known and felt firsthand. Their stories tell of how they interacted with Maharishi, of what they observed and learned from him, and of why he had such a lasting effect on their lives and ultimately on the world. This book will enthrall you, draw you into itself, and, as you will soon see, be hard to put down. You will feel impelled to read just one more chapter, and yet another, and another. And then read them all again.

George Ellis conceived the idea for this book and labored several years to endow it with muscle and marrow, strength and sensibility, and a heart whose pulse permeates every page. The result is a living tribute to Maharishi. It is also, as George envisioned, a legacy to link generations a hundred or a thousand years from now to these first recipients of Maharishi's knowledge who are, in Maharishi's words, the Pioneers of the Age of Enlightenment. They who share their stories here come from many backgrounds and were among the first to break old boundaries and explore the new frontiers of human consciousness that Maharishi opened to them. They are artists, authors, and musicians; scientists, Cenacle Sisters, and civil servants; preachers, professors, and even prisoners—all of whom have been inspired to give to others the gift Maharishi has given to them.

Maharishi saw the world not merely as it is but as it might be, and he gave those around him his vision of possibilities and the means to achieve it. With his TM and TM-Sidhi programs he put forward the formula for world peace in which there would be victory before war—but more than that: for law and order, there would be rehabilitation before crime; for health and wellbeing, wholeness before illness; and for religion and ethics, right action before sin and misfortune. He paid particular attention to all levels of education where his prescription is to expand the knower before inserting the knowledge. Each of these aspirations, which Maharishi patiently nurtured in us, is among the most honorable and altruistic the world has known, and this book helps us steer the ideal course he set to continue his work of transforming possibility into reality.

And, of course, this book contains many stories of personal encouragement that Maharishi gave us. If ever we felt lowly or insignificant in such an enormous universe, as if we were a forgotten speck of flesh on some distant fleck of dust, he reminded us that we are each the pinnacle of creation blessed with an unbounded awareness capable of comprehending within itself the entirety of the universe and more. If ever we seemed overwhelmed by the darkness around us, he taught us not to fight the darkness, but simply to introduce the light, first within ourselves and then to the world. If ever we wondered about our spiritual progress, he brought forth objective scientific methods to demystify, validate, and explain our subjective spiritual experiences. Of particular gratification to me as a Christian has been the manner in which Maharishi's gift of TM is able to foster and enliven the noblest yearnings of any religion. You will find all of this chronicled in these pages.

Having known Maharishi personally or even living while he lived is a privilege, and receiving his knowledge is a gift. But not a gift to keep to ourselves, nor a privilege to be indulged in by a few. It is to be passed on to others who will pass it on to others still who, in turn, will pass it on yet to others until this knowledge is available to all for all time. This book gives impetus to that process, and those who appear in it will continue to be the friends and benefactors of readers in ages to come.

George was the right person to have scored the many voices and melodies within this book into a splendidly crafted symphony. He is indefatigable. He is a man of sizable talents and credentials whose life has been filled with a fascinating assortment of educational pursuits, entrepreneurial ventures, and humanitarian projects. He is also an excellent communicator—both an engaging writer and a gifted orator. He brought all these skills and achievements to the making of *A Symphony of Silence*.

I have known George for more than thirty-five years, and I know that no one else would have attempted or could have accomplished such a monumental tribute to Maharishi and a momentous legacy for ages to come. He knew Maharishi personally and he personally knows each of the contributors to this book. He sought out and found the right balance of diversity that would give it substance and vitality as well as authority and endurance. Simply scan the table of contents and see how the contributors cross the borders of generation and gender, race and religion, education and occupation.

Many books flash for a moment against the horizon like a roman candle and then are gone; but precious few grow and last like the dawn. Every good book, it is said, writes itself—meaning the writer was merely the instrument of an idea demanding to be heard. This is one such book, and it will endure simply because it deserves the acceptance it is destined to receive. Centuries and millennia hence, when people wonder what it was like to have known Maharishi, to have studied under him, or to have worked with him, they will consult *A Symphony of Silence*, as you are now doing, and be delighted to hear from those who were there during the season it all began.

What a wonderful time and place to be alive—and how wonderful it will continue to be. Call it nature, destiny, or divine providence, but the time was right on this tiny planet for Maharishi to appear, for this book to be written, and for you now to be opening it.

Sit back and enjoy the symphony!

Introduction

This field of inner silence is where a person's true Self resides, and he or she experiences their greatness, if you will—it is the gift of life, the great mystery, which is life.

—Paul Horn[1]

Every human being seeks happiness. We seek far and wide to understand the purpose of our lives. From the echoing halls of high security prisons to the quiet sanctuary of an artist's studio, the diverse stories we read here are founded on a common experience: that of inner silence. Each contributor to *A Symphony of Silence* has experienced this inner stillness of Transcendental Consciousness and is sharing it with us through his or her own unique perspective. Each inspires us to discover, or rediscover, our own self-awareness.

A symphony is a harmonious combination of sounds emerging from silence. It is the antithesis of the cacophony that is engulfing humanity. The voices in this book lift the heart and awaken the intellect beyond the dissonance. Their experiences point to the mystery and beauty that is resting within us all.

I have observed that individuals, regardless of circumstances, carry an inner beauty and optimism. However, the pressures upon us of economic survival, political upheaval, health, and education often subvert this innate positivity and generate conflict between people and among cultures. In response to these observations, my passion was to search for solutions that were less obvious, and yet common among all cultures. I was looking for the missing element.

Our global challenges catapult us toward harmony or catastrophe. This has always depended, and will always depend, upon the quality of individual and collective consciousness.

Creating harmony begins with welcoming differing points of view. It progresses by recognizing these differing perspectives as valid. And here we find the missing element: bringing the light of coherent consciousness to remove darkness. Only then can we illuminate the pathway to a more enlightened

---

1 Please see interview with Paul Horn on page 8.

society. The inner light is within us. Each individual has an infinite reservoir of intelligence, creativity, and love, unfolding in an unending process of evolution. Collectively, we have the ability to find creative solutions to all the challenges we meet.

Maharishi Mahesh Yogi, founder of the Transcendental Meditation (TM) program, stated that his intention was to bring a universal and scientific technique that would cultivate the full potential of the individual, and thereby support all traditions of knowledge or systems of belief. This experience of expanded self-awareness is not foreign to us, but depends on the nervous system being free from the stress that restricts our full potential. Glimpses of the experience of inner silence, as well as stories of its unfoldment, are shared from many perspectives, including artists, musicians, philosophers, politicians, scientists, religious leaders, and prisoners. Their stories describe how they developed their own experience, and how they made it available to enrich the lives of others.

The underlying thread of *A Symphony of Silence* is the experience of uncovering the ineffable power within. The experience of transcendental stillness gives a person a fuller perception of reality. We often look at the world as if through colored glasses, which affects the validity of our perception, distorting our intellectual and emotional evaluations of inner experiences and the objective world. *A Symphony of Silence* transcends distortion and compartmentalization, presenting a unity of understanding and experience. Self-knowledge is the first step of integrating the various disciplines of knowledge and human development. As William Blake wrote, "If the doors of perception were cleansed everything would appear to man as it is, Infinite."

Once this takes place, it is like a seed that should be watered regularly. This experience of stillness facilitates the blossoming of knowledge of who we are, the purpose in our lives, and the infinite connectedness of every component of human existence, nature, and consciousness. The awakening that emerges leads to compassionate and creative solutions to the challenges facing ourselves and society, which are resolved in direct correlation to our state of Self-actualization.

The book traverses diverse dimensions of knowledge, experience, and practical application, and in it we see that the experience of Self-knowledge is accessible to everyone. We see a vista of evolving human life juxtaposed with an enlightened vision. We glimpse golden rays of awakening within society. This affirms the infinite potential that we each have, the realization of which is now on the doorstep of humanity. This is our birthright.

The author hopes that the insights and experiences presented in this book will enliven the majestic reality of human life, helping to resolve the uncertainty that walks beside us throughout our life. May readers come to understand that the special moments in their lives of an expanded state of consciousness can become a permanent reality.

Part I of the book shares intellectual and experiential insights of an enlightened vision, which includes a journey from India to the college campus of UCLA. The wisdom of "following your bliss" echoes through the music of legendary artist Paul Horn and the paintings of Vincent van Gogh and Debbie Arnold, demonstrating the universal experience of unfolding creative intelligence.

In Part II members of the Cenacle Sisters (a Catholic religious order) describe their innocent surrender in wordless prayer. A tender conversation between a father and daughter, graduates of Harvard programs in religious studies, explores spirituality and higher states of consciousness. A Catholic deacon examines Catholicism and TM in service to humanity. A college professor provides brilliant insight into the universality underlying religious experience around the world.

Part III describes an exciting new paradigm for science, presented by David Orme-Johnson, Ph.D., a highly regarded research scientist.

Part IV presents the power of human transformation from the perspectives of justice and leadership, and the human stories representing the dark corners of society, such as Folsom and San Quentin Prisons. Part IV concludes by highlighting the compassion of bringing the private sector to play a role in social transformation by recognizing that "change begins within."

Part V honors the strength of women. Their perspective and inner silence highlight that strength can be as delicate as a snowflake and contain the power of the wind. In Guatemala, a daughter and her family touched the hearts of the Mayan Indians and their children when she introduced the TM technique to orphanages for the nation's abandoned children. She also encouraged government, military, and business leaders in her country to begin a process of change based on human development. In Vermont, a wealthy entrepreneur created a developmental model of an ideal society applicable to developing nations. Beginning as teenagers, twin sisters volunteered in prison work, and years later compassionately involved themselves with projects bringing TM into the prison system. An international singer-composer tells her story of setting aside fame and fortune to become a healer through music. A 92-year-old businesswoman, after practicing TM for more than three decades, delightfully communicates what aging can look like. She has come to clearly experience the gradual integration and stabilization of Transcendental Consciousness in her life.

In Part VI an African-American poet and a social scientist share insights into the value of transcending cultural boundaries, while enlivening cultural integrity. Former defense attorney Candace Martin describes her experiences teaching TM to reduce hypertension in African-American women through an NIH-funded program. In Part VII, several individuals share spiritually transforming experiences that range from early childhood to mature awakenings of inner beauty.

In Part VIII, the author's final reflections consider how light can remove darkness and how enlightenment transforms ignorance. Every generation has aspired to enrich life and to prepare a bright and fulfilling future for its children. The intention of *A Symphony of Silence* is to inspire people to understand that the quiet, special moments experienced throughout their lives indicate a hidden wonder waiting to emerge: the unbounded nature that is their birthright.

George A. Ellis

Part I

Inner Vision:
Music, Literature, Art, and Philosophy

Chapter I

Follow Your Bliss

Paul Horn

I had the opportunity to first meet Paul Horn when he was giving a concert in San Francisco. For decades his music has reflected the inner beauty of his consciousness and compassion for humanity. He was born in New York City and now resides in British Columbia, Canada. Paul is a Grammy Award-winning artist, and has been playing music since he was four years old. In our conversation we discussed some of the highlights of his spiritual journey, which he expressed beautifully in his book entitled Inside Paul Horn: The Spiritual Odyssey of a Universal Traveler. *In 2011 a new CD was released, entitled* The Stillness Inside: The Meditation Music of Paul Horn. *Paul Horn is a kindred spirit whose music gently reflects the universal and mysterious melody underlying life.*

We are traveling in historical time, from the present to the distant past.
We are traveling inwardly as well, through the music of meditation.

— Paul Horn (1990)

George Ellis (GE): You stated in your book that Miles Davis made an observation about people playing too many notes, and the space between the notes being important. The space between the notes is a field of silence and a junction point between notes and impulses of thought. Could you elaborate this insight in the context of meditation?

Paul Horn (Paul): It's a paradox: we are given all this energy, we are given a mind which can think, ponder, try to understand, and the questions that arise in the mind result in an internal dialogue almost continuously in our life. The great value of TM is that it gives me the experience of silence and through my studies with Maharishi I gained the intellectual interpretation of the silence and the process of transcending. The test for evaluating the benefits of transcending is not what experiences you have in your meditation, but how your life is going, and then you will see the value of TM. We come to see the real value is that you get out of the way, and let it happen without effort. You experience the silence, and in that silence when the mind can be still, even for a few seconds, we transcend and that experience is a personal experience; it is the experience of deep silence where all the potential is located—the field of unlimited potentiality.

GE: I am wondering how you correlate your experience in music and your meditation, particularly the concept of experiencing the space between notes. For example, you started playing the piano at 4 years old, and throughout your life, before meditating, music must have given you some experiences and insight into this transcendental experience. Is that correct?

Paul: Certainly I did not view it that way or think in those terms when I was 4 or many years after that, but that is right—the experience of being quiet.

GE: I read your beautiful book, *Inside Paul Horn: The Spiritual Odyssey of a Universal Traveler,* and you say: "We are traveling in historical time, from the present to the distant past. We are traveling inwardly as well, through the music of meditation." In the book you tell the story of your own life and journey. Could you share the essence of what you expressed in that book? What were you trying to communicate to the reader?

Paul: Music is organized sound. Sound is the basis of creation. The whole universe is comprised of sound. Music, being organized sound, is the vehicle through which you travel as a musician—and everyone relates to music in whatever way. Our essence is sound, the vibration, which is music— organized sound, organized vibration. In all the travels I have done, I do not think I have met anyone who does not enjoy music in some form because it is in our basic nature; it is what we are composed of—sound. I believe the value of music is that it allows us to transcend the thinking process. If you really get into the music, people have a transcendental experience, they lose themselves for a few seconds, maybe a few minutes, maybe even longer, and that is silence. People who practice TM are comfortable with that silence, but normally most people do not experience it from the time they wake up in the morning until the time they become unconscious at night, and place the head on the pillow. There is always motion, thought, or something going on. We need to get to a point where we can experience deep silence without fear. The unique experience of deep inner silence can make a person who is not familiar with it insecure and ask themselves—what do I do with it? A person becomes insecure with silence because they are accustomed to something going on all the time, and find themselves alone with his or her self, and questions—what do I do, and what is this experience? It is important to have a qualified person provide guidance in these areas because it is uncharted waters for most people to consciously be moving in and out of the silence. The paradox is to get out of your own way, and see the value in our daily lives. The experience of transcending into the silence and eliminating fear through knowledge requires a guide, a master, or a teacher to make you feel safe when you move into this unfamiliar area. This field of inner silence is where a person's true Self resides, and he or she experiences their greatness, if you will—it is the gift of life, the great mystery, which is life. We need to stand still, be quiet, and let these feelings emerge, and appreciate and value them. I believe everyone has these experiences sooner or later while watching a sunset, having a walk by the seashore feeling the warm sand under your feet, the sun on your back, and the glory of it all—most of the time we are too busy for this. We are fortunate to have a technique available where you go into the quiet, unafraid, and know intellectually the value of what you are doing. As a result we see the experience and the benefits of TM in our own life manifesting in terms of experiencing and understanding the process of developing inner silence in activity.

GE: Did you experience this inner silence prior to meditating?

Paul: Probably I did without intellectually knowing, because it was related to music. I fell in love with sound, which is music, and it reshaped my life; it made me aware of abstractness—music is abstract. It is the most abstract of all the arts.

GE: Why do you believe people are afraid of silence, and how does it affect musicians?

Paul: It is uncultivated territory for most people. Most of us are subject to the waking, dreaming and sleeping states, and that is life. A conscious awareness of the experiencer normally is not present in these states of consciousness. We are experiencing objective reality all the time and our senses are bombarded during the waking state, they are lost in the dream state, and then unconsciousness in deep sleep—you run out of conscious thoughts. I think we find eventually through our lives when suffering sets in, in its own way that something is missing—I do not believe we intellectualize on that issue. For example, we can have good health, a roof over our head, food on the table, and the basics are covered. Additionally, maybe we are succeeding in what we want to do in life; whatever our goals are we are moving in that direction, and yet an inner voice is asking—why am I not happy? That is what happened to me one day. However, I was fortunate to meet Maharishi and went to India to explore the answer to this critical question.

GE: When did you learn TM, and how did you arrive at that decision?

Paul: I was always interested in philosophical issues, and mainly—what is the underlying mystery of life? My wife Ann Mortifee just finished a book which is out now, called *In Love With The Mystery*. If everything is going well in your life and you are moving toward your goals and succeeding, then how come you are not smiling from ear to ear 24 hours a day? I think that unhappiness and suffering can be a catalyst that pushes a person to say: "I better look into something." Suffering can be on so many levels, but basically it would stand for not being fulfilled—that was my experience. I was looking in the mirror one day in my early thirties, and reflecting that I am achieving all the goals I set out to do, and I am not happy. How come I am not smiling from ear to ear? I had been reading about spirituality, human development, and meditation. I also tried to sit down and meditate on my own with minimal success, and at that time Maharishi appeared in my life.

GE: Where did you first learn TM and when did you meet Maharishi?

Paul: That happened in the early sixties, around 1964. I had been reading about meditation without success; I thought this is difficult and not for me. I met some old friends I had not seen for a while; they were a couple and seemed very happy. I posed the question, what is going on here? They responded they had been meditating. I said, that is interesting because I have been reading about it, tried it myself, and it does not seem to be an easy thing to do. They explained the benefits of TM, and there was a teacher in Los Angeles who would come and teach when there were enough people in that area to learn. There were not many TM teachers in those days. I learned TM and I started to feel good, but no lights went off and then I heard that Maharishi was coming to town to give some public lectures and be in Los Angeles for a while. In those days Maharishi traveled around the world once a year to expand the knowledge of his teaching.

I met Maharishi because I was meditating and felt comfortable with good benefits from the TM practice. However, I did not appreciate the subtle positive influence the TM technique was having on my life until I stopped meditating for a little bit because I was on the road and playing music, in Las Vegas and other venues. I got into my old habits again, and I was not meditating. When I came back to Los Angeles about a month later I found myself leaving my bags by the front door—I am still leaving my bags by the front door—sitting down on the coach, and spontaneously starting to meditate. A little voice in my head said "If you do not do this every day for the rest of your life you are going to die," and that was the catalyst for me (mutual laughter). The impression was very strong. The contrast of practicing the technique, not doing it, then coming back to it made me realize the profound value. The process of transcending is subtle, fireworks may not go off right away, and a person may question the benefits, but the value is in the person's experience in his or her daily life: sitting down, closing the eyes, and transcending. Maharishi emphasized we normally do not talk about experiences during the process of TM because it is so personal; a person does not judge the success or value of TM during the practice, just do it and "the proof of the pudding is in the eating." I saw how my life was going, and that was really clear. Shortly after that experience Maharishi came to town, I met him and it was wonderful. I decided to go to India, so did my friends, the man and the wife who were the catalysts for me to learn TM.

My trip to India was fantastic, in fact even better for me because this was a Teacher Training Course. I want to back up a little bit because you just do not pick up and go to India to be with Maharishi. I asked my friends how I could arrange to go to India. Maharishi was coming to town and I went to see him. I mentioned to him that I would like to go to India. Maharishi asked some basic questions such as how long I had been meditating. I had been meditating only three months and the meditators in the group, who were preparing to travel to India, had been meditating three years or more. In my mind I believed this was a lost cause. I mentioned to Maharishi that even though I had been meditating a short time I have experienced fantastic changes happening. I said to him, I believe if I could be in your presence a little longer, and if you would allow it, it would be just magnificent. Maharishi asked if I was married, and what did I do in life. I tried to explain a freelance musician to him (laughter) and it was not so easy. I told him I was divorced and I had a couple of children; he asked who was going to take care of the children while I was gone. I mentioned to Maharishi that I was a responsible person and they will be taken care of, they will be OK. Maharishi was trying to check out that I was not just running away and that everything will be OK. Then there was a long silence and Maharishi stated OK it will be good that you come, but do not expect anything (laughter). Then I said that is good advice. "Don't expect anything" are good words—if you live your life like that it will be pretty good.

I went to India and everyone was concerned about becoming a teacher, but I had never thought in those terms. I just wanted to be near Maharishi, and it was an amazing experience meditating under his protection. Deep meditation in India in those early days with Maharishi could be long hours. Little by little we were able to meditate longer hours, sometimes days at a time and I had an epiphany, something happened and it changed me.

GE: When you say you had an epiphany, what do you mean?

Paul: I experienced a perception of Unity Consciousness often expressed as: I am That, you are That, all this is That. Yes it was an awakening. In those days you could sit for long periods of time in deep inner silence. The way we did it then was that you worked up to it because there was too much stress in a person's nervous system and you could not just sit for a long time at once. After a month, little by little individuals increased the time. In the morning, a couple of hours, and again in the afternoon a couple of hours, and then eventually you would meditate all morning and all afternoon. You did not have to, but the time was set aside to do that. Little by little it became more comfortable to sit in deep inner silence for a long time. If you became tired you just kept your eyes closed and switched between the bed and the chair. Someone would bring you an apple, a piece of bread, and some tea once or twice a day, whatever you wanted. You would tell someone that you will be meditating for a while—it was quite wonderful. I did it for 5 days once and then someone said, "Maharishi wants you to come out now" (laughter).

GE: Did Maharishi meet with everyone every evening on those courses?

Paul: We did meet in the morning and the evening with Maharishi and time was set aside for meditation. It was quite magnificent.

GE: You were in India in 1967 and went back in 1968 when the Beatles, Donovan and other artists were there. How was the 1968 course?

Paul: It was very different, and I am glad I was there the year before because it was quiet. Maharishi was not a household name all over the world. Just a few people knew about him. The year before, there were only 35 people there from 12 different countries. It was quiet. The world was not up in the trees with photographers.

GE: Was Jerry Jarvis there?

Paul: He was, and he was the instrument for me becoming a TM teacher because he talked to Maharishi when everyone was becoming teachers. I was not the least concerned with any studying because it was never my intention to become a teacher. Jerry communicated to Maharishi that there was such a big movement with the students at UCLA and Berkeley and he needed some help. The people on the 1967 course did not include many from the United States: it was a quiet time. Jerry suggested maybe Paul could become a teacher because he is younger—I was in my mid-thirties. Furthermore, Jerry remarked that many of the students knew me because I was a well-known jazz musician. I became a TM teacher, helped Jerry initiate people, and I loved it. There were so many students and we were initiating about 8 hours a day, 7 days a week in Los Angeles. Jerry and I would travel to Berkeley and follow the same routine, and then return to Los Angeles to continue the process of teaching people to meditate. I was not playing much music. I did not miss it at all, I was really enjoying teaching TM, and I was very happy.

GE: That period of time after the epiphany in India and teaching all those people TM—it must have had a wonderful effect on your consciousness.

Paul: I was never happier or feeling more fulfilled, comfortable; I was just enjoying. I guess I was a type-A personality. I was driven to be a musician and pursue my music. This desire for greater fulfillment motivated my trip to India and being with Maharishi. I was successful in achieving my life-long professional desires. Nevertheless, prior to India I asked myself why I was not feeling fulfilled and smiling 24 hours a day. These reflections propelled me into searching, which led me to Maharishi and the whole story so far that I have been telling you.

GE: Did the albums *Inside* and *Cosmic Consciousness* come after your time in India?

Paul: *Cosmic Consciousness* came as a result of my first trip to India. I went back to New Delhi and recorded those albums.

GE: What was the back-story to that beautiful picture of you with Maharishi and the Indian musicians?

Paul: We were in Kashmir and Srinagar. This was the third Teacher Training Course Maharishi had given. It becomes very hot in India—Maharishi said let's go somewhere where we can enjoy. We went to Dal Lake located at a high elevation and it was beautiful. The picture was taken on the roof of the houseboat. During my time in India I expressed to Maharishi that I would like to do a documentary on him and what I had just experienced with him in India when I returned to Los Angeles—he said to go ahead and see what happens. I organized a film crew and we went back when the Beatles were there, not to film the Beatles, but Maharishi. I did not know the Beatles would be there. Of course that fact became news all over the world—the film people became excited and I made it clear that this was not a film about the Beatles. I wanted it to be a film of the experience I had the previous year with Maharishi and the phenomenon that is taking place. Unfortunately, the film was not completed because the situation was too chaotic. However, there is 100,000 feet of footage of Maharishi that the TM movement has somewhere in their archives. Alan Waite was a producer with me.

GE: Paul, I bought the album *Cosmic Consciousness* and I loved the picture on the cover of your album with you and Maharishi on Dal Lake, it is so beautiful. When did you do *Inside the Taj Mahal?*

Paul: It was the year when the film crew was there. We had a 16-man crew and one of the location sites was the Taj Mahal. I had originally gone into the Taj Mahal to record it as a memento just for myself. When I came back to Los Angeles I played it for some friends, and they enjoyed it because it was a great

Maharishi on Dal Lake with musicians including Paul Horn (far right)

sound, which I knew it was from the previous year—that is how all that came about.

GE: That album sold a million copies, I believe.

Paul: *Inside*, yes.

GE: So destiny is interesting, isn't it Paul?

Paul: Very interesting!

GE: You go over to India with a pure heart and good intentions to film Maharishi and your gift is *Inside the Taj Mahal!*

Paul: Yes and the film that I wanted to produce on Maharishi did not turn out.

GE: I heard you have a new album coming out in September?

Paul: My wife Ann organized the new album. Ann took my various albums and listened to them; she pulled out the ones she liked, and put them together. It was not an easy task, but Ann did a wonderful job. I am happy with what she accomplished. She put together the music in what she felt would be a good sequence, various tracks from different albums, which was a challenge because they are all so different and yet the album, *The Stillness Inside: The Meditation Music of Paul Horn*, sound like they belong together.

GE: I saw a photograph of you playing music to a whale. I can imagine that must have been an extraordinary experience, playing music to a killer whale that seemed to love it (http://www.obmg.com/timeline/paul-horn-and-haida.html).

Paul: I moved to Victoria, British Columbia, Canada with my two boys, who were 10 and 13 at the time. I was divorced and had obtained custody of them and moved to Canada, where I had visited a couple of months previously and thought "This is it." In British Columbia there was an aquarium that had two killer whales. My neighbor owned the aquarium and we became friends. A researcher was conducting experiments on killer whales trying to measure their intelligence. One of the elements the researcher wanted to explore was music, how would they respond to music, and in what way. I just became a part of the experiment; they asked me to come down and play my flute to see what happened.

I was with the trainers on the feeding platform playing my flute. There were a male and a female whale; at first I was not certain what was going on because they were swimming around individually, and spending a moment or two in front of the feeding platform, and then swimming off again. One of the trainers suggested I do what they did as trainers, which is called reinforced normal behavior. When the whales came and stayed with me, I would play the flute, and when they would leave, I would stop playing. The researchers wanted to observe if the whales came and stayed longer because they were interested in the music; otherwise we would not know.

I did that and it worked. When they swam away I would stop playing the flute, and when they came back I started playing. Sometimes they would stay longer, which indicated that they had an attention span and they were interested. I continued participating in the research and the National Film Board came out and filmed the process—it became news all over Canada. The story highlighted that these whales responded to music and were very intelligent. It affected me too, because when I was playing music for the whales my head was in an entirely different place. I was not thinking in any musical terms at all; it was my way to communicate feelings to them. I knew we were conversing through the sound of music. I got a sense for their consciousness and believed they were intelligent beings in many ways, and I was feeling it, but unable to articulate it. The music was just feelings coming out, so whatever notes I was playing in my head—not thinking about any of those notes I was playing; it was an interesting experience for both of us.

GE: Paul, in one of the videos it appeared that the killer whale had kissed you?

Paul: Well he did, but that was in another aquarium.

GE: How did that happen?

Paul: That was an aquarium outside of San Francisco—by that time the word had spread that I played flute to whales (laughter). The aquarium staff asked me to come down and play, so I said sure. The whale was used to moving back and forth when he was being fed. However, when I started to play the flute the whale was not being fed; the reinforcement was tied to the music. I knew the music was in some way communicating on a nonverbal level my feeling of respect and appreciation.

GE: The whales communicate through sound.

Paul: Exactly.

GE: This must have been extraordinary.

Paul: It was.

GE: This is such a beautiful story. When I saw that and I watched the whale almost turn on his back as you were playing for him—it was amazing.

Paul: That was very sweet; there were two whales there, a male and a female. The trainers isolated the female in a smaller area of the pool and the male was the one out there. The male whale would go back and forth to tell his girlfriend, who was held in a little pen, that he was not abandoning her. He seemed to be saying "hi" to her, and informing her that the music was interesting, as he would come and listen to the flute, and then go back and see the female whale. It was very sweet to observe, at least this was my interpretation.

GE: The experience with the whales reflects the universality of intelligence and love, which I believe was expressed in those moments you articulated so beautifully. How do you think that the experience of transcending impacts your music?

Paul: I came to a place where I was more comfortable and interested in doing solo concerts. My music became different—quieter. I love jazz. I was surrounded by jazz musicians and the art of improvisation that was revived in the 20th century under the name of jazz, and now it is the 21st century. During the time of Bach and Mozart they all improvised. However, it dried up, and for some reason classical musicians stopped including improvisation as part of their training. Jazz came along and used the art of improvisation, and I was always interested in that. It is freedom; you express yourself through the language of music.

GE: Unless an individual plays a musical instrument he or she may not fully understand the internal influence on our consciousness. How do you define your experience when you are playing with a group of people and you all start to ride the same wave? Although the group is made up of individuals there is a synchrony where the individual members seem to share one consciousness. Can you describe that experience—is it transcendental for you?

Paul: Yes, I would think so, that is why I have had my own groups in the past. Somehow like souls gravitate as much as the music because you are philosophical and on the same wavelength as far as enjoying delving into the mysteries of life. The band members would have interesting discussions along the way as we were traveling through the different countries. The relationship in the group reflects in the music, which is hard to articulate, but there is a feeling among us as a group, not just the music.

GE: Many artists struggle because of their sensitivity, and they go through so many troubled times because of their sensitivity, and then they become confused, thinking that they have to suffer to be creative. How do you interpret that perspective?

Paul: I do not know logically if you could equate the two, but I do not think you have to suffer to be creative. I do not think many people can go through life without some kind of suffering. It does not have to be material suffering; it can be emotional, breakdowns and confusion, all kinds of things. We are here to learn—it is a big school. Some kind of suffering forces you to ask what you are really here for, and that's an individual consideration.

GE: I believe your music lifts the human spirit. Just like that beautiful story of the whale—it brings people to a new feeling level. At this point, what is behind your motivation in creating music?

Paul: Thank you, music has been an instrument of pleasure throughout my life. I was fortunate that I could make a living with it and do what I loved to do. I often talked about the joy of music when I used to go to schools, high schools in particular. Many of the students wanted to go into music, but their parents and teachers did not support it because they would often say: look, it's an insecure career, and how are you going to make a living? I started music because I loved it and that is what I shared with the students. Just go for what's in your heart. Follow your bliss, and do not be afraid to do that. If you cannot make a living playing music then you wind up not making a living through that art form, but there are other benefits. If you find you need to make a change, you make a change. Don't live life with fear of failure. That is not what life is about anyway. Follow your bliss and give it a try.

GE: How do you feel regarding the connectedness between your consciousness, your breath, and the sounds that you put out?

Paul: When I am playing I am usually in another place and always have been. That is why I love improvisation. Although I have had a lot of schooling, it started as a child with an innovative approach to music, and remained with me throughout my professional career—that is the essence of jazz: it's the art of improvisation. I prefer to use the word transcend when I play the music, especially when I am improvising. If you are playing music that you memorized and then have to perform it, obviously you are thinking in terms of not making mistakes—all of that disrupts the flow of the music. That is why I love improvisation, because none of that is there. I am not afraid to make a mistake, there is no mistake, this is what I believed in that moment, and I am using the language of music to express how I feel. I think any musician who does not have that in his or her experience on the road to becoming a musician is strictly classically trained—you don't improvise—and he or she is missing an important part. I just show up and play, I do not worry about right or wrong, if anyone is going to like me or not, or if the critic is going to like it or not like it. Transcending is exactly what I was doing. If you are improvising and involved in the music then it takes you somewhere; if you are playing a piece of music that you have memorized, right or wrong will exist. For example, if you do not play a particular note at a specific time, then you will have made a "mistake" and you do not want to make mistakes.

GE: You have created beautiful music and lived a magnificent life.

Paul: I have been fortunate.

GE: Your music is transcendence in action. The essence that I feel and see in your music is thoughtless, wordless Being. Your life has been a platform for uplifting humanity. Do you have any thoughts you could share in that regard?

Paul: I never thought of it in those terms, using the word platform. If my life could be an example of following your bliss then that would be good. We are all different. We are all here following our karma. We are hoping to graduate, the sooner the better, and move on, by becoming enlightened, and aware of the deep value of life. We are here to learn and to help others. My book, *Inside Paul Horn: The Spiritual Odyssey of a Universal Traveler,* was written 20 years ago. I was thinking about it the other day. When someone writes a biography, which I was asked to do, it is normally toward the end of your life. Well it is 21 years later and I am still around. The last 20 years are not much different from the first. I would hope that others would find the courage to follow their bliss, which is an essential message in my book. It is never too late; a person needs to look into his or her heart and ask the question: what do I really want to do? The answer to the previous question will define an individual's purpose in life because that will come from within.

If you have a deep feeling for something, then do it and follow it. It is not so much in a person's success or lack of success, but what you learn along the way. We are all in school, and we are supposed to graduate at some point.

Maharishi said value your human life, don't waste it! Part of not wasting it is following your bliss because that is telling you where you are supposed to be. If you see and feel the world you will be successful in serving others. If you want to be of service, you need to see the great gift of life. "They also serve who only stand and wait" is a wonderful saying. Just take a moment to be still, use your senses and look out there in the world; it would be nice to experience the stillness in a park, nature, down by the seashore, a lake, or something that is beautiful. Move away from the hecticness, take a breath, and breathe in and breathe out through your nose; just hear life and realize that someday you are going to do that, but you will not be able to breathe in. Our time here is limited, and you need to be still in order to have that thought, let alone that experience, which will add to your happiness and effectiveness in life.

You have to take a picture of yourself and appreciate and value who you are—you have to appreciate what is there. If you do not have that appreciation, you are sort of lost. It has nothing to do with what you are doing professionally in life, but it is more about the value of the gift of life itself, and to try and get out of the way—TM helps that to happen. After a while you do not have to think about it because you are appreciating the gift and the value of life automatically. You do not have to be an old man or woman to see and get the picture. The only question is why I am here, and pursue this as a gift.

I have one more chapter to add to my book, which is 20 years later and I do not know if I have any more to say other than I have met my soul mate, which is just wonderful, with Ann; it took my whole life to find her. It is fortunate if you can meet someone where you never argue, never have any fights, and never go through those things that you do when you are younger, and enjoy a relationship based on respect and appreciation. That is a great gift; it took me a long time to gain that experience, and I am having it right now. If you are fortunate enough to meet your soul mate, that is astonishing. If not, you travel on the path alone; I did that for many years, too. Either way, life is an unbelievably precious gift. That's about it, George.

GE: That is beautiful, Paul.

Paul: I really look forward to your book, and I am proud to be a part of it.

GE: I am honored to have had this conversation because it is all about love. This was a pleasure and a joy for me.

Chapter II

Literature and Self-Reliance

Rhoda Orme-Johnson, Ph.D.

Rhoda Orme-Johnson was one of the founding faculty members of Maharishi International University (MIU), which is now called Maharishi University of Management (MUM). She holds an undergraduate degree from Vassar College where she studied Mathematics and Philosophy and has an M.A. and Ph.D. in Comparative Literature from the University of Maryland. Rhoda taught at MUM for 19 years. She was Chair of the Department of Literature and Languages and supervised programs in literature, writing, drama, French, Spanish, and professional writing. She transcribed and wrote the general introduction to The Flow of Consciousness, *a collection of lectures by Maharishi, which provides profound insights into the processes of writing, reading, and teaching literature. She edited the volume with her colleague Susan Andersen, and wrote the introduction to the lectures on literature, summarizing how Maharishi viewed the mechanics of literature. She followed her academic achievements with a successful and prosperous business career. Dr. Rhoda Orme-Johnson is committed to facilitating the creation of an enriched humanity on a continual path to becoming better men and women.*

Philosophy was my interest from a teenager. I wanted to know what life and what God was all about. I had issues with God because I wondered what kind of God would create a world with so much suffering. It started when I was a child in Sunday school, and my teacher said that God hardened the heart of the Pharaoh so he would not let our people go. I raised my hand and asked, what do you mean? Why didn't God make the Pharaoh a nice person? I did not receive a satisfactory answer and soon persuaded my father that Sunday school was not for me. However, I read widely in works of religion and philosophy during my teenage years and it continued to be a larger abiding interest of mine.

I majored in mathematics because I was good at it and it was fun for me. My father was not college educated and as a young man he worked hard at physical jobs. When he attended night classes and entered the warm classroom after working all day in the cold, he just fell asleep. He knew he could not do it. He could not acquire an education and a better job, but he wanted his children to go to college. He wanted me to learn something practical and important so I could earn a good living.

Vassar is a liberal arts college and we did not really understand what that meant at the time. It does not offer degrees in engineering or any practical areas; nevertheless, I majored in math, which my Dad thought was wonderful. Neither of us knew that you needed a Ph.D. in math to obtain a professional job. Math without a Ph.D. does not automatically lead to a good job. I did it for my father, even though I preferred philosophy and literature and took all my electives in these areas. When I graduated I did manage to secure jobs in practical areas, with the engineering group of the New England Telephone Company, and after that in computer programming in Washington, DC working on abort trajectories for the Apollo project. However, my real love was literature. My career in literature started when I was working in DC and began going to graduate school in comparative literature.

Regarding TM—if it had not been for my husband David, I may not have learned to meditate. He took me to a lecture on TM and I was not impressed. It promised a lot, but there was no proof, no scientific research. How did I know it was the real thing? But David wanted to learn, because he had seen the proof in an old friend who had started, so I said, "OK, you learn and I will see what happens to you." David learned the TM technique, and I immediately observed dramatic changes in him. I recognized the value, and I learned a few months later, when the next TM teacher came to town. To me, a purpose-driven life is necessary. I need a purpose. I do not engage in random behavior. I do not know how to have fun very much. Once I started TM, I saw that it was changing me, and thus it intersected with another major interest in my life, self growth. What propelled me through my teenage and college years was finding myself, growing, evolving, and changing through knowledge and self-knowledge. After I learned TM I had a word for it—evolution, and I had a path for it—meditation. This interconnected not only in the search for truth but growth in truth. They came together.

I have been meditating 41 years. I am nicer. I was mean; I am not so mean now. I was too critical, and I am now more accepting. I feel better, happier, more energized, and I feel the stresses leaving. One example of how this came about: my father died unexpectedly and much too young, several years before I started TM. When I started meditating I would cry in meditation and thoughts in meditation would be that someone near to me died (like a child) and the grief would overwhelm me. It took some time for me to realize that I was healing from the grief of my father's death. It took me a while to figure that out.

Maharishi explains that in meditation the mind does not sustain a mood on an abstract basis; it attaches that emotion to something more recent, or close by. So I attached it to something in the close environment. But that is not where it originally came from; it came from the deep grief over the loss of my father. I realized that I was healing. Now I can think of my father with love, and some regret that he was not able to enjoy my interesting life, but the pain is pretty much gone. So that is the story. A lot of healing has been going on over the years, on many dimensions.

Through TM, ignorance and suffering leaves us quietly; one does not always notice the lack or absence of pain, because it is natural to be happy and healthy. I find the scientific research very heartening and validating of my personal experience. My coherence, my appreciation, understanding, and ability to enjoy life have been growing. No question, I completely appreciate the evolutionary process and results.

I met Maharishi in the summer of 1971, at a course on the Science of Creative Intelligence at Humboldt College in Northern California. We were invited because my husband David had just published one of the first scientific studies on TM. I did not understand what Maharishi was talking about, either experientially or intellectually, or what he meant by Being. Nevertheless, I understood that it was important and I wrote it all down. I recognized I needed to know more of it. I dutifully took notes and David and I would look at each other and shrug, and say that maybe we will understand it later. It was completely new to me, from my materialist and scientific perspective, but Maharishi was so appealing personally. He had such love and humanity. I knew I was sitting in the presence of a great man.

We were later invited to join Maharishi's international staff in Switzerland, based on David's contribution to the scientific research on TM. David had an ability to make the research understandable to ordinary people, which came out when David interacted with Maharishi in Italy on our TM Teacher Training

Course. In the four years we lived in Switzerland, I personally had the opportunity to interact with Maharishi almost daily regarding the various tasks he gave me to do. One major job was to collect course fees from the students who were there to study Vedic Science. He needed someone to evaluate their situations. The task fit my practical, motherly, teacherly nature. It seemed that a lot of the students were in arrears and I was to see if (a) they were living on a promise, (b) there was money available, (c) they were spending money they did not have, and so forth. If the students did not have the money, they needed to go home and make it. If the learners were spending money they did not have, they should stop it. If students had it, they should pay the cost of their room, board, and tuition. But because of me there were soon fewer Ph.D. students. Anyway, Maharishi liked what I was doing and when he saw me riding up and down the mountain from my hotel to the students' housing in taxi cabs he provided a car so I could get around more easily, and he gave me other jobs.

Literature is an engine for self-discovery. When I read and saw how characters lived life, I lived and grew through them. I did not have to commit adultery and throw myself under a train, like Tolstoy's Anna Karenina, but I could see how her suffering resulted in such outcomes.

Regarding creativity, Maharishi said that suffering does not drive creativity. Creativity is an escape from suffering. The artist may be having a miserable time in his or her life and then some impulse comes to paint, or write, and it is so blissful or joyful. The artist moves in that evolutionary flow and it's an escape, a relief, and the artist or writer creates something wonderful. The suffering does not inspire the work or create the work. In fact, suffering interferes with work. We all know that. Suffering is not essential for art, and the best thing you can do as an artist is to get yourself out of suffering. Start meditating and increase your ability to deal with your stresses and enhance your inner happiness. Live a happy, successful, and creative life!

Literature impacts my consciousness and is an engine of self growth. Emily Dickinson said that you know when a poem is good, because it blows the top of your head off. It really does. So it was like that; I experienced in literature a means to evolve. Maharishi explains in the lectures we collected in our book, *The Flow of Consciousness*, how evolution occurs through the writing, reading and study of literature. Self growth comes partly from the knowledge, and the truth in the work of literature. Emotional growth comes through the emotional truth in the work, and from the power of its language. Most important, Maharishi explains, literature swings the reader's awareness from concrete images to abstract ideas and emotions, and the jerks and jolts one's consciousness experiences through these swings cultures and purifies the mind, the intellect, and the emotions, and can lead, in fact, to higher states of consciousness, and enlightenment.

During my readings I experience a sense of going deeper inside, my consciousness becoming subtler and subtler. In the process of experiencing quieter levels of the mind and staying there for some time, I definitely transcend. For example, the other day I was reading in the living room and my husband David was working on framing the wood around the new wall air conditioner. When I finally looked up from reading I noticed he had completed it, and I remarked that it was fortunate that he did not have to cut the pieces the contractor had left and could just put them right up. David was shocked. He told me he had been sawing the wood and then hammering up the frame. How had I not heard that? I looked at the floor, and saw that there was sawdust on the floor. Where have you been? He laughed; he could not believe it. I was deep inside. I was not aware of hearing anything. It has always been like that for me. I start reading and the movie starts rolling. I think this is true for many readers, and also for those deeply involved in research, in solving a mathematical equation or developing a scientific theory. The mind goes inward and lives in the inner depths for some while. It has to be evolutionary; nevertheless, transcending through reading is not as profound as transcending with TM. However, any experience of Transcendental Consciousness is valuable and evolutionary.

I believe that transcending through the TM technique deepened my experience and understanding of literature. Through my experience of transcending during TM I became familiar with slipping inward, and as a result I gained a deeper comprehension of literature than I ever had before. My vision became broader, more comprehensive. I saw that as a teacher, with this knowledge and understanding, I could help others to see more deeply into something, become better perceivers, seers, readers, and experiencers, and become more deeply engaged. That is what I tried to share. I tried to lead my students to see more deeply and take note of what they were seeing. I would give quizzes with questions on what happened, small but important details, and then we would discuss the meaning of those details. I tried to help them become better noticers. I was helping them learn to read literature, and I was sure the evolution would take care of itself.

In the context of academia, I started to work on a book entitled *The Flow of Consciousness* when I was teaching at MIU because it was my job to connect literature and consciousness to Maharishi's knowledge. Maharishi helped the faculty at his new university make these connections by giving lectures with examples of how to do it and how to think about it. We often played the tapes of these lectures to the students, and we all tried to become better readers and literary critics using his knowledge. These tapes were very useful to the students and to the faculty, but they were not easily accessible because they were video and audiotapes that could only be played in a classroom or in the library. For example, accessibility is necessary for scholarship. I am not a musician and when I hear a piece of music, it goes through me like a river and when it comes out the other side I cannot tell you anything about it. I cannot listen like a musician. Even with literature or speech, I cannot fully understand and intellectually process what I hear as well as I can when I can see it, and read it. I have to see it with my eyes to be fully engaged. So I knew that these lectures had to be written down. The students also needed to be able to cite them in a scholarly way and to go back and forth between the literature and Maharishi's knowledge.

I asked Maharishi if I could transcribe these lectures and bring them out as an aid for the students in studying literature. Maharishi thought it was a wonderful idea and gave me the go-ahead. I transcribed all the tapes that my colleague Susan Andersen and I chose, and I have to tell you, it was like sitting with Maharishi again, sitting in the presence of an enlightened man, being drawn into his consciousness, and transcending to subtler levels. I think the reader has this experience reading the transcripts as well.

We put all the transcripts together and I wrote an introduction to the volume. I thought this book might be given to someone's aunt, an English teacher, or a poet who knew nothing about Maharishi and who he was. The new reader needed an introduction to Maharishi, to the TM movement, and Maharishi's major ideas, like states of consciousness. Additionally, there was the scientific research, and topics from physics; therefore, footnotes were needed. I edited and introduced the literature section, and Susan edited and introduced the language section. I regret to say that we finished the book about 17 years ago and I printed 10 copies. I visited Maharishi when he was based in Holland and gave him a copy to approve, but he was busy dealing with governments and other major projects, and a book on poetry and literature could wait.

Some years later Dr. John Fagan, who was inspired by Maharishi to investigate the hazards of genetic engineering, was visiting him in Vlodrop, Holland and while he was waiting to see Maharishi he was asked to wait in a room that Maharishi used for puja (a traditional Vedic ceremony of gratitude). After meditating he began to look around; he saw my book sitting on a puja table and he told me about it when he came back home. This meant to me that Maharishi had given it a place of honor and had not forgotten it. I was very heartened by this news. I mentioned it to Dr. John Hagelin, the head of the TM movement in North America, after Maharishi passed on, that for every physicist we have in the movement we must have 1,000 people more interested in reading about literature.

John Hagelin thought it was a fabulous idea to bring out the book, it was approved, and MUM agreed to print it. The introduction was 15 years old (and quite a lot had occurred with the TM movement over that time), as was the scientific research. I had to bring both of these subjects up to date. I worked on the book for another two years, added an index, and it finally came out in 2010. The lectures in the book date from 1972 to 1976 because those were the years that Maharishi was helping his university get off the ground; he was giving lectures in all the disciplines to help the faculty determine how to teach their area in the light of consciousness. During that period he held symposia and spoke about different fields of study. After the symposia he went on to discuss government and collective consciousness. For literature, art, and music that was a special period in which the relevant tapes were recorded. Soon a book of Maharishi's lectures on art will be available. Another treasure!

I would like to make a comment about the different energy and power of women and literature, although I am not sure I can define it. I derive a certain enjoyment just being around women. There is a comfort level I have found around women, and also in my career I gravitated toward teaching works by women. I had been reading dead white men all my life, and I thought I was one of them. It took me a while to learn, to experience, that I was not. First, I needed to know who I was, and what it means to be a woman, and a woman in society. What I prefer and enjoy most is reading works by women, which

I pretty much always do when I read for myself. I do occasionally read something by a man. I really enjoyed *Driftless* by David Rhodes recently when my book club chose it.

I had an interesting experience regarding the difference in teaching men and women. For a time at MIU the women and men were in separate classes, only the first year students, because the classes were so large. It was a totally different experience. It was so much better to have them separate. When the young students were together there was all this mating, and dating, note passing, flirting, tickling and carrying on with minimal paying attention to the course. When they were separated, the girls, who always did their homework and read the book, would be right there and totally focused. They would have wonderful insights and were marvelously responsive students. The boys, although it was like driving a team of 16 wild horses, were basically there also, and when the girls were not there to distract them, all the wasted energy disappeared. The students became better learners; they focused more deeply on the knowledge.

In the world, women can come into in an area and soften it, but the world can also make women harder. My experience is that having a woman in a power position is not going to change it that much, because that change can work in both directions. What I see is that TM is the experience that can change it. It helps men be better men and women be better women. Both will become better, more effective people. I think the issues focused on by the women's movement—equal opportunity, equal pay and so forth—are important issues. Nevertheless, real change has to come from another place. It is the same situation with civil rights: change has to come from another place. You cannot legislate prejudice away. Consciousness has to change. The legislation is vital, because it creates the opportunity to be with and learn from the feared "other," but real change will only come from a change in consciousness. Look at today's younger generation. They grew up with women in charge. They grew up with kids of all races and orientations, and they see the world differently from how their parents did. Their parents may talk a good game, but inside they are still fearful and prejudiced—I know mine were. Meditation can change that.

Maharishi was aware of the women's and the civil rights movements, but he did not speak publicly about either. He stayed out of the political areas, because he was working in a deeper region. He knew that what you had to do is change a person's consciousness. He was not unsupportive of anyone working for civil rights or the women's movement; he just placed the emphasis on the development of consciousness. It has come to pass that he was absolutely right; only evolution of consciousness can produce lasting change. You can legislate, you can litigate, but real change can only be facilitated through the development of consciousness. Thus, I became less interested in social movements and more interested in consciousness, because that is most profound. I had a professor at Vassar who was very interested in women artists. It opened my eyes in that area. Now when I go to a museum or a gallery I notice all the works by women, pretty much unknown women, who are really good. I believe they were always there, just swept away or forgotten by the men who created the anthologies, what we call the canon of important works. When you read about history you read that women were not in business, that they stayed home. But the real history of it is eye opening. Almost every time a man died without a grown son, his wife took over the business. When fathers needed a level head in the business, the daughter would take over the accounting, but she often did not receive credit for it and took her training on the job. Women have always stepped into these roles, but the history of it becomes lost. When we look back in time we see there is no her-story, just his-story. Nonetheless, women have always been in the deepest areas of society and social change, working behind the scenes if they had to. A correction in this imbalance and injustice, I believe, is happening now.

The rise in collective consciousness being brought about by the large groups of meditators in the U.S. and India is bringing all those situations into the public sight. They are no longer hidden from view. The light is being shown on these dark, hidden areas, and then change is possible. We still have a long way to go. I see the rise of the collective consciousness as supportive to all movements seeking justice and fairness in society.

After my work at MIU, I went into real estate, in which women outnumber men, or at least are as common as men. My boss was a man but it was a very comfortable and welcoming world for me because it was full of successful, vibrant, dynamic women. Several of them mentored and helped me to close my first few big deals. Because of TM, I was flexible, able to learn the business quickly, and not burn out. Women are very good at helping people find a home. Women are interested in homes and so I think people are comfortable with a woman; they are looking for a house to live in and the wife is looking for a kitchen. A woman understands what the wife wants, a place for the children to play, a yard. It is a shoe that fits. For a woman it is a natural situation to help another woman and her husband buy a home. Although, I have to say that most of what I accomplished was to sell resort real estate, second homes, and investment property. People respected my Ph.D. and trusted me on a deep level to be honest with them.

Another aspect of the business that favors women is the erratic pay. If you happen to be married to someone with an income, then your income can come and go but you can still continue. At the time I became a realtor my husband was working on a grant and we lived off his salary and we pretty much invested my real estate money. It was a little slow at first, and then it picked up and we invested almost everything I made. I was very comfortable as a woman entering that business. I did not feel any prejudice or glass ceiling. There is nothing keeping you from making as much money as anyone else, so that was an easy transition. I was always practical, but I did not have any business experience. I had to learn the business and to brand and promote myself. I learned from the women around me and from my experience. It was a dynamic time. The salmon were running and I realized that now was my time. I would be a fool if I were not out there up to my chest in water, wielding my net. I was working seven days a week. I was able to do it, and I felt driven to do it, because I knew this was my moment in time to make money. When we left MIU, now MUM, we did not have much money and very little Social Security, because we were mostly volunteers. I felt nature had provided this opportunity and was supporting me in this new professional activity; because of my daily TM I could keep up the pace.

I worked hard, but I never missed a meditation. Other people around me would become angry or upset because of deals falling through, or difficult customers, but not me. I was calm and I was even. The entire office admired me. They knew I was meditating and they recognized that quality in me, that I had a steadiness. They saw that I rarely lost my temper. I realized I could not have accomplished our economic independence and survived the intensity of that real estate environment without all the years of meditating and being an even-tempered, cosmic soul. My practice of TM allowed me to accomplish what I did in a short time, without burning myself out.

I have been seeking self growth and its practical value was clearly apparent in my business life. I could not have succeeded in achieving my business goals without meditation and the consciousness I had developed. It enabled me to do what I had to do, but it also enabled me to evolve through this very dynamic activity. I grew in self confidence and in other qualities. It was evolutionary for me to work in business at that time of my life. My self-knowledge and self growth continued in that activity, supported by TM. When I finished those hectic years and the market slowed down, I realized who I was and what I could do in the world. You wonder about that when you spend your life cloistered in the academic world.

I was fortunate to spend 20 years to help build MIU, now MUM. However, you do not stand up and say you are going to dedicate the next 20 years of your life to a project. That is not how life works. You wake up day by day, working on project after project, and one day you realize, I've invested 20 years into this project. At the time it was very normal, fun, inspiring, and we could never think of anything better to do with our time and energy. Our young son was always more interested in money, brand names, and having stuff. He would say, why don't you and Dad go out and search out jobs and make a lot of money? I would say, we could do that, but then we would save our money to come back to MIU and round (periods of deeper meditation), and while we are here we have it all. I have spent 40 years in the subtle, transcending to refined states of consciousness. It adds up. The scientists would tell you I have increased coherence of my brainwaves. It has made me a nicer person. I have a more precise intellect, broader comprehension, and I am a better person. Someone asked Maharishi what happens to criminals when they start to meditate. Would they become better criminals? He said they would become better people, and a better person is less of a criminal. I am less of a criminal, I am smarter, I am nicer, and I am more generous. It seems like a small change, to be nicer, but it is not a small issue. It is a very big transformation to become a better person. I cannot think of anything else I would rather be.

Chapter III

Art and Creativity:
van Gogh to Maharishi

Man is not on this earth merely to be happy, nor even to be simply honest. He is here to realize great things for humanity ... Art is not vague production, transitory and isolated, but a power, which must be directed to the development and refinement of the human soul. The artist must have something to communicate, since mastery over form is not the end, but instead the adapting of form to internal significance.

— Vincent van Gogh (Graetz, 1963)

Creativity is the nectar that nourishes our intelligence and sweetens our lives. The artist climbs a hilltop to gain more vision of human capability. The enlightened artist, like the ancient Rishi, urges humanity to climb the mountain and share the vision. The unique value of art lies in its ability to articulate and evoke the full range of consciousness. Maharishi provides a technology to unfold and access the inner reservoir of creativity and intelligence, beyond duality in pure unbounded consciousness. On the practical side, artists, after they learn TM, report remarkable benefits including increased richness of perception, expanded imagination, and effortlessness in realizing ideas. In Maharishi's book *The Science of Being and Art of Living* (Maharishi Mahesh Yogi, 1966), he discusses the experience of speaking from the level of Being. This is an experience that applies to any field of knowledge. It is a unique state of consciousness, with moments of unity, in which everything flows effortlessly—it is a great gift to the artist in particular; it is the centerpiece of the creative process:

> The artist has to be a man of fully developed heart and also fully developed mind. With full development of his heart, his life will blossom in fulfillment, and with full development of his mind, his life will be in harmony with everything around him and should be the quality of his

art. The piece of art should speak of life, should blossom in life, should radiate life, and that life should be in harmony with everything in the environment (SCI, 1972).

The father of abstract art, Wassily Kandinsky, in his book *Concerning the Spiritual in Art*, affirms Maharishi's perception of the purpose of art. Kandinsky believed that art was an expression of internal necessity. Every artist has something that demands personal expression, and as a child of his or her time is impelled to reflect the age and style of that time. Every artist is a servant of art, and this is a constant in all ages (Kandinsky, 1955).

Maharishi, in *The Science of Being and Art of Living*, emphasized the interconnectedness of knowledge with the individual. In my graduate years, I studied van Gogh because I was impressed by his love and compassion for humanity. Furthermore, after exploring Maharishi's insights on the origins of creativity, and reading van Gogh's letters to his brother Theo, I determined that the source of his creativity had nothing to do with suffering. Therefore, it was natural to juxtapose van Gogh with Maharishi because all human beings are connected on the level of pure consciousness. The enlightened Maharishi and the troubled seeker van Gogh share the universal nectar of creativity, but from different levels of consciousness and perception.

Maharishi was permanently experiencing the unity of individual and universal consciousness—the origin of creativity—and van Gogh was seeking to find it through his art. The similarity that I wish to highlight is the compassion for humanity, the guiding force of love that each individual expresses from his unique perspective. The artists and visionaries of every age add their voices to the human choir, and touch humanity as they pass through. The essence of significant art is the unity of ideas and material realization, which fulfills its purpose by touching the soul of another through the senses. Creativity and inspiration interlace with one another and are the quintessence that makes art such an enjoyable and uplifting experience.

Art is an instrument of human transformation because through it we can glimpse the transcendent. The ability of every human being to transcend is inherent, and the vehicles vary. Some methods are more efficient than others in facilitating the process of transcending, such as the TM technique. Art is a process of experiencing a pause of silence between each thought, in which the origin of creativity is hidden. The expressions of art can influence human perception and consciousness like a mandala, a marriage of form, color, sound, and silence in the depths of awareness. The function of art is expressed by Robert Schumann, who declared art should send light into the depths of the human spirit, and is the artist's vocation (Thomas, 1964).

Van Gogh was an expressionist and in every painting he was sharing his visions of life, reality, and his purpose. Van Gogh felt his mission as an artist was to bring solace and love, and to transcend human boundaries and suffering. Artistically he illustrated these aspirations through two famous paintings, *The Potato Eaters* and *Starry Night*. Van Gogh stated:

> "Art although produced by man's hand is something not created by hands alone, but something that wells up from a deeper source out of our soul. Art is something greater than our cleverness or knowledge of science . . . the painted portraits have a life of their own, which comes radically out of the painter's soul" (Graetz, 1963, pp. 209-210).

Van Gogh through the tools of color and form took the observer into his heartfelt compassionate perception of reality and helped him transcend the immediate and grasp the essence. The excellent book entitled *The Symbolic Language of Vincent van Gogh* (1963) highlights the symbols employed by van Gogh to express his experience of Transcendental Consciousness, and his love of using his paintings as instruments to console humanity. Van Gogh remarked in a letter to his brother Theo that:

> Love is something eternal. It may change in aspect but not in essence. And there is the same difference between one who loves and the same person before he loves as between a lighted lamp and one that does not burn. This love is the light of the world in which we live. (Graetz, 1963, p. 19)

The Potato Eaters is an example of this sentiment: at first the painting appears dark, but the longer one looks, the lighter it becomes. The stable-like room with five people sitting around a table eating their supper of steaming potatoes is painted in a greenish-gray color, which produces warmth based in restfulness (Graetz, 1963). Although the figures seem isolated from one another by their glances and gestures, there is one unifying feature—the light of the lamp.

The lamp throws light on everyone in the room and brings out the warming effect of the steam from the hot potatoes and coffee. This was the light of love, which emerged in the silence between each brush stroke, often described by van Gogh as the source of his creativity. The burning lamp is van Gogh's symbol of love, and is the means to console them in their loneliness (Graetz, 1963).

The Potato Eaters

Van Gogh states:

I have already said a few words about humanness. I am not ashamed to say that for my part I have had and always shall have the need to love another creature. I find it something so natural and self understood that I cannot understand that people can usually be so indifferent to one another. (Graetz, 1963, p. 207)

In van Gogh's *Starry Night* his soul reigns in its spiritual transcendental domain and the life of the sky becomes the real life as opposed to the world of humanity. Van Gogh painted himself in the giant cypress trees that unite with the spiraling stars and clouds (Graetz, 1963).

The painting was a self-portrait of van Gogh's quest for transcending the burdens of the world, and experiencing the inner silence of spiritual awareness. Van Gogh's empathy and his attempt to eliminate human suffering were noble.

Starry Night

A contemporary example of the juxtaposition of art and Maharishi's knowledge was observable behind the granite walls of Folsom Prison (Ellis, 1979). For example, the Folsom art program was an attempt at locating the reservoir of creative intelligence described by van Gogh and Maharishi. Art is a silent language experienced in the quiet depths of consciousness and manifest in the silence of the canvas. This silent medium was the instrument whereby captive voices could transcend their physical circumstances by expressing their innermost thoughts and feelings. In listening to the prisoners and observing their visual creations one is deeply moved regarding the value of freedom, and realizes the importance of being loved, and loving. George Hannaford, an art instructor at Folsom, remarked: "Art restores a man's self image as they find that they can accomplish something aesthetic for themselves and others" (Ellis, 1979).

Many artists in contemporary society have had the idea that they are expected to be temperamental and subject to excesses of emotion. Some artists have assumed that suffering and tension are necessary for artistic development, and falsely attributed that perception as the source of van Gogh's creativity. But this thinking is the reflection of those who lack the creative intelligence to express themselves without struggling. When one has less access to the reservoir of creative intelligence, he or she naturally strains. The artists of Folsom refuted the need for suffering—they knew its effect too well. An artist from Folsom nicknamed PeeWee states:

> Art is a way of bringing out one's true being, which results in a sense of accomplishment. If I am tense, that mood comes out in the painting. When you are uptight, you force more and that affects the quality of your painting. I strive for a unity with my work. At times, when painting, I become part of the painting itself. (Ellis, 1983, p. 56)

Marquez, another artist at Folsom and successful painter, remarks:

> Because of tension and stress, it is hard to obtain ideas. Also, due to lack of outer stimuli, originality is difficult to achieve. One problem in being original is due to the lack of inspiration. Thus one's subject is done over and over in different ways, resulting in repetitiveness. (Ellis, 1983, p. 56)

Color can be an avenue for expressing emotions; it is well known in art theory and from common sense perception that more somber colors express and create depressed moods, and brighter colors symbolize joy. Marquez shuts off his outer negative world and chooses the brighter colors to express an emotional effect reflecting a joyous celebration of life, rather than focusing on his present condition. Most of the artists at Folsom were self-taught. Perhaps their accomplishments are a reflection of the understanding that art unfolds because it is a natural organic part of being alive. Even in the midst of human tragedy, the inner joy of life is significant to everyone. The TM program offers to the artist a greater resource from which to draw. The mind is fundamental in integrating our perceptions and feelings; it is essential to intuitive insights. The combination of intellect and feeling enriches imagination, thereby enlivening one's originality. As stress is reduced, energy increases, and an individual naturally comes to all activities more refreshed and alert. It is important that an artist become less bound by his media during his or her creative process. Alertness is essential in order to grasp the intangibles that make a work of art significant.

On the individual level the TM technique, by increasing a person's creative abilities, allows him or her to make maximum use of the environment, both subjectively and objectively.

Van Gogh echoes the universality of this truth—that art is guided by an internal dictation in intuition and quietness. An artist creates because he must. Van Gogh in his passion and love for humanity expressed:

> I sit down with a white board before the spot that strikes me, I look at what I have before my eyes, I say to myself that white board must become something . . . I see in my work an echo of what struck me. I see that nature has told me something . . . I am searching for a great thing . . . I look for the root origin of so many things at the same time. (Graetz, 1950, p. 38)

Van Gogh, because of his experiences of inner creative silence, had insights into the origin of creativity. He is an inspiration as an artist, but he suffered as a man. He had no system to integrate and intellectually understand how that silence could become a permanent feature in his life, which could have minimized his personal suffering. Maharishi has provided a practical tool for every artist and non-artist to enliven and integrate the full value of that inner silence. The experience of a unified field of creative intelligence does not compromise the uniqueness of each individual. Maharishi's simple TM technique allows the blossoming of an individual's full potential.

Chapter IV

Love Lifted Into Light

Debbie Arnold

Debbie Arnold lives in Boone, North Carolina, and her artistic process can best be described as a stream of consciousness. She has produced more than 400 paintings over the last 35 years, expressing fluidity and lightness learned through the years as a watercolorist, which she combines with the ability of acrylics to be layered. The process creates unique paintings with as many as 15 to 20 layers of transparent paint. Debbie remarks that she normally has no preconceived ideas or plans when starting a painting. She presently does not use drawings, models, or photographs, and begins a painting spontaneously with color and texture, but without a subject, employing different techniques. Debbie continues to layer transparent colors and textures to form a veil painting—rendering an effect that is like looking through water (Arnold, 2011). Her accomplishments include several one-and two-person shows, and numerous juried and invitational exhibits. Debbie's paintings are included in several public, private, and corporate collections.

Debbie is a hidden jewel with an inner wisdom and insight into the human condition. Her work, as the work of many artists, is a self-portrait telling the story of an evolving soul. She recognizes her innocent role as a contributor to a better world by unfolding her own inner silence and beauty, and sharing it with the world through color and form. Debbie's art and creativity whisper a message of illumination that the transcendental flow of consciousness is within and accessible to everyone; she creates a visual rendering of its manifestation. Selected paintings have been included in this chapter to highlight her immense talent. Debbie's extensive collection can be viewed at her website: www.arnoldfineart.com

---

Debbie: What is the purpose of *A Symphony of Silence?*

George Ellis (GE): One purpose of the book is to elucidate that the experience of Transcendental Consciousness and inner stillness is available to everyone, and is fundamental to a fulfilled life. We need to find tools and knowledge that can accelerate the process of integrating the inner silence of pure consciousness in our daily thought and action. The TM method integrates the inner stillness of pure consciousness, and breaks the illusion of duality through the embrace of unity. Regarding your paintings, they are beautiful and reflect an evolution of consciousness, and we want to tell that story. From early childhood did you know you wanted to be an artist?

Debbie: Yes, according to my mother, as soon as she handed me anything I would start drawing. Art has always been a part of my life, and I have been passionate and focused. I have had experiences throughout my life of expanded awareness because of my connection with nature, and I believe the first time I thought of it consciously, I was 5 years old. I remember being outside, barefoot, running through the grass and clover. I came inside, and my mother told me I needed to put shoes on because I might step on a bee, and the bees would sting me. I considered this statement one of the most shocking comments anyone had ever said to me, because I knew that the bees and I were friends, and I questioned—why they would sting me? I asked my mother why they would do that because the bees were my friends. The disparity between her viewpoint and mine made me begin to realize how different my world-view was from everyone around me at that time.

Celestial Gardener©

I was born with an innocent sense of spirituality and throughout my childhood experienced joy, connection, and passion. I believe most children share this innocent experience—you are born with this inner reality and then people talk you out of it. As a child it was just there, a deep connection to everything around me, a deep love. I was fortunate to be born into a very loving family. I had a wonderful childhood and support for my art from my parents. My art has evolved through different stages. For example, because of limited resources I used myself as a model for *Celestial Gardener*, which I consider a self-portrait of my inner feelings; it was like putting together a puzzle.

In *Celestial Gardener*, I was thinking about how flowers have their own light, and trying to convey the idea that the flowers were forces in life. I also had an interest in different textures. It was the creation of a subconscious puzzle of textures. Everything was fabricated out of my imagination. Most of my paintings came from my inner inspiration because I did not paint directly from nature. My paintings often were the result of images emerging from within my consciousness. At the time, I was making a transition from watercolors to acrylic. *Celestial Gardener* was a transitional painting where I was learning how to use acrylic as watercolors. I strongly relate to color more than any other component in my art. I do not make color choices consciously. I will sometimes use color in mixtures to convey different feelings. In *Celestial Gardener*, I wanted to convey the feeling of light. For example, there are purples and yellows in the painting, which are subtle; yellow makes purple more purple and purple makes yellow more yellow, and the mixtures helped me to convey the feeling of light. I wanted to make the colors in the flowers and the moon brighter. I have been painting for over 35 years, and I do it both consciously and unconsciously.

GE: Kandinsky (1947) in his book *Concerning the Spiritual in Art* discussed the spiritual power of color and form. What is your experience with color and form?

Debbie: Color is like eating chocolate cake, or smelling a wonderful fragrance; it is a three-dimensional vehicle. I love color; it is a passion.

GE: Color within form creates movement. If you take certain colors such as blue, it will pull the spectator into the painting, and yellow moves outward to embrace the spectator. Van Gogh used color with form as an instrument to express his love for humanity. Color moves in different directions, and according to Kandinsky when you put it into a structure it has different effects.

Debbie: I do not analyze or choose color based on an emotion that I am trying to express. A color chooses me.

GE: If I am interpreting you correctly these colors are emerging from within you?

Debbie: Exactly, my job is to get out of the way.

GE: That is what the legendary musician Paul Horn said about jazz improvisation.

Debbie: I have read some of what he said, and it seems we work in a similar way. I would do things to keep my mind occupied or listen to the radio while I was painting. It sounds strange to people because I was trying to move my individual consciousness out of the way. Does this make sense?

GE: It is not that you moved your consciousness out of the way because you are consciousness.

Debbie: The ego part of myself.

GE: TM is a technique to transcend thought and effortlessly helps the artist to move out of the way. Have you noticed that there are moments during your creative process where there is a sense of non-attachment, and everything is happening almost automatically?

Debbie: Yes, that is the entire point. I have learned through the years to get out of my own way.

GE: The practical benefit of TM for an artist is that it naturally cultivates a different style of functioning of the nervous system. An individual can transcend the boundaries of the senses and become an observer of his or her creative process. If that experience is available during the creative process the artist effortlessly does not create obstacles in the process. The diversions you were speaking about had the intent of accomplishing that goal, but they actually could defeat the objective because they divided the mind and required effort.

Debbie: I had been trying to trick myself into moving my individual ego out of the way.

GE: This is exactly what I was discussing with you when we began our conversation. People complicate the process because they do not understand intellectually that setting aside the individual ego during the creative process can be cultivated to happen spontaneously. TM cultivates higher states of consciousness in which the individual spontaneously witnesses the creative process and activity in general. Higher states of consciousness increase in the artist the experience of refined perception, and identification with a non-changing field of Self-knowledge. In other words, an individual is no longer controlled or dominated by experiences through the senses, and the individual identifies that their true nature is unbounded. That is also one reason your painting *Celestial Gardener* caught my attention; it reflects an inner beauty and a refinement of perception.

Debbie: Many of my paintings are like that and reflect the inner reality from where all of my artwork emerges.

GE: In your website Galleries your paintings are listed under Intuitive, Landscapes, the Feminine Mystique, and so forth (Arnold, 2012). I assume they represent your evolution as an artist. Does the Intuitive artwork represent a unique step in your evolution?

Debbie: The intuitive pieces represent creation without preconception, which is a journey that I have been on for many years. *Celestial Gardener* was a visioning process. It was an idea of a feeling, but it was still a conception; it was pre-conceptualized and formulated in my mind, and then I would deliberately create it.

GE: Nevertheless, it emerged from within you.

Debbie: Yes, but it was a deliberate creation. I posed for the *Celestial Gardener* painting; I drew it, and so forth. They all come from within me. About 10 years ago I stopped painting for some time, almost seven years, because I had a child, and wanted to devote my full attention to my child. I quit because I was obsessed with painting, and when I had a child I wanted to be a good mother. It did not have to be either/or, but it was simply a choice. When I came back to painting, I decided I could find a balance. At first, when I began to paint again, I believed I was out of practice because the painting seemed to be taking over. I would have a conception or an idea about what I wanted to create, which was a deliberate creating process. However, I found the painting process was taking unexpected directions from my original idea or feeling. The painting process was moving in a direction that I was not consciously planning. It appeared that I was driven by my inner Self to let go, but at first it did not feel like a choice. I would be going along, and I knew what I wanted to do, but it felt that I was not allowed to do it. I could not consciously create in the same way I had been. I finally realized the inner message was to let go of the process—let go. It took a while, but over the course of a couple of years the intuitive paintings emerged with no preconceptions when I started to paint. My job was to remove my individual ego out of the way, create from a totally subconscious level, and remove the boundaries.

I needed to remove the boundaries, the judgments, the idea of something not working, and that I should try something else. I had to learn to create with no judgment. It took time, but all the paintings in the Intuitive Gallery were created by letting the process take over; it was an amazing experience, and I began to take photographs of the process. It was like being in a darkroom and developing a photo, and watching images emerge. You put the negative into a fluid and what you observe is that images gradually emerge; the images then appear on different parts of the negative, and eventually the artwork becomes a complete image. I was in awe of what was taking place. I had no idea that I could do what I was doing. I might have been working on the painting upside down or sideways from what eventually ended up happening. I did not make any judgment regarding what the painting would become, until maybe halfway through the process, when I would start seeing what it was. My job was to keep my ego out of the process, and let the canvas become what it wanted to become. The complicated pictures came together and told a story of a spiritual process.

When I look at the Intuitive Galleries they are telling stories. In September of 2001, I began a painting that I called *The Blue Wall* (Arnold, 2011). I was going to paint a lily pond, but when I originally started the painting it was a beautiful peaceful place; it was more about the colors than anything to me. I added a blue mountain wall because I believed I needed to feel safe from the world. Something within me pushed me to do it, although I did not want to do it, but it had to be done. This happened right before September 11, 2001. After September 11th, it made perfect sense that I needed to be secluded and safe. It was with this painting that I began to become cognizant of the intuitive process.

After the Blue Wall painting, I did not paint intuitively again until the spring of 2005. The painting *First Sign of Spring* represented light breaking through in a dark place. It was a self-portrait; I was going through a difficult time in my life, and I realized that what I had to do was to let go. That painting is a manifestation of letting go in the creative process. This was the first intuitive paining I had ever done. I just started with color and let whatever happened, happen. The next intuitive painting *Out of the Woods* was fascinating because the figure in the painting was just standing there. I thought this was a landscape of color and texture. Then I looked and saw a shape in the center of the painting, and I just enhanced the figure. I did not draw it; it was just there.

GE: From your observations on the creative process, you are describing yourself as an instrument to manifest creative intelligence.

Debbie: Exactly, I was just the conduit. *Out of the Woods* was completed in 2007. I have always been a spiritual person, but at this moment a large life passage began to take place and accelerated my personal and artistic evolution.

First Sign of Spring©

GE: It appears that your process of creating art is reminiscent of a mandala.

Debbie: Yes, that is a great way to put it because I am intuitively being led forward, and I have no clue, but it is a very specific direction.

GE: When you say you are being led, I interpret it to mean you are surrendering to a higher level of consciousness within yourself, which is directing your life rather than being controlled through your senses. Would that be correct?

Debbie: Yes, and that has become my path to walk, and I walk it through intuition. As I continue to walk down this path, situations arise. When I finished the painting *Out of the Woods*, it reflected back to me that I was emerging from a period of my life in which I had been completely focused on the three-dimensional world. I had passed through a period of my life where I had been focused in a world I did not like very much. The physical world has never made a lot of sense to me. It has never felt right. We focus on all the wrong things in life; it was like a suit that did not fit me very well. When I finished the painting *Out of the Woods*, the message to me was—you are coming out of the darkness into the light. I then moved to the next level of development, which was to seek to arrive at the Self. I was fortunate to participate in a community of spiritual ladies who provided the support and strength to move forward. It is similar to when people come together to practice the TM-Sidhis and you raise your vibration, which is harder to achieve alone. I understand, now that I am self-sufficient, and have the capability to accelerate my inner evolution.

In the summer of 2007 the next intuitive painting *Butterfly Dream* was created. This painting reflects an inner message to renew the TM experience to accelerate and integrate the process of my evolution. I looked at *Butterfly Dream* as a meditation painting. That is when I began to let go and move completely into the intuitive painting process. That was the message that came to me from the painting. Although this was happening to me personally, I felt something was happening to the planet. The paintings seem to follow a planetary guideline or evolution of consciousness.

GE: Kandinsky, in his book *Concerning the Spiritual in Art*, speaks of the artist as being a servant of his or her time, and they have no choice but to express an internal necessity as a voice of the time.

Butterfly Dream©

Debbie: Exactly. When I first started thinking about what I was doing with the intuitive paintings the feeling I had was that I was creating beauty and light. I was attempting to bring beauty and light into a world that needed it badly. I believed I was transmuting energy in some way. As I created the intuitive paintings, it was not that the paintings in themselves were important, but instruments to ground positive energy into the planet containing love, light, and beauty. The intention behind the paintings was similar to the efforts of many people helping to raise the vibration of the collective consciousness of the planet to create balance.

In 2007 a shift began in my life with the three-dimensional world, which led to nowhere. It seems like I needed to look somewhere else, and the only other place to look was within. *Drifting Thru the Day* is about surrender, it is about letting go and surrendering completely to the process. That is the way I saw *Drifting Thru the Day*, it was an intuitive painting, but it was also co-creative because the background was intuitive, and the woman in the water, I believed, needed to be there. When I finished looking at this painting, I realized it was about surrendering completely. The aspect of the painting that bothered me for a while was that the woman in the water did not look alive, she appeared dead. No matter what I did she did not look alive. But then I realized that this is what death is. Death is the ultimate surrender to the light, to the Divine—the returning to the great consciousness. When I looked at this painting, I reflected that you get to a place in your life where you cannot plan and cannot force, or push; so what you do is you surrender, and let the water support you. It is like you are floating, and the support of nature is always there, but if you do not surrender to it, you are not allowing the natural evolutionary process of life to happen. I believed I needed to control my life; my ego thought that I needed to be in charge. However, I recognized I could not do it anymore. *Drifting Thru the Day* is about surrendering to the God-force; it is about drifting and flowing with the stream; it is about letting your canoe go downstream. Insights emerge in my consciousness during the process of creating these paintings, but the knowledge or understanding came once the paintings were created.

I have begun to increase my trust in the process and the path. After I completed the painting dealing with surrender, the next step in my artistic evolution was *Leap of Faith*. In *Leap of Faith* the turbulent water is flowing over

Drifting Thru the Day©

rocks; it looks very dangerous but the woman in the painting is making a leap of faith.

The woman featured in the painting is preparing to let go, and that was the *Leap of Faith* taking place within myself. I was prepared to follow wherever my creative process would take me. In August 2008 I created *Celestial Bodies*, which I considered to be significant. The reason that I believe it was significant is because it reflects the inner energy beginning to rise within me. The time of just surrendering and letting go was past, and the inner vibration of consciousness was rising; I felt a growth of consciousness, and that is what this painting represents to me, an expanded growth of consciousness. Most of the paintings after the creation of *Celestial Bodies* have been about the growth of consciousness. In 2008, my paintings became completely intuitive. I began with collage, or sometimes an old palette, and would smear it on a new canvas, completely in an unformed way. It did not seem to matter how I started. I would start

Leap of Faith©

with a random composition, with whatever color was available. I created an underpainting, and when I looked at the canvas, I would become attracted to something, a line, a color, or whatever. Many times it was very subtle. Then I took it one step at a time. It was like walking down a path in the woods at night, and you can only see the next step you are taking; that is how many of my intuitive paintings were created. With several of them, I started realizing what was happening during the creative process. I began to photograph the process, and when anyone looks at the photographs, he or she can see the development unfolding—you can see how one step leads to the next. This is how most of the intuitive paintings in the gallery were created because they emerged with no preconceived notion. I completed a painting entitled *Transformation*, which was full of symbolism. Before *Transformation*, I believed that my perception during the creative process was not fully in my control. After *Transformation* a shift in my consciousness put the ball completely in my court. I realized I was leading myself. I came to understand that what I had perceived as an abstract guiding force was an experience of connecting with Divine Intelligence or the inner stillness of pure consciousness. At first, it felt as if something had been taken away from me. The process of my continued artistic evolution and expansion of consciousness found expression in two stages of *Eruption of Water.*

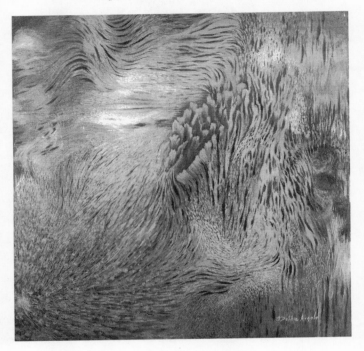

Eruption of Water©

I photographed the beginning stage of evolution of *Eruption of Water,* and a second image represented the finished product. *Eruption of Water* was a strange piece. It was like two paintings trying to exist on the same canvas, and I could not reconcile them with each other for about six months. The left side was a peaceful image of a sunset and a waterfall, and the right side was an explosion of energy. It felt like new energy was pouring into the planet but could not be absorbed. When the time was finally right I completed the work very quickly. The images that reflected the beginning of my non-representational period were very gentle and beautiful. I felt like new or more refined energy was coalescing into matter. I had a new state of awareness, in which the veil was lifting. The abstract art that I am creating at this time is new to me, and the creation process is easier, lighter, more fun, and with much less attachment. The art reflects the evolution of my consciousness.

GE: Human beings should appreciate that each one of us can open a door to ourselves through an innocent shift in our attention. Art helps us not to become trapped by our intellectualism, or the inner cacophony caused by our own thoughts.

Debbie: Brilliant thoughts are fun, like a pretty dress; they are window dressing for the ego and can fool us. The delicate intuitions, the inner voices of silence are the ones that whisper to us like children. We need to change the channel we have been listening to. As we change the channel, we expand our consciousness, and thereby change everything about our life. During the process of my life, I have realized that I have been growing and enlarging my sense of self—it has not been an easy process. There is a process of rest and activity as in all of nature. Rest has been important to my development. Stillness in my mind transcends the intrusions and demands of living. There needs to be lightness, a creative play matched to balance the challenges of life. Intuitive thought is experienced during the creative process of discovery. Instinctive thought often comes with strong emotions that propel us into action. The deeper inner intuitive voice is without emotion, more subtle and gentle in comprehending the stillness. We turn to pure energy beyond thought as a flower turns to the light seeking natural nourishment. We sense the answers, and the habit of the experience is facilitated by methods that effortlessly allow us to transcend the boundaries of duality.

GE: Life is full of miraculous moments—we call them miracles because we do not understand the mechanics of nature. For example, we see the transformation of a butterfly, or the human functioning of the body, and it all appears miraculous, but it is natural law unfolding. You described transcending the boundaries of duality and contributing to society. I concur because we create from the invisible center of our consciousness making visible our ideas, and manifesting our compassion in the process. Compassion is love lifted into light. Love resonates beyond the emotions from the inner stillness of pure consciousness. Empathy modifies our vibration to touch humanity, and love raises the vibration of the person touched by kindness.

Debbie: As an artist, I recognize I can play and contribute to the visual history of civilization. Each generation builds upon the last. Even in the middle of so much negativity in the world, highlighted through the media, the positive is dominant. I heard a beautiful expression: divine intelligence and natural law will not take us where the grace of God will not protect us. In these difficult economic times people have become afraid. However, pressures can force us to turn within for answers and rely on our inner strength. My artistic process and TM have been an instrument of transcending; the experience and habit of transcending have perpetuated the cultivation of consciousness and the refinement of perception. My voice expressed through art enriches my life, expands the inner silence, and awakens an innocence previously lost.

I am trying to do more documentation of my process. I wish I had started earlier, but as I stated, the intuitive paintings originally felt like a fluke to me. I think I was rejecting the process because my ego thought it was impossible. I am finding that there are a lot of "impossible" things that I am doing. You asked me if I thought I was transcending while I painted. The answer is yes, during the co-creative work in which "I" am involved in the decision making. I would say that I paint in a transcendental state part of the time. I lose track of time. I am in a joyful state for the most part; I am calm and centered. However, when I am doing the intuitive painting, it is more like being pregnant. I sense that the painting is there, but I have to be extremely patient and let it evolve naturally. I work on these paintings for several months, working on them only when I feel the impulse to take the next step. It is more like a dialogue within me. "You want me to do what?" "That looks stupid," "I could do that far better than this" and the answer I receive is: "Just do it." That is why I said that my main job is to get out of my own way and listen to the deep inner prompts. I have grown to love the process; it is like giving birth, but you don't know until the end what you have created. The child is part of you, but he or she is not your property or possession; the child came through you, but has an individual identity and independent existence. When I look back, I see that I was learning lessons about myself in the process of creating my art. I have done several pieces over the years that were premonitions of important events in my life. Sometimes it takes years to see what a painting is saying to me. I also know that if I were less skilled, and did not have the experience of years of painting, I could not do this.

GE: As an experienced and accomplished artist, what is your message to other artists and the public regarding creativity?

Debbie: Creativity is simply allowing the greater consciousness to flow through. It is being in a place of non-resistance, and allowing the joy and the passion of life to flow through. All life is an expression of the greater consciousness; it is life flowing through in a different way. Creativity is the way for the artist to connect on a very deep level of trust and allowing surrender. From my experience that is where the deepest level of creativity comes from; it requires trusting the process, by removing the ego, judgments, and comparisons. I knew this experience as a child, and it has evolved to a level of understanding where I realize it is a way of life. A true transcendental experience can be integrated within a person's consciousness, and become a permanent feature of daily life. Life is not something that happens to you; it is a flowing toward home. My art has helped me to be like a flower that opens, grows, and strives to move in the direction of the light, which nourishes life. My journey is taking me into a deeper and deeper place allowing me to live in a three-dimensional world with an expanded consciousness. That is what art and transcending through TM does for me, and that is also where mankind is headed. Humanity needs to bring that expanded consciousness into a three-dimensional world.

Debbie's creative process affirms her artistic and personal desire to spontaneously create art as a natural flow from her experience of Transcendental Consciousness. Debbie shared that she had many moments of non-attachment and witnessing herself in activity, which can be a symptom of a higher state of consciousness. These experiences have been expressed by artists, poets, and philosophers throughout human history. Her experience represents the universal nature and existence of the ineffable inner stillness that is shared by all of humanity. TM provides a systematic method to enliven Self-awareness, and science offers empirical credibility regarding the repeatability of the experience. Debbie also mentioned the importance of rest and activity in her life. TM provides a unique restful alertness through the experience of transcending to finer levels of mental activity. The activity of the creative process is a complement to the inward process of transcending and can be an instrument for developing Cosmic Consciousness, a state of consciousness in which non-changing Self-awareness is not lost or overshadowed by the world of the senses. The development of Self-knowledge in the context of art can result from the interacting balance between experiencing the inner silence of pure consciousness through TM, and the activity experienced in the creative process.

Debbie in the process of creating her art cultivated a refined attention and innocently had moments of transcending. Additionally, her experience with TM created a natural memory in the nervous system of settling to quieter levels of mental activity. She became comfortable and familiar during her creative process, which has expressed itself in her paintings and tells the tale of a *Celestial Gardener*.

My conversation with Debbie enlivened my memories of the writings of Herman Hesse, in particular his discussions of the internal struggles faced by human beings between their inner life of self-referral, and the outer world as experienced through the senses. Just as the paintings of Debbie were self-portraits, the literary work of Herman Hesse reflected his inner evolution and understanding of life. In Hesse's literary work *Narcissus and Goldmund* he symbolically explores the journey of the active life versus the contemplative life. Hesse tells the story of the human journey to gain self-knowledge and explores the process of inner awakening. Hesse's spiritual journey was beautifully expressed in his book *Siddhartha* (1951) that presented the journey of two friends traveling their individual paths. The book highlights the power of experience and intellectual understanding. In *Siddhartha* there is the enlightened ferryman Vasudeva, who helps seekers cross the stream of life, achieve Self-knowledge, and become stream winners. Hesse immersed himself in studying the sacred teachings of the East in search of Transcendental Consciousness and enlightenment.

In contemporary society certified teachers of TM, similar to Vasudeva in *Siddhartha*, employ the tools of ancient Vedic wisdom along with modern technology to help seekers to cross the stream and transcend the duality within human consciousness. Debbie in her description of her artistic process is describing the same journey of inner awakening that everyone is seeking. The goal of enlightenment as expressed in *Siddhartha* is mirrored in the artistic aspirations of Debbie; they are fulfilled through the wisdom and legacy of Maharishi's knowledge and system for experiencing Transcendental Consciousness.

Chapter V

Philosophy: Love of Wisdom

Jonathan Shear, Ph.D.

Jonathan Shear is Affiliated Associate Professor of Philosophy at Virginia Commonwealth University (VCU), where he has taught since 1987. He received his Ph.D. in Philosophy from the University of California at Berkeley, where he was a Woodrow Wilson Fellow. He also was a Fulbright Scholar in the Philosophy of Science at the London School of Economics. Since the early 1960s his work has focused on the use of meditation practices and related scientific research to expand our knowledge of human consciousness. He has published and lectured widely in North America, Europe and Asia, and was the founding Managing Editor of The Journal of Consciousness Studies.

George Ellis (GE): I could not think of a more appropriate person than you to speak about philosophy. In the first section of the book I wanted to deal with the humanities, and philosophy is a cornerstone. What happened in your life that put you in the direction of seeking deeper knowledge, such as tai chi and meditation?

Jonathan Shear (Jon): To tell the truth, in the beginning I was not interested in anything spiritual. Then in college I began studying under a deep philosopher, Herbert Marcuse. Marcuse argued that a great percentage of the problems modern society faced resulted from its superficiality, and the fact that we had forgotten all of the deep levels of inner awareness where Being, bliss, and the deepest values of the heart are located. I read his work, and he made sense to me. In the summer of 1961 I experimented with some methods that produced altered states of consciousness. The experiences caused me to reflect that if this is evocable in someone as unaesthetic as me, it must be in everyone. I started to write about these experiences.

Soon afterward a friend took me to a lecture being given by Alan Watts at Brandeis University, where my friend and I were students. The talk was very interesting. At the end of the lecture I went to the back of the hall and threw out the manuscript I was working on. Four of the manuscript's six metaphors turned out to be traditional Eastern metaphors about consciousness, and it was obvious to me that what I had been writing about was not a new topic, but had been studied extensively by Eastern traditions for millennia. Writing anything further on my own now seemed to be a waste of time. What I needed instead was further study, and I decided to look deeply into the subject as soon as I graduated. This led me to the study of Zen and Judo, a Zen art, the next year when I was Fulbright Scholar in the Philosophy of Science in London. Later, of course, I started TM.

GE: What led you to start the TM technique?

Jon: I practiced Zen an hour a day for five years, along with my Judo practice. During this time I also became aware of Maharishi's teaching. Then, while I was working on my doctorate at the University of California at Berkeley, a close friend of mine asked me about Maharishi's meditation, and I told him I thought it seemed authentic. My friend went to an introductory lecture, which was given by Maharishi himself; he started TM, and I could see immediate changes within a day or two. I learned myself at the next available course, in February 1968. I was not impressed the first day, but after two days I was very impressed, and within two weeks I was totally convinced that this was a very profound technique. When Maharishi came to the United States to give a course that summer in Squaw Valley, California, I took time off from my work at Berkeley. It was obvious to me that Maharishi had brought something that was very real, not just words. Instead of being simply good-sounding talk, the stuff of most philosophers, what Maharishi brought was real experience. With his technique the average person could easily settle deep inside to that level of pure consciousness.

I was one of those lucky people who happened to get good results from Zen. I knew how to concentrate. I had already had plenty of practice with extreme inner concentration while working towards my degree in pure mathematics. Nevertheless, I would only experience transcending once every two or three months after years of practicing with Zen. However, most people have a lot of difficulty concentrating like that. Zen teachers would say maybe one percent of the population might experience deep transcending, even after years of hard work. So I was really surprised when after only two or three days of practicing TM I found myself as deep as I had ever gotten, which was very infrequent with Zen. It is clear that TM allows the majority of people to begin to have these types of experiences in just a few days. It's effortless and immediate. The contrast with Zen couldn't be greater.

GE: To step back for a moment, what is your family background? It seems you had excellent academic capability and became a scholar studying at eminent institutions throughout the world.

Jon: Yes, my family background created a solid ground for this. My father was the first person in America who showed and proved that chemicals and environmental pollutants could cause cancer. He headed up research on chemotherapy for the National Institutes of Health for decades. When he passed away, newspapers called him "the father of chemotherapy." My background valued intelligence. Conversations at the dinner table regularly included guests who were international scientists. I was born in Washington, DC and raised in Bethesda, Maryland. My father had moved there to help set up the National Institutes of Health.

GE: In regard to philosophy, many people believe it does not have practical relevance to their life because it seems that it is just arguments about justified belief and knowledge. How do you address the superficiality in philosophical discourse being taught in most universities?

Jon: It is not the philosophers' fault. Western civilization made a big change as it emerged from the plagues into the modern world in the beginning of the 17th century. The ancient knowledge was lost, the medieval "age of faith" was shattered, and modern science seeking to be based on knowledge, rather than faith, evolved. Science relies on the two things that usually appear most certain, namely logic, which includes mathematics, and direct experience; it is also very democratic because anyone following the appropriate methodology should be able to obtain the same results. The deep inner life that was at the heart of wisdom in the ancient world was not accessible systematically, and most people couldn't find it no matter how hard they looked. Hence, many of the influential ancient discussions regarding the self and wisdom now just seemed to be mere speculation-based opinions rather than reliable *knowledge*.

So modern philosophers from Descartes, Hume, and Kant onward began to focus on the fundamental question of what knowledge really is. Knowledge, of course, is a function of consciousness. So understanding knowledge requires understanding consciousness. Without knowledge of how to explore the inner domain systematically, philosophers have had to rely on speculation, words, and arguments to address its fundamental problems.

What is needed is a way to investigate inner life systematically, and this is part of why I found Maharishi's approach so exciting—it seemed to offer us just the sort of systematic, culture-independent approach to investigating consciousness that modern science and philosophy need. Modern philosophy does very good work in logic and epistemology, but on the whole, as you noted, it often seems to be an unanchored web of words. So what is necessary is to turn inside systematically. Knowledge, the topic of epistemology, is a special kind of relationship between the knower and the known—so if you do not know what the knower is, it is hopeless to try and figure out what knowledge is.

GE: Jon, this is an important point because I was in a doctoral program in organizational leadership and they offered a course in epistemology. The first two weeks of the course the students were disturbed because they were reading what appeared to be nonsense. The business students assumed that philosophy had minimal value for their profession because most of the texts' authors were just playing with words. We also were studying the Greeks in philosophy, and I know you have written and published extensively on Plato. Therefore, I am curious regarding your opinion on whether Socrates was a real historical figure, or was he just an invention of Plato?

Jon: People argue about it, but I believe there is little doubt that Socrates existed. Most—but not all—of what we know about Socrates does come from Plato. Plato wrote his dialogues over a forty-year period after Socrates died. Plato remarked that the Socrates of his later dialogues should be understood as Socrates "made modern." It appears that the Socrates of his earlier dialogues was intended to be an accurate portrayal. It is of particular interest that Plato described Socrates as a meditator, who employed well-known meditation techniques, including the use of an *epidos* or mantra. It appears Socrates had deep transcending experiences and special abilities similar to those described in Patanjali's *Yoga Sutras,* and reported by people practicing the TM-Sidhi program as taught by Maharishi.

The texts are very clear here, and obvious to any philosopher who has even a little experience of transcending and knowledge of the relevant techniques. Although, not having this kind of experience and knowledge most modern philosophers ignore things like the facts in the *Republic*—Plato's most widely read dialogue. Plato emphasizes repeatedly that the *main theme* of philosophy is to learn to redirect your attention and go inward to the source of thought, and insists that without doing this one will not have wisdom. Similarly clear but almost universally overlooked points can be found in other widely read dialogues such as the *Phaedo* and the *Symposium*.

GE: Can you find these aphorisms in the writings of Plato?

Jon: They stand out. I used to travel and give lectures and presentations to philosophy departments' colloquia on this subject. At one colloquium held at Dartmouth College some thirty-five years ago, after my talk, the head of the department turned to his expert on Plato and asked him what he thought. The professor, a Greek scholar from Greece, replied: "He knows his texts." He was familiar with all the texts I was explaining, but he had never thought about how to interpret them literally, as I was doing, because he had lacked the experience of transcending and knowledge of the relevant techniques. His reply opened the whole colloquium to a very lively, friendly, and satisfying discussion of Plato's texts and their implications, ancient and modern.

GE: There is a debate in epistemology between *a priori* and *a posteriori* knowledge. How do you think scientific discoveries on Transcendental Consciousness synthesize all of these unnecessary debates between these philosophers?

Jon: Debates have a value in clarifying the issues and making theories clear. Science makes an effort to clarify theories and then goes about testing and defending them. Let me discuss *a priori* knowledge. What is *a priori* knowledge? *A priori* means "prior to experience," so *a priori* knowledge refers to knowledge that is supposed to be built-in and brought *to* experience, in contrast to knowledge that is gained *from* it.

Plato believed in *a priori* knowledge, and many people in the modern world have argued against it, with very intelligent positions. Their general idea was that the mind is merely a "blank slate." This was the dominant view in much of European and American philosophy fifty years ago. Two ways that science has challenged this thinking follow from the existence of computers and from work in neuroscience. First, by analogy with computers: computers have to have built-in "knowledge." Unless there is a "read-only" memory, and there are hard-wired categories and operations, the computer cannot learn anything or compute at all. Logically, the case for the mind appears to be similar. Second, with neurophysiology we are now uncovering innate neurological structures related to *a priori* knowledge. Such considerations now appear to make it clear that the mind has its own *a priori* knowledge.

GE: I was sitting with Maharishi, in a private meeting at Humboldt University, when a couple of educators brought up John Locke and his theory of the mind being a blank slate. Maharishi closed his eyes and sat in silence for a few seconds; he opened his eyes and stated that John Locke was speaking about pure consciousness. When you say that *a priori* knowledge is prior to experience, does that change when you transcend the duality of thought and the individual self is merged in the transcendental self? Is that not another type of experience?

Jon: Yes, but when philosophers say "prior to experience" they are referring to the idea that when a child is born he or she has a kind of knowledge "built in." This built-in knowledge is not of particular things. It amounts to an automatic reflex to structure things in a certain way. Transcendental Consciousness, as Maharishi describes it, is the ground of all experience. Thus, even though it can be experienced in meditation, it would be *a priori* in the sense of existing prior to all the kinds of experiences philosophers ordinarily refer to. So it's both prior to experience and *experienceable*.

Ordinary knowledge, as Maharishi's tradition analyzes it, arises from the *interactions* of sensory and other inputs with pure consciousness. Pure consciousness seems to have nothing in it—no colors, sounds, taste, feelings, thoughts, and so forth, but it is full of potential, like a seed. Therefore, when pure consciousness interacts with sensory inputs it produces the conscious experiences. Just like a computer: you enter data, the data interacts with what is built into the computer, and you receive outputs in response—calculations, images on your screen, and so forth. Similarly, it is the interactions of consciousness with the world, through the senses and other built-in mental faculties that structure our knowledge.

GE: This is a beautiful description, your explanation is exquisite. When you look at this battle that went on among philosophers, your description appears to resolve this dilemma in philosophy between the two extremes of empiricism and rationalism.

Jon: It resolves part of it, but more is needed. The experience of Unity Consciousness, in which, according to Maharishi, you can experience the *mechanics* of the interaction of consciousness and its inputs, rather than just the product of these mechanics, might well be able to address many of these further philosophical questions. This would be an empirically based approach. In modern Western philosophy, Kant and others who have argued for the existence of *a priori* knowledge by contrast have generally only argued on purely logical grounds. Thousands of years ago Plato took a more experiential approach.

GE: How does Plato differ from Kant?

Jon: There is no doubt that Plato emphasized the importance of direct meditation-related practices and experiences. We do not know whether he had such experiences himself. Nevertheless, his texts clearly described standard meditation practices, and experiences such as removing attention from the senses and the world, then from sensory-oriented thinking, and finally turning it away from all thinking whatsoever until one comes to experience the inner *source* of thought and experience. Plato calls this source "the Good," describes it as intangible, beyond color and form, identified with existence itself, and associated with pure unbounded bliss. In many ways the practices Plato describes parallel aspects of the TM and the TM-Sidhi programs. However, there is one all-important difference: Plato makes it clear that the practices he describes are extremely difficult, and unlikely to produce the desired experiences even after decades of effort, while the techniques of the TM and TM-Sidhi programs are, as we know, virtually effortless and surprisingly effective. Plato even discussed Socrates having and teaching the employment of a method similar to TM's use of a mantra as a vehicle for transcending.

GE: What do you mean about Socrates having a mantra?

Jon: This is in the dialogue *Charmides*. In the Middle Ages, I'm told, this was the first Platonic dialogue people usually studied, but now people seldom read it. In this dialogue Socrates is described as having received an *epidos* from the doctors at the court of the king of Thrace. The technical definition of *epidos* is "a word which when repeated is said to bring health to the body, wholeness to the mind, and fulfillment to the aspirant." This is obviously equivalent to what we call a mantra. Plato describes Socrates as knowing how to teach people to use this *epidos* not only to help cure headaches, but to produce *sophrosyne*, the highest virtue of the Greeks, associated with temperance, wholeness of mind, self-knowledge, and wisdom.

GE: How do these practices relate to the question of *a priori* knowledge?

Jon: Plato believed that for every single idea we have, there exists a structure built into the nature of intelligence. That is what Plato's pure "Forms" are, *a priori* structures of intelligence. They are supposed to exist on a transcendental level, much deeper than any thought, even deeper than the deepest abstractions of mathematics and logic. According to Plato a person needs to "reverse" the direction of inner awareness, and leave all thinking behind to enter into the realm of these deep structures of intelligence. This is a standard description of meditation in traditions as diverse as Zen, Yoga, and Vedanta; it is one of the most important features of Plato's thought. His four-stage account of cognitive development described in the "Divided Line" of the *Republic* makes this very clear. The first three levels involve what we can call (1) picture-thinking, (2) common sense understanding, and (3) abstract thinking of the sorts used in physics, logic, and mathematics. These levels display striking parallels to those of Piaget and others in modern developmental psychology. Plato's fourth level, the level of Forms, goes quite beyond anything normally discussed in developmental psychology today. To reach this level one has to learn to turn one's inner awareness in an "opposite direction," taking it away from all thinking and redirecting it toward the source of thought. This, he says, is necessary to gain awareness of the Forms, the *a priori* transcendental structures supposed to underlie thought in general. Without knowledge of this fourth level, he says, we will never really be able to understand how thinking works—or indeed, what we really are. Plato's famous Allegory of the Cave is intended to illustrate this, and Plato emphasizes that real understanding is impossible without direct experience.

GE: How do you differentiate what Kant was talking about versus Plato?

Jon: Kant had none of these deeper experiences. He was only able to *reason* regarding the foundations of how we think and act. Reasoning about the preconditions of knowledge, he concluded, like Plato, that there has to be a built-in, structural basis in the mind. The mind needs to have built-in operations, like a computer, even to be able to think at all. Kant was sure we couldn't *experience* the transcendental ground of mind, and he was very disturbed about this fact.

GE: How do you deal with Hume and his skepticism trying to set aside the mind?

Jon: Two big steps. Hume was very scientific, and when he attempted to investigate the internal domain of the mind, he could not locate anything intellectually like the pure self that Descartes talked about. Descartes, of course, also described specific meditation techniques that he used to come to his conclusions about self, but Hume could not discover the relevant experiences, no matter how hard he looked. I once gave a talk at a conference in the late 1970s that Maharishi chaired. After the talk Maharishi complemented Descartes, Hume and Kant for their genius—and added that it was not their fault that they did not have effective techniques to experience finer levels of consciousness systematically. In other words, the way to deal with skepticism is to expand access to the realm of internal experience in a systematic way.

GE: Is this why Descartes' only method was to try and create an argument and then refute it to prove "I think, therefore I am"?

Jon: Actually that was not Descartes' method. It is a common misinterpretation that arises when people do not have enough experience to take Descartes' texts literally. He himself was quite clear that his "I think, therefore I am" was *not* to be understood as an inference or product of an argument at all. It was (as he emphasized in letters published along with the *Meditations*) to be understood as a single, simple "intuition" gained by practicing the methods described in his *Meditations.* Two of these methods amount to meditation techniques widely practiced in Asia. One of them is a process in which a person attempts to ignore entirely both the senses and thoughts related to the senses. This is a very difficult practice, and Maharishi once remarked that a person would need to be highly evolved and no longer disturbed by passions to gain success with it. That is why most people obtain no results with these techniques; indeed it's not even healthy for most people to practice. We can also note that Descartes remarked he was at a stage of life where he was no longer bothered by his passions, so he appeared to fulfill the requirement for success with this technique. Descartes' "methodological doubt" also brings to mind the Zen technique of "raising the doubt sensation" as an all-encompassing feeling to help leave the intellect and verbal thinking behind and arrive at Transcendental Consciousness—another very difficult technique.

GE: Where did the doubt sensation method originate?

Jon: It was a standard Ch'an (Chinese Zen) technique, much recommended, for example, by the eminent master Hsu Yun a century ago. Regardless of the particulars of Descartes' methods, it's clear that he described himself as closing his eyes, sitting in contemplation, and becoming aware of himself as consciousness, or "a conscious being," as Anscombe and Geach translate it. In other words, as Anscombe and Geach point out, the accurate interpretation of "*cogito ergo sum*" is "I am *conscious*, therefore I am," not "I *think*, therefore I am." Descartes states explicitly in his "Replies to Objections" that this is *not* a syllogism reasoning from premises to conclusion, but a single simple "intuition" or inner experience that the mind "sees, feels, and handles." Descartes' experiential language could hardly be clearer. The *cogito* on his account was something experienced as indubitable self-awareness—the self aware of itself. Descartes then asserted he became aware of unbounded infinite consciousness as the context of his individual awareness in this same "simple" and "indubitable" way, and finding in this experience "the highest bliss" humanity is capable of. Descartes is very clear in his description of these standard meditative procedures and experiences, but it takes a person who knows something about them to recognize what Descartes is talking about, and interprets his philosophy properly, regardless of our final opinions about his arguments and conclusions.

GE: This analysis completely takes the studies beyond what is being presented in most universities. You have deep thinkers with inner knowledge, and then you have skeptics like Hume. I assume you believe that Hume just lacked the technique?

Jon: That's right, if you look at the mind there are different layers we can experience as we transcend in meditation: the sensory level, the layer of thinking and words, a deeper more abstract pre-verbal layer, and a level beyond the individual self—pure consciousness. When we read different philosophers it becomes clear they had different levels of inner experience, and that a particular philosopher was familiar with this or that level and not others. It becomes clear why each philosopher would be likely to develop a particular kind of philosophy. Maharishi praised the genius and the detailed accuracy of the way each of these great philosophers described the particular levels of mind that were open to them. Instead of criticizing them, he suggested how much more they might have contributed if only they had had a technique to experience the full range of inner awareness.

GE: This brings us back to scientific research on higher states of consciousness that is being conducted on people who practice TM. How do you interpret what is taking place in that research, and its practical value in under-standing philosophy?

Jon: Many people are talking about consciousness now, but as Maharishi stated, anyone can *say* anything. Therefore, anyone who is a hard-headed inde-pendent thinker wants to know what is real and what is not. So research is fun-damental; for example, people often challenge the validity of claims of having experiences of pure consciousness, assuming that they reflect little more than people's imagination and/or wishful thinking. This challenge is very reason-able, given the highly unusual nature of the experience. Even people who grant the general possibility of the experience often raise serious questions because they know how rare the experience is generally reported to be in most tradi-tions. So they are often very skeptical about reports that the TM technique produces the experience so quickly and easily. Given their general knowledge, this skepticism is very reasonable. One value of empirical research is that it can provide very strong reason to take these reports of experiences of pure consciousness seriously.

GE: Can you elaborate on the empirical perspective?

Jon: Throughout history people have described physiological correlates of the experience. For example, metabolic rate is described as dramatically reduced, and breathing as very refined and even suspended entirely. Zen and the Taoist traditions sometimes simply use the phrase *ch'i-shi* (which means "the breath is suspended") to refer to the experience itself. We now know from research on TM practitioners that refinement of breath and suspension of perceivable respiration are correlates of reports of experiences of pure con-sciousness made by those practicing TM in laboratory settings. Research also shows that the oxygen and the carbon dioxide levels in the blood remain con-stant, making it clear that the suspension of respiration is a product of sharply decreased aerobic metabolism, rather than any attempts to control the breath. This kind of research provides strong evidence that the reports of pure con-sciousness made by TM practitioners and the reports in the literature of other traditions do, in fact, reflect the same psycho-physical state, although the fact is that the experience is gained so easily and so often with TM.

Research also shows that there is an increase both of alpha-1 power and pre-frontal alpha coherence as a person comes close to the experience of Transcendental Consciousness. The work to isolate such correlates is just beginning, but I think it is very important. When I was a Fulbright scholar in the Philosophy of Science so many years ago, I found that in culture after culture, different traditions with different metaphysical belief systems described what appeared to be exactly the same experiences at the depths of inner awareness. This suggested to me that these experiences had to reflect something universal about human consciousness, rather than culture-dependent variables such as wishful thinking and metaphysical beliefs. It seemed very unlikely that all these different traditions with their different and often opposing metaphysics would come up with the same unique experiences simply by chance. The research on physiological correlates supports this observation. It also makes it harder for serious philosophers to dismiss the experiences out of hand.

GE: What do you mean by opposing metaphysics?

Jon: Metaphysical systems that make opposing claims about the nature of consciousness, the self, and the universe. These systems can interpret the experience of pure consciousness very differently, and take it to be of very different things. For example, one may interpret it simply as experience of one's individual nature; another may take it to be experience of God, and another of nature itself with no personality at all. It would not seem reasonable that such opposing systems would report the same experience, much less report it in conjunction with the same unusual physiology, unless there were something universal and belief-independent about the experience and associated physiology. Research now supports this observation; it indicates that far from being a creation of metaphysically inspired beliefs and expectations, the experience is the natural correlate of the physiological state. The capacity to go deep inside and have this experience is, in other words, natural, belief-independent, and built-in.

GE: The essence of what you have been describing is that regardless of station in life this experience is a fundamental property and birthright of humanity.

Jon: It is. It's everyone's inner nature, everyone has it, and it is described throughout the world, and experiencing it has all sorts of benefits. The analogy of a stereo may help explain this. If you turn the media (programs, etc.) off, and turn the volume of a well-functioning high-fidelity stereo up, you should hear no sound at all. If you hear static, the system is not high-fidelity. Pure consciousness is pure silence, the ground state of our inner awareness;

when we experience it and tune ourselves to it we become more high-fidelity with everything we experience and do. Additionally, this experience is one of pure satisfaction, pure comfort, ease, and bliss—feeling OK, "no problem." The high fidelity awareness is what we are all looking for, even if, as Plato noted, we might not know it until we gain the experience.

In our modern world we often find that a child goes to the refrigerator, opens the door, sees that it is full of food, and nevertheless turns to his or her mother and says, "There's nothing to eat." The refrigerator is full of food. So what does this mean? It means that the child wants something to eat, but does not quite know what it is. Without knowing what he or she wants, the child is all too likely to continue eating without satisfaction. When we do not know what we truly desire—satisfaction itself—we tend to go through life stuffing ourselves with what we happen to find in front of us. This is the general condition in the modern world, going through life overstuffed with objects and possessions without ever satisfying our hunger for satisfaction. What is needed, of course, is knowledge of satisfaction itself.

GE: Let's take another direction. If you look at the political debates, the entire approach is to throw mud on their opponent. The politicians will do almost anything or say anything to achieve power. It appears there is no ethical core. In this context how do you see philosophy having a practical value in society?

Jon: Philosophy—"love of wisdom," literally—has always really been about how best to live. As Plato pointed out, if we do not know what we want, we wander around bumping into one another, often highly destructively. Until we experience what we are deep within, we remain ignorant of what true satisfaction is, and thus of what we want. An unsatisfied person is always in a sense hungry, and a person who is always hungry may be likely to do all sorts of things to satisfy his or her hunger. A person who is already satisfied will naturally be less likely to be prompted by selfish cravings to do harmful things. A well-fed person won't be driven by hunger to steal food. We have two basic instincts: self-preservation and preservation of the species. To the extent that we feel satisfied internally, our natural impulses to act for the welfare of others become freer to express themselves. One's "cup," one's happiness, naturally "runneth over," so to speak. This happens automatically. I'm reminded of the man, Pat Corum, you taught to meditate at Folsom Prison long ago, who remarked that before learning TM the only time he felt powerful was when he had a gun in his hand. When Pat Corum realized this experience of inner bliss was within him, his view of humanity changed. This inner satisfaction frees our natural reflex to care more deeply about others. This is the heart of ethics, both private and public, and it grows naturally as we grow in self-awareness.

GE: There is so much conflict between religions, even though they are all branches on the same tree. As a person who has dedicated himself to philosophy, exploring truth, and justified belief, what is your response to the situation?

Jon: This is due to ignorance. People usually gain their religious beliefs from other people who have no direct knowledge of the real depths of religious experience themselves. This has been the case throughout the world, generation after generation. So their understanding is often superficial and when they hear someone say something different from what they have been taught, they can easily take him to be an enemy of life's eternal truths. Highly evolved people of all religions of course recognize that there is a common core at the depth of all the world's religions, but you have to experience this to really know it. You need teachers, clergy, and preceptors of all the different religions to gain higher levels of consciousness, understand it, and pass it on to others.

GE: Have you had an experience of expanded consciousness that transformed your philosophy?

Jon: I would probably say, "informed and affected," rather than "transformed." One experience happened before I learned TM. I was practicing Zen techniques at the time. I had an experience of unboundedness, infinity, in meditation. I had been a serious mathematics student, and thought infinity only meant you can always add one, without ending—in other words that there is no real infinity. However after this expansion of consciousness I saw that this was wrong. I realized infinity can be experienced. I was trained as a scientist, and consequently when I had an experience that falsified my previous hypothesis, my response was to leave it behind, and move forward.

After learning TM I also had other important experiences. These included experiences of bliss. One type of bliss was of being bathed in rich, warm, utter satisfaction, permeated with a sense of "Ahh; this is what I really am!" Another was just of simple, quiet fulfillment, and another was an incomprehensibly thrilling, golden *ocean* of delight that seemed to display the essence of pure happiness. All of these experiences naturally had a significant effect on my sense of what life is really about, making it ever clearer that happiness is something in itself, quite distinct from all the things we usually associate it with.

Not long after I had learned the TM-Sidhi program (an advanced TM technique) I had another experience worth mentioning. I was having a conversation with some distinguished individuals when I noticed that the space around us seemed to be alive in a certain sweet way. I had the thought that the *purpose* of life was to personally maintain and help everyone else have this experience of *life itself*. Before that I had never worried about the "purpose" of life. I just believed life was simply to live, but now it seemed clear that the purpose of life is for that delicate loving feeling, that soft tenderness deep within each of us, to be cultured everywhere. The insight was clarifying. I had never even wondered about the purpose of life, but it seemed to be obvious since that moment. I've been meditating for many years, so naturally there have been other experiences as well.

GE: Where did you first meet Maharishi?

Jon: I first met Maharishi at a course he led at Squaw Valley, California in 1968. It was a one-month course, but I was only there for two weeks. Throughout the course when Maharishi was lecturing, I remember putting in my notes again and again that this was the *real* Zen. This is exactly what I have been studying all these years. It also seemed obvious that Maharishi is one of these remarkable figures that come around only every few centuries. The experience I had the first time I went to the microphone to say something to Maharishi was really remarkable. When I reached the microphone, I begin by saying, "Maharishi," and the next thing I knew, I was experiencing an enormous expansion of consciousness. I felt my consciousness filled the entire auditorium, bright, glowing, filled with life and empty of thought—a state I had been seeking to gain for years. I eventually spoke with Maharishi briefly, and when I turned to return to my seat I felt like I was floating, and everything was glowing. It took all of my Judo practice simply to put one foot in front of the other; it was very impressive. It was an overwhelming state of bliss.

GE: Do you have any idea of how these phenomena occur?

Jon: I have only the traditional explanation, which is that a fully enlightened teacher influences all the space that he is in. An ordinary, less coherent person is like an iron filing that becomes more coherent in the presence of a magnet. The internal magnetic domains line up coherently in one direction, and hold that direction for a while, temporarily becoming a magnet itself. In this way ordinary individuals are said to become more coherent for a while in the presence of an enlightened teacher's unbounded coherence.

GE: How do you compare Eastern and Western philosophy and their approaches to knowledge?

Jon: They are very different both in what they take to be basic and in the methods they use. Western philosophy focuses on intellectual analysis of the world of the senses and the realm of thought. Eastern philosophy traditionally adds systematic meditation procedures and examination of levels of consciousness deeper than the realm of thought.

In the history of Western philosophy you will of course find some major thinkers who were clearly reflecting on the depths of consciousness and enlightenment as well as ordinary life. Plato describes Socrates as experiencing and reflecting on the crucial significance of higher levels of consciousness. Parmenides was described similarly. The writings of leaders of Plato's academy for hundreds of years contain very clear descriptions of higher states of consciousness, and structures of awareness similar to those traditionally described in Yoga, Vedanta, and elsewhere in the East. However, that knowledge was generally lost in the West after the Barbarian invasions, and remained lost during the medieval age of faith, and the three plague-devastated centuries that followed. Then in the 1600s the modern West as we know it began, and it's only now beginning to really understand its own ancient roots. Thus, to return to the original question, modern Western society needs to regain—and to reevaluate from its own perspective—what it once had at its basis. Plato was very clear when he said we would never resolve the intellectual and social issues we have been struggling with for centuries without the deeper levels of experience. My own work over the last half century has been to suggest how modern Western philosophy can become powerfully transformed with even a little knowledge and experience of transcendence.

GE: You just mentioned "social issues." Can you say something about your ideas on the social significance of experiences that TM produces?

Jon: It is really crucial, especially now. We live in a society, a world, where affluence is becoming the norm for a large part of the population on nearly every continent. When income rises, according to the World Health Organization, people become happier to the point where income becomes comfortable. However, after that, significant mental problems, rather than happiness, are what typically appear to go up significantly. There is a reason for this. Put in the context of Maslow's "Hierarchy of Needs," we can see that people have different kinds of needs. The most basic are meeting physical needs, having enough food, safety, and so forth. Once these most basic needs are fulfilled, middle level needs, such as social acceptance, esteem, respect, love and so on, arise and become dominant. As these needs become fulfilled, higher, "self-actualization" needs come to the fore. With affluence this growth has taken place in advanced economies all over the world, and our higher, self-actualization needs have become more and more influential. Fulfilling these needs requires the kinds of experiences we have been talking about, and most people have no idea that these experiences even exist—much less how to gain them. Growing dissatisfaction and psychological problems in the midst of prosperity are a natural result. Young, well-educated people throughout the world report feeling lost, stuffing themselves with games, food, and useless things without achieving satisfaction.

This is a big problem, and it's growing. The only way it will be addressed is when we employ techniques for self-actualization by going deep within. People need to gain clear knowledge of the value of self-actualization, and establish research to determine precisely which techniques produce what results on what people. TM is the most conspicuously successful of these methods so far, and we need to find ways to produce this kind of growth or the human race is doomed to consume itself out of existence. We are like people in a new environment who do not know which new foods will be satisfying, and eat more than we need, and get fatter and fatter without satisfaction. We are eating up the environment in a useless way. The only solution is to find out who we are, and what we really need by going deep within. This is the crying need for the planet, the need in terms of ecology, politics, wars, and conflicts between states. It's a matter of education and transcending.

GE: What you have articulated requires a more educated generation. Can you provide your perception of the type of education that you participated in during the founding days of MIU? I believe you were one of the pioneering faculty members in developing MIU.

Jon: I helped Nat Goldhaber write the original letter to Maharishi suggesting the idea of the University, and headed up its Philosophy Department for a dozen years. The early days at MIU were a priceless and peerless experience. In those days a byword among educators was "interdisciplinary education." In the attempt to avoid the narrowness of overspecialization, universities would try to cross boundaries by mixing disciplines, for example mathematics and physics, but this eventually would simply generate another field, mathematical-physics, and so forth. No one seemed to be able to develop real interdisciplinary studies. Interdisciplinary studies at MIU took a very different approach. The idea was that every intelligible discipline has in common the fact that it is intelligible, and it fits the nature of our intelligence or consciousness. As Maharishi explained, "knowledge is structured in consciousness." Maharishi reasoned, if you have a student body that is turning inside and experiencing finer levels of consciousness, this experience is placed in the context of specific understanding, and unfolds to produce knowledge in general. We formulated an educational system that illuminates the deeper levels of every field of study simultaneously. All fields of knowledge studied in this way would become relevant to the students' own experience of whom and what they really are.

As it turned out, the experiment succeeded remarkably well. The research that the ETS (Educational Testing Service, the College Board people) conducted on the students at MIU, for example, was just amazing. The median College Board scores of incoming freshmen over the five-year period the tests were conducted were 55th percentile. By the time they were graduating and evaluated by the ETS their scores were in the 78th to 80th percentile nationwide. The entire university went up nearly 25% in its national standing over a five-year period. MIU was created as a model for other universities to follow, and it was ignored. Imagine today if our entire university system had incorporated MIU's programs, what the standing of U.S. education in the world today would be! MIU was an astonishing place to be and teach. So many young people enjoying direct growth of consciousness!

GE: You are teaching at VCU now, and it must be extraordinary for your students because of your depth of knowledge, even without your students learning to meditate. Each one of your students must leave your courses shaking their head, and full of questions.

Jon: They do shake their heads, and some also learn to meditate.

GE: Can you say something about your work after your days at MIU?

Jon: I've continued to work on the basic ideas from that time, refining and applying them in different ways. I've also been doing some work on categorizing different types of meditation, and trying to bring together researchers from different traditions to evaluate objectively what really produces what effects. TM at present appears overwhelmingly to be the most efficient for developing pure consciousness, but other procedures also produce useful results. So we really do need collaborative research, conducted by people associated with all sorts of traditions, to determine which procedures produce what results on what populations over what time frames. Such collaborative research, I think, is needed to directly address suspicions of bias that are often raised in the field of meditation-related research. It could have enormous practical results, making it clear to everyone what meditation practices are credible in terms of the benefits to the individual and society based on scientific research. It could also have very important theoretical results. For example, extensive cross-tradition research showing, as Maharishi indicated it should, that correlations between reports of pure consciousness and physiological correlates remained the same regardless of differences of belief, metaphysical context, and meditation practice. Science can provide much stronger evidence regarding the universality and validity of the experience.

GE: People are at different levels of human development and have different types of attachments and biases. This includes fundamentalists attached to the literal interpretation of their traditional texts, resulting in a fearful sector of the population who resist change.

Jon: Maharishi made it clear that the best way to help such individuals is to demonstrate that you have no intention of threatening them. For example, I observed how Maharishi would handle fearful individuals who would come into a lecture with the intention of disrupting things. He would always treat them with great respect; he would never, for example, simply say the word "Jesus" by itself; he would say "the lord Jesus," and there would be an enormous energy of love and compassion emanating from him. Maharishi would only encourage all their love for their tradition, and their attacks would be completely diffused.

GE: In the context of your profession, what is your perception of Maharishi?

Jon: Maharishi has given us previously unheard of insight on the effortlessness of transcending and knowledge of the experience of pure consciousness unavailable for thousands of years in the West, and in all of modern philosophy. He made clear that a person needs to explore the mind systematically from the surface to the depth. He wanted the results of these explorations to be examined empirically, using the belief-independent methods of modern science. He encouraged the use of direct inner exploration combined with scientific protocols to inform major philosophical issues. He provided a path to make plausible the existence and implications of transcendental experiences, and to move major philosophical theses from the realm of mere argument to that of scientific investigation. He provided a practical technique for producing new experiential data capable of corroborating and/or falsifying such theses directly, which is an enormous contribution.

GE: What thoughts would you like to share with the readers who are seeking knowledge and techniques to enrich their lives and society?

Jon: I would encourage people to sit down and turn within. Enjoy TM because it is effortless and effective; do it for a little while and you will be surprised. TM is very quick. Within two to three days the average person really begins to settle down. Deeper levels of awareness open up, and satisfaction increases. That's all that one can say. Satisfaction increases, life gets better. Different states of consciousness open up on their own.

GE: You have had glimpses of this inner awakening. It is as if a veil is pulled back and all of a sudden you gain an insight into our capacity.

Jon: That is beautifully put. Yes, and we see our potential. I recall an analogy from Maharishi. He described an overcast day with heavy clouds. Then the clouds part and you see the sun stream through. Even if the clouds go back together you know the sun is still there; as a result your attitude and your feelings change. I have had a special experience of expansion of consciousness, unbounded awareness that has remained with me for decades—not flashy, but subtly satisfying. Although I recognize that there are much more profound levels beyond it, I found that cravings for growth somehow eased and no longer put pressure on my life. Growth is wonderful, but attachment to it somehow melted. Something relaxed deep inside.

GE: That is beautiful because it is right; it does unfold over a lifetime. The process you describe above seems so simple, and people ask, how can this process work?

Jon: It works because it is so simple. It is like pushing a child on a swing—when you get into the swing of it, the child goes faster effortlessly. It seems as if you are doing nothing. This is also a principle of many internal martial arts; when it works it seems as if you are doing nothing. This seeming like you are doing nothing is a hallmark of an optimum technique—it works gracefully when you are moving with the nature of the system. One should expect the most efficient technique to be as close to effortless as possible. Even with the grindingly intense concentration of some Zen techniques, masters may tell students to concentrate harder, but at the same time tell them that when they get it, it will be natural. Maharishi made it effortless from the beginning. It is simply a matter of a higher level of knowledge of how to practice, an astonishingly systematic way of teaching the technique, and thorough training of teachers, so people can practice it so efficiently.

GE: Everyone who learns the TM technique interprets it from his or her own reference point, how they are living and seeing the world. The gift of enlightenment happens innocently. It is a gift resulting from the purification of the nervous system.

Jon: It is a gift of our nature—and whatever created us. What we usually think we are is some surface personality. As a child, a teenager, and a young adult, one is likely to spend a lot of time and effort trying to determine who one wants to be; we fantasize about different personalities, picking up and putting down this one and that, and eventually putting one on and wearing it, perhaps for the rest of one's life. Even mature adults may do this. All of these personalities however are not what one really is. What one really is exists deep within. *That* level of inner awareness is what is busy creating and trying on all these personalities in the first place. The gift you describe comes from deeper than one's personality. Whether this source is nature, one's true self, or God is a difficult question to answer; nevertheless, the important thing is to get the process right, and let it unfold.

GE: The title of the book is *A Symphony of Silence.* People like you and others in the book have experienced that inner stillness, and have gained an enlightened vision from it. This book was written out of love and compassion for humanity. What would you communicate to the reader regarding your journey?

Jon: It is very easy to settle down, find yourself, and be yourself. Very easy, and it just relaxes one's life, it empowers life. It allows a person to become more intimate with life itself. It is so simple that almost anything I can say is just too much. Just try it.

Part II

Consciousness, Religion, and Spirituality

Chapter VI

Searching for the Rishi

Jerry W. Jarvis

Jerry Jarvis first met Maharishi in 1961 and immediately began to study and work closely with him, helping to build Maharishi's U.S. and global TM teaching organization. For most of the next two decades Jerry served as US National Leader for the TM organization and was among those instrumental in establishing over 400 teaching centers and organizing numerous teacher training courses in the U.S., Europe, and India where Maharishi trained more than 12,000 TM teachers, thereby making the TM program available to everyone. During this time more than a million individuals in the U.S. learned Maharishi's TM technique.

Jerry pioneered the Students International Meditation Society, which brought education and science together to enliven the experience of the previously ineffable wisdom of ancient knowledge, to remove the mystery and to make it accessible. I first met Jerry as an undergraduate student when he gave a lecture at the University of California, Davis. I recall two aspects of the lecture. First, Jerry remarked that the TM program would help to create a proper sense of values. The second aspect was Jerry's own inner peace, and his explanation that the experience of Being, the conscious source of thought, was the natural result of transcending through the practice of TM, and that it would enrich human life.

From early on I had a desire to know the truth of life and to understand life in all its aspects. My inner impulse was to gain spiritual realization, and everything else was secondary. I had heard that a Rishi (holy sage) had been in the U.S. for many years, but was not here now. I had the hope that some-day I would meet a real Rishi and that it would help me in my quest. In September 1961 I saw an announcement in the newspaper that Maharishi Mahesh Yogi would be giving a lecture in Los Angeles. I researched what the prefix "Maha" meant and found it meant "the great." My wife Debby and I were living in Malibu, California. I said to Debby—let's go and hear him. The lecture was held at the Wilshire Ebell Theater. We entered the lecture hall and were walking down the aisle to our seats. Maharishi was already sitting on the dais. My first sight of him was enough to recognize his attainment, and with all his wisdom, power, and grace, he fulfilled for me the status of his name. After hearing the lecture I wanted very much to meet him. When it was later announced that we could sign up for interviews we were quick to do so. I must admit that I did not understand that he was teaching an actual technique that you practiced. I believed that this would be a chance to talk with him. I soon discovered that the interview was a step toward learning the TM practice. At the end of the interview he told us to come the following morning, when he instructed us in TM.

When we learned TM from Maharishi I recognized that the experience and the teaching were what I had been seeking all my life. I then thought how great it would be to express this knowledge, to be able to teach it. During those days we would meet in the TM center every evening with Maharishi for checking of the practice and advanced lectures. One evening it was announced that Maharishi would be holding a three-week meditation guide training course on Catalina Island, which is an island 25 miles off the coast of southern California. I attended the course and after one of the meetings the course leaders asked who could assist in transcribing tapes of Maharishi's lectures, and I quickly volunteered. The next day I informed Maharishi the transcript was ready, and he said—good, come up after lunch. I began to read the transcript to Maharishi and it became a pamphlet called "The Divine Plan." It was a transcript of a lecture he had given in London about a year before and this was the first time I had worked with him closely, and it was an experience beyond description. Maharishi's enlightened vision for humanity was in that lecture. I felt that Maharishi had total knowledge, and therefore everything he said was from that enlightened state. The earliest talks and writings contained all the teaching of the Veda, the total knowledge of life: life is bliss, and suffering abides in weakness. First transcend and Be; then, established in That, perform action, and swiftly come to the supreme.

Maharishi's earliest lectures and pamphlets express all the principles of total knowledge. We can understand through the analogy of learning carpentry. An apprentice can learn from a master carpenter, or he can learn from a carpenter who knows 70% of carpentry. As the student, he will learn in the range of the carpenter's capability. A master carpenter looks at the work and his assessment will certainly be different from that of a carpenter who has limited knowledge.

Maharishi was a master of the total knowledge of life and he inherited that knowledge in its totality from his teacher, His Divinity Brahmananda Saraswati, Jagadguru Bhagavan Shankaracharya of Jyotir Math, Himalayas (Guru Dev), who embodied the Vedic knowledge and tradition. Maharishi always acknowledged all gratitude to his Guru Dev and the Holy Tradition, offering Guru Dev's blessings to the lovers of life desirous of enjoying all glories, worldly and divine. In the Bhagavad-Gita, which Maharishi called the pocket edition of the Veda, Chapter 4, verse 34, he states: "Know this: through homage, repeated inquiry and service, the men of knowledge who have experienced Reality will teach you knowledge." Maharishi spent 13 years with Guru Dev and naturally all elements of this verse were in full enlivenment. Maharishi said it took about two to three years to attune his mind with Guru Dev's mind. Then in 1953, when Guru Dev passed, Maharishi went to Uttar Kashi in the Himalayas to live the life of a fulfilled yogi.

Maharishi did not plan to teach. He was a fulfilled yogi and the story of how this all came about is beautiful and innocent. After several years in Uttar Kashi a thought came to Maharishi that he should visit a particular temple in southern India; this was rather strange because in Uttar Kashi, the tradition is that there is no need to ever leave that place, but the thought persisted. After he completed his visit to several temples in southern India he began his return to Uttar Kashi by way of Trivandrum. In the town a man asked him to give some of the wisdom of the Himalayas to the people who lived there, as he recognized Maharishi to be a wise Yogi from northern India. Maharishi had never given lectures so they worked up seven subject titles. Maharishi observed that the people were not achieving their spiritual quest or enjoying life fully. He commented to them: either the Vedas are wrong and you are right, or the Vedas are right and you are wrong. The Vedas express that life is bliss, and the audience was not experiencing that reality; they had their teachers, their meditation techniques and spiritual practices, but were not obtaining significant results. Spiritual practices and meditation techniques had been taught in India for thousands of years, but they mostly required effort, renunciation, and control.

Maharishi pointed out that this was a tragic misinterpretation of the Vedic texts. He taught people how to transcend effortlessly and easily using the natural tendency of the mind to go to a field of greater happiness, which was the exact opposite of what they had been taught in the name of spiritual development. Maharishi explained that many of the interpretations of the Vedas and other systems for spiritual and human development were incorrect and did not produce the desired results, fostering the excuse that suffering was therefore necessary to life. Maharishi's teaching is that life is bliss, and its purpose is the expansion of happiness—and he began the revival of the Veda. The simplicity of the TM technique Maharishi taught and its immediate effectiveness produced enormous results for the people learning.

When Maharishi first began teaching the technique he called the transcending process Sadhana, which means "the practice that takes you to the goal." People were delighted with the outcomes, and they began to tell their friends. Maharishi spent the following few years teaching people the technique and the knowledge of an enlightened life, which has nothing to do with suffering—only with expansion of happiness and enlightenment.

In 1957, in honor of Guru Dev's 89th birthday celebration, Maharishi held a Congress of Spiritual Luminaries in Madras. During the Congress he was reviewing the progress that had been made and how many thousands of people had started this practice throughout India; he announced that with the revival of this teaching, the spiritual regeneration of the entire world could be achieved. People were so inspired that they applauded enthusiastically. During the applause the manager came to Maharishi and inquired why he did not inform him that he was going to announce the founding of a worldwide movement, because he would have generated more publicity. Maharishi responded: "I didn't know I was going to announce it." This is another example of the beautiful innocence of all his teaching and activity.

Toward the end of the Catalina Island course I told Maharishi that I wanted to give lectures on TM and wanted to express them accurately and completely. He said he would write out seven lectures for me to read. The extent of the TM organization in the United States for the next several years was Maharishi coming each year but during the rest of the time I would read out the seven lectures to a few people, and Mrs. Beulah Smith, who was the only American teacher who had trained with Maharishi in India in 1960, would come and teach the people TM. Maharishi came again to Los Angeles in 1962 and conducted another course on Catalina Island, which both Debby and I attended. In the days following this course I was waiting for Maharishi to leave for Europe and India, and someone came and informed me that Maharishi wanted me to come up to the mountains near Los Angeles where he was going to write a book. I was of course ecstatic. That book became *The Science of Being and Art of Living* and it was completed in about six weeks. Maharishi first dictated the table of contents and then each night he would speak a chapter into a tape recorder. In the morning I would transcribe the tape and then read it back to him. He made very few changes. On the weekend Debby, who was then working as a technical editor, would come up and help with the manuscript.

In 1963 Maharishi did not come to Los Angeles but instead conducted a course in Canada, which Debby and I attended. In 1964 Maharishi gave another course in Canada, and at the end of the course he asked me to meet him at Lake Tahoe in California where he planned to finish the translation and commentary on the Bhagavad-Gita, Chapters 1-6, which he had been working on for the last four years. I read out the manuscript and he said he was satisfied with it, and it was ready to be published. Then as time permitted he worked on the rest of the chapters of the Bhagavad-Gita. We left Lake Tahoe after six weeks and Maharishi gave a brief advanced course in Los Angeles, then on to Europe and India.

I went back to Los Angeles and continued to proceed with the seven-lecture courses. At the end of 1964 as I was giving these courses a young college student asked me if I would come down to Manhattan Beach and meet with about 15 of his friends, as they all wanted to hear about TM. They were so eager to learn that I gave the content of three or four lectures all in one session. Then we met again and they received the content of the rest of the seven lectures. Beulah Smith came up to Los Angeles and initiated all the students. I found out later that the student, Steve Weldon, who had invited me to Manhattan Beach, had a reputation of never smiling. And his friends began to notice he was smiling to himself. They asked him why he was smiling. He told them he had been hearing about TM. He had not even started TM at that point. I like to think that the student movement began with a smile.

In January in 1966 Maharishi's new academy near Rishikesh, India was sufficiently completed to hold a Teacher Training Course. Debby and I attended the course with about 35 others from several countries. To be in India under the direct guidance of Maharishi for four months of teacher training went a long way toward fulfilling my aspirations for spiritual guidance. In addition to our personal progress we learned how to teach the principles and practice of TM. When I returned from India to the U.S. as a trained TM teacher, we hit the ground initiating.

In the summer, we started the Students International Meditation Society (SIMS) at the University of California, Los Angeles (UCLA), which was established as an official student organization and authorized us to offer a six-week elective course on the principles and practice of TM. The 65 people who took the course became well grounded in the understanding of TM; those students were from all over the country, and from different colleges. Later, these students began calling me and asking if I could come and give lectures on the knowledge and practice at their campuses. During the rest of 1966 we held courses throughout the U.S. This is how the growth of SIMS rapidly took place.

In 1967, Maharishi lectured at UCLA, UC Berkeley, Yale, Harvard, and other institutions of higher learning. By 1968 there was a very active student TM movement, and about a hundred teachers had been trained in India. The same year, Maharishi organized a course in India, which included creative individuals such as Mike Love, Paul Horn, Donovan, and the Beatles. When the Beatles and other artists started TM, there was a large surge of interest.

Simultaneously with the increased response to TM, a major discovery took place. Dr. Keith Wallace was attending UCLA, and helped create SIMS on campus to provide educational TM courses. Keith switched his major from physics to physiology because Maharishi was very interested in conducting scientific research on those practicing TM. Keith found that during the practice of TM there were significant changes in the physiology that substantiated what Maharishi had predicted in regard to the existence of a fourth state of consciousness. The fourth state of consciousness has a completely different structural, chemical, and metabolic basis to it as compared to waking, dreaming, or deep sleep. Maharishi knew we were in the scientific age; he employed the language of science and later remarked that through the window of science we would see the dawn of the Age of Enlightenment.

When science appreciates the ultimate intelligence of the universe, they will appreciate that behind and within every movement of any particle

In 1968, Jerry and Debby Jarvis organized a one-month advanced course on the TM program conducted by Maharishi Mahesh Yogi in Squaw Valley, California.©

there is intelligence that is guiding the entire process. In the process of evolution everything is changing; creation and destruction are taking place simultaneously. Maharishi often used the analogy of the bud and the flower. The bud is simultaneously being destroyed as the flower blooms. Evolution is taking place all the time. An individual can have the experience of higher states of consciousness, but without proper understanding it can be misinterpreted.

In the film *Sage for a New Generation*, Maharishi was asked by a scientist what he wanted to be remembered for. Maharishi paused for a moment, and said: "Nothing, because everyone will remember me in the way they want to." All the great teachers revived the same truth of life. Maharishi did not make up what he was teaching, nor did Krishna, Jesus, Moses, Buddha, Shankara, or others. In this scientific age with all the technology, there is an opportunity for tremendous advances in reviving the age-old truth of life and making it available to all people once again. Life can be transformed from suffering, shortcomings, and sickness—to fulfillment. Human beings are built for fulfillment; they have all the technology to achieve enlightenment, but the operation manual had not been clearly defined until Maharishi appeared. He provided the knowledge of how action becomes more effective when an individual is functioning from the level of Being.

Throughout human history great sages arrive in the world and revive this ancient wisdom. They bring the same wisdom and teaching, always in accordance with the language of the time. It is the technique of skill in action. The teaching in all its profundity is found in the Bhagavad-Gita, which is the science of the Absolute, the scripture of yoga, the complete science of Vedic Knowledge. The Gita describes an intelligent and powerful leader of the day coming to a situation where he is not able to decide on a course of action. The essential teaching of the Gita is the teaching of skill in action: what is required is to first "Be" and then established in Being, perform action. Yoga is defined as skill in action. The real meaning of Yoga has been lost throughout the world. Maharishi revived the complete teaching of Yoga. The beauty of Maharishi's translation of the Gita is another example of a master carpenter in that he can see the complete value of knowledge and express it. There are 165 translations of the Gita in my library and none of them come close to Maharishi's insights and revival of the real teaching that has ultimate usefulness for all human beings. In India Maharishi was asked about the rightness of his perspective, and he responded:

> When I see your life, I am only concluding that this new voice is correct, and the older voices, wherever they came from, must have come from a field of ignorance. We do not know who said it but whosoever advocated concentration, control, and the need of detachment and renunciation for enlightenment, whomsoever he was, did not know what he was talking about. Whoever is talking such nonsense, we should politely ask him to please stop.

Maharishi declared that the interpretation of the Veda, the Upanishads, the Gita, the entire philosophy of Vedanta, the philosophy of Yoga, was in a mess.

In 1970, a summer conference was held at Humboldt State College near Eureka, California. Maharishi was giving a lecture to about 1,500 participants. He explained that with all the experiences on our personal level, we had come to understand that the great seer Patanjali, who cognized the Yoga Sutras, from which the teaching of Yoga emanates, advocated transcending thought as the basis for successful and fulfilling action. Maharishi further elaborated that this is the soul of Yoga philosophy and we are not responsible for the misunderstandings that have become common and we need to refresh the entire atmosphere. Maharishi stated: "We hope with this voice of revival, which is such a simple and natural system, to give the experience of inner reality so clearly that the misinterpretations will be eliminated. We have one solution—the transcending process through the TM program—and we do not concern ourselves with the darkness." We can spend the next 100 years analyzing problems and their symptoms because you cannot eliminate problems on the level of problems, just as you cannot eliminate darkness by researching the source of darkness. There is no source to darkness—darkness is simply the absence of light.

Maharishi's approach was to bring the light of knowledge. There is a recent example of this principle. An inner-city middle school was about to be closed because of the violence, absenteeism, and lack of focus or motivation by the students. School administrators did not have any answers as to why the students were absent, or the multiple sources of all the problems. The principal became aware of TM; he investigated the program and started the technique. He experienced for himself that the TM technique worked, and then made it available to his students and faculty.

Today, the formerly troubled school is flourishing. A few years after the program started, the principal won the award for the best middle school principal in the U.S. He simply brought the solution; it was so simple, the entire quality of life in the school improved, beginning with the academic performance of the students. Moreover, the faculty has their own quiet lounge area in which they can practice the TM technique. It is a powerful illustration of how the introduction of this one technique was like switching on the light in a dark room, and this can be duplicated throughout the world.

When a person is instructed in TM, he is guided to allow the natural process of transcending to occur; he or she then comes out to act in a more life-supporting manner. It has been found that the inability of a person to permanently maintain Transcendental Consciousness is caused by impurities in the chemical and structural setup of the nervous system through which we have our experiences. We have five senses, plus the organs of action, and mind, intellect, and ego. All of these are aspects of a human being. So through transcending, the purification process begins and this is why people have such diverse experiences. Each nervous system is different.

There are different states of consciousness and the nervous system has a unique style of functioning in each of these various states. In addition to waking, dreaming, and deep sleep, Maharishi defined the fourth state of Transcendental Consciousness, a field of unbounded awareness; the fifth state, Cosmic Consciousness, in which Transcendental Consciousness is maintained permanently along with activity; the sixth state, refined Cosmic Consciousness, where a person has the ability to experience the most refined aspects of the objects of sensory perception; and the seventh state, unity, whereby one eventually begins to live the unity of life, which means you begin to experience everything in terms of the Self.

Maharishi often pointed out that when a person begins to appreciate the inner and outer reality through knowledge based on experience, one then can attain enlightenment based on knowledge. There are two important components in developing an enlightened vision: experience and knowledge. Experience without understanding is an incomplete picture. The Yoga Sutras distinguish between two kinds of knowledge—pure knowledge (transcendental) and phenomenal knowledge (expressed). Pure knowledge has three components: perception, inference, and traditional teaching. Perception means experience through the senses; inference means deciding what the experience is through the intellect; traditional teaching provides the authority whereby one can verify one's understanding. Maharishi has said that knowledge is based on experience, and enlightenment is based on knowledge. When we study Maharishi's teaching we are verifying our understanding and facilitating the growth of enlightenment.

Maharishi emphasized that the only way the teaching of TM will remain effective for centuries to come is to uphold the purity of the teaching, and then the benefits will be maintained 100%. If the procedures of teaching are changed, even slightly, the benefit to the student becomes diminished. The purity of the teaching is of utmost importance. A major aspect of Maharishi's genius—which I believe is unprecedented in history—is how he transferred the ancient knowledge and methods so carefully that the purity of the teaching is maintained. The teaching can automatically be transferred to any individual independent of the level of consciousness of the teacher.

Maharishi stated that if a person can think a thought, he can transcend that thought. He developed an efficient system of training teachers and charged them with the responsibility to maintain the purity of the teaching down through the ages. To teach this universal knowledge is an enormous responsibility, and we are doing well when we uphold the purity of the teaching. When Maharishi first started teaching, he faced tremendous ignorance throughout the world. He said that the impulse that kept him moving forward was knowing that he had a technique that could bring ultimate value to any human life—no matter what the status, health, wealth, or worldly situation.

Since 1959 Maharishi's lectures have been audio- and videotaped. There are more than 30,000 hours of Maharishi's knowledge, which will serve to maintain the purity of the teaching. A vital component of gaining enlightenment is to verify our understanding by having access to total knowledge. It is fortunate to have this vital resource of Maharishi's teaching, generation after generation. Maharishi has laid out a plan for establishing an enlightened age and his vision is being fulfilled through the commitment of his trained TM teachers. We can envision the ultimate enlightenment of all mankind fulfilling the very purpose of life.

1968, Gulmarg, Himalayas, Maharishi Mahesh Yogi, Debby and Jerry Jarvis©

Chapter VII

Silence is the Universal Refuge

Rev. Roger Wm. Johnson, Ph.D. and Cynthia E. Johnson

Cynthia E. Johnson is a certified teacher of TM. She has taught the TM program in Cambridge, MA, and Washington, DC. She has also taught in schools using Consciousness-Based education, including an inner-city school in the nation's capital. Cynthia received her Master of Theological Studies from Harvard Divinity School.

Cynthia's father, Dr. Roger William Johnson, is a retired Protestant minister. Roger received his Ph.D. from Harvard University's Graduate School of Arts and Sciences. He served churches and taught in Massachusetts, Minnesota, Illinois, and New York. He grew up in the Midwest within the religiously conservative church of his Swedish parents and grandparents (Evangelical Covenant Church), and later transferred ordination credentials to the United Church of Christ to be open to progressive values. Roger characterizes himself—and feels this applies to most people—as being conservative regarding preserving the best of human values, and liberal, willing to learn and change. His ministry is characterized by dedicated social activism and his life by profound spirituality.

Cynthia and her father discuss spirituality and Transcendental Consciousness. Their dialogue reflects a tender synchrony of love between a daughter and her father. It is a brilliant clarification of the value of TM and Transcendental Consciousness in the context of a progressive vision of Christianity.

Finding the Path

> *Silence is the universal refuge, the sequel to all dull discourses and all foolish acts, a balm to our every chagrin, as welcome after satiety as after disappointment.*

> — Henry David Thoreau

Cynthia: Dad, I want to talk with you about the value, beauty, and necessity of inner silence for transforming our lives. Some of my earliest memories of the experience of silence have to do with you. I remember one summer when

I was four years old and you were the chaplain at a camp in New Hampshire. The sanctuary was in a pine forest clearing. You spoke at the altar with pine trees and sky above you, and I sat on a wooden bench with a soft carpet of needles under my feet, breathing in the fresh scent of early morning stillness. I was in a state of wonder, soaking in the hushed holiness of the atmosphere.

It was during this time of your life, when you were a young father, that you had a couple of transforming experiences of a transcendent nature—what you refer to as peeks into the divine mystery. But before discussing those stories, let's talk about how the need for inner silence grew as time went on—in your life and in my life as well. You were juggling many things in your early adult life. You served churches full-time in the Boston area; you were starting a family; and then you began to take courses at Harvard that were offered free to ministers in the area. You then were encouraged by the faculty to do a full-time Ph.D. program, which you did. In addition to having three small children, you discovered you and Mom were expecting twins. How did you do all this?

Roger: I was so stimulated and exhilarated by everything I was doing! And I was disciplined with my time. I often began my day at around 3 a.m. when the twins would awaken. I would change their diapers, give them their bottles, and put them back to bed. Then I would go across the street to have coffee and a doughnut, sharing a bit of camaraderie with the deliverymen and policemen—the only other individuals awake at that time. Then I did some studying and work in the church. I used to study whenever I could, such as when stopped at red lights on my way to visiting parishioners.

Cynthia: That is discipline! I know you finished your doctoral degree in almost record time—two and a half years.

Roger: It was necessary because I had a family, was a pastor, and a student. But I loved what I was doing, so that is what made it possible.

Cynthia: I remember visiting you in your study at our church, next door to where we lived in the parsonage. I enjoyed just being there, basking in the atmosphere of your study. Even though this was a middle-class/working-class urban area, there was a sense of sacred, scholarly stillness in the church and your study.

Roger: Yes, the whole Boston area had that mingled atmosphere of scholarliness and sacredness.

Cynthia: I remember sitting on the steps of the church, built in the classic

New England style with white pillars, brick walls, and a steeple. I could hear the most beautiful sound of choirs singing. Sometimes it would be from our own church, but other times, it was fainter, and sounded like angels to me.

Roger: Perhaps you heard a choir practicing at one of the other churches nearby.

Cynthia: I used to love to visit the Catholic church down the street with my best friends, who were part Irish and Italian. The church was dark, but illuminated with candles, and had a lovely spicy scent. I loved the feeling of quiet, mysterious holiness.

Roger: Yes, I remember you visiting there; in particular, when you went to light a candle for our bird that had died. How old were you then, maybe five?

Cynthia: I think so. Mom gave me a Velveeta cheese box, which was a perfect coffin for our parakeet Amy. Off I went in my Easter hat, white gloves and shorts, holding Amy to light a candle for her at the Catholic church. That kind of hands-on ritual was very helpful to me as a child to deal with death. As I reflect upon the situation now, I realize how supportive and comfortable you and Mom were with my visiting the Catholic church.

Roger: We lived in an area with many houses of worship, and your mom and I appreciated both the diversity and the common experience of spirituality.

Cynthia: Let's fast forward 10 years or so. The busy pace of your life continued.

Roger: There was a lot going on in my life and in the world in that next decade—from the early 1960s through the '70s. During that time we moved to Minneapolis where I served a church and taught part-time at a seminary for a few years. Afterward, I was recruited to be the chaplain and professor of philosophy of religion at a small private college in Rockford, Illinois—my hometown. That was an intense time in America. I was involved in the civil rights and peace movements.

Cynthia: I recall when you were at Rockford College you supported conscientious objectors to the Vietnam War. I was around 13 at that time, and I was so proud of you for doing that.

Roger: Yes, but it got me into trouble with the president of the college, who was very conservative, and my contract was not renewed. After that I received several offers, including from a church in Scarsdale, New York, where we moved in 1970.

Cynthia: In Scarsdale, you continued your involvement in many avenues of social activism, such as antiwar, ecumenism, civil rights, public education, and prison work. Didn't you get arrested during this time for an antiwar protest?

Roger: Yes, I participated in an antiwar demonstration and was arrested in front of the White House on Veterans Day in 1972.

Cynthia: I love the story about your ride from the jail.

Roger: After spending the night in jail and posting bail, we were released, but there was no public transportation available in the area. So I, along with two other protestors—a college professor and a college freshman—spotted a bus several blocks away. We ran down the road and discovered it was a school bus filled with the football team of the United States Naval Academy! It was serendipity that they were going to the very parking lot where our car was, and they agreed to give us a ride. As we rode along, my colleagues and I conducted an ad-hoc seminar about the Vietnam War. These students were not familiar with the other side of the war situation, and they seemed to listen with interest and respect.

Cynthia: While you were deeply involved with the Church and your social activism, I was a busy student in the 9th and 10th grades, trying to follow, in some ways at least, in your footsteps. I was very conscientious academically—my goal was to go to Harvard. I was involved in volunteer projects such as the Head Start program for underprivileged children, projects to raise funds for the hungry, and so on. However, I was unhappy—full of anxiety, and with terrible insomnia. On the weekends, to blow off pressure, I did some wild partying, which only exacerbated things. Both of us were getting burned out and not getting any help.

Roger: Yes. I was putting in 90-100 hours of work each week, and sometimes not sleeping well. As a parish minister, I saw myself as a helper. For a long time, I did not realize that before I could be an effective helper, I needed to be helped. I had grown up with the awareness that we should love God and our neighbors; anytime I thought about myself, I used to feel "Now I am being self-centered," and felt guilty.

Cynthia: So you did not take care of yourself. You kept giving and giving and pushing on, not taking time to rejuvenate.

Roger: Right. It was Erich Fromm (1956)—the Jewish psychologist and philosopher—who got through to me about this. It was his writing that made me realize that self-love was necessary in order to "love thy neighbor as thyself."

Cynthia: Right. How can you love others as yourself if you don't love yourself properly, if you are filled with exhaustion, anxiety, and self-criticism? During that time of my life, I became seriously depressed. I could see that when I was unhappy, my ability to help others was ineffective.

Roger: Your well was dried up.

Cynthia: Exactly. You and Mom arranged for counseling, which was somewhat helpful, but barely scratched the surface.

Roger: What about your relationship to the Church and Christianity at that time?

Cynthia: At that time, I perceived Christianity as a body of ethics: principles for compassionate behavior, which were obviously correct. Moreover, I felt that I was trying to live in accord with them. However, I didn't see anything that would alleviate my own suffering, and enrich the source of compassionate behavior, but I was seriously seeking. Around age 13, I had started seeking for something more—beyond the status quo. I knew there was much more potential for human joy and creativity than what I was currently experiencing and seeing around me. I attended lectures on yoga, and went into Manhattan once and participated in some strange program where you stared at each other and talked in gibberish! In 9th grade I started reading the existentialists—and could relate to the "nausea" described in a book of that name by Jean-Paul Sartre (1964), but that did not help me.

Roger: In 11th grade you began to attend the Scarsdale Alternative School.

Cynthia: Yes, the Alternative School had just started as part of the public high school in Scarsdale. That was, and is, such a great place. It fills a gap in education, nurturing the students by providing close mentoring relationships with teachers and leaders in the community, who taught classes or provided apprenticeships.

It was at that time I saw posters with a picture of Maharishi, announcing TM introductory lectures, but I thought TM was another Indian fad, and it did not attract me. I did not want to become involved in any kind of cult, and I thought it was like the McDonald's of meditation. However, one day a vibrant young woman with long red hair came to our school and gave an introductory lecture on TM. She was such an authentic, intelligent, warm, and interesting person. She had a lot of vitality and ease. When she described the principle of the technique, it felt right. You did not even have to believe in it; it was a straightforward procedure that allowed the mind and body to experience a fourth state of consciousness—restful alertness. I remembered those times in my life when I had felt very settled, yet quietly awake—times when I was in nature, or in a sacred space. I wanted more of that experience, for sure! Also, the scientific research on TM gave me more confidence in the validity of the technique.

Additionally, what impressed me as much as the research was that the TM teacher embodied the qualities that she was talking about. She had a refreshing openness. I will never forget our exchange that day. After the lecture, I bounded up to her, enthusiastically asking questions. Despite my 1970s teen persona with knee-high black suede platform boots, a bunch of scarves tied around my neck, and wild eye makeup, she said to me, I like you, you are so innocent! No one had said anything like that to me in ages.

So I learned TM. Nothing flashy, but I noticed I started feeling more stable inside. I was not as vulnerable to getting thrown around by whatever was going on in my life. I began to sleep better; the anxiety and depression steadily dissolved; the drinking and smoking gradually tapered off.

Roger: Yes, Mom and I noticed that you were feeling more secure and happy, much to our relief. From our perspective, these healthy changes were immensely significant.

Cynthia: Beyond the stress release, what was compelling to me was the possibility of enlightenment, or Cosmic Consciousness—where inner silence and deep bliss would be unshakeable. And even more fascinating was something a friend told me a couple of months after I had learned TM. We were at a party, and while our friends carried on around us, he and I sat on the floor and he described to me higher states of consciousness. I found myself increasingly riveted as he told me about refined Cosmic Consciousness or God Consciousness, where perception and emotions become so refined that you have the most highly-developed appreciation of God's creation. My friend further explained that refined Cosmic Consciousness flowers into Unity Consciousness, where the infinite value of everything in creation is cognized, and is as intimate as one's Self. I wanted that experience!

Roger: Then you went to Cornell University for your freshman year, but midway through the year you wanted to go to Maharishi International

University (MIU). At first Mom and I were skeptical and encouraged you to stay at Cornell, at least for a year. After that we thought you would check out MIU for a semester and return to Cornell.

Cynthia: I did finish my freshman year at Cornell. Although I enjoyed some of my classes and the beautiful campus, it was the usual college thing: studying bits and pieces of fragmented information, and the standard routine that burned us out. Every semester students would jump into the gorges that cut through campus—to end their lives, which was so sad. We used to say at exam time when we felt stressed, "I'm going to go gorge out." Like most colleges, it was not a place for nourishing the instrument of knowledge—the nervous system.

The Soul of the Whole

> *We live in succession, in division, in parts, in particles. Meantime within man is the soul of the whole; the wise silence; the universal beauty, to which every part and particle is equally related ...*
>
> — Ralph Waldo Emerson (1841)

Cynthia: I had heard about this new university where growth of consciousness was a fundamental part of the program, and where common patterns of natural law were explored within all disciplines, and within human consciousness. This sounded like an incredibly fascinating place, and so I went to MIU (now called MUM) after I finished that year at Cornell. After traveling from New York to the Midwest, through miles of farmland, we drove onto campus on an autumn evening. The sun was setting and pouring golden light through the campus. I felt as if I were coming home after being in exile my whole life.

I loved life at MIU. The professors were passionate about their disciplines and were superb teachers. We would sit together over meals—teachers and students—and discuss consciousness, physics, music, biology, economics, art, literature, and so on. The regular routine at MIU is designed to cultivate the instrument of knowing—the quality of our consciousness and the body—by setting aside time for meditation and obtaining a good night's sleep. The creativity of the students was off the charts, and we had so much fun together. As David Lynch (2006) says, we found we were far more creative without the usual college haze of exhaustion, drink, and drugs.

Roger: Now that you are a parent yourself, you can imagine how significant your transformation was to Mom and me. A few years earlier you had been unhappy to the point of serious depression—and now, you were healthy, enthusiastic, and happy. And another thing: it was during this time you began to show interest in Christianity.

Cynthia: I began to read the Bible, and it started to become meaningful to me. Verses like this: "But seek first the kingdom of God and His righteousness, and all these things shall be added to you" (Matthew 6:33, New King James Bible). "The kingdom of God does not come with observation; nor will they say, 'See here!' or 'See there!' For indeed, the kingdom of God is within you" (Luke 17:20-21). Or a childhood favorite psalm, " . . . He makes me lie down in green pastures. He leads me beside still waters; he restores my soul" (Psalm 23:2-3, Revised Standard Version). I began to see and relate to the richness of profound spiritual truths in the Bible.

Roger: We began to talk more about my own interest and experience in deeper, spiritual values of Christianity. For example, I shared with you how at Harvard I had a friend and fellow student, Walter Pahnke, who had a degree in medicine and was now working on his theology degree. He particularly was interested in so-called mystical experiences. We were interested in the idea that the great spiritual teachers throughout time were speaking of the transformation of consciousness. Mystical experience was transformative for human consciousness, and needed as a foundation for life-enriching behavior.

Cynthia: So your interest in Christianity was not only as a system of ethics, as I had perceived in my teen years.

Roger: Absolutely. Compassionate behavior has its roots in something much deeper. Paul in Galatians (5:23) speaks of the *fruit of the Spirit*—love, joy, peace, forbearance, kindness, goodness, faithfulness, gentleness, and self-control. Well, what was the nature of this Spirit, and how can it be experienced in order to give rise to these ideal behaviors? You and I began talking about things like this. I thought of the qualities I saw growing in you and others who practiced TM in the Pauline sense—fruit of the Spirit.

It was around this time that you became a teacher of TM, and you taught Mom and me to meditate. Because I was a clergyman, you taught it in the context of the Science of Creative Intelligence Course, which was a requirement at that time. (This is a 33-lesson videotaped course, taught by Maharishi, in the study of the source, course, and goal of principles of creative intelligence that govern the growth of the universe and human consciousness.)

Cynthia: What did you notice from your starting TM?

Roger: A few things: I felt more at peace with myself; I felt less anxious striving. I've been prone to feeling a lot of anxiety, but when I have been meditating regularly, it has given me a source of serenity that feels very good. Of course, if you are serene, there is a dimension of joy in that. Joy is not something apart from serenity—they are intermeshed. A line from one of my favorite hymns is "the silence of eternity interpreted by love." I love that line. (He recites from memory): "Dear Lord and Father of mankind, forgive our feverish ways. Re-clothe us in our rightful mind; in purer lives, thy service find . . . O calm hills above! Where Jesus knelt to share with Thee, the silence of eternity, interpreted by love." And this verse makes me think of TM: "Drop thy still dews of quietness, till all our strivings cease; take from our souls the strain and stress, and let our ordered lives confess the beauty of thy peace" (Whittier, 1996, p. 397).

Cynthia: That's so beautifully appropriate, Dad. So, after you started meditating, would you say you began to experience some of the "still dews of quietness" in your feverish life?

Roger: Yes, like you, it was gradual, but very significant. It helped me with some serious health problems at that time, related to depression, exhaustion, and anxiety. As the anxiety drained away, I started feeling more whole and healthy.

Cynthia: It is interesting, how health, wholeness, and holiness are all related.

Roger: Right. When we feel anxious, we feel torn apart, scattered—the opposite of wholeness, holiness.

Cynthia: And then we are thrown around on the surface waves of life. Lack of integration can carry with it a deficiency of integrity.

Roger: That lack of integrity is contrary to our nature, and is what gets us into trouble. This discussion makes me think of the detainees I worked with in the 1970s, when I volunteered at a house of detention in the Bronx. I was impressed with the intelligence and goodness in the men I encountered. In the process of trying to find fulfillment, they had taken shortcuts and had made some bad choices.

Cynthia: Yes, it is a helpful perspective. I remember a story you told me once about some prisoners comparing you to a great historical figure.

Roger: That amazed me. I used to walk away sometimes from these meetings with these men, feeling more ministered unto, than ministering to them. They were so articulate, and had such good sensitivities. One day, two detainees I had been working with—two African-American men who had grown up on the streets of the Bronx—greeted me by saying: "We have figured out who you remind us of. We think you are a reincarnation of Henry David Thoreau!" I so was surprised! Not only by this great compliment but also by the fact that they were familiar with Thoreau and reincarnation.

Cynthia: Why do you think they said this about you?

Roger: There were certain issues we discussed that we all shared. We all valued silence, and had a profound appreciation of nature, and an open mind concerning spirituality.

Cynthia: Those are certainly qualities that I know you greatly respect.

Roger: And they did as well. But of course, it was so hard for them because they had no opportunity to be in the healing atmosphere of nature. They had no silence in their environment—harsh noise constantly amplified and echoed off the walls—it was horrendous. I think I would have gone crazy. That is why I really can see the value of TM for prisoners, giving them an opportunity to experience the silence within.

Cynthia: Even in that harsh, chaotic atmosphere the experience of inner silence softens their emotions. The stories these people have shared are extraordinary (Ellis, 1983). Don't you wish TM was available in every prison?

Roger: Yes. The silence that Thoreau (1985) called "the universal refuge . . . the balm to our every chagrin" (p. 318) could unfold within the prisoners.

Cynthia: Yes, and it seems that has been the case with the prison programs, and for everyone feeling locked away from peace. While we are speaking of Thoreau, I want to share a quote I found recently on a visit to Concord, Massachusetts. I had just walked through the beautiful old moss-covered Sleepy Hollow Cemetery to visit the gravesites of Thoreau, Emerson, and other Transcendentalists. I was so deeply moved. Then I walked over to a used bookstore, where there was a huge two-volume set of Thoreau's Journals. I opened the Journal and was quite amazed to read the following from his entry on July 16, 1851:

In youth…I can remember that I was all alive, and inhabited my body with inexpressible satisfaction, both its weariness and its refreshment were sweet to me. This earth was the most glorious musical instrument, and I was audience to its strains. To have such sweet impressions made on us, such ecstasies begotten of the breezes! I can remember how I was astonished. I said to myself—I said to others—'There comes into my mind such an indescribable, infinite, all-absorbing, divine, heavenly pleasure, a sense of elevation and expansion, and [I] have naught to do with it. I perceive that I am dealt with by superior powers.' This is a pleasure, a joy, an existence, which I have not procured for myself. I speak as a witness on the stand, and tell what I have perceived . . . The maker of me was improving me. When I detected this interference, I was profoundly moved . . . (Torrey, 1906, pp. 306-7).

Roger: That is beautiful.

Cynthia: It reflects his highly developed sensitivity, and I am so moved by his awed acknowledgement: "The maker of me was improving me." Also, it is poignant that it took Thoreau a long time to discover others who had similar experiences. He further wrote on that same day:

I wondered if a mortal had ever known what I knew. I looked in books for some recognition of a kindred experience but strange to say, I found none. Indeed, I was slow to discover that other men had this experience, for it had been possible to read books and to associate with men on other grounds (Torrey, 1906, p. 307).

He felt alone, and I could relate to that. This is partly why it was such a relief to attend MIU—where others valued this kind of experience, and where refinement of consciousness was central to the education.

Roger: I feel I can relate to what Thoreau is describing from an experience I had once. It also involved the sense of hearing.

Cynthia: I would love to hear about it!

Roger: When we lived in Boston in the early 1960s, Mom and I had received tickets to a concert by the Boston Symphony Orchestra at Symphony Hall, which had superb acoustics. I was familiar with these acoustics from my own experience there, several years earlier. When I was a student at Augustana College, our college choir had sung a concert in Symphony Hall—a thrilling experience. One of the pieces we sang was Randall Thompson's "The Peaceable Kingdom" (1936). I remember I had shivers up and down my spine, especially when we sang "and gladness of heart" several times in succession, starting with double pianissimo and gradually building louder and louder in a spine-tingling crescendo until Symphony Hall vibrated with our voices. So that college choir experience was in my awareness as we took our seats that evening, four rows from the front on the center aisle. There was a guest conductor, and I was immediately struck by similarities to my father—you remember he died when I was only 15—who had directed two very large church choirs. The conducting styles of my father and this conductor were similar—very smooth and flowing.

As I listened to the opening selection—Haydn's Oxford Symphony—I went from a state of being enthralled, to a state of ecstasy, to a state which made me think of St. Paul's description of being taken up to the second or third heaven (2 Cor. 12:2). Such joy I felt. Indescribable! In this state of ecstasy, I imagined my father in heaven singing and directing a huge choir. This was one of the three or four most vivid states of consciousness I have ever had over the years. It can be described only as mystical or transcendental. I told no one about it at the time because words paled in comparison to the experience.

Cynthia: How very beautiful! How did you feel afterwards?

Roger: I felt I was almost walking on air for about two to three weeks until it gradually subsided. I was living in the aftermath. It was not just an emotional experience; it was a different mode of being. From within this experience, the secular was transformed into the sacred, the ordinary into the extraordinary.

Cynthia: This refinement is an important aspect of what Maharishi taught concerning development of consciousness. After all the stresses and strains are released, our machinery of perception becomes increasingly more refined. There is a positive feedback cycle where we appreciate more, which means our hearts are more loving, and that in turn further refines, nourishes our perception, and so on. Your experience at Symphony Hall sounds like you gained a peek into a higher state of consciousness.

Roger: Yes, it is true—when the heart is fuller, we appreciate more. Beauty is in the eye of the beholder. This experience makes me think of what Jesus referred to as the kingdom of heaven, which he said is within, about, among us

(Luke 17:20-21). It is hard to put into words, and you cannot put boundaries on it—it is an experience of the unbounded. Living within boundaries is an everyday experience of being human, but to some, from time to time, is given the gift of transcendence. You do not control it.

Cynthia: That is the value of a practice—regular cultivation of the mind and body, and it is true: the development of consciousness is not based upon control. With TM, you take the proper initial condition, like diving. You let go, and nature takes over and allows you to dive deeply. It is this naturalness that makes TM effective. It makes use of our innate tendency to be drawn toward fields of greater charm, and more subtle layers of consciousness have more charm.

Roger: That describes my experience with meditating, and you are right about the value of regular practice for refinement of our awareness.

Cynthia: There was another journal entry by Thoreau that I wanted to share with you, where he again describes his very refined sense of hearing. This is from July 21, 1851:

> There is always a kind of fine Aeolian harp music to be heard in the air. I hear now, as it were, the mellow sound of distant horns in the hollow mansions of the upper air . . . far away overhead, subsiding into my ear . . . . what a harp this world is! . . . There is an immortal melody that may be heard morning, noon, and night, by ears that can attend, and from time to time this man or that hears it, having ears that were made for music (Torrey, 1906, p. 330).

When I discovered this I was excited, because his words give a flavor of experiences I had as a very young child. For example, when I was about four or five, during an apparent dream, I saw and heard a choir of angels singing. The beauty of the sound and the experience of intense ecstasy were on an order of magnitude beyond anything—it was sheer glorious ecstasy. Like Thoreau, it took me many years before I encountered anyone, either in books or in person, who had such a similar experience. That's why I was so captivated when my friend at that party told me about refined Cosmic Consciousness, or God Consciousness, where one's appreciation of God's creation is highly developed. But unless you have had a glimpse of this experience, it can sound a bit unbelievable.

Roger: That experience planted a seed for you, didn't it? For your deep knowingness that there was something more to life than the mundane.

Cynthia: Yes, and that it was possible to dissolve suffering and experience joy in life.

Roger: Your angel-choir experience reminds me of the hymn *This is My Father's World*: "This is my Father's world, and through my listening ears, all nature sings and round me rings the music of the spheres . . . " (Babcock, 1996, p. 57). Whenever you visit, I love to have you sing the hymn *O Holy Angels Bright*:

> O holy angels bright, who wait at God's right hand, or through the realms of light fly at your Lord's command . . . Sing thou the songs of love . . . Let all thy days, till life shall end, whate'er He send, be filled with praise . . . (Baxter, 1996, p. 760)

Science tells us there are innumerable contrapuntal sounds surrounding us—in the way of radio waves and the music they carry. In a similar way my intuition tells me that in the silent spaces there are a multitude of energy forces, which are full of wisdom and creativity, going on all the time. Creation is not just in the past; it is endless and infinite. Angels are a symbolism that points to this reality. You need a poet's sense to see the inklings or inclinations of these foci of energy—they could be called the hearts and minds of the entities around us, symbolized by the concept of angels. Angel means a messenger. There are infinite possibilities of messages or messengers, including from the past, which are literally there in our brains, a kind of cosmic brain.

Cynthia: Wow, Dad! That is quite an interesting way of understanding the possibility of angels! You mentioned the cosmic brain. One phrase I have heard Maharishi use for the pure field of creative intelligence is the "cosmic computer."

Roger: That is a fascinating term.

Cynthia: When we sing these hymns together now, I can appreciate that being exposed to such beautiful hymns did indeed help refine my perception as a young child. The music in the church, the images, and metaphors in the Bible stirred something deeply in me. As I said before, I loved the mysterious sacredness of the Catholic Church. Our own church had a different flavor of holiness. It was like liquid sunshine—joy and warmth flowing through my veins.

Roger: This is an experience not only in a church context. You can feel it hiking in the mountains or walking in the early morning or at sunset—feeling quiet, awake, and alive. Many of the psalms are songs of praise about God's creation. "This is the day the Lord has made, let us rejoice, and be glad in it!" (Psalm 118:24).

Cynthia: Isaiah wrote: "For you shall go out in joy, and be led forth in peace; the mountains and the hills before you shall break forth into singing, and all the trees of the field shall clap their hands" (Isaiah 55:12).

Roger: I love that!

Cynthia: The sense of wonder and appreciation unfolds as softness and silence unfold within our consciousness. If we are full of fatigue and anxiety, it coarsens both our perception and our hearts. Our ability to love tends to suffer in spite of our good intentions.

Roger: I think of Rabbi Jesus' teaching that you must be as a child to enter the kingdom of heaven. "Truly, I say to you, unless you turn and become like children, you will never enter the kingdom of heaven" (Matthew 18:3). Thoreau described—and perhaps lamented—that it was in his childhood that he was most awake and aware. Jesus addresses this with the teaching to be as a child *now*. We have the potential, at all times in our lives, to become childlike in terms of appreciation, wonder, love, and trust.

Cynthia: The New Testament uses a very interesting word, *metanoia*, usually translated as "repent," for how this transformation takes place. Can we explore the meaning of *metanoia* in the context of discussing a theologian, Paul Tillich, who has had a profound influence upon you?

The Ground of Being

> *The name of infinite and inexhaustible depth and ground of our being is God ... And if that word has not much meaning for you, translate it, and speak of the depths of your life, of the source of your being ...*

> — Paul Tillich (1948)

Cynthia: I remember that when you learned TM and took SCI, you immediately saw parallels with Paul Tillich's theology. In your doctoral program in the early 1960s, you had taken one of Tillich's last seminars at Harvard.

Roger: Paul Tillich (1963) is considered one of the most influential Protestant theologians of the 20th century. He was one of only four faculty given the title of "University Professor" at Harvard at that time, which meant that his learning was considered deep and broad enough to be applicable to all of Harvard's schools: Divinity, Arts and Sciences, Medicine, Law, Education, and Business. I was privileged to have participated in one of his last seminars. The seminars were held in his apartment in Cambridge, so it was a comfortable setting, conducive to sharing.

Cynthia: I remember that for your doctoral dissertation, you read almost everything he had ever written, which was significant.

Roger: Yes, including all he had written in German!

Cynthia: What did you like about Tillich?

Roger: As a young man, I had an uneasy conscience about traditional Christianity. The traditional Biblical language left me puzzled. Tillich enabled me to recognize how realistic, practical, and relevant that inherited theology is. With Tillich I constantly experienced that "aha" feeling when I read his interpretation of Biblical language. He spoke in a language that was universal. Tillich defines God as *Being Itself*, the divine ground, source, and power of life. Fundamentally, Tillich said it is not doctrine or teachings that are the essence of religion and spirituality. Religious doctrine points to the Truth, which is a state of Being beyond any activity or thing. He viewed intellectual understanding as complementary to direct spiritual experience. Similarly, Maharishi speaks of the transcendental field of Being, which we can only experience when we transcend mental activity.

Cynthia: Where we experience pure awareness, pure consciousness, as expressed in Philippians 4:7—"the peace that passes understanding." I recently saw a couple of translations that interpreted this verse as the peace of God, which transcends all understanding (New International Version), or powers of thought.

Roger: That adds more clarity. I recently was rereading one of Tillich's sermons called "What Is Truth?" from his book, *The New Being* (1955). Tillich writes that Jesus' life was "a life which never lost the communion with the divine ground of all life, and . . . which never lost the union of love with all beings" (p.74).

Cynthia: That is a beautiful way of describing the life of Jesus.

Roger: Yes, and I remember from the SCI class how similar Tillich's analysis was to Maharishi's description of higher states of consciousness. As with the life of Jesus, love for all beings springs from communion with the ground of all life—what both Tillich and Maharishi call Being.

The universality of Tillich's and Maharishi's teachings concerning "love" greatly appealed to me as well. In one of Tillich's sermons (1955), he quotes from 1 John 4:16: "God is love, and he who abides in love abides in God, and God abides in him." Even so-called unbelievers can relate to this. The philosopher and mathematician Bertrand Russell (2000) said at the end of his life that he came to recognize that the greatest of all values was love. Not romantic love—*eros*; not even just brotherly or sisterly love—*philia*; but unconditional love—*agape*.

Cynthia: One practical teaching of Maharishi is that the ability to love fully is based on inner fullness, inner Being. That is something you and I both had to learn.

Roger: Psalm 23 expresses the restorative power of the Divine. "He makes me lie down in green pastures. He leads me beside still waters; he restores my soul . . . my cup overflows" (verses 2-3, 5).

Cynthia: When we are restored, compassion for others is natural; it overflows from communion with the Divine.

Roger: I agree. Returning to the point about Tillich defining the Divine as the "ground of Being": he was criticized by some because when he defined God in this way, many people were turned off. They felt it sounded too abstract, but it is another way of saying that God is the dynamism within the structure of Being. The dynamism is the energy or spirit in which we participate.

Cynthia: This is very similar language to Maharishi's. He speaks of the nature of Reality as "silence and dynamism." In Unity Consciousness we experience or cognize the silence within dynamism and the dynamism within silence.

Roger: Interesting! Also Tillich said: It is impossible to deny the personal dimension of Ultimate Reality. What it means to be a human being is such an amazing phenomenon, and so, of course, God must contain the personal attribute, so to speak; at the same time, there is an impersonal dimension (Tillich, 1951).

Cynthia: Maharishi (1973) in his *Science of Being and Art of Living*, discusses there being two aspects of God, the personal and the impersonal. "The impersonal aspect of God is formless, supreme; It is eternal and absolute Being" (p. 272). The personal aspect of God is the Supreme Being who "governs and maintains the entire field of evolution and the different lives of innumerable beings in the whole cosmos . . . If the individual . . . can succeed in attuning himself with Him or Her, then certainly his unevolved . . . life will be blessed by God's all-powerful, merciful nature" (pp. 278-9).

Roger: At one point, I wanted to do my doctoral dissertation on the personal and impersonal dimensions of God, but I eventually realized it was too broad a topic and would require a lifetime of writing.

Cynthia: That's very interesting, because that is a topic with which I have been intrigued for years as well.

Roger: Yes, we certainly have many overlaps in our interests! Regarding the impersonal dimension of God, it is the source of the pulse of creativity, which is omnipresent throughout creation, and yet transcends time and space. This represents the impersonal impression that we may have when we try to understand God. I use the word "impression" because we cannot comprehend the infinite with our finite intellects.

Cynthia: However, we have the capacity to experience the infinite on the transcendent level of our Being, where we have transcended mental activity. Discussing this reminds me of an especially clear experience I had of transcendence. It was as if I fell through a trapdoor into Being, pure awareness, where I was utterly immersed in a state of limitless joy, freedom, power, and all possibilities. It was very powerful . . . something way beyond words. As part of this experience I sensed something: merciful compassion, or total and utter acceptance and love. I had been going through a very challenging time in my life, and this experience flooded me with profound relief, freedom, and joy. It was incredibly transformational. I discussed this experience with a Christian monk who is also a TM teacher—about whether he thought this was an experience of the personal or impersonal aspect of the divine. The experience was completely devoid of anything sensory—I had not seen or heard anyone. But my friend pointed out that my experience appeared to contain qualities of both the personal and the impersonal aspects of God. So the division between personal and impersonal, perhaps, was my own conceptual overlay onto a unified reality.

Roger: Beautiful, and I agree about the conceptual overlay.

Cynthia: The effect upon my life of this experience was enormous. The bottom line was that it was absolutely self-evident that fulfillment in life comes from the inner Divine Source, not from any thing or person outside.

This direct experience gave me the freedom to stay in a challenging situation, and transform it through love and positivity.

Roger: Your cup overflowed from the fullness of the experience.

Cynthia: Absolutely.

Roger: I had a somewhat similar experience, except that mine came during a time of great contentment. It was one of the several experiences that I call "Peeks into the Divine Mystery." In 1952-3, as my final requirement in preparation for the ministry, I was doing my internship at two small churches in Massachusetts. It was a happy time for me. Mom and I planned to be married when I returned home in the summer (she was teaching school back in Rockford, Illinois). My mental, spiritual, and physical health could hardly have been better. And so it happened that on a quite ordinary day, temperature comfortable, trees and bushes in full bloom, as I walked along, I was thinking about what a privilege it was to be alive and well in this remarkable world. All of a sudden, there was an instantaneous awareness of . . . (pausing, trying to find words) . . . the eternal dimension, which broke through the boundary walls of ordinary consciousness. It was as if a kind of veil opened to another dimension; it was extraordinary, ineffable, infinite, and unbounded—impossible to put into words. We have only finite words to describe the indescribable. I cannot recall perceiving any specific things. I stopped walking, stood still for a few moments as if time itself did not exist. I was awestruck. Time and space lost all form. Then, just as suddenly, this other dimension was no longer there. I recall wondering, "What the heck was that all about? Strange! Very strange!" I could not discuss it because I did not know what to say.

Cynthia: Sounds like a very clear experience of pure consciousness.

Roger: What comes to mind is Tillich's (1963) "eternal now," which sounds like a contradiction, but it is not. It was an awesome, pure bliss kind of moment. It was a mystical experience, transcending ordinary awareness or consciousness. It was profound joy, holy joy.

Cynthia: Beautiful! Like Rudolph Otto's (1958) *mysterium tremendum et fascinans*, the mystery that is awe-inspiring and fascinating.

Roger: My words are so inadequate because reality itself was transformed for a brief period. When we refer to that dimension of life, we can only use the word "transcendent." The word transcendent meant so much to me even before I became acquainted with TM, because that is as good as language can get to point to this sacred dimension. I have tried at various times to put my own experience down in words, but I finally gave up because there was no language to describe it.

Cynthia: That is the value of having a teacher. A teacher can help to explain, provide a roadmap, give a vision, and help us cultivate our consciousness by providing a technique for regular practice. That is what I value about Maharishi and his teachings regarding the development of higher states of consciousness.

Roger: Yes, and so that it is not just a once in a lifetime experience, which has been the case for many people, leaving them with a poignant yearning to recapture that experience, as William James (1958) recorded in his seminal *Varieties of Religious Experience.*

Cynthia: How did that very clear experience transform you?

Roger: Even though I cannot adequately describe that experience, I can still feel and know what it was all about. I would say that the deepest effect of the awareness of the Infinite is a sense of awe, astonishment, and wonder about life. Later, when I encountered TM, this experience was a reference point when I heard Maharishi describing pure consciousness.

Cynthia: Dad, do you think this could be what is referred to as *metanoia* in the Bible? Would you agree this is one of the central features of the teaching of Jesus? It is usually translated as "repent," but the original Greek word was *metanoia*.

Roger: And *meta* means beyond, *noia*, mind. As you say, this is usually translated as repentance, and sometimes understood as meaning "a change of mind." But in light of our discussion, perhaps a more accurate understanding is of "going beyond the mind," which then transforms our lives in a positive direction (Grof, 1988, p. 125).

Cynthia: Yes—going beyond mental activity to inner silence. The Hebrew term for repentance is *teshuvah*, which literally means "return"—to our communion with the Divine (Schneerson, 2011). If we lose this connection, our lives become chaotic, weak, and unhappy.

Roger: Isaiah states: "In returning and rest is your salvation; in quietness and trust is your strength" (30:15). We return to that reality which is at the very heart, being, and soul of our lives.

Cynthia: What do you see as the value of *teshuvah?*

Roger: In so doing, we return to our sanity, to the inmost center of being human, to the mode of Being which God intended for human beings. "Be still, and know that I am God" (Psalm 46:10). We especially need this teaching today because we tend to get so distracted by a myriad of unimportant things. This is an issue one of my favorite theologians, Howard Thurman, discussed, and wrote about.

Inner Silence

There is very great virtue in the cultivation of silence,
and strength to be found in using it as a door to God.
Such a door opens within.

— Howard Thurman (1953)

Roger: Mom and I read something the other day about our need to relax our hold on everything that dulls our sense of God. You remember Howard Thurman, the African-American theologian? In the 1960s, he was chaplain and professor of religion at Boston University. I used to listen to his weekly radio "meditations," and each word he spoke was so calm and deliberate, like a pearl on a string.

Cynthia: Several years ago I found on your bookshelf Thurman's book, *The Search for Common Ground* (1971). I loved this book! He had a fascination with the common ground that all living beings share—the interconnectedness of all of nature. He was very interested in cultures that had this perspective—Asian, African, and American Indian. He recounted amazing stories of people who had communicated with animals, for example. Thurman was very sensitive to the wonders of life.

Roger: I recently read something that I used as a responsive reading in church, based upon a poem by Thurman (1978). He said that we must all let go and experience that freedom that is at the deep core of us. We need to relax our hold on everything that dulls our sense of God, and that comes between us and the quiet, inner awareness of His presence in our lives. Thurman said that we become filled with wonder as we sense the ways God glorifies all the common aspects of our lives.

Cynthia: That letting go is central to how TM works. As we talked about before, it's like diving—we take the proper angle and let go, and spontaneously dive into our refreshing inner silence. The dullness dissolves, and clarity unfolds. We have more of a sense of wonder in life.

Roger: Yes, I notice that from my meditation. I am also struck by his phrase about freedom—deep at the core of us.

Cynthia: Yes, the experience of unbounded freedom is a characteristic of enlightenment. To me, this inner freedom relates to the ability to forgive—another core teaching of Jesus.

Roger: I can relate. I have had the experience where an uncomfortable interaction left me gripped with negative feelings toward someone. But after some deep rest, from a good night's sleep or from meditating, I found I was free of its grip.

Cynthia: When you are at peace within, you don't get snagged like Velcro by negative experiences. Eventually, it's like water flowing off a duck's back, and you are spontaneously liberated from the hold of negativity.

Roger: This is profoundly practical for the teaching of Jesus: to forgive each other over and over again, to not get locked into negative feelings. I have had many experiences with parishioners who seem to hang on to bitter feelings. That is one reason I have recommended TM to parishioners.

Cynthia: When you are happy, it is easy to forgive, see the best in each other, and to move on.

Roger: It is as healing—perhaps more—for the forgiver as for the person being forgiven. When you forgive, you are liberated from the internal pollution of bad feelings within. There is a line from a hymn, *Love Divine, All Loves Excelling*: "Set our hearts at liberty" (Wesley, Charles, 1996, p. 439).

Cynthia: Inner freedom comes from inner security—being rooted in the deepest foundation of ourselves. Maharishi uses the phrase "mother is at home" for this experience: you come home to yourself. That unshakeable inner at-home-ness is a source of creativity. When the parent is at home, the child feels free to play.

Roger: He or she feels secure.

Cynthia: Exactly. Haven't you found that when you feel peaceful and secure, you feel most creative? It is the opposite of the neurotic, deeply anxious artist.

Roger: One thing that comes to mind about creative thinking and letting go: when preparing for a sermon, I will have some seed idea, and then I won't strain on it—I let it go entirely and do other things. Then out of the blue, ideas just start flowing.

Cynthia: So you notice your creative springs come out of silence, rather than strain. It is the creative process: preparation, silent incubation, illumination, and then the creative product. This is a principle of Consciousness-Based education. Modern education, piling on information, stifling creativity, needs to wake up to this. There are some schools pioneering this, but every student should be able to use this.

So the inner field of silence is not empty in the sense of being impotent. It is a field of creative intelligence, where creative springs of life are accessed.

Roger: Thurman (1953) wrote, "There is very great virtue in the cultivation of silence, and strength to be found in using it as a door to God. Such a door opens within" (p. 18).

Cynthia: In this passage, Thurman (1953) speaks of encountering the presence of the Divine as a child:

> As a child I was accustomed to spend many hours alone in my rowboat, fishing along the river, when there was no sound save the lapping of the waves against the boat. There were times when it seemed as if the earth and the river and the sky and I were one beat of the same pulse . . . There would come a moment when beyond the single pulse beat there was a sense of Presence which seemed always to speak to me. My response to the sense of Presence always had the quality of personal communion. There was no voice. There was no image. There was no vision. There was God. (p. 95-96)

Thurman is describing how he became receptive to "the still small voice of God."

Roger: Yes, and so we return to the source of our strength. We access guidance—reliable guidance that is beyond our individuality. Thurman (1953) also wrote: "There is strength beyond our strength, giving strength to our strength . . . Sometimes in the stillness of the quiet, if we listen, we can hear the whisper in the heart" (pp. 95-6).

Cynthia: I always liked a term of yours—spiritual radar. It is fascinating to consider why the experience of silence allows us to access a profoundly intelligent guidance system.

Roger: This is what Socrates called the inner voice, which he said was infallible as long as he followed it.

Cynthia: Maharishi sometimes refers to the pure field of creative intelligence as the "cosmic computer." Physicists describe increasingly more subtle layers of creation, and beyond the finest, they theorize, is the unmanifest unified field of natural law. Similarly, we as humans can experience increasingly more quiet layers of awareness, until we experience the most settled level of consciousness. This is cosmic intelligence—nature's intelligence that governs life.

Roger: That's why when we need some direction in our lives, we let go. If we fully let go and experience that inner stillness, as Thurman says, we are more able to hear "the whisper in the heart" (1953, pp. 95-6).

Cynthia: The other day I read in a sermon that the translation of the Biblical "still small voice of God" is more accurately translated from the Hebrew as "a sound of fine silence" or "sheer silence." The minister referred to 1 Kings 19:12, "It is in the stillness of silence that Elijah encountered God. Not in the earthquake, not in the storm, but in the silence" (Crowe, 2005, p. 3). That fine or sheer silence is potent with cosmic wisdom. Its unmanifest structure is cosmic intelligence.

Roger: We see this in the Prologue of the Gospel of John: "In the beginning was the Word." What is this "Word?" The Greek term is *Logos*. " . . . and the *Logos* was with God, and the *Logos* was God" (John 1:1).

Cynthia: I did some research for a paper at Harvard on how *Logos* was understood at the time the Book of John was written. It meant essentially the pre-existent ultimate reality through which everything in creation was made and constantly renewed (Johnson, 1987).

Roger: It is like what the Taoists call the *Tao*—the underlying natural order of the universe. It is the source of all manifest creation, but in itself it is unmanifest (Chan, 1963).

Cynthia: Yes! This is what the Vedic tradition calls the *Veda*: the blueprint of creation—not only in the beginning of creation, but also the underlying source of continuous creation, recreation, rejuvenation. *Veda* is that which is constantly guiding the galaxies in the cosmos, the DNA of all life, and the coordination and evolution of everything in creation. In the Bhagavad-Gita, which Maharishi says contains the essence of Vedic knowledge, *Veda* is said to emerge within the "self-illuminant effulgence of life"—when the field of unmanifest consciousness becomes aware of itself (Maharishi Mahesh Yogi, 1967, p. 206). So, returning to the idea of the experience of silence: when we go beyond mental activity, or experience *metanoia*, we open ourselves to that field of divine or cosmic intelligence, which directs our lives in the most life-supporting way.

Roger: We are made in the image of God. We have that God-given nature within ourselves. A phrase from that favorite hymn I always ask you to sing when you come home, *O Holy Angels Bright*, comes to mind: "a well-tuned heart" (Baxter, 1996, p. 760). It is like re-setting the system, from chaos to order. The "well-tuned heart" comes from attunement to the Divine.

Cynthia: There is a Vedic phrase: *Yatinam Brahma bhavati sarathih* (Maharishi Mahesh Yogi, 1996, p. 512). When a person takes recourse to pure consciousness—the totality of natural law—their life becomes guided by divine intelligence. Just as Tillich taught, it is not through learning of dogma that our lives become in tune with divine will. It is an automatic, experiential way of living that flows out of functioning from within that field of cosmic intelligence.

Dad, in closing here, how do you see the value of Maharishi's teachings in relation to the visions and insights of spiritual traditions, such as Judeo-Christian, and spiritual teachers from Thoreau to Tillich and Thurman?

Roger: In this frenetic world, everyone needs inner silence. TM is a practical tool for what Thoreau, Thurman, Tillich and many others are trying to awaken in us: the need for silence and the anchor of Being. When you think about the word "salvation"—from *salve*—it refers to health, and health refers to wholeness, holiness. TM helps uncover our wholeness, and within inner silence, we sense the spiritual radar, the inner voice, the still small voice of God. We become settled in "the peace of God which passes all understanding" (Philippians 4:7). The coarseness of our hearts melts and our hearts open, and we naturally begin to "abide in love [so] we abide in God..." (1 John 4:16). I think it is only from unfolding the authentic inner core of love within the individual that we are able to create a peaceful world. As written in 1 John, "... if we walk in the light, as he is in the light, we have community one with another ..." (1:7).

I greatly appreciate TM for the transformative value of silence and rejuvenation.

Cynthia: And I value you, Dad, for your rare openness to beautiful truth and practical wisdom, wherever you find it.

Chapter VIII

The Cenacle Sisters

The mission of the Cenacle order is to awaken and deepen faith. The Cenacle Sisters and their supporters, empowered by their spirituality, desire to nurture their inner lives as they seek deeper connection with God, society, and all of creation. Their desire is to be so filled with the love of the stillness of Divinity that through their ministry the fire of this inner awareness kindles and deepens their faith. I had the pleasure of teaching the Sisters TM and the joy of observing how it enriched their religious beliefs and experience of the divine silence within their life of service to others.

Simultaneous to my teaching the TM program in prisons and residential treatment facilities, I conducted periodic weekend in-residence courses for the meditators in the local community to accelerate the refinement of the nervous system. In selecting an appropriate facility in Carmichael, California for the in-residence course, we chose to work with the Cenacle Sisters. The Cenacle is defined as the upper room where Jesus joined with his followers who wanted to leave a legacy of love and service. The Cenacle group has their unique nomenclature, as most religious orders do, but the essence of sharing and engendering unconditional love is expressed to the world through prayerful solitude (Cenacle, 2011). The intention is admirable—in a world full of division and mistrust, they saw a unification of the world by unfolding the mystery of the invisible; they spoke about a *sacred space*. The Cenacle Sisters wanted their mission to flow out of the consequence of prayer (Cenacle Sisters, 2009). They were a group that understood the experience of transcendental silence.

The Cenacle Sisters permitted the use of their facilities for TM in-residence courses, and since they also conducted Catholic retreats, they quietly observed our activities. After we had offered a couple of in-residence TM courses, the head of the Cenacle order at the retreat house invited me to meet with the entire group of Sisters. The Sisters asked me what we were doing to keep the course participants in their rooms, because this was difficult for them to accomplish at their retreats. I shared with them that it was the charm of the inner peace and bliss that motivated the participants to continue in the quiet meditation experience. The Sisters asked if they could learn the technique, and I made arrangements to teach them. I explained that the TM technique was simple and not intellectual but experiential. I instructed the Cenacle Sisters, and completed the four days of instruction that comprised the TM course. After we meditated, they said: you have just taught us how to experience "thoughtless, wordless prayer." It was a beautiful moment. I reflected on the purpose of religion throughout the world and science itself, and how they were interconnected with our own consciousness. One definition of the purpose of religion is to bind one back to the source (Maharishi Mahesh Yogi, 1966). In this innocent moment with the Sisters, I could appreciate that there is one tree of knowledge with many branches, and that we are all seeking the exploration of our essence.

A couple of months later there were two extraordinary moments that have stayed with me all my life. I was conducting a TM checking procedure with the Mother Superior of the Cenacle Sisters to ensure that she was meditating correctly. As we were meditating, I began to experience deep inner silence, and I felt the inner presence of pure expanding love. I had the innocent thought that I wished the nun could also have this experience. When I opened my eyes the nun turned to me and said in her religious context, "You had the experience of the presence of God, and you shared it with me." This was a simple moment of connectedness, invisible and yet visible, indescribable in its simplicity, and yet tangible, but beyond words to describe. As we move through life we are given these gentle surprises from within.

As the nun and I continued with our brief conversation, we discussed enlightenment becoming a permanent link with the infinite on the level of our consciousness. She remarked that enlightenment was the result of grace; it was a gift of our commitment to the journey itself. As Maharishi once remarked, God Consciousness results from our growing appreciation of the artistic expression of the creator. Maharishi used the analogy of the artist (Divine Intelligence) who creates a work of art, and discovers an individual appreciating the art so profoundly that the creator of the artwork chooses to pay a visit—and awakening happens innocently when we answer the knock at the door.

A second insightful moment took place with an 83-year-old Cenacle

Sister who thought she had insomnia. She expressed her concern and I asked a few questions about the experience:

Cenacle nun: I believe I have insomnia.

GE: Why do you assume you have insomnia?

Cenacle nun: Well, I just do not remember sleeping.

GE: And how do you feel in the morning?

Cenacle nun: Full of energy, happiness, and love.

After listening to the nun's descriptions of her inner experience, I reflected on Maharishi's explanation of the signs of Cosmic Consciousness, and it appeared she was resting in the embrace of spiritual Stillness, or unbounded awareness. The nun had been a witness to her sleep and her dreams; she described that her body and mind were asleep, and yet she was awake inside—to the essence of her pure consciousness. She was awakening to the continuity between each breath, each thought, each transition or state of awareness that hides our beautiful Self, infinite and without the boundaries of the body, time or space. The nun's experience has become common throughout the world in the lives of TM practitioners; the infinite is whispering to us in our sleep—another reality that walks with us and within us at every moment of our life. For a moment, the individual, like a wave on the ocean, realizes that the ocean and the wave are the same. The unbroken transcendental reality that underlies our individual consciousness quietly becomes apparent. The power of intellectually understanding the experience is critical for our spiritual and human development.

Dr. Evan Finkelstein in his doctoral dissertation discusses a universal principle underlying the religious experience. Finkelstein's (2005) examination concluded that all the religions he studied emphasized the need to transcend both the inner subjective and outer objective boundaries of the space-time-bound relative world. The development of higher states of consciousness is the cornerstone of the success experienced through the practice of the TM technique regardless of age, sex, race, religion, or ethnicity. The contribution to the clergy, religious orders, and the faithful laity is the development of higher states of consciousness and perception through the TM technique, which removes the obstacles created by anxiety and tension.

As the mystic Evelyn Underhill (2002) expressed, Christian mysticism aspires to apprehend spiritual truths inaccessible through intellectual means.

Underhill (2002) suggests in her writings that the illuminative or contemplative stage unites the aspirant with the inner spiritual presence of divine love or intelligence—a pure consciousness empty of duality but full of vibrating silence. The vibrating silence is a supreme manifestation of that indivisible power of knowing which lies at the root of all spiritual satisfactions. Within the ineffable experience beyond duality is a fusion of individual thought and love resting in the embrace of divinity. The fusion of individual and universal consciousness is not an act of reason, but of the whole personality working under the stimulus of mystic love. Hence, the experience results in feeding every aspect of the personality, including the self and its cognitive powers; we pour ourselves inward toward the overpowering experience of transcendental unconditional spiritual love. The Christian mystic would conclude that whatever the reality may be within this experience, it is given to us, and we know it, but we cannot know it by the ordinary devices of thought. Instead of sharply experiencing the fragments of perception, we apprehend the solemn presence of the whole (Underhill, 2002).

Christian texts declare that the Kingdom of Heaven is within and among us. Maharishi has encouraged the cultivation of pure consciousness for individuals of a religious nature for deepening prayer life and a living experience of the scriptures. In the beautiful experiences of the Sisters we see that the TM technique is an innocent instrument to support and facilitate the spiritual growth of aspirants in any religion.

Chapter IX

Truth, Transcendence, and the Upper Room

An Interview of Arthur John Anderson by Cynthia E. Johnson

The synergy between Art Anderson and Cynthia Johnson created a profound insight into the value of the TM program as a supportive tool to achieve the spiritual aspirations of Catholicism and religion in general. The interview covers a range of interesting faith-related topics, including several thoughtful discussions on the experience of transcending and the ways in which TM fostered, clarified, and enlivened Art's faith. It reflects a universal respect for truth in different religions and the interconnectedness of humanity, regardless of differing philosophical or religious perspectives. This interview is a call for unity and a recognition that diversity does not have to be divisive but can be instrumental in creating a human tapestry in which our differences are like threads woven together to create an outcome greater than our individual preferences.

Brother Elias Marechal, a Trappist Monk in the Monastery of the Holy Spirit in Conyers, Georgia, reviewed the completed interview and helped edit it, offering his sagacious observations and suggestions from a Catholic perspective. Michael Willbanks, a full-time TM teacher for over thirty-six years, also carefully assessed the interview from the viewpoint of the TM program and made incisive yet sensitive editorial recommendations. We thank each of them.

Cynthia: To prepare for this interview, I reviewed your website and read your curriculum vitae. You've had an exciting professional and academic career. You obtained your college education from the Jesuits, graduated Harvard Law School and received an appointment to its faculty as a Teaching Fellow, held influential positions in government, served on a variety of boards and commissions, worked closely with Bill Clinton while he was in state politics, became a TM teacher, lectured throughout America and Europe, won writing awards, and were a successful trial attorney. And that's just some highlights. From talking with you beforehand, I know you've done other fun things like driving Chicago transit buses, working as a construction laborer, a train conductor, a housepainter, a salesman, and a criminal investigator. You were even a bartender. You packed a lot into life. And then you became an ordained Catholic deacon with seven children and managed a Midwest farm operation. Those are some big leaps. How did you transition from all that to this, especially from a career in law to a vocation in ministry?

Art: Compressed into a few sentences, it now sounds like a lot, but it didn't seem that way then. I was focused on whatever I was doing, one thing at a time, yet always ready to move on to the next challenge. Law had been my main focus but, in retrospect, I think it was more an intermission than a career. Even an interruption, because in midlife I finally understood that my true vocation, the one I had begun pursuing as a teenager, was and is the ministry. Sometimes we have to be hit over the head to realize, even more so to accept, what God is calling us to do.

Cynthia: Tell us a little about that calling.

Art: I had just turned fourteen when I entered Quigley Preparatory Seminary in Chicago to begin studying for the Catholic priesthood. I loved my life as a seminarian and was in love with Jesus. I spent many hours with him in prayer and devotion in our seminary chapel and felt his presence throughout the day in class and in other activities. I especially loved our chapel. It wasn't large, but it had vaulted ceilings and stained glass windows and looked like a miniature cathedral. It was the heart of the seminary. There were only two ways to enter, each from a different part of the seminary structure. One of them was a dark entry in the rear under the choir loft, which was how I usually came in. A number of years ago, I started having a recurring dream in which I would find secret passageways into the chapel, and I had the same dream again just last night. I loved being in the chapel, praying in the chapel, feeling close to God in the chapel, and in my dreams I long to be back in the peace and joy of that little chapel.

Cynthia: When were you first drawn to involvement with the Catholic Church?

Art: I'm a cradle Catholic. I became an altar boy the summer I turned nine. Back then, we had to memorize a lot of Latin to qualify, so much of my summer vacation was spent learning Latin prayers. My family lived on the West Side of Chicago, in a section dotted with factories. When I served as an altar boy at the 6:30 Mass, I would leave at six in the morning and walk five or six city blocks to church. In the winter, the streets were still dark and often covered with snow. I remember trudging past the factories and wondering if someone was going to jump out of a dark corner and grab me. It was spooky, but not scary. I never felt in danger because I knew God was watching over me. Besides, I kept reciting my Latin prayers out loud as I trudged along.

Cynthia: Why did you leave the seminary?

Art: Curiosity. During my fifth year—by then I was in the new intermediate seminary in Niles, Illinois—I decided to see what the outside world was like, even to explore the possibility of marriage, which I could not do as a seminarian. I discussed it with my rector. He said the seminary would always be there if I chose to return, but that life would pass me by if I stayed. I left and continued my education in mathematics, philosophy, and theology, which somehow led me to law school, a demanding legal career, and eventually to starting TM. In the meantime, I had become a very lax Catholic but, after learning to meditate and attending six months of TM teacher training courses in France and Switzerland and then working with Maharishi in Seelisberg, something deep inside me came to life. I began having a vague sense of what it means to be born again. My understanding of Jesus took on new dimensions and relevance in my life, even a surge of urgency, and my desire for him quickened ever more fervently in my heart.

Cynthia: It sounds like you broke through some boundaries.

Art: That's exactly what happened. It's popular for business coaches to talk about taking their clients to "a whole new level." Well, that's what Maharishi did for my Catholicism, and I found myself yearning to return to the religious life, but this time in a monastic setting.

Cynthia: What happened during your time with Maharishi that triggered a religious renewal?

Art: I gained a perspective on life, both intellectually and experientially, that I had not known before. It was as if my edifice of neatly accumulated knowledge and past experiences had been gently dismantled and reconstructed so that I could now see the world—law, religion, reality, all of life, everything, especially God—in a fundamentally different way. I was able to grasp on a small, yet radical, scale the underlying interconnectedness of all things in a harmonious, homogeneous whole. This discrete shift in understanding profoundly affected my values and the way I perceived reality so that the world never again looked the same.

Cynthia: What do you mean by a discrete shift affecting your values and perception? How did it take place?

Art: An inner transformation occurred. It wasn't any specific experience that I could point to. Passing experiences in or out of meditation were not important. The enduring changes that took place were what mattered. Let me try to explain it this way. When our children were young, I would often spend Christmas Eve night, after they were in bed, assembling toys to put under the tree. Sometimes the pieces had to be connected with fasteners that, when pressed together, snapped into place and could never again be unsnapped. It was like that. Once the shift occurs, you can't go back. It's permanent. The world is forever different because your understanding of it, and therefore the way you perceive it, changes. That's what happened to me after learning TM, studying under Maharishi, and just being around him. I was truly amazed at the difference this new knowledge made in my life. I had studied in some depth mathematics, philosophy, and theology, looking for answers, for explanations, for the intellectual alchemy that would unscramble life's mysteries. But the decoder's key had always eluded me. Now, with the experience of Transcendental Consciousness, I felt as if I had been the fish in the ocean looking for water. It was there all along, all around me. I just needed someone to open my eyes.

Cynthia: What kind of difference did it make in your life?

Art: Seemingly impenetrable questions that I had pondered since youth about the nature of reality were being answered by Maharishi or they simply opened up and resolved themselves on their own. But it's one thing to be given the answers, and quite another thing to understand them. That's what was so amazing. I understood what Maharishi was talking about because I had the experience of Transcendental Consciousness as my reference point. It was my decoder's key for the apparent mysteries of life. I now saw everything, myself included, as part of the same dynamic and, yet, undifferentiated whole. Once this shift snapped into place, it permeated everything within and around me, making it impossible ever again to see things the way I had before. Some years later, when I again began studying for the ministry, the first major paper I wrote was entitled "The Interconnectedness of All Things in Christ," in which I attempted to analyze this shift from a Christian perspective. When we recognize ourselves and all others as participating in the same divine reality, everything, ourselves included, is ennobled with new and immeasurable value in our eyes.

Cynthia: It sounds like a fundamental shift in your experience of the world.

Art: It was a change in perspective that has consistently colored the way I perceive the world. I cannot look at anything without considering the broader frame of reference in which it exists. The missing piece had been supplied, and things finally began making sense. It was an expanded and deepened awareness of the underlying sameness or unity of all things, and it came about from my experience in Transcendental Meditation coupled with listening daily to Maharishi give us a vision of possibilities. I don't think any of this is unusual because everyone who meditates grows in an awareness, both intellectual and experiential, of the inherent unity of all things.

Cynthia: Did this shift have immediate effects in your life?

Art: Yes. It was reinforced and put into focus by opportunities Maharishi offered me to speak internationally on the application of TM to criminal rehabilitation and, more fundamentally, to the prevention of crime. I was at the time involved in the administration of criminal justice, and the seemingly unsolvable problems we faced no longer appeared hopeless to me. I now saw crime, its causes and effects, from a very different perspective, and I wanted to tell the world about this new and fuller way of seeing reality and dealing with problems. I wanted to share this feeling of renewal. It was like the feeling of falling in love. It has that kind of freshness and vitality.

Cynthia: What about your desire to continue studying for the priesthood?

Art: It gently persisted in the background. I was particularly drawn to the Trappist Abbey of Gethsemani in Kentucky.

Cynthia: I'm familiar with it. My friend, Brother Elias, is the Novice-Master at the Trappist Monastery of the Holy Spirit in Conyers, Georgia. It's an outgrowth of the Monastery at Gethsemani. Before entering the Abbey, he also worked closely with Maharishi, and even taught courses in religion at what was then Maharishi International University.

Art: Maharishi has a way of bringing to the fore our deepest spiritual yearnings. I experienced that, and perhaps Brother Elias did, too. I've read and reread Brother Elias' enchanting little book, *Dancing Madly Backwards: A Journey Into God.* It's often by my bedside for nighttime reading. It's disarmingly profound, insightful, even poetic. Especially poetic. You don't read the chapters; you listen to them, each one a condensation of the transcendence into word-droplets of sound and meaning. Sound that's porous with silent spaces in which to ponder. Meaning that's part you and makes sense only when your part fits neatly into the rest. You grasp meaning in the transition between his words and your own past experiences that you bring to them. Meaning happens in a flash, like the joy felt before an unexpected apparition fades; and you release it to be reabsorbed into its source, not sure how much you've received or retained. But you are satisfied, satiated. I've not experienced another book quite like it. Brother Elias is a beautiful man. A compassionate man. A mystery writer. A monk. His words follow you around.

Cynthia: I certainly agree. I've read his book, too, and found it delightful and uplifting. But you didn't enter Gethsemani. What happened?

Art: I prepared myself spiritually while continuing to practice law: daily Mass and Holy Communion; daily spiritual reading; and a daily prayer life that included TM. I read everything I could find by Fr. Thomas Merton, a mystic who had been a monk at Gethsemani. This went on with greater or lesser fervency for quite awhile, and then something unexpected intervened. I met Annie, fell in love, and my desire for monastic life politely stepped aside. Eight months later we were married. It's not that I previously hadn't met any wonderful ladies. I had, and I was particularly fond of one of them. But marriage always eluded me. Ironically, or perhaps providentially, I met Annie when I was least interested in marriage. We are blessed with seven children—six girls and a boy—and what a delight they are! I loved my contemplative life as a seminarian, but nowhere near as much as I love my amazing life as a Daddy.

Cynthia: When did you become an ordained minister?

Art: I continued to be drawn to the ministry and, six years into marriage, with Annie's consent and support, I began a program of study and discernment for the Permanent Diaconate, a Catholic ministry of service to others that is open to married men. Annie was there, participating and encouraging, at every step of the way. After ordination, I divested myself of my law practice and focused on family, farming, and ministry.

Truth, Transcending, and Spiritual Growth

Cynthia: You mentioned that your prayer life included your practice of TM. The Catholic Church seems to be very conservative in its quest for truth.

How does the practice of TM, which is derived from the ancient Vedic tradition of India, relate to Catholic dogma?

Art: It relates well, precisely because the Church is dedicated to knowing, preserving, and unfolding spiritual truth. The Church does not claim a monopoly on truth, but strives to embrace all that is true and to ensure that all it professes is true. If TM leads a Catholic to truth, then I would say that for him or her TM is Catholic. *The Declaration on the Relationship of the Church to Non-Christian Religions*, a 1965 document from the Second Vatican Council, clarifies this. Referring to Eastern religions among others, it states: "The Catholic Church rejects nothing which is true and holy in these religions." I want to be clear, however, that Transcendental Meditation is not a religion nor does it involve a system of beliefs, but it can be an aid to any religion. Later, in a 1989 letter to the Catholic Bishops entitled "Some Aspects of Christian Meditation," which was issued by the Congregation for the Doctrine of Faith and signed by Cardinal Ratzinger, now Pope Benedict XVI, Transcendental Meditation is specifically listed in the first endnote as one of the Eastern meditation practices that can be "...a suitable means of helping the person who prays to come before God with an interior peace, even in the midst of external pressures."

Cynthia: Is there no conflict, then, between TM and Catholicism?

Art: From a Catholic perspective, conflict occurs if we fail to integrate the practice of TM harmoniously into our Catholic beliefs, or if we use TM to replace those beliefs or to create a syncretistic amalgam of beliefs. But, again, I want to emphasize that TM is simply a technique. It neither contains nor requires any beliefs. If, as Catholics, we incorporate TM into our prayer life, we enrich our Catholicism, new dimensions of the mystery of our faith open to us, and clearer insights and deeper experiences abound. In "Some Aspects of Christian Meditation," Cardinal Ratzinger said, in reference to Eastern techniques of spirituality, that Catholics could "...take from them what is useful so long as the Christian conception of prayer, its logic and requirements are never obscured."

Cynthia: You have obviously found TM useful.

Art: I've found that transcending is not only useful but even essential to my spiritual growth. TM provides me a natural, predictable, and reliable way to experience Transcendental Consciousness daily. And it doesn't conflict with my beliefs. The Catholic Church rejects nothing that is true and holy; and who, having experienced Transcendental Consciousness, can deny the truth and holiness it contains? Cardinal Ratzinger went on to remark that some Christians use these spiritual techniques " . . . solely as a psycho-physical preparation for a truly Christian contemplation." This reminds me of a short interview I heard a while back of Father Leonard Dubi, a Catholic priest in a parish outside Chicago, in which he talks about doing TM in the morning before celebrating Mass.

Cynthia: Yes, I heard it, too. It was a very dear and sincere discussion of TM.

Art: Father Dubi and I were in the same seminary at the same time, but we were in different years, so I didn't know him. But I'll bet he loved our chapel as I did. In his interview, he talks about TM as a technique he uses for deepening his religious commitment, for empowering prayer, and for making conscious contact with a power greater than himself. For Christians, he says, that is the spirit of Jesus. I love the way Father Dubi describes his experience in TM of getting "deeper and deeper and deeper." He ends by saying that he is a better Christian and a better priest because of the TM technique. This dovetails with a 1971 video I once saw of Maharishi discussing Christianity. It was from the Teacher Training Course he gave in Mallorca, Spain. He said, "I love Christ very much" and that "TM is a special friend of Christianity" because it takes us to the kingdom of God within, which, he said, is what Jesus wants everyone to find and enjoy.

Cynthia: Is the experience of Transcendental Consciousness something that happens each time you sit to meditate?

Art: Because TM is a completely natural process, the body and mind receive in each meditation exactly what they need at the moment, whether that's transcending or really deep rest. Our experiences will vary from meditation to meditation, but each time there is usually some degree of transcending, at least from the surface level of mental activity to more silent levels of awareness. We may not have clear experiences of Transcendental Consciousness, but that doesn't mean we're not transcending. Sometimes we transcend all mental activity, sometimes we don't. Sometimes we might transcend and not be aware of it. And sometimes we might even feel restless and not very settled, but scientific studies have shown that even then transcending is taking place in

TM. At first, whenever I experienced meditations that seemed to be somewhat restless, I wondered if I was meditating correctly; but then I heard Maharishi assure us that something good is happening. The mind and body always take what they need from each meditation. Usually we feel some settling of the physiology, at times quite deep, along with a corresponding refinement of our breathing and thought process. Like Father Dubi said, he gets "deeper and deeper and deeper." But the important thing is not to look for anything because that only keeps the mind engaged rather than allowing it to follow its natural course into the transcendent. We just take it as it comes. Something good is happening, and that we can always be sure of.

Cynthia: What did you mean, then, when you said that transcending is predictable in TM?

Art: This is something I want to be very clear about from the outset. What is predictable is the setting of conditions for transcending to occur. That's what TM does. It makes transcending possible in a very predictable way. It keeps the mind lively but undirected so that it can follow its natural tendency to experience transcending. It happens automatically. We don't do anything from our side. We simply step out of the way and allow it to occur. We take it as it comes. In any given meditation, we may have clear experiences of transcending or we may simply settle down to varying degrees of silence. Or we may transcend and not realize it. There is no right or wrong experience, and we don't analyze anything, especially not while we're meditating. That keeps the mind directed, which can create an obstacle on its path to Transcendental Consciousness. The idea is for the mind to be free to follow its natural course into the transcendent. TM provides this freedom. It sets the conditions for us to transcend, and that is what is always predictable. It not only opens the path to Transcendental Consciousness, but by releasing deeply rooted stresses, it also clears the path along the way. Maharishi refers to this as "purification of the path." The more we meditate, the clearer the path to the transcendent becomes. No other technique that I'm aware of does this. That's not to say that transcending can't happen in other practices. Sometimes it does, but not in the predictable way that TM makes it available to us.

Cynthia: Did you ever experience transcending before you learned TM, either as part of your religious training or during liturgical functions or in any other setting?

Art: In retrospect, I realize I often did, especially during my seminary years. I said the rosary daily, usually by myself in the silence of the chapel or the privacy of my room. It was always a very peaceful experience. The rosary has five decades, each representing a mystery associated with the life of Christ. We repeat prayers, mostly the Hail Mary, and use rosary beads to keep track of where we are, fingering them one at a time. As I repeated the prayers, my mind would sometimes, without me knowing it, drift off into a momentary—how do I say this?—a vague kind of unknowingness in which I would forget I was saying the rosary. I would then come out of it on a stream of extraneous thoughts, not knowing what had happened or how much time had elapsed. I would get irritated with myself for not concentrating better on the repetition of the prayers. Yet I couldn't help it. I had absolutely no control over these periods of slipping away into the transcendent.

Cynthia: How would it happen?

Art: My focus on the prayers would seem to get thinner and thinner and then disappear. Years later, after I began to experience transcending in TM, my memory flashed back to saying the rosary as a young seminarian, and I realized I had been transcending all along. I have since wondered whether the rosary was originally intended to be a means for transcending. Perhaps—and this is mere conjecture on my part—the rosary was at one time a form of meditation whose purpose, or one of its purposes, was to bring us to Transcendental Consciousness.

Cynthia: Do Catholics understand transcending as a purpose for the rosary?

Art: I doubt it. We're taught to concentrate on the meaning of the words in the prayers we repeat or to contemplate the meaning of the mysteries represented by the five decades. Concentration and contemplation are suitable forms of prayer in the right circumstances, but they can also impede transcending. Maharishi tells us that concentration and contemplation keep us on the surface level of thinking, whereas TM allows us to dive deep within to the source of thought.

Cynthia: Then why are Catholics taught to concentrate on the rosary?

Art: Despite the obvious value of transcending for spiritual growth, few Catholics I know have the slightest idea what it is, let alone how to initiate the conditions for it to occur. We're taught to concentrate instead. I suspect this is true of all religions and, so, transcending happens only randomly, if at all. We need to regain the knowledge of, and the means for, transcending. With the TM technique, Maharishi has provided both to all religions.

Cynthia: Maharishi says that the knowledge of transcending is lost from time to time.

Art: That's why he's put in place precise procedures both for the teaching of TM and for the training of TM teachers.

Cynthia: Do you think Jesus taught his disciples to transcend?

Art: The Gospels don't record any explicit account of that but, having experienced the profound spiritual effects and implications of transcending, I cannot imagine that he didn't. I once heard someone speculate that this might have been what the Apostle Peter was referring to in the Gospel of John when he said that Jesus had the "words of eternal life." But who knows for sure? There's also a saying attributed to Jesus: "Empty thyself and I shall fill thee." I don't know where it's found, perhaps in a non-canonical gospel, but it's a good description of transcending from a Christian perspective.

Cynthia: Do you know whether transcending was ever a part of Christian liturgy?

Art: I don't know, but certain things suggest that it may have been. For example, Gregorian and Ambrosian Chants, which we sang in Latin in the seminary, have enjoyed a prominent liturgical function, particularly prior to Vatican II, and still do in monastic communities. While singing these chants or simply listening to them, the physiology settles down. Incense, which mellows the atmosphere, is commonly used in many Catholic liturgies. Chanting and incense may have been used to set the tone for transcending. Some liturgies include the recitation of long, repetitive litanies that have a gently calming effect. Also, the idea of entering into the transcendent in worship is implicit in Christian architecture.

Cynthia: Architecture?

Art: Have you ever wondered why churches have steeples and spires? They reach to connect earth to heaven, but there's a deeper symbolism. Shaped like spears, they pierce through the profane space of the world to separate it from the sacred space of God. When we come to church and enter that sacred space beneath the spires and steeples, we are to leave worldly concerns at the door, become oblivious to space and time, and experience the infinite and eternal presence of God. Sounds like Transcendental Consciousness, doesn't it? To answer your question, it seems that one of the purposes of at least some of our Christian liturgy may have been to set the conditions for transcending to occur.

Cynthia: Why do you suppose the Church hasn't preserved and passed down the knowledge of transcending?

Art: It has, but only in isolated quarters such as monastic communities where ancient chants, repetitive prayer, and contemplative practices are more commonplace and where, as I understand it, the rosary had its origin. I've learned from Brother Elias that there are also certain forms of prayer that lead to Transcendental Consciousness. They involve contemplation, but probably not the kind that Maharishi says will inhibit or impede transcending. What the Church calls contemplation may be a form of meditation.

Cynthia: So the Church has a tradition of knowledge regarding Transcendental Consciousness?

Art: Yes. This knowledge is rooted in the writings of the early Fathers of the Church. A treatise entitled *Mystical Theology*, written by Dionysius the Pseudo-Areopagite who is known as the Father of Mysticism, dates back to the fifth century. The Church has, through the ages, developed a rich history and understanding of the transcendent. The terminology it uses to describe it, such as "mystical union," differs from Maharishi's, but the experience is the same. The content of mystical theology is both doctrinal and experiential. It's not something that receives much attention among the Catholic faithful. It seems to be considered the province of saints, the desert fathers, Christian mystics, various Fathers of the Church, and contemporary contemplative orders of men and women. The substance of what Maharishi teaches is not new to Catholicism. Maharishi complements it by offering us a simple technique by which the goal of Catholic mystical theology can be reached by anyone, not just contemplatives.

Cynthia: Catholics are not generally familiar with mystical theology?

Art: No. It's a discipline the ordinary Catholic knows nothing about. In mystical theology I think that transcending is considered to be a grace or a gift that's bestowed primarily on very devout people, in particular those pursuing a contemplative lifestyle. Yet, I suspect that ordinary Catholics sometimes, perhaps often, experience it serendipitously in their prayer life as I did. The fact is that anyone can transcend, but Catholicism and other religions do not teach their adherents a systematic way to do so at regular intervals in daily life. Various kinds of prayer certainly can settle the physiology, clear the mind, and open the way to transcending; but this process is more elaborate and unpredictable—and for some more cumbersome—than simply sitting down for twenty minutes twice a day and quite quickly and effortlessly experiencing Transcendental Consciousness. What's been missing from Catholicism and other religions is a simple technique to accomplish this, and that's why TM is a valuable addition to any religious practice.

Cynthia: Why do you suppose the knowledge of transcending contained in mystical theology is not provided to ordinary Catholics?

Art: I know very little about mystical theology as a body of Church doctrine or scholarship. I have never studied it and have read very little about it. I am familiar with some of the writings of a few Church mystics like St. John of the Cross. The best I can tell, it's not something that's promoted or fostered by the Church. I suspect it's considered a fairly esoteric, perhaps abstruse, field of theoretical study and even more arcane in its practical application. There certainly does not seem to be any effort to filter it down to ordinary Catholics.

Cynthia: Why do you suppose that is?

Art: Perhaps—and, again, this is only conjecture—the Church feels it is suitable to the lifestyle of people living in monastic communities who can devote their lives to prayer and contemplation, but not appropriate for those living in the world who are busy with professional and family obligations. As far as I know, the Church does not have a simple and efficient delivery system to bring to the ordinary Catholic the experience of transcending. But now with TM it's easily accessible to anyone. I think the Church needs to bring TM into its liturgical practices and make it available to the faithful so that everyone, not just those in monastic communities, can experience Transcendental Consciousness.

Cynthia: The contemplative environment of monasteries was probably seen as an ideal atmosphere for meditation.

Art: Convents, too. When I became a teacher of TM, I offered to instruct my older sister. She belonged to the Felician order of Catholic nuns and lived a communal convent life. After I gave her an introductory and preparatory lecture, she said, "But I already do something like that. We learned a similar meditation technique in our novitiate." She was not speaking specifically of TM, although TM has been taught in some Catholic monastic settings.

Cynthia: You obviously feel quite strongly that TM fits into your faith and should be used as a spiritual practice.

Art: Transcending quickens spiritual growth. Although Catholic theology is familiar with the experience of Transcendental Consciousness, it doesn't offer the ordinary Catholic a way to attain it, but TM does. TM provides a simple, systematic means of transcending that can be easily introduced into the practice of anyone's faith. It's a natural fit. As the Catholic Church teaches, we don't reject anything that is true and helpful.

Cynthia: Although the Gospels may not contain an explicit indication of Jesus teaching his disciples to transcend, is there any evidence elsewhere in the New Testament to support the practice of transcending?

Art: In his epistle, the Apostle James writes that we should draw near to God, and He will draw near to us. This sounds like what happens when we transcend. Reciprocation emerges. God wants us as much as we want Him. Even more. Infinitely more. Maharishi likens it to a mother and lost child. When their eyes finally meet, they begin running toward each other and, the closer they get, the faster they run. Don't you know the mother is always running faster to embrace her lost child? So, too, with God. His love and yearning for us come first. But it takes both. If we sincerely desire Him, He draws us near to Himself. James cautions us that we must be pure of heart and not "double-minded."

Cynthia: That's an interesting phrase.

Art: Pure of heart or double-minded?

Cynthia: Both.

Art: By transcending regularly, we experience refinement of heart. Jesus called the pure of heart blessed and said they shall see God. In Transcendental Consciousness, what else is there to see but God?

Cynthia: And double-minded?

Art: I think it refers to a divided mind torn between the riches of the outer world and the richness of the inner world. In the Sermon on the Mount, Jesus relates this ambivalence not to the mind, but to the heart. He tells us that we cannot serve both God and mammon because, where our treasure is, there also will be our heart. He admonishes us not to lay up treasures on earth where thieves will steal them and rust corrodes them, but in heaven where our treasure is eternal and indestructible. And he tells us that heaven is within, which is why we can experience heaven on earth—as within, so without. Jesus points to the birds of the air and the lilies of the field and chides us for our foolishness in worrying about what we will eat and wear. He's not telling us to disregard or renounce our earthly needs but, rather, he gives us the formula for enjoying the treasures of both the inner and outer worlds: "Seek ye first the kingdom of God and his righteousness and all these things shall be added unto you." And he also assures us that we will succeed: "Seek and ye *shall* find." All the biblical translations of this passage imply a certainty that what is sought will be found. But, from our side, we must seek.

Cynthia: Maharishi tells us to enjoy 200% of life: 100% of the absolute, and 100% of the relative.

Art: He uses the image of capturing the fort, which is the inner world of the absolute, and the whole village, which is the outer relative world, will be ours. It's the same idea. When we experience Transcendental Consciousness, the kingdom of God within, we transfer harmony, order, and beauty from the inside to the outside, and our world changes accordingly. Maharishi often tells us the world is as we are. We bring with us the flavor of Transcendental Consciousness from our meditation, and our world becomes seasoned with the absolute. The Yoga Vasistha points out that, for the person who wears sandals, the world is paved in leather. When we leave meditation and return to activity, we pave our outer world with the love, compassion, and justice acquired in Transcendental Consciousness, and we come to realize the futility of focusing our attention solely on the outer world. As Jesus said, "What does it profit a man to gain the whole world but suffer the loss of his soul?" Once we begin meditating, we quickly realize the value of nourishing the outer world of activity with regular excursions into the inner world of silence, the kingdom of God.

Cynthia: As Maharishi says, "Water the root to enjoy the fruit." Both worlds, inside and outside, are important.

Art: The Yoga Vasistha also points out that it takes two wings for a bird to fly. Difficulties arise when we get so absorbed or entangled in the relative side of existence that we ignore or abandon the absolute. Then we miss what life is really about. Maharishi tells us in his commentary on Chapter Six, verse 32 of the Bhagavad-Gita that the ultimate objective is to live in the fullness of the absolute and the fullness of the relative—the 200% of life that you mentioned. He says the Upanishads refer to this as *purnamadah-purnamidam*. To achieve this, we need a way to move easily from the relative to the absolute and back again, like through the wardrobe in C. S. Lewis' *The Chronicles of Narnia*. As in Narnia, "The further up and the further in you go, the bigger everything gets. The inside is larger than the outside." With TM we enter the kingdom within, a world of bigness, of richness and beauty. Most religions have forgotten to teach us how. So, Maharishi came and said in effect, "Here, try this and see what happens." He gave us a key to Transcendental Consciousness, a key that is often missing or hidden in the obscure dogmas or esoteric practices of religion. I've wondered if, when Jesus gave Peter the keys to heaven, one of them was for entering Transcendental Consciousness, the world within the world, the taste of heaven on earth.

Cynthia: Did you ever experience transcending other than while saying the rosary?

Art: Yes, and I suspect that many people experience random instances of transcending but don't know what they are. Transcending is a natural part of life. Our nervous systems are designed to transcend. It's a means by which we become pure of heart and attain higher states of consciousness. Transcending is, I think, necessary to accelerate our spiritual journey; and, if necessary, then natural. When we learn TM and begin to transcend, we might experience a sense of familiarity, of belonging. It may trigger, as it did for me, memories of past episodes of random transcending, or it may be a delightful and completely new experience. Either way, there may be a sense of "Oh, yes, this feels so right."

Cynthia: You're saying the random instances of transcending you had are the same as what happens in TM?

Art: This is something else I need to be very clear about. The TM technique provides a systematic means of transcending each time we sit to meditate, whereas there is nothing systematic or predictable about the random instances I'm describing. But the actual experience of transcending was very similar. The point I want to make is that the mind naturally seeks to transcend, to go beyond itself. It's this natural tendency of the mind that the TM technique uses to make transcending easy and accessible to all. Transcending can then be realized as both a cause and an effect of spiritual growth.

Cynthia: What were other early experiences of transcending that you had?

Art: When I entered the seminary in my early teens, my voice had not yet changed and I was selected to sing in a boys choir. We sang regularly at the Holy Name Cathedral in Chicago. Those were some of the most joyful times of my life. My joy was often so great that I couldn't tell if it was in me or I in it. A few times I got so washed away in the ecstasy of singing at a Solemn High Mass that I would fall into that vague unknowingness, a kind of emptiness. It was similar to what happened when I said the rosary, but more sudden, more discrete. I would lose all sensation of where I was and, when I came back, we would be at a different part in the song and, yet, my singing apparently had not been interrupted by this falling in and out of Transcendental Consciousness. These experiences while singing, although they were fewer, were more lucid and distinct than the more frequent ones I had while saying the rosary. I remember they would—how do I describe this?—not frighten but surprise me at first. I would wonder what had happened. Where had I been?

Cynthia: Have you had random instances of transcending as an adult, especially after learning TM?

Art: Yes. As a deacon, I often assisted my pastor at the altar when he said Mass. Occasionally, I had experiences similar to those as a choirboy. They were empty of content and were preceded by a pervading feeling of joy and ended with a refreshing sense of renewal. My pastor noticed this happening, and I described for him the experience. He said it's what the Church calls ecstasy. Maybe so, but it's something we all can regularly, not just randomly, experience in the practice of TM. I think it's what Maharishi refers to as bliss consciousness.

Cynthia: I noticed that in each of these experiences you speak of sensations of peace or joy as preludes to the experience of transcending.

Art: Yes, I hadn't thought of that before. But you're right.

Cynthia: You say that transcending is essential to spiritual development, yet it's often missing from our religious rituals and practices.

Art: Transcending is natural to the mind, and not only necessary for spiritual growth but, I think, unavoidable as we grow, which is probably why it sometimes happens randomly if there's not a way to facilitate it regularly. In TM, Maharishi gave us a religion-neutral technique that makes transcending systematic, predictable, and available to all so that it can be confidently integrated in regular intervals into daily life. As Maharishi said, "TM is a way to experience the message of every religion." The brilliance of TM, which sets it apart from all other meditation practices, is that it capitalizes on the natural tendency of the mind to arrive at the experience of Transcendental Consciousness. This makes TM completely effortless, which ensures its immediate effectiveness because effort of any kind defeats the purpose of meditation. It also makes TM enjoyable and self-motivating, which fosters our adherence to it and thereby enables its long-term success.

Cynthia: And this has the potential to open us up to a fuller experience of our religious sensibilities.

Art: Maharishi tells us that the purpose of life is the expansion of happiness. Jesus said that he came that we might have life and have it in abundance. He also said that he wants his joy to be ours so that our joy might be complete. He invited us to experience that joy by becoming one with him and the Father. Happiness is the purpose of life, the reason we were born. Complete happiness, the full abundance of life, can be found only in union with God. We are always seeking it, desiring it, yearning for it above all else. God-realization is our most powerful instinct. It is our very nature to want and seek God, and that's why it's natural to transcend.

Cynthia: A more powerful drive than self-preservation or preservation of the species?

Art: More powerful and personal, more intimate and intense. Self-preservation extends only to our finite, mortal life. God-realization reaches for the infinite, the eternal, the divine.

Cynthia: TM has obviously given you deep insights into your Catholicism.

Art: Yes, but I want to be clear that, although I've studied theology, I do not pretend to be a theologian because I am not. And although I have been ordained, I do not presume to speak for the Catholic Church because I do not. I'm only presenting, as an ordinary Catholic, my impressions of how TM has fostered, clarified, and enlivened my faith. After learning TM, I realized that the depth, majesty, and power that I now perceived in Catholicism had been there all along, but it took Maharishi to open my eyes to them. I felt like a new convert, because that's what happened. With the regular experience of transcending, I was reconverted to a deeper understanding of my Catholicism.

Cynthia: That's a profound statement.

Art: But not as profound as the actual experience. I might draw an analogy between it and the experience of the Apostles Peter, James, and John at the Transfiguration. Jesus took them up Mount Tabor where he became gloriously radiant before their eyes, and they saw him talking with Moses and Elijah, who stood alongside him. After I began to meditate, it occurred to me that perhaps the Transfiguration was not so much a matter of Jesus suddenly becoming glorified and Moses and Elijah abruptly appearing out of nowhere but, rather, that the eyes of Peter, James, and John were for a blazing moment opened to see what was always there but invisible to mere physical vision.

Cynthia: What a beautiful insight!

Art: Something more was needed, something finer, yet more profound, than their ordinary senses. Let him who has eyes see. Jesus opened the eyes of the three disciples to see what had always been there, and they thereby experienced his true, ever-present reality. In an analogous way, Maharishi opened my eyes to a fuller experience of Jesus. I saw what was there all along but previously unavailable to a vision not yet refined by the experience of transcending. Now I saw Jesus more clearly and understood more fully what he was saying. As the song goes, I was blind but now I see. I re-embraced my Catholic Christianity with the intensity and sincerity of a young seminarian, to the point of leaving my law practice and becoming an ordained deacon. I think this says a lot, not just about the compatibility of TM and Christianity, but even more so about TM being a powerful catalyst for fuller Christian experience, commitment, and steadfastness. Transcendental Consciousness is the key. It's something that has to be experienced because it can't be grasped intellectually, or even adequately discussed in an interview.

Knowing God or Merely Knowing About God

Cynthia: You're saying the experience of Transcendental Consciousness can't be known on the level of the intellect.

Art: The intellect can be a bridge to God, but also a barrier; and failing to grasp this can be a stumbling block for religion. That's why the Catholic Church and other Christian denominations, and probably all religions, exhort us to prayer, where we leave the mind behind and seek the presence of God existentially. All the preached sermons and theological treatises in the world cannot equal the experience of God. Whatever we think we know about God is not God. St. Thomas Aquinas, a Doctor of the Church who is regarded as the greatest of all theologians, had profound spiritual experiences later in life, including episodes of levitating while in ecstasy. Shortly before his death, he stopped working on his most profound thesis of all, the "Summa Theologica," which even in its incomplete state is considered by many to be the most comprehensive theological treatise ever produced by anyone in the history of the Church. When asked why he stopped, he replied: "Everything that I have written seems like straw to me compared to those things that I have seen and have been revealed to me."

Cynthia: That's beautiful!

Art: I want to read something Aquinas wrote: "The only-begotten Son of God, wanting to make us sharers in his divinity, assumed our nature, so that he, made man, might make men gods." I think this understanding must have come from his experience in the transcendent. St. Athanasius, an earlier Doctor of the Church, and St. Irenaeus, a contemporary of Athanasius, made similar statements.

Cynthia: What is meant by "make men gods"?

Art: It refers only to sharing in God's divinity. Maharishi once said something to the effect: "Never do we become God!" Brother Elias said: "As our consciousness evolves, we experience God more clearly and realistically, and not merely as a projection of what we think God is like." Sharing in God's divinity seems to be a common thread that runs through the Church's understanding of the relationship of man to God, beginning with the Apostle Peter who, in his second epistle, said that the Word became flesh to make us "partakers of the divine nature." Before I began meditating, it struck me as outlandish, even blasphemous, to say that men can become like God. And, yet, isn't this what Genesis implies when it says God made us in His image and likeness? We only need to discover the Godlikeness within us, but I don't think this is something gained intellectually as much as from our direct experience of God, as we come to know Him in Transcendental Consciousness. I think this is what Aquinas was telling us.

Cynthia: Aquinas lived in the thirteenth century, didn't he?

Art: Yes, his intellect was prodigious, and his writings prolific. They are still studied in seminaries around the world. His life testifies to the fact that to truly know God we have to get beyond dogma, which is intellectual, and into Transcendental Consciousness, which is experiential. Theology is mind stuff; transcendence is soul stuff. The scholastic tradition of theology, which attempts to illumine the truths of faith through the aid of reason, primarily Aristotelian logic, will take us only so far. We can accumulate an extensive assortment of theological knowledge, but it's horizontal and indirect, and it alone won't get us to God. For that we need vertical knowledge, a way to dive beyond thought and into direct contact with God, to know Him not as a theological concept, but as a personal experience. Maharishi discusses this in his commentary on Chapter Six, verse 30 of Chapter Six of the Bhagavad-Gita. Let me quote from it:

> We remain thinking of God, or trying to feel Him, only so long as we lack knowledge of Him, so long as we do not know how to break through the phenomenal field of experience and enter the realm of transcendental bliss, the pure kingdom of the Almighty.

Cynthia: Jesus tells us the kingdom of God is at hand and we should therefore repent. What does "repent" mean in this context?

Art: Sometimes the flavor of what is said is lost in translation; sometimes the loss is even more fundamental than that. Brother Elias captured the lost meaning of "repent" in this context when he said:

You may be familiar with the passage in the Gospels that reads: "Repent. The Kingdom of God is within you." The word translated as "repent" is metanoeite: Meta, "beyond"; and noia, "the mind." The meaning is: Go beyond the mind . . . as well as the imagination and sensations.

To enter this silent realm of Transcendental Consciousness, where our human soul seeps into the divine presence, we must repent, that is to say leave our minds behind, as if putting our shoes outside the door before entering a holy place.

Cynthia: It reminds me of the verse from Psalm 46, "Be still and know that I am God."

Art: Stillness implies an absence of thoughts or words. Everything we think we know about God is just a preconception, a bundle of thoughts and words. How can they contain God? Thoughts have boundaries; words have tight little meanings. There's not enough room in them for an infinite, eternal God. This is true of all intellectual knowledge because, being relative, it's localized in space and time. Conceptualizing God can become a subtle kind of idolatry if we don't get beyond our concepts. Thoughts and words, dogma and doctrine can point the way to God but, if we become fixated solely on them, they end up hiding God from us. It's like the ancient adage about the master pointing to the moon, and the disciple mistaking his finger for the moon. We must guard against mistaking our concepts of God for the reality of God. To do this, we need to get beyond the clamor of our mind and meet God in the silence of our heart. That's why I said earlier that I felt one of the purposes of the rosary was to get us beyond words and into the transcendent. This is what happens in TM. When we transcend, we leave thoughts behind, including all our fears, desires, and expectations because the silence of Transcendental Consciousness doesn't admit them. Maharishi also addresses this in his commentary on Chapter Six, verse 30 of the Bhagavad-Gita, where he says:

> Thought that remains thought obscures God-consciousness. Emotions likewise hide the blessed bliss. The thought of God finds fulfillment in its own extinction. And emotion too has to cease in order to let the heart be full in the unbounded love of God.

Maharishi had already specifically discussed the emotion of fear in his commentary on Chapter Six, verse 14 of the Bhagavad-Gita:

> [O]n the path of increasing happiness during meditation there is no chance of fear. . . . The mind, during the inward stroke of meditation, begins to lose the sense of duality, begins to move away from the field of fear.

This harkens us to the words of the Apostle John in his First Letter that " . . . perfect love casts out fear." He also says, "God is love." In meditation, as we transcend and experience the presence of God within us, we become emptied of fear and all else that is not God, and we're filled with love, which is God. This experience is much like that elegant little saying attributed to Jesus: "Empty thyself and I shall fill thee."

Cynthia: But the idea of becoming empty can be off-putting. Who wants to be empty?

Art: No, it's not that. Emptiness is simply looking at fullness from the inside out. The experience in Transcendental Consciousness is one of complete fullness. The emptier we get the fuller we become. Complete emptiness is total fullness. It resonates as bliss—an imperturbable peace that really does surpass all intellectual understanding. At this juncture, where the fullness of the Absolute and the emptiness of the relative meet, we experience God's presence, as someone once put it, where we leave off and He begins. The fullness in our emptiness is the presence of God, Whom we experience not as a theological concept but as Supreme Being. It's what Christian contemplatives mean by a loss of self or dying to the self. When we experience the presence of God in Transcendental Consciousness, we momentarily lose the experience of self. But who cares? The trade-off is wonderful! Maharishi says that, when a man is taken from a hut and given a palace to live in, he doesn't mind leaving the hut. This is how we begin to share in God's divine nature, as Aquinas, Athanasius, Irenaeus, and other Church Fathers spoke of. In Transcendental Consciousness we leave our small localized awareness and step into the divine.

Cynthia: So the experience is not an empty emptiness?

Art: No, it's the other way around. It's the complete fullness of pure consciousness. Think of emptiness as a grand openness, an unbounded panorama without horizon or limitations that is capable of containing all there is. In a sense, if we think about it, only emptiness can contain the fullness of everything in its virtual or undifferentiated state. If we try to introduce anything discrete into emptiness, we immediately set limitations and transition it from the absolute to the relative. Infinity and eternity cannot exist within boundaries but only in the endless expanse of emptiness from which everything takes form. Emptiness is how we experience God Who is infinite and eternal. Brother Elias describes it as being " . . . drawn into an immense internal spaciousness, so vast that you could walk for miles and miles and find no one . . . but Christ." And Christ is everywhere you look.

Cynthia: Maharishi speaks of pure consciousness, which is what we experience when we transcend, as the home of all possibilities. It contains everything in virtual form.

Art: Pure consciousness, which is the basis of all material existence, has no physical content or components. In that sense it is empty. Maharishi said: "Emptiness is the potential of everything." Pure consciousness is the "great void" in Genesis from which God created everything. Just as the statue is already present in the uncarved block of marble and the bracelet in the uncast lump of gold, each awaiting the sculptor or goldsmith to call them forth and give them form, so also do all possibilities, all that will ever exist, already reside in pure consciousness. Genesis tells us that in the beginning God the Creator called forth from the great void all relative creation and gave it form. The great void, then, is really a complete fullness, but not in the way we ordinarily think of fullness. It's not jam-packed like a can of sardines with everything that can possibly be but, rather, it contains all possibilities of what can and will be. It's the potential for everything. That's why pure consciousness is the wellspring of creativity, why artists and architects, writers and poets, composers and inventors, people of all callings experience a surge in creativity after learning TM. When we transcend, we enter this vast realm of pure consciousness, the fullness of emptiness, the potential of everything, and we appropriate this source of creation to the specific characteristics of our own lives.

Cynthia: Does Christianity have its own set of terms and concepts for what Maharishi calls pure consciousness and Transcendental Consciousness?

Art: There's an equivalence both in Christian thought and experience. I think mystical theology has developed its own vocabulary for distinguishing between merely knowing things about God and actually knowing Him, which is not accomplished by accumulating intellectual facts about Him. It talks about a mystical union with God so intimate that it can be described only by the term "spiritual marriage." The experience is one of bliss or ecstasy, but without intellectual content. Christian mystics and contemplatives sometimes describe it as unknowingness or becoming empty. Because terms like unknowingness and emptiness are devoid of intellectual content, they help us bypass the logical contradiction in trying to understand intellectually that which can be known only experientially. Just as emptiness is not empty, unknowingness is not an absence of knowledge or certainty. It's pure knowledge without form, and complete certainty without substance. It needs no name because it has no object. In fact, it has no distinct subject. It's beyond the subject-object dichotomy. It just is. It's a state of pure is-ness. And that's bliss. A gentle, buoyant bliss. I think Brother Elias expresses this in various places in *Dancing Madly Backwards*. Let me quote from it:

> *Dabar* engages the whole person, beginning at the level of "not knowing": the way that lies beyond the fiftieth gate of knowledge in a loving silence beyond concepts or images. And from there it sweeps back through all the other gates: feelings, imagination, senses . . .

Dabar, Brother Elias tells us, is Hebrew for "word" but connotes a "dynamic happening" that carries us into "a festival of deeper life." It reminds me of John's use of *Logos* in the Prologue to his Gospel.

Cynthia: We're constantly struggling to describe that which can only be experienced.

Art: Exactly. Descriptions have boundaries that can't contain the infinite vastness in which we meet our eternal God. Words are not able to convey the experience, so talking about the fullness of emptiness or about unknow-ingness as pure knowledge will seem paradoxical to anyone unfamiliar with Transcendental Consciousness. The quandary is that we can speak only of that which we know; whereas regarding unknowingness, only silence knows and can speak. But there's a little poem that I think comes close to giving us a feel for this paradox. It's by Johannes Scheffler, a Polish-German Catholic priest, who wrote in the seventeenth century under the name Angelus Silesius:

> God, whose love and joy
> Are present everywhere,
> Can't come to visit us
> Unless we aren't there.

It's another way of saying: "Empty thyself and I shall fill thee." It reminds me, too, of the insight Brother Elias offers us in *Dancing Madly Backwards* when he says: "Here, to be 'No One' is to be 'one' in the purest sense: one with one-self, others, creation, the Secret One." Sometimes poetry says it best because it says it least.

Cynthia: Some of the Christian mystics spoke primarily in poetry, didn't they?

Art: One of the best examples is the sixteenth century Spanish priest and mystic, St. John of the Cross. He tells us that the soul proceeds by unknowing rather than knowing. Let me read one of his poems that clearly and profoundly expresses the difference between intellectual knowledge of God and the actual experience of Him in the transcendent:

> I entered into unknowing,
> and there I remained unknowing,
> transcending all knowledge.

1

I entered into unknowing,
yet when I saw myself there,
without knowing where I was,
I understood great things;
I will not say what I felt
for I remained in unknowing,
transcending all knowledge.

2

That perfect knowledge
was of peace and holiness
held at no remove
in profound solitude;
it was something so secret
that I was left stammering,
transcending all knowledge.

3

I was so 'whelmed,
so absorbed and withdrawn,
that my senses were left
deprived of all their sensing,
and my spirit was given
an understanding while not understanding,
transcending all knowledge.

4

He who truly arrives there
cuts free from himself;
all that he knew before
now seems worthless,
and his knowledge so soars
that he is left in unknowing,
transcending all knowledge.

5

The higher he ascends

the less he understands,
because the cloud is dark
which lit up the night;
whoever knows this
remains always in unknowing,
transcending all knowledge.

6

This knowledge in unknowing
is so overwhelming
that wise men disputing
can never overthrow it,
for their knowledge does not reach
to the understanding of not understanding,
transcending all knowledge.

7

And this supreme knowledge
is so exalted
that no power of man or learning
can grasp it;
he who masters himself
will, with knowledge in unknowing,
always be transcending.

8

And if you should want to hear:
this highest knowledge lies
in the loftiest sense
of the essence of God;
this is a work of his mercy,
to leave one without understanding,
transcending all knowledge.[1]

Cynthia: That is powerful.

Art: Powerful, I think, because it leads us away from the intellect and toward the experience that he's describing. Because you and I have experienced

---

1   St. John of the Cross, *The Collected Works*, Trs. Kavanaugh & Rodriguez, Thomas Nelson & Sons, London, 1964, pp. 718-719.

Transcendental Consciousness in TM, we can identify with what he says. The Catholic Church has a rich tradition of intimacy with the transcendent, and Maharishi has made this experience, once known only to mystics and contemplatives, available to everyone through the practice of TM. I think TM will soon be seen as the missing link that will join all Catholics to the mystical tradition of their Church. For many, many centuries, we've had this body of mystical theology, but there has been no practical way to enter into it and, so, it's not been available to ordinary Catholics. Now all that is changed because we have TM, which not only makes it easily accessible to everyone but also demystifies it so that it can be understood by anyone. Wouldn't it be wonderful if, as we studied Church doctrine, we also learned to meditate and thereby gained firsthand knowledge of what the Church is teaching—not just word-knowledge, but the actual experience of the kingdom of God within?

Cynthia: What you were saying about emptiness reminded me of something I once read by Meister Eckhart. He said that knowing God is a matter of subtraction, not addition.

Art: That's a beautiful thought. The more we take away who we think we are, the more we discover who God is because deep down, beneath all the superficialities, we are His image and likeness. This idea of negation or subtraction is found in sacred writings, both East and West. Thomas Aquinas used a process he called *Via Negativa*, the way of negation, to describe the nature of God by listing what He is not. In fact, so did Dionysius many centuries earlier. We don't find God within ourselves by adding new chunks of theology to our intellectual reservoir of facts, but rather by subtracting from ourselves everything that is not like God. Then His image and likeness reflect in us as He says He is: I AM WHO AM, the Pure Being that is before all else. As John the Baptist said of Jesus: "He who has come after me has been set above me because he was before me." And as Jesus said of himself, "Before Abraham was, I Am." Throughout the Gospels, Jesus invites us into this fullness, to become perfect even as the Father in heaven is perfect, to have life in abundance, and to know his joy in its completeness. Finding this fullness within is always a process of subtraction and negation. Sages of India, ancient and modern, refer to it as "Neti, Neti," not this, not that. We strip from ourselves, as we would from an onion, all the superficial layers of the self and, like in Narnia, as we " . . . continue to go in and in, each circle is larger than the last," until we get to the world within the world, the I AM WHO AM, and realize that we each have a share in divinity, that we are each included in the WHO AM of the I AM.

Cynthia: Emptiness, then, is a prelude to fullness?

Art: It *is* fullness. The process is simultaneous. For Christians, as we experience Transcendental Consciousness and become more and more empty of ourself, we become more and more filled with Christ. This gives a whole new meaning to the idea of selflessness. Perhaps this is what John the Baptist was describing when he said, "I must decrease and he must increase." Or that pithy statement: "Empty thyself and I shall fill thee." We are the emptiness of Brother Elias' "No One," and the fullness of his "Secret One." It is not emptiness that we experience in Transcendental Consciousness, but the fullness that supplants it. Christians have the experience of union with Christ in Transcendental Consciousness precisely because it is an emptying of self that is filled with Christ. As St. Paul says in Galatians, "I live, yet not I but Christ lives in me." In Ephesians he exhorts us to put away the old self, be renewed in spirit, and put on a new self. I believe this is what Jesus referred to as dying to the self and why Paul tells us in Philippians that "to die is gain." When we transcend, we are transported from the hut to the palace . . . and we don't mind leaving the hut and gaining the palace.

Cynthia: But this is not something we can make happen or wish into existence.

Art: No, that would amount to mood-making. We can't manufacture, prod, or manipulate Transcendental Consciousness into happening. Trying to do so only keeps it from happening. When we meditate, we merely set the conditions for it to happen, let go, and, as Maharishi says, take it as it comes. The TM technique keeps the mind lively but undirected, thereby allowing it to transcend according to its own natural tendency. We don't enter meditation with an agenda or a list of expectations or personal ambitions. By letting go of all that, we are easily drawn into Transcendental Consciousness. We innocently let go into God and, as we draw unto Him, he draws unto us. If we simply take it as it comes, we are led to this selflessness, this dying to the self, and we begin to realize that, at our core, we are this stillness or emptiness in which everything else happens. Maharishi tells us that stillness is at the core of motion and silence at that of commotion. The dimensionless center of the axle never turns. Even in the hectic tumult of daily life, the stillness we experience in

Transcendental Consciousness remains silently, even if only imperceptibly, in the heart of our being; and the more we meditate, the more we become aware of this stillness in the midst of our activity.

Cynthia: Stillness and emptiness, unknowingness and dying to the self all refer, of course, to the spiritual world. How do they translate—what are their effects and implications—in terms of the material world?

Art: For one thing, we gain a new perspective on material possessions because, paradoxically, by giving up everything in Transcendental Consciousness, we gain everything. As Paul says, to die is gain. This idea is captured in the old adage that a person who is content having no possessions owns the world. It has also been said quite perceptively that the wealthiest person is not he who has the most, but he who needs the least. Jesus, who owned nothing, told us that all power in heaven and on earth had been given to him. Perhaps that's why Jesus commends to us the birds of the air and the lilies of the field. It's why he asked the rich young man to sell what he had and give the proceeds to the poor.

Giving away his riches would, of course, only be of momentary benefit to the poor, but the rich young man would himself be the eternal beneficiary of his divestment. He would no longer be possessed by his possessions or, for that matter, enamored of his youth because youth, like riches, is just another possession that we vainly try to hold on to, but it slips away anyway. The true art of life is not in acquiring and holding on, but in relinquishing and letting go. Had the rich young man done what Jesus asked, he would have realized, clearly and conclusively, that happiness is the eternal essence of his being, and he would have found it from within and no longer sought it from riches, youth, intellectual knowledge, or anything else outside himself, outside his true Self. It is, as preachers often point out, the difference between life *with* abundance, which is what the rich young man could not relinquish, and life *in* abundance, which is what Jesus promises us in return.

Cynthia: The two aren't mutually exclusive. Jesus isn't saying that we have to give up everything to enter heaven.

Art: Yes and no. Yes, we do momentarily give up every "thing" to gain everything when we experience Transcendental Consciousness, the kingdom of God within. But, no, there's nothing inherently wrong with having material possessions, and that's not what Jesus is telling us. His advice to the rich young man does not mean we should discard our possessions, renounce our wealth, or deny our personal needs. The rich young man was so inextricably entangled and fully self-identified with his wealth that only a complete severance would have freed him from its grip. That's why he's identified in the Gospels simply as "the rich young man." His wealth and youth completely define who he is. For us, the lesson means only to relinquish our attachment to extraneous things, both physical and emotional, including our fears and desires, recognizing that they are not who we are, that they do not and cannot define who we are, and that they will one day fall away. This includes our body, around which all our other extraneous things accumulate. We should not get too attached to it because it, too, will fall away, and we will stand naked before God, which is the way we are in essence and the way He sees us and we see Him in Transcendental Consciousness—invisible to less discerning eyes.

Cynthia: Would you elaborate on what you mean by momentarily giving up everything in Transcendental Consciousness?

Art: Maharishi tells us in his commentary on Chapter Six, verse 10 of the Bhagavad-Gita that, when we sit to meditate, we should not try to hold on to anything. He explains that:

> [M]editation is a process which takes the mind from the consciousness of possessions to the consciousness of Being. In terms of possessions, it is a process of becoming possessionless: the Self is left by Itself. The mind loses consciousness of the surroundings and the body, leaving [the meditator] quite naturally without any consciousness of possessions.

This, I think, is what dying to the self means. By dying to the self in Transcendental Consciousness, we get a taste of heaven on earth. In Transcendental Consciousness, we are debrided of all those things with which we identify in daily life, including the awareness of our bodies, and we find out that they are not who we really are. That's quite a liberating discovery! Here's something else worth considering. We remain fully alert in Transcendental Consciousness, and yet we lose any trace of externally distinguishing characteristics, even of the sensation of our body. This gives us a taste of what eternal life will be like when we pass from this earthly physical existence—a kind of dress rehearsal without the dress.

Cynthia: The idea of dying to the self is mentioned often in Christianity.

Art: And we do it daily in TM. I think this experience is what Jesus spoke of in the Gospel of John when he said that "Unless a seed of wheat falls to the ground and dies it remains just a seed, but if it dies, it brings forth abundant fruit." He then warned that he who loves his life shall lose it, but he who hates his life in this world shall keep it unto life eternal. Isn't the reference obvious? Life in this world is the small self, the person we think we are, but not who we really are. If we're gripped by the small self and blindly identify with it, we miss eternal life. But, by dying to the small self in Transcendental Consciousness, we simultaneously experience and gain eternal life. I hear the words of Jesus echoed in *The Science of Being and Art of Living* in which Maharishi says: "[L]overs of life may find life in losing it and may find God in losing themselves in God-consciousness." He explains this further in his commentary on Chapter Six, verse 45 of the Bhagavad-Gita:

> If we analyze what happens when the individual mind gains cosmic status in Transcendental Consciousness, we find that the individual ceases to exist—he becomes pure Existence. On coming out from the Transcendent, individual life is regained.

Maharishi does not mean that we cease to exist in a literal sense. Rather, we lose the sensation of body and surroundings. As Brother Elias puts it: "Everything about our individuality remains, but sets itself apart during the experience of Transcendental Consciousness." Maharishi goes on to explain that each time we come back out of Transcendental Consciousness, it's like a rebirth to individual life. His description of our experience in Transcendental Consciousness complements the Christian idea of dying to the self—and perhaps also the idea of being born again. Each time we die to the self, we are then also, as Maharishi says, "re-born to the world." Here is what he says in context:

> [We are] . . . perfected through the continued practice of repeatedly gaining Transcendental Consciousness and thus being re-born to the world many, many times until Cosmic Consciousness is gained.

Cynthia: Some Christians interpret being born again as a reference to Baptism.

Art: Yes, we believe that's what Jesus meant when he said: "Truly, truly, I say to you, unless a man is born of water and the Spirit, he cannot enter the kingdom of God." This seems to be a specific reference to the Sacrament of Baptism. But being "born again" might also have a broader application. In the same chapter of John's Gospel, Jesus says in more general terms: "Unless a man is born again, he is not able to see the kingdom of God." If the kingdom of God is within us, as Jesus said, and if we see it, so to speak, in Transcendental Consciousness and, further, if this occasions a continual rebirth, as Maharishi said, then being born again might also refer to the "continued practice of repeatedly gaining Transcendental Consciousness."

Cynthia: Does all this have any practical effects in daily life?

Art: Dying to the self, like the seed of wheat that falls to the ground, brings forth abundant fruit, as Jesus tells us. In the Gospels of Matthew and Mark, Jesus cursed the fig tree that bore no fruit. Maharishi said we must water the root to enjoy the fruit. All of this, from a practical perspective, relates to seeking first the kingdom of God inside and thereby also having all our outer needs fulfilled. It's the 200% of life that Maharishi speaks of. When we transcend and die to the self, we bring back into our daily lives the flavor of Transcendental Consciousness. If everyone experienced transcending on a regular basis, what would happen to bigotry, rivalry, and persecution?

How could we discriminate against one another based on apparent differences that recede into nothingness in Transcendental Consciousness? They become irrelevant. In the unity of the Absolute, we quickly come to see the folly of using the diversity of the relative to justify intolerance or hatred, or to permit anything but love for one another. Who is there to war with or discriminate against in Transcendental Consciousness? Loving others as our-Self, including our so-called enemies, becomes a reality in Transcendental Consciousness because it's the only option. And, each time we come out of Transcendental Consciousness, of having died to the self, we are reborn with a little more of the image and likeness of God that shines through in our activity.

Cynthia: These are intriguing insights from a Christian perspective.

Art: If we take the tenets of our religion and view them through the lens of Transcendental Consciousness, they come to life in our daily affairs in ways we had not before envisioned. Not only are TM and our Christian beliefs compatible but, even more so, they complement one another. Conflict,

I think, arises from insecurity about one's beliefs. I am a Catholic. Period. I love and profess my Catholic faith and, being secure in it, I can, without getting fearful and fidgety, appropriate to it all that is true, harmonious, and helpful. This includes practicing TM daily. Should anything inconsistent with my Catholicism ever arise, it simply falls to the side.

Cynthia: I like how you see TM as a way to help our Christian faith grow and be fruitful.

Art: The practice of transcending gave me a better insight into what Jesus was talking about when he compared the mustard seed, the tiniest of all seeds, to the kingdom of God. The mustard plant in Israel, unlike its counterparts in other areas of the world, can grow to well over ten feet in height. It must have been a marvelous metaphor for Jesus. When this tiniest of seeds is planted, it soon digs roots deep into the earth and sends toward heaven a stem that branches out and cascades into countless more branches, producing copious leaves and eventually exploding into a profusion of bright yellow flowers. From one tiny seed, the most prolific and prodigious of all plants emerges. So, too, when the seed for transcending is whispered into our awareness, the kingdom of God begins to blossom and flourish within us.

Cynthia: And we experience Him, as you said earlier, not as a theological concept but as Supreme Being.

Art: I think this is another reason why emptiness is a useful image. By defying description, it implies the futility of over-intellectualizing about God, of grabbing at God solely with theological concepts or religious doctrine instead of allowing Him to happen to us spontaneously in Transcendental Consciousness. Angelus Silesius wrote another little poem to capture this:

> God is the purest no-thing,
> Untouched by now and here;
> The less we reach for Him,
> The more He will appear.

Grabbing for God conceptually is self-defeating due to our limitations of mind, language, and logic. But, the moment we begin Transcendental Meditation and let go of any compulsion to possess Him, He gently begins to possess us. We experience His presence within us, and it continues to grow, like the mustard plant, until we no longer know God as a cluster of thoughts but as the Supreme Being with Whom we are intimately and inextricably entwined.

The Eucharist and the Upper Room

Cynthia: You said that, before learning TM, you experienced random instances of Transcendental Consciousness. You described them as happening in religious settings. Have you experienced them elsewhere?

Art: No, I have no recollection of spontaneous or random transcending apart from praying the rosary or during liturgical celebrations. I mentioned these episodes only to show that transcending is both natural and necessary to spiritual growth. If we don't have a predictable way to transcend regularly, it may happen randomly on our spiritual journey. But, then again, it may not. With TM, however, we don't have to gamble about something so important. Maharishi made TM available to all religions so that their adherents can regularly experience transcending and thereby enjoy rapid spiritual growth in the context of their own system of beliefs.

Cynthia: Did you find any liturgical settings in Catholicism to be especially conducive to deeper levels of silence?

Art: Yes, the Eucharistic celebration. The times I experienced transcendence as a choirboy and as a deacon were during the Eucharistic celebration. Our hearts and minds yearn for union with God, and the Eucharist is a direct taste of that union.

Cynthia: You're speaking of Holy Communion. What exactly is it?

Art: Seven Sacraments are at the center of the Catholic Church, and central to these Sacraments is the Eucharist, commonly called Holy Communion. The word "communion" means "union with." Holy Communion is union with Christ and, through him, union with one another. It's very beautiful. It's an experience of wholeness. We believe the Eucharist is the real presence of Jesus. You're familiar with the concept of *darshan?*

Cynthia: It can refer to the grace, or blessing, or other benefit received from being in the presence of a spiritual master.

Art: If merely being in the presence of the Master has profound spiritual effects, can you imagine what it is like to be in intimate communion with him in the Sacrament of the Eucharist?

Cynthia: What do you mean by the Eucharist as a Sacrament?

Art: A Sacrament, which is a visible sign of an invisible reality, effects an inner transformation through the transmission of grace. That's not an official definition but merely my simplified explanation. Jesus, while on earth, was the

Sacrament of God—the visible sign of the invisible reality of God, as Paul tells us in Colossians. When Jesus knew he would no longer be physically present on earth, he left us the Sacrament of the Eucharist, the visible sign of his continuing invisible presence among us. But it's not just a sign. It is his real presence. Like Transcendental Consciousness, which can't be adequately described in words, the Eucharist, which means "Thanksgiving," defies rigid definition. Sidestepping technicalities, I would say that, when we receive the Eucharist, we bring the real presence of Jesus within our own bodies and get a taste of divinity within ourselves. It's not so much that we take Jesus into ourselves; rather, he takes us into himself. We enter into his divinity. Just as the bread and wine are transformed into him, our life becomes transformed into his as we come to share in his divinity. As St. Paul says, "I live, yet not I but Christ lives in me." The Eucharist is endless in the grace and goodness it bestows.

Cynthia: What kinds of experiences do people have when receiving the Eucharist?

Art: It's very personal and varies from individual to individual, depending on his or her relationship with Jesus. I suspect that some people might even transcend, with varying degrees of clarity, perhaps without realizing it. The experience of transcending may be faint and fleeting, or it may be more discernible and sustained. By tradition we sit or kneel quietly upon receiving the Eucharist and contemplate the presence of Jesus within us. In these moments of deep silence, I suppose it wouldn't be uncommon to transcend and experience the flavor of Transcendental Consciousness. But please understand that the Eucharist is the real presence of Jesus, the Son of God. That's a profound realization! It's transformational in and of itself. By receiving the Eucharist, ". . . we come to share in his divinity as he has humbled himself to share in our humanity." These words are from a prayer said by the priest or deacon at the Offertory of the Mass. It's what Aquinas spoke about in that quote I mentioned earlier: "The only-begotten Son of God, wanting to make us sharers in his divinity, assumed our nature, so that he, made man, might make men gods." The Eucharist, if properly received, brings this about.

Cynthia: You mentioned other saints who had also said something similar to Aquinas.

Art: The words of St. Irenaeus may be even more apropos to the Eucharist:

"For this is why the Word became man, and the Son of God became the Son of man: so that man, by entering into communion with the Word and thus receiving divine sonship, might become a son of God." Irenaeus speaks specifically of communion with Jesus who, of course, is the Word, as described in the Prologue to John's Gospel. John tells us in his Prologue that " . . . to as many as receive [Jesus] he gave the power to become sons of God." The Eucharist is for Catholics the direct, tangible means of receiving Jesus, communing with him, and sharing in his divinity.

Cynthia: Would you be more precise in describing your personal experience in Holy Communion?

Art: Keep in mind that the Eucharistic experience is personal, not magical, and will vary from person to person depending on his or her predisposition or level of receptivity. My experience in the Eucharist is different from what I described having while saying the rosary or singing in the choir or serving at the altar as a deacon. I'm sure I've had episodes of unknowingness when receiving the Eucharist, but that's not what dominates the experience. Instead, the Eucharist gives me a sense of grounding, of great refinement and all-embracing satisfaction. The experience is more one of completeness than of unknowingness, of wellbeing and wholeness, as if nothing else is needed. And for some people nothing else is needed. There are recorded instances of saints subsisting for years on just the daily reception of the Eucharist with no other nourishment taken.

Cynthia: There are similar accounts of saints in India who do not have to eat to survive.

Art: It requires a highly purified nervous system. It's not a feat of self-abnegation, nor something a person can do by trying to do it. In fact, someone recently died foolishly trying. The ability to live without food is rare and is the result of gradual inner purification in which the impulse to abstain from food comes naturally, without a sense of sacrifice or denial. It is definitely not something about which to entertain foolhardy pretensions.

Cynthia: Meditation refines the nervous system. Do you find that the Eucharist does, too?

Art: Yes, definitely. Religion sometimes forgets that there is a physiological component to spiritual growth. In its emphasis on the soul's eternal hereafter, religion must not diminish or trivialize the importance of the body in the here and now. We must diligently care for the body because through its faculties, its organs of sensation and action, we are able to purify the soul.

Cynthia: In the East it's called *tapas*—purification.

Art: The Eucharist purifies our physiologies as well as our souls. It nourishes both. Since my seminary days, I have often felt when receiving Holy Communion a gentle, yet sustained, sense of physical wellbeing. It's very subtle, yet very peaceful and satisfying. After I learned TM and experienced Transcendental Consciousness in a systematic way, I came to appreciate more fully the Eucharistic as a universal unction for body and soul. I began receiving it daily as I had in the seminary, and the feeling of completeness and wellbeing became more and more pronounced in my daily life. Just as a single meditation has manifold benefits, so, too, with receiving the Eucharist. But, as with meditation, the true benefit is in its regular reception. There is a cumulative effect, and each reception prepares a person for a fuller experience in subsequent receptions. Those who live in seminaries, convents, and monasteries receive the Eucharist daily, as do many Catholics who work in the world. There is a reason and a reward for this kind of dedication and devotion.

Cynthia: So, the experience isn't the same each time the Eucharist is received?

Art: It varies depending on a person's disposition at the moment. But we can always be sure that something good is happening, which is what Maharishi says about meditating. I have found that the more regular I am in receiving the Eucharist, the more consistent the experience becomes, all the while drawing me closer to Christ.

Cynthia: Some denominations hold that the words of Jesus when he instituted the Eucharist were merely symbolic, but the Catholic Church believes he really transformed bread and wine into his body and blood, doesn't it?

Art: Some symbols are just that—symbolic, just so much imagery. Other symbols actually contain what they symbolize. The consecrated bread and wine are the reality they symbolize. While retaining the outward appearances of bread and wine, they are transformed in substance to the body and blood of Jesus. The Eucharist is the real and continuous presence of Jesus, his divine omnipresence. Throughout the centuries, as well as presently, this belief has had its ridiculers and detractors. What cannot be argued against, however, is the actual experience of receiving the Eucharist and the effect it has on our lives. A pervading sense of wellbeing, even ecstasy, might be experienced that we carry with us into activity. It has a purifying effect on everything we encounter and do. But, like Transcendental Consciousness, we can't make it happen or pretend that it is happening and, so, we must guard against mood-making. We receive the Eucharist, remain quiet with it for a period of time, and then return to activity. Gradually it transforms our lives.

Cynthia: But I suspect some people might wonder if bread and wine can really be transformed into the body and blood of Jesus.

Art: Why not? Jesus raised people from the dead. He cured dreaded and deadly diseases. He gave sight to the blind and unlocked the limbs of the lame. He transformed five loaves into enough bread to feed five thousand with twelve baskets left over. And, most importantly, he forgave sins. As John says about Jesus in the Prologue to his Gospel: "All things were made through him and without him was made nothing that has been made." He made the bread and wine and every molecule and atom that make them up. He made his own body and every cell in it. Certainly he can transform one into the other, keep the appearance of bread and wine but make it into his real presence. And he can ordain and empower his disciples to do the same throughout all ages to come. "Do this in memory of me." I have no problem accepting this. And the proof is in the Eucharist itself.

Cynthia: The Eucharist sounds both mysterious and inviting.

Art: It's mystery and majesty. And, yes, it does beckon us. It helps, I think, to put it in context. The Eucharist was instituted by Jesus at the Last Supper in the Upper Room, which Jesus asked his disciples to prepare beforehand for the celebration of the Passover. This scene is replete with meaning, resplendent with possibilities. Passover is the transition from bondage to liberation. The Last Supper is both beginning and end. It's the culmination of knowledge and the elimination of ignorance. It was the first Mass. The Upper Room was lit with love, filled with the impassioned effulgence of self-sacrifice. Jesus was about to lay down his life for his friends. "Greater love than this no man has." Now, centuries later, when we celebrate the Eucharist, we, like the disciples, retreat with Jesus to the Upper Room of our consciousness where the ordinary becomes the extraordinary, where bread and wine become the body and blood of Jesus, where we partake of his real presence, just as did the disciples. We become his disciples, intimately and ultimately One in Christ.

Cynthia: I especially like the image of the Upper Room lit with love. It was, of course, a physical location in the Gospels, but it can refer to a place in our consciousness, too.

Art: Jesus spoke elsewhere in the Gospel of the "inner room," telling us to retreat into it when we pray. If we keep the imagery consistent, then Upper Room refers to an even more refined level of consciousness than inner room for the purpose of celebrating the Eucharist. It is the place within our heart that is self-effulgent with love.

Cynthia: It's all fascinating imagery.

Art: Imagery offers a deeper grasp of the significance of the Passover, of the Last Supper, and of the Upper Room in the context of the Eucharist and in relation to Transcendental Consciousness. When we meditate and transcend, we, like the disciples, are readying our Upper Room so that, when we celebrate the Eucharist, we are better prepared to pass over from bondage to liberation and, as in the Last Supper, to witness the ending of ignorance and the ascendence of knowledge. The bread is composed of many grains of wheat and the wine of many grapes of the vine, all brought together as one in the Eucharist, exemplifying our unity in Jesus. The consecration of bread and wine into the body and blood of Jesus is, however, more than mere imagery. The bread and wine become what they symbolize. They are the reality behind the symbol as expressed in the very words of Jesus when, giving thanks to the Father, he took bread, blessed and broke it, and said, "Take and eat, this is my body." Then, taking the cup, he gave thanks, blessed it, and said, "Take and drink, this is my blood." He meant what he said, and he bids us to become One with him in the Eucharist and, through it, one with each other. He empowered his Apostles and their successors to perform this Sacrament of transubstantiating bread and wine into his body and blood when he said: "Do this in memory of me." In this manner, he has made himself physically present to us until the end of time.

Cynthia: If the Eucharist contains what it symbolizes and is more than imagery, then there seems to be quite a bit hidden under the appearance of bread and wine.

Art: Bernadette Roberts offers an engaging perspective on the Eucharist. She is a contemporary Catholic contemplative who describes her spiritual journey into higher states of consciousness in language that, although drawn from the parlance of our Catholic faith, sounds strikingly similar to Maharishi's description of Cosmic Consciousness, God Consciousness, and Unity Consciousness. In *What Is Self?*, her third book dealing with growth in consciousness from a Christian perspective, she observes, speaking about the Eucharist, that there's no great mystery in a nonmaterial spirit not appearing to the senses, but there is enormous mystery in a material body that does not appear to the senses.

Cynthia: Meaning?

Art: We have to ponder her meaning. She explains that the Eucharist, which is material and therefore apparent to the senses, comprises, as did the historical person Jesus, the totality of his Being, which is not apparent. The Eucharist comprehends not only all the characteristics of Jesus' humanity but extends to the unbounded entirety and enormity of his divinity, and encompasses the Trinity, which is the true nature of Godhead. It also incorporates his Mystical Body, consisting of the entire Christian Church on earth. That means the Eucharist embraces the ultimate mystery of our own bodies. That's an awful lot to be hidden, as you noted, under the appearance of bread and wine. And yet, it's all there.

Cynthia: I have a feeling there's even more to the point she's making.

Art: There is. She draws an interesting insight about the Eucharist. She says it tells us that the body—not just Christ's body but also our own—is of a different nature than what we ordinarily see and know, that our true body is what we do not see or know, in the same way that the Eucharist is infinitely more than just the visible bread and wine. She says this is a tremendous truth to ponder because it means there is no separation between who we are eternally, which we do not see or know, and our physical body, which we do see and know. Her discussion gets somewhat technical here, but the gist is that the Eucharist informs us of how incomprehensibly intricate and immense our own being is and that death is not what it appears to be. It's not a disintegration of the body as much as a transition into all we are that is not apparent to the senses. Just as the enormity of what is hidden behind the bread and wine of the Eucharist is incomprehensible to our physical senses, so also is the enormity of what is hidden behind the appearance of our own bodies. In death, nothing of whom we are is any longer available to the limitations of physical perception because we have now been transitioned into the considerably fuller awareness of all of whom we are. She concludes by saying that whatever Christ reveals to us—and here the revelation is the Eucharist—is our truth, and not merely his truth. Bernadette Roberts offers us a beautiful perspective on life, death, and fuller life. All this from the Eucharist.

Cynthia: And a lot to try to grasp.

Art: She suggests pondering, not grasping. She then explains how the Ascension of Jesus, forty days after his Resurrection, vividly reveals this truth. As Jesus physically ascended into heaven, he seemed to those who were watching to fade away from sight, yet he remains ever present. Where did he go? He went nowhere, which is non-localized and, therefore, he continues to be everywhere. I would compare it to the Transfiguration event, which I spoke of earlier, and to the Resurrection, both Jesus' and our own. In the Ascension, the visible became invisible. In the Transfiguration, the invisible became visible. In the Resurrection, both are joined, the visible to the invisible, earthly life to eternal life. But it's really all a continuum. Everything about Jesus is always there, always the same—yesterday, today, and forever. We change, not he. The only thing different is our perception of him. The crossover line between visible and invisible is the limitation of our ability to see. Our eyes are either open, or they are not. We see, or we don't. Jesus said, "Let him who has eyes see." But first our eyes must be opened. Paul said in First Corinthians: "For now we see through a glass, darkly, but then face to face; now I know in part, but then shall I know even as also I am known." And Brother Elias said:

> [B]ut better still is to expand into the vision of the Witness who watches without judging. Faith is the Friend looking out from the eyes of a heart that has always seen, without realizing that it was seeing.

It's an echo of Plato teaching allegories from the cave.

Cynthia: Paul implies that we will become purified so that we comprehend all of truth, including the entire reality of Jesus. What do you suppose Brother Elias means?

Art: I only know what it is that I mean when I read his words. That's the joy of *Dancing Madly Backwards*. Brother Elias' words are as much possibility as they are substance, with lots of open spaces, little tabernacles of silence, in which to meditate and insert our own meaning—whatever our own experience brings to his words. Transposing his words into my context allows me to see reflections of my own meaning from different angles. The meaning I get is that what is looked upon with faith is already there, really there, always there. It's not what's seen by us, but through us. It's the vision of the Witness who watches from my heart, and yours, without judging. It's the certainty—not faith, but certainty—that all of Jesus, visible or not, is present in the Eucharist. And it's the knowledge that death is a matter of perception. Isn't that the beauty of the Resurrection, both Jesus' and ours?

Cynthia: Is this something you get from the Eucharist?

Art: Yes, and from meditation, too. They both give me a fuller sense of my own resurrection. Shortly after beginning to meditate, I noticed that my fear of death had faded away. Vanished. I enjoy thinking, feeling, and perceiving through my body, but I'm ready to let it go whenever I'm called to do so. I've come to realize that my passing body is just something to float in and out of as it moves on by. It's a joy for the moment, but hardly the meaning or measure of my existence. I am the life in my body; and it's merely my temporary wrapper. This was a pretty big realization. We like to think of life after death as a kind of continuation of what it was like to live on earth, having the same sensations, perceptions, and movements. But I think that's a very limiting perspective. It will be a much fuller life, much more profound and complete, not bounded by space, time, or causation. In Transcendental Consciousness, where the senses are drawn in like the limbs of a tortoise, as the Bhagavad-Gita says, we get a taste of the fullness of existence without the limitations of the body. With this experience, death loses its sting, as Paul notes. The glory of it all is that without bodily limitations our awareness, in the form of pure knowledge, is unbounded, and we can then comprehend all of Jesus and all of us. Perhaps this is the meaning of being resurrected into a glorified body, one without physical limitations so that there will no longer be for us a dividing line between the visible and the invisible.

Cynthia: That's beautiful.

Art: This is the spiritual confidence we acquire in meditation and from the Eucharist. While we are still bound to the grosser aspects of our physical senses, our perceptions are not refined enough to comprehend the totality of our own being, let alone the presence of Jesus among us. And, so, he left us himself in the Eucharist, which is available to our senses but, even so, our physical senses can never penetrate the enormity of what is hidden under the appearance of bread and wine. As we continue to receive the Eucharist in an attitude of devotion, we steadily gain the vision of the "Witness" mentioned by Brother Elias. It's like what Maharishi says about purification of the path. The Eucharist gives us a continuous taste of the goal as it clears our path to it. It's very beautiful and, as you said, mysterious.

Cynthia: It's an intriguing point to ponder.

Art: That's why it's a mystery. Bernadette Roberts' insight into the Eucharist resonated with me because I remembered from my studies in the seminary that the Aramaic word for "body," which Jesus used when he instituted the Eucharist, was *"basar."* It's a dynamic word that doesn't refer just to the physical body but comprehends the entirety of who Jesus is. When he took and broke bread, he said, "This is my *basar.*" It means this bread has now become who I am in my completeness.

Cynthia: You said earlier that receiving the Eucharist sometimes gives you a sense of completeness.

Art: Maybe that explains why. The word *basar* sparkles with imagery. In its masculine form, it translates into "flesh"; in its feminine form it means good news. The connection in meaning is significant. The Israelites often sacrificed, and then shared, the flesh of an animal when celebrating special events, instances of good news. As Jesus, the Word made flesh, instituted the Eucharist at the Last Supper, he knew he was to be crucified the following day. The Upper Room must have been dazzling in the love radiating from the heart of Jesus. The self-sacrifice of his *basar* that he was about to offer, both in the Eucharist and on the cross, made it possible for us to celebrate and continually share in the good news of redemption. The Eucharist comprehends all of this, not just the presence of Jesus as man and God, but also the entirety of the Good News. *Basar* implies unification, as when God said in Genesis that the two shall become one *basar.* It means more than a physical union of man and woman. By using the word *basar,* Jesus in effect says that we are to become completely one with him in the Eucharist. He shares his divinity with us. He invites us into all of who he is. We could ponder endlessly the implications of this.

Cynthia: I like the way the word *basar* implies completeness.

Art: Yes, Jesus offers the totality of himself to us in the Eucharist in an act of complete giving. When he says, "Take and eat . . . Take and drink," he is saying in effect: "Here, take me, take all of me, eat and drink of me, I am completely yours." And the following day he gave up his life, completely giving of himself on the cross. It seems to me that Jesus accepts no bounds in his desire to share his divinity with us.

Cynthia: Thank you for explaining all this. I never understood the enormous implications of the Eucharist. I think few do. You're right, we could ponder it endlessly.

Art: Bernadette Roberts' insight is also significant to me from the perspective of Transcendental Consciousness, which is unity, wholeness, completeness. Transcendental Consciousness is not something we individually possess, but something we are. It's not mine but, rather, I am it. We are all one in Transcendental Consciousness, just as in the Eucharist we are all One in Christ. Truth ultimately implies unity which is found both in the Eucharist and in Transcendental Consciousness; and, so, I believe that the Eucharist, which we call Holy Communion, and Transcendental Consciousness, which we might describe as a holy unity, are entwined in the same sacred Truth.

Cynthia: I see what you mean about TM and your Catholicism being mutually complementary.

Art: The goal of each is union with God and, in tandem, they accelerate that process. I sometimes hear people say, "Now that I've begun meditating, I have no further need for my religion." And I say, "No, please stay with your religion, too, and find in it the joy, magnificence, and fulfillment that have thus far eluded you." Maharishi does not offer TM as a religion or as a substitute for religion. He makes it clear that TM is not a religion and tells us to practice our own religion. TM opens our awareness to the deeper mysteries of our religion. It's a means of spiritual growth that is synergistic with whatever religious practices we profess. And for me, the pinnacle of my Catholicism is the Eucharist.

Cynthia: How does the Eucharist relate to the emptiness by which you described Transcendental Consciousness?

Art: Exactly the same way. It's nicely explained by that maxim: Empty thyself and I shall fill thee. We prepare ourselves for the experience of the Eucharist through the subtraction of Meister Eckhart; the *Via Negativa* of

Thomas Aquinas; the letting go of the small self that Maharishi speaks of; the decreasing of self that John the Baptist refers to; and Paul's idea of gaining from dying to the self. The less of us there is when encountering Jesus in the Eucharist, the more we can receive of him.

Cynthia: How do we bring this about?

Art: This is not something we can make happen; it is only something we can let happen. In the Prologue to his Gospel, John tells us that, to as many as receive him, Jesus gives the power to become sons of God, to those who are born " . . . not of the will of man, but of God." We cannot will ourselves into becoming sons of God, we can only allow ourselves to be drawn into divinity, to be born of God. If we are looking for something to happen, pretty soon we'll start prodding it to happen; and what happens then is born of the will of man, not of God. When receiving the Eucharist it's important, just as in meditation, to remain innocent and not fall into moodmaking. We are to be like little children whom Jesus calls unto himself, for of such is the kingdom of heaven. From our side, we remain available for Jesus to come to us by simply allowing everything to be as it is and not creating any obstacles. Moodmaking is a major obstacle.

Cynthia: In the Catholic tradition, how does a person prepare to receive the Eucharist?

Art: Basically by remaining innocent, what we refer to as being in the state of grace, free from serious sin. The Catholic Church prescribes specific guidelines for the reception of the Eucharist. They're not meant to be an encumbrance, but to foster in us the proper disposition because that determines how fully we receive Jesus.

Cynthia: Is it true that only Catholics are invited to receive the Eucharist in Catholic churches?

Art: Generally, yes, with a few carefully defined exceptions. But everyone is invited to become a Catholic and then receive the Eucharist with us.

Cynthia: Why is it restricted just to Catholics?

Art: The Eucharist is the center of our Catholic doctrine, liturgy, and experience; but it has different meaning in various other Christian denominations. Some believe, as do we, that the Eucharist is the real presence of Jesus. But for most others the bread and wine are, and remain, just symbols that are not consecrated into his body and blood. In the Catholic Church, we reserve the Eucharist for those who are One in faith with us, who share the same belief in the Eucharist as the real presence of Jesus. The Catholic Church also prescribes guidelines for the proper disposition to receive, accept, and enjoy communion with Jesus and each other. In this way we assure the best possible experience for everyone who receives the Eucharist while also maintaining the purity of our faith. It's similar to Maharishi putting into place certain requirements and procedures for those who wish to learn to meditate and experience Transcendental Consciousness. He does so to assure the best possible experience in TM while maintaining the purity of his teaching.

Cynthia: Why should a person's disposition influence the experience he or she has in the Eucharist? Maharishi tells us that the disposition of the meditator is irrelevant to the benefits that meditation bestows.

Art: Sacraments are self-efficacious. With respect to the Eucharist, that means Jesus becomes present regardless of the holiness of the person consecrating the bread and wine or of the disposition of the person receiving them. But the grace and joy we experience when receiving the Eucharist depends very much on our disposition. What we personally bring to the Eucharist matters. We see this in other areas of life. For example, why do some people feel enraptured by a Beethoven concerto while others are bored? Why do some get lost in contemplating a Rubens painting while others pass it by? It's because the composer and artist create only part of the aesthetic experience. The perceiver, with his or her unique matrix of sensitivity and receptivity, creates the rest. It's in the joining of the two that beauty emerges. This is what I find so captivating about Brother Elias' writing. And this is the way it is with the Eucharist. Jesus is always present, but are we always ready to receive him?

Cynthia: You're saying that the Eucharistic experience, like the aesthetic experience, is not a one-way flow.

Art: Beauty emerges in the interaction. It's not just a matter of what Jesus brings to it, because he brings everything. The more relevant question to the quality of our Eucharistic experience is: What do we bring to it? How big is our container to receive what Jesus offers us? When we are properly disposed, the union of his giving and our receiving is filled with grace and joy. Jesus said he came that we might have life in abundance, and he said he wants his joy to be our joy so that our joy may be complete. Only we can prevent that from happening. Our disposition is important. The greater our faith and innocence in receiving the Eucharist, the more of himself Jesus communicates to us. I find, as I mentioned earlier, that each time I receive the Eucharist it better disposes me for the next reception.

Cynthia: Was receiving blessings from Jesus while he was on earth also dependent on a person's disposition?

Art: Think of all the cures Jesus performed. Almost every time, he said to the person healed: "Thy faith has saved thee." Isn't Jesus telling us that the person's inner disposition of faith was the power that effected the healing? He could have imposed the cure from outside the person, but wasn't it better to implement it, to set things aright, from within the person by way of his or her own faith? Like those in the Gospels who were touched by Jesus, we bring our faith, our inner disposition, to our encounters with him in the Eucharist. Reality takes place for each of us within the confines of our own awareness. That's where Jesus' miracles occur and where union with him is experienced. The fuller our awareness, the greater our capacity to receive Jesus. That's why a proper inner disposition or receptivity is an indispensable component to the fullest reception of grace in Holy Communion. I still clearly remember a song we used to sing as little children each time we were getting ready to receive Holy Communion:

> O Lord I am not worthy,
> That Thou should'st come to me,
> But speak the words of comfort,
> My spirit healed shall be.
> Repeat:
> But speak the words of comfort,
> My spirit healed shall be.

Cynthia: I can just picture a group of sweet young children singing it as they approach the altar to receive Holy Communion. But the part about being unworthy troubles me. Children aren't unworthy. Where does it come from?

Art: You're right. Children are innocent, and I can see how the sentiment of this song can be misunderstood. Jesus said we must become like little children to enter the kingdom of God. It's the same innocence we need in meditation to transcend and experience the kingdom of God within. The few lines I recited of the song are only its first stanza. It's meant to bring our awareness to the incomprehensible holiness and wholeness of the Eucharist and to express our unqualified reverence in approaching it. That stanza is a loose paraphrasing of an event recounted in the Gospels where a centurion requested Jesus to heal his servant who was sick with palsy. Jesus asked to be taken to the servant, and the centurion replied that he was not worthy for Jesus to enter under his roof but that Jesus only needed to say the word and his servant would be healed. Jesus responded that it would be done according to his faith, and the servant was healed. Jesus then praised the centurion's great faith. That stanza of the song is a tribute to faith. In fact, the entire congregation recites it at every Eucharistic celebration just before receiving Holy Communion. It is meant to align our faith with that of the centurion and, should our spirit lack sufficient innocence, Jesus need only speak the words of comfort and our spirit will be healed. The idea of Jesus speaking words of comfort to heal our spirit reminds me of Peter's comment about Jesus having the words of eternal life. It is a very sweet song.

Cynthia: I remember Maharishi once mentioning Holy Communion. It was during a talk he was giving about the nature of spontaneous union with the Almighty. He said that union is not experienced on the intellectual or emotional level but on the level of the reality of life, of the totality of our awareness. He made a reference to Holy Communion in describing that delicate link between our individuality and the divine reality. The link, he said, becomes complete in the unbounded awareness of Transcendental Consciousness. He said we should live our lives so that, no matter what we do, we strengthen that link.

Art: It's interesting that Maharishi used Holy Communion as a way to express that delicate link between man and God, a link that's neither intellectual nor emotional but encompasses the totality of our awareness. This is a good explanation of why the Eucharist is central to the Catholic Church, why the Catholic Church carefully prescribes the conditions for the proper reception of the Eucharist, and why we have a special celebration when a youngster or an adult convert makes his or her First Holy Communion. We honor the Eucharist because, as the real presence of Jesus, it is a direct link to the divine reality and, through it, our lives grow into complete and continuous union with God. The effects of Holy Communion become more profound as we continue to receive it, just as transcending becomes clearer as we continue to meditate. Purification of awareness occurs in each. I think Maharishi makes the point I've tried to explain about maintaining the proper disposition for receptivity when he says that we should live our lives so that, no matter what we do, we strengthen the link between us and God. That link for us as Christians is Christ, and we enter into that link in Transcendental Consciousness. As Catholics we also enter into that link in the celebration of the Eucharist, and we live our lives in a way that nurtures in us a disposition worthy of its reception so that we continue to strengthen that link.

Cynthia: For Catholics, how does this joining to God work with Christ as the link?

Art: I don't know what the formalities of Catholic theology would say, but I do know what my experience as a Catholic tells me. As Irenaeus indicates, Jesus is the link between God and man—the connection, the point of contact. Jesus tells us that he is the Way, the Truth, and the Life, and that no one comes to the Father except through him. Many Christians argue that this means salvation is open only to Christians, but I think that argument overlooks the fact that we all, by the very act of coming into being, bear the fingerprint of Christ, the Word incarnate through whom all things were made, who has touched each of us in the act of creation; and, therefore, we all have within us the means of living a Christlike life. I cringe whenever anyone tries to fence in Christ, as if he's solely our possession and prerogative. Christianity is not an exclusive country club.

Christ became man for the salvation of all, and I wish we could find better ways to share him than to insist that, to be saved, everyone must adopt our theology and doctrine. In the Prologue to his Gospel, John tells us that in Jesus " . . . was life and the life was the light of man. It was the true light that enlightens *every* man who comes into the world." Jesus tells us in John's Gospel that he has other sheep to tend to who are not of this fold. Before putting "Private Property" signs around Jesus, we should listen more closely to what is being said in the Gospels.

Cynthia: Christians consider Christ the link between man and God.

Art: Yes, and Christians can come to know Christ in Transcendental Consciousness. It's a link to God the Father that's available to all Christians—and to everyone else regardless of religious affiliation. Brother Elias has a nice way of explaining this. We described earlier the experience of Transcendental

Consciousness as one of unknowingness or emptiness that is paradoxically a complete fullness, and we compared it to the "great void" in Genesis, from which God draws forth all that is or ever will be. Here's how Brother Elias ties it all together:

> One comes to realize that the void has a source: and the source is Jesus. . . , the Inner Guest. And He is opening up the way to an even more immense and limitless and bottomless void, which is the Father.

Cynthia: And the Eucharist is a link.

Art: Yes, we also know Jesus in the Eucharist, a physical link that he gave us to his divine presence. After all, we are both spirit and matter. On the physical plane, what more intimate form of communion is there than the Eucharist, which joins flesh and spirit, earth and heaven, and man and God?

Cynthia: You said earlier that the Eucharist gives you a sense of physical well-being.

Art: It nourishes us physically as well as spiritually, and I'm not referring merely to the effects of the nutrients in the bread and wine. The nourishment is more fundamental and comprehensive than that. Each time we receive the Eucharist, something transformational occurs. It's very subtle, but the nourishing effects of the Eucharist gather and accumulate within us. This reminds me of an interesting thought I once had long ago. While Jesus was on earth, he was the Sacrament of God, the visible sign of the invisible reality of God among us. Now that Jesus is no longer on earth, he left us the Sacrament of the Eucharist, the Body of Christ, as the visible sign of the invisible reality of his continuing presence among us. The Mystical Body of Christ, comprised of all Christians, is also a Sacrament in that it, too, is a visible sign of Jesus' invisible reality among us. The Eucharist, then, is the Body of Christ nourishing the Body of Christ, a Sacrament enlivening a Sacrament.

Cynthia: Ah, that is a beautiful thought.

Art: The Eucharist is being celebrated continuously throughout the world. It's impossible to imagine how many trillions of times the Eucharist has been received during the past two millennia or how many trillions upon trillions of times it will be in ages to come.

Cynthia: You've described your understanding of how the Eucharist brings those who receive it to a fuller knowledge of God, of actually partaking in divinity. How do you understand the experience of Transcendental Consciousness as a process of coming to know God?

Art: It's the beginnings of that knowledge. In the unknowingness of Transcendental Consciousness, the knowledge of God is being knitted, so to speak. Maharishi tells us that Transcendental Consciousness eventually becomes an all time reality in Cosmic Consciousness so that it coexists with the three ordinary states of consciousness—waking, dreaming, and deep sleep. Cosmic Consciousness then develops into God Consciousness, and it is in this state that Maharishi speaks of actually knowing God. God Consciousness, in turn, reaches its final fulfillment in Unity Consciousness, which is what I think Aquinas must be referring to when he says we become gods. We partake directly and continuously in divinity.

Cynthia: So Transcendental Consciousness blossoms into a fuller experience or knowledge of the Divine?

Art: I think God gives us tastes of Himself in Transcendental Consciousness, and we begin to experience Him here, there, and everywhere in activity along our spiritual journey home to Him.

In Transcendental Consciousness, He keeps our hunger for Him lively. In this way, we stay on course and begin to grasp how intimately we are connected to Him. We realize that He can be known and loved only in our own awareness, in the silence of our own being, which is our entrance into the Supreme Being. As Christians, we come to know this juncture point as the presence of Jesus within us, and we begin to understand more clearly why Jesus said it is through him that we come to the Father. When we experience Transcendental Consciousness, the teachings of our religion begin to fall into place, sometimes quite suddenly. We comprehend a deeper beauty and majesty of our religion. Our minds are opened to understand Scripture, similar to what Jesus did for his disciples as recorded at the end of Luke's Gospel.

We come to know the joy Jesus spoke of, a joy that becomes complete in higher states of consciousness where we live life in abundance. And we grasp the continuity of life through death. With the experience of Transcendental Consciousness, coupled with the knowledge about it that Maharishi gives us, everything finally makes sense and the tightly knotted mysteries of life begin to unravel.

Our eyes are opened. The world is transfigured. Let him who has eyes see. And we can't help but to smile at everything around us, for it has taken on a new hue of beauty, of richer meaning and value. The world has become as we are: Christlike.

Laws of God and Laws of Man

Cynthia: Religions usually involve rules of behavior to guide us to live in tune with the Divine. How do you understand this in relation to the simple technique of transcending?

Art: Religions typically interpret revelation, promulgate doctrine, and codify standards of conduct as well as the laws needed to support or enforce them. The idea is that, by obeying certain laws and acting good, we thereby become good. Maharishi tells us that acting good to become good confuses the path for the goal. Right action is not the means to attain goodness; rather it's the natural result of already having attained goodness. Jesus said: "Ye must become perfect even as your Father in heaven is perfect." Brother Elias points out that the Hebrew word for becoming perfect connotes maturity or a process of maturation. It's a ripening. The ripened fruit is already contained in the green nub. And that's the secret to perfection. It's already there, waiting to be discovered. It's not something we create in ourselves by practicing being perfect. That's not possible. We become perfect, not by adhering to rules or trying to act perfectly, but by eliminating, stripping away, simply letting go of, all that is imperfect. This happens automatically in Transcendental Consciousness. Maharishi said that TM creates perfection in life. By relinquishing the imperfect, perfection shines through. We become pure of heart. We are blessed. We see God.

Cynthia: So what's the point of all the rules? Why do we have them?

Art: Because we need them while we're still on the path to perfection. To say we don't become perfect simply by acting perfectly doesn't mean we need not obey laws or bother to act in wholesome, life-supporting ways. We should, but it's not the laws or the actions they prescribe or proscribe that bring us to perfection. For that we need the purification offered in Transcendental Consciousness and in receiving the Eucharist. But that's not to say laws are unnecessary. Being derived from the system of beliefs of each religion, they guide its adherents along the path to God. Laws also preserve truth and safeguard the purity of each religion as it is passed from one generation to the next. But laws don't make us good. Maharishi discusses the role of religious laws in *The Science of Being and Art of Living*. He says:

> [Religion is] . . . a direct means of enabling human beings to evolve to the level of the Divine. Religion dictates the do's and don'ts of life in order

to channel the activity of the individual to attain the high purpose of human existence. All these do's and don'ts of religion are meant to provide a direct way to realization of the ultimate reality, or, freedom in God Consciousness . . . The purpose of religion should not only be to indicate what is right and what is wrong, but its direct purpose should be to elevate man to a state of life so that he will only go for that which is right and by nature will not go for that which is wrong.

Cynthia: The point you're making is that we don't become good simply by following rules or outwardly acting good, but rules keep us on the path as we progressively become inwardly good by regularly immersing ourselves in Transcendental Consciousness.

Art: Yes, well said. The fully realized man lives truth. He doesn't need it imposed from the outside when it spontaneously emerges from within. In the meantime, guidance is necessary as we progress along the path, and we should take care not to jettison prematurely the rules, doctrines, and codes of conduct that keep us headed toward God. The safe way is to let God do our housecleaning for us. If from our side we decide it's time to ditch adherence to religious rules, that's a pretty good sign we still need them. It's a delicate, gradual, and often precarious transition we are making from piecemeal seeking after God to being embraced in His bosom in full God-realization.

Cynthia: And you feel that the Church has the inherent authority to make these rules?

Art: The Church has not only the right but also the duty to teach, sanctify, and govern in the name of Jesus. It is responsible for preserving truth, pointing us in the right direction, and keeping us on the path to the goal. All organized religions have the responsibility to guide their adherents to God, but they must be vigilant in the exercise of such prerogatives. At one time or another, almost every religion has seen its teaching devolve into accusing, its sanctifying into condemning, and its governing into persecuting. The integrity of any religion must be conscientiously guarded because it provides fertile ground for unscrupulous charlatans or misguided fanatics to pervert and exploit it to their own self-serving and opportunistic purposes.

Cynthia: What do you feel is the best way for religion to promulgate and promote its guidelines for life-supporting behavior?

Art: Not through fear, as has often been the case. Maharishi is very explicit about this. In *The Science of Being and Art of Living,* he says:

The true spirit of religion is lacking when it counts only what is right and wrong and creates fear of punishment and hell and the fear of God in the mind of man. The purpose of religion should be to take away all fear from man. It should not seek to achieve its purpose through instilling fear of the Almighty in the mind.

This brings us back to the words of the Apostle John that I mentioned earlier:

There is no fear in love, but perfect love casts out fear. For fear has to do with punishment, and whoever fears has not been perfected in love.

Fear, especially fear of punishment, should have no place in religion, and yet it is used to secure adherence to rules.

Cynthia: How else can religion encourage its followers to live in accord with its guidelines?

Art: Perhaps by recognizing that prescriptions for right action are ultimately self-implementing. I think religious institutions must acknowledge, and remain constantly mindful, that beneath all our human frailties and failings is the perfection of the Father silently working its way through to the surface. We need to give credence and respect to that process, facilitate it, and let it have its way. The insistent push from the Church should not overwhelm the gentle pull from God. Religion should seek to enliven orderliness from within rather than imposing it from without. Jesus told the Pharisees that they had the Law of Moses because of the hardness of their hearts. That's a brilliant insight. Isn't it better to melt hearts with love than to perform heavy-handed heart surgery on them? Anything not motivated by love risks decaying into ignorance and abuse. That goes especially for exploiting fear in the name of God.

Cynthia: Why do you suppose Jesus spoke of hardness of the heart?

Art: The Pharisees confronted him—the Bible says tested him—with a tricky legal dilemma about divorce, specifically: "Can a man put away his wife for any cause?" Jesus answered in a way that raises important considerations about law, both that of church and that of state. The issue of divorce had been widely debated among scholars of the day without any consensus, and it had delicate political overtones because Herod Antipas had divorced his wife to marry, illicitly and incestuously, his half-brother's wife who was his niece. John the Baptist's outspoken criticism had cost him his head. Jesus adroitly sidestepped the inherent pitfalls of the dilemma by saying: "Do you not know that the Creator made them male and female to come together and no longer be two, but one flesh? What God has joined, man may not put asunder." Jesus didn't take sides with the Pharisees or the Herodians who were also present but simply stated God's position on the matter as recorded in Scripture. Who could argue with that?

Cynthia: But that wasn't the end of it.

Art: Hardly. The Pharisees now thought they had Jesus trapped and triumphantly pointed out that the Law of Moses permits a man to divorce his wife for various reasons. If Jesus stuck with his original position regarding the impropriety of divorce, not only would he provoke Herod prematurely—he does that later with silence—but, worse yet, he would be accused of advocating a disregard for Mosaic Law. If, however, he retracted his statement, he would lose credibility with his followers. Either way it was a win for the Pharisees.

Cynthia: But it wasn't.

Art: That's where this brilliant insight of Jesus comes in. He said: "You have the Law of Moses because of the hardness of your hearts. It was not that way in the beginning." In other words, because they were no longer responsive to the subtle, silent, spontaneous impulses of natural law—God's Law—reverberating within their very being, they needed large doses of the Law of Moses, with its list of moral mandates as well as compromises and accommodations, to give them direction on how to live their lives. The Old Testament was a Covenant of Law, the New Testament is a Covenant of Love, a return to the "beginning" where external law is not needed because, when we're filled with love, we carry right action in our hearts. As John tells us in the Prologue to his Gospel, "The Law was given through Moses; Grace and Truth came through Jesus Christ." The emphasis is not on codes of conduct imposed from the outside, but on right action spontaneously emanating from within.

Cynthia: Is that what you mean by law reverberating in our being?

Art: Yes. In a book I'm currently writing, I say something to the effect that precise patterns in nature organize and regulate everything in the world. We call them the laws of nature. They are the codification of God's will written in each blade of grass, in each leaf of every tree in every forest, and in the hearts of each man and woman who has ever lived. These imperceptible laws are the blueprints for happiness. For most of us, our hearts have become too hardened to feel the faint impulses of these laws moving within us. Yet, at all levels of creation, from the grandest galaxies to the smallest subatomic particles, they are quietly at work. There's a cause for every effect, an action for every reaction, a reason for every occurrence. No event in life is without its invisible meaning.

Cynthia: That's an elegant, even noble, take on natural law.

Art: And I believe an accurate one. Years ago, while reading very early Christian writings, I came across the expression of natural law in terms of grass and leaves on trees, and it has stuck with me. Similar writings are found in other cultures and traditions. The idea is that, when we align ourselves with the laws of nature, our lives are balanced from within and flow smoothly. When we don't, we lose our bearings, stumble, and need laws from the outside to tell us what to do, and to make sure we do it.

Cynthia: How do we align ourselves with the laws of nature?

Art: It develops spontaneously as we experience Transcendental Consciousness, and the easiest and quickest way to do this is by regularly using the TM technique. Transcendental Consciousness, as Maharishi tells us, is the home of all the laws of nature. Each time we meditate, we bring more of this inherent orderliness out into activity. This gives us a clue to the meaning of Jesus' enigmatic words: "It was not that way in the beginning." I think we often misinterpret what "in the beginning" is referring to. In preparation for a series of speeches I gave some years ago, I traced its use and meaning in both the Old and New Testaments. The first words of Genesis are: "In the beginning God created the heavens and the earth." The first words of John's Gospel are: "In the beginning was the Word . . . without whom was made nothing that has been made." Both Testaments link the phrase "in the beginning" with creation. And Jesus said, speaking of the hardness of our hearts, "It was not that way in the beginning," meaning at the moment of creation.

Cynthia: In other words, the Law of Moses was not needed in the beginning because, at the moment of creation, our hearts had not yet become hardened.

Art: Yes, but what moment is the moment of creation? What does "in the beginning" really refer to? I found what I think is the key to its meaning in the Greek word ἀρχή, pronounced ar-kay, which John used in the Prologue to his Gospel and is transliterated into English as *arche*. In Greek philosophy, *arche* means the root cause or first principle of that which exists. The first word in John's Gospel was later translated into Latin as *"in principio"* and then into English as "in the beginning." But *arche* more accurately means "at the source." This is an important distinction that may have been inadvertently glossed over in translation from Greek into Latin and then from Latin into other languages, including English. By referring back to *arche*, the shift in meaning in each phase of translation becomes obvious. The Latin term *"in principio"* could be translated as "in principle," referring to the first principle of existence, or "at the inception," or "in the beginning." For some reason, and I do not know why, it was translated into English as "in the beginning." Perhaps it's easier for us to think of an inception in chronological terms, as in the beginning of time, rather than in ontological terms, as in the fact of existing.

Cynthia: That's a good point. Can you explain a bit further what the difference is and the significance of this shift in meaning?

Art: It's commonplace to say that nuance or gradations of meaning are lost in translation, but here, I think, the shift is even more fundamental with far-reaching implications and ramifications. I don't presume or pretend to have any skill or experience as a translator, because I don't. Yet the Greek word *arche* suggests so clearly, at least to me, that the term "in the beginning," as Jesus used it and as it appears as the first words of both the Old Testament and John's Gospel, does not refer to an historical point in time but, rather, to a point common to all time—the ever present juncture of time and eternity. *Arche*, which means "at the source," relates to the finest point in relativity, a point without beginning or end, where creation is always taking place and the laws of nature are continuously being structured. In this sense, "in the beginning" as used in Genesis and in the Prologue to John's Gospel, is happening right now. It's happening all the time. The Greeks even attributed divinity to the concept of *arche*. It is, in the ceaseless process of creation, the divine source, the ever-present point of inception, at which God's will is codified as the laws of nature and implanted into all that comes to be. And this is where Justice first makes its appearance and proceeds to order reality.

Cynthia: Meaning?

Art: *Arche* is the point at which creation occurs. Unity manifesting as duality creates parts and a relationship between them, and this requires the infusion of justice to establish order—a harmony and balance—between the duality of parts to keep them from mutually destructing. Justice therefore is, and must be, the first attribute of creation. Justice is the essence of *arche*. From nothingness, God perpetually creates somethingness and continuously infuses justice—His divine will—into the nature of all things. This primordial justice, inherent in the act of creation, manifests as the laws of nature or the will of God. We don't need to impose it from the outside because it's already there on the inside. Like the invisible imprint of a picture on a strip of film, it simply needs to be exposed under the right conditions in a darkroom, and it will appear. And that darkroom is our inner silence.

Cynthia: And we can get there through TM.

Art: Yes. And for Catholics through the Eucharist, too.

Cynthia: Is *arche* similar to what we call pure consciousness?

Art: The Greek philosopher Anaximander introduced another word for that: ἄπειρον, which is transliterated into English as *apeiron*. It refers to the underlying reality from which all physical existence emerges. *Arche* is the point of divine transition where the undifferentiated unity of the *apeiron*, or pure consciousness, is transformed into the discrete multiplicity of phenomenal creation.

Cynthia: So, getting back to what Jesus is saying, in the beginning, or at the divine source as you put it, man-made law isn't necessary because justice, or right action, is inherent in creation?

Art: Exactly. Man is by nature—or at his divine source—responsive to the silent impulses of God's will, the natural law written in his heart. Jesus was pointing out that, at the source of creation where orderliness is the very flow of existence, we don't need the Law of Moses because lawfulness springs naturally from our unhardened hearts.

Cynthia: But isn't some man-made law, like the Law of Moses, inspired by God and not really man-made?

Art: Yes, and I need to be very careful about how I distinguish natural law from man-made law, which is commonly referred to as positive law. All of Mosaic Law is inspired by God through Moses. Consider the Ten Commandments written on tablets of stone to emphasize God's authorship. Perhaps a better way to make the distinction is to speak of the laws that spring from within our very being, as opposed to those that are imposed on us from without. Natural law springs from within; positive law, whether inspired by

God or the mere edict of man, is imposed from without. Mosaic Law, although inspired by God, is imposed from the outside inward, whereas natural law, the codification of God's will in our hearts at the moment of creation, resonates from the inside outward, if the hardening of our hearts has not blocked it.

Cynthia: What are the practical implications of all this?

Art: The understanding that orderliness, like perfection, is already there has revolutionary implications for criminal justice and rehabilitation because at the base of even the worst misconduct is perfect orderliness. What has been missing is a way to tap into that orderliness, to clear away whatever obscures or obstructs it. Our criminal justice system typically tries to impose orderliness from the outside inward through man-made law. We seek to achieve lawfulness through police force. We call it law enforcement. The common denominator is force. We use, as we deem necessary, violence to fight violence, with the net result being more violence, leading eventually, and often quickly, to a proliferation of violence. We can't eradicate violence with violence or even neutralize it with non-violence. That's the frustration of pacifism. Violence can be disarmed only with silence. Maharishi has shown us that the means are more efficient, and the results more permanent, if orderliness is released from within rather than imposed from without, and he gave us the science of silence with which to do it.

Cynthia: In Transcendental Consciousness in the practice of TM.

Art: Yes. The secret to orderliness is that it's already there. Through the steady refinement and purification we experience in Transcendental Consciousness, we eventually reach a point where all our thoughts, words, and actions are spontaneously in accord with the laws of nature, with the will of God, and we become unhardened of heart. Blessed are the pure of heart, for they shall see God.

Cynthia: This is what Maharishi calls spontaneous right action.

Art: St. Paul says in Romans that it is becoming a law unto ourselves. Different words for the same reality. We are ruled from within. As we experience the orderliness of Transcendental Consciousness, we begin acting in accord with divine law. As Maharishi says, our actions are spontaneously in accord with all the laws of nature. We do what's right not because we are told to or out of fear of punishment, but because what's right flows naturally from within. We gain a clearer understanding of what Jesus meant when he said the Sabbath was made for man, not man for the Sabbath. We don't have to keep trying to be good when everything we do is spontaneously synchronized with the will of God. All our thoughts, words, and actions are right for the moment and in harmony with our surroundings. They are naturally life-supporting and mesh seamlessly with the needs of our environment. Paul also tells us in Romans that, "All things work together for the good of those who love God, those whom he has called according to his plan." This finds fulfillment in spontaneous right action. Whatever a person does is harmonized with all of nature—and he thereby receives nature's full support—so that all things work together for his good.

Cynthia: And transcending gets us there?

Art: It refines all aspects of our being. Our hearts become unhardened and, pure of heart, we see God by experiencing His presence within.

Cynthia: I remember Old Testament references to the law being written in our hearts. In Jeremiah 31:31, he prophesied that God would make a New Covenant with the people of Israel and place His law within them and write it upon their hearts. It's one of my favorite passages.

Art: Yes, and Ezekiel, anticipating the New Covenant, said that God would give us new hearts, taking from our bodies our stony hearts, placing in us natural hearts—meaning unhardened, as they were "at the source"—and putting His spirit within us that we may live by His laws. These prophesies refer to Jesus transforming the Covenant of Law into a Covenant of Love. I find Psalm 95 particularly apropos. It begins by beckoning us to make a joyful noise in gratitude to God. It then goes on to implore us: "If today you hear his voice, harden not your heart." We are to be responsive to the gentle impulses of the law of God, "our maker," who implanted His will in our hearts at the moment of creation. It's a very beautiful Psalm. The law of God is written in our hearts. Everything we need to live successfully is already there. We need simply enter into Transcendental Consciousness and hear His voice.

Cynthia: So, with unhardened hearts we won't need man-made laws?

Art: We do for matters of convenience or convention. Being in tune with all the laws of nature doesn't necessarily tell us what side of the street to drive on. The distinction between the laws of God and the laws of man, which Jesus drew in his response to the Pharisees, highlights society's ultimate frustration in the enactment and enforcement of its laws. It's a misguided notion that we can regulate human behavior by man-made laws, that we can somehow "make" people be good. We can't. Laws do not create justice; rather, justice, which is infused in all creation at its "source," naturally expresses itself as lawfulness. Even if laws could somehow assure right action, the law-making enterprise would nonetheless prove to be futile. The problem is that no Moses—neither the law-givers then nor now—can anticipate, evaluate, and legislate every possible ramification of every possible alternative to every possible situation that may eventually be processed through the awareness of each individual who might come under the rule of law.

Cynthia: So, lots of things go unlegislated.

Art: That's right. If a person's sense of justice depends solely on adherence to the law's letter, there's still lots of room for him to perpetrate injustices with impunity. Besides, each human mind is ultimately as intricate as the universe itself—and who could presume to regulate the universe? Or to make it be good? Such an approach to justice can only engender a proliferation of man-made laws, which leads to an enormous enforcement nightmare.

Cynthia: I suppose there are already too many laws to enforce.

Art: All you need to do is visit a major law library. You'll see floor after floor, aisle upon aisle, row after row, shelf upon shelf, book after book, page after page, line upon line of laws telling us, word for word, how to live our lives. If the proliferation of man-made law represents in any proportionate way our lack of knowledge of God's will, then our law libraries are glaring monuments to our ignorance.

Cynthia: Is this all just theory or does this distinction between God's law and man's law have any social significance? I don't mean the difference between church law and governmental law. I'm talking about the subtler distinction that you're describing.

Art: Much of church law, at least to whatever extent it may be man-made falls into the same category as governmental law. But the more subtle distinction between natural law and man-made law has been recognized and appreciated in many civilizations. I once traced the etymology of this distinction through diverse cultures in various time periods and found a surprising consistency in the manner in which societies, despite geographic or historic differences, have conceptualized and contrasted them. People from diverse social systems have understood from the dawn of civilization that there is an inherent, fluid natural law that governs all phenomenal existence and an extrinsic, rigid man-made law that gives direction to daily affairs.

Cynthia: How is this distinction described? Does it have substance, or is it just theoretical?

Art: Languages in the cultures I looked at, both modern and ancient, use very different words with disparate meanings to designate and distinguish the law that flows from within and the law that is imposed from without. My favorite is from the ancient Greeks who had a rich, enlightened understanding of reality. Our Western philosophical and scientific knowledge had its origin in ancient Greece, and there is scholarly speculation that some of the pre-Socratic philosophers studied in India. Much of their dictum reflects Vedic knowledge. I think this is especially true of Anaximander whose insights, which survive only in fragments, are remarkably parallel to Maharishi's teachings. But it was Solon, the ancient Greek lawgiver, who first distinguished *nomos* ($\nu\acute{o}\mu o\sigma$) from *kosmos* ($\kappa\acute{o}\sigma\mu o\sigma$), the former being the laws made by man and the latter those that pre-exist within the universe. Many years ago I gave a lecture entitled "The Cosmological Concept of Justice" in which I explored these issues from the perspective of both Pre-Socratic philosophy and Vedic knowledge.

Cynthia: These are fascinating insights from one of the world's richest traditions of knowledge.

Art: Heraclitus, a subsequent Pre-Socratic, refined this cosmological concept of justice by introducing into it the *Logos* ($\Lambda\acute{o}\gamma o\sigma$)—the "Principle of Reason" that pervades, interconnects, orders, nourishes, and gives meaning to all existence. The *Logos* was later personified in the first century writings of Philo of Alexandria. The Apostle John, in the Prologue to his Gospel, took the final step and personalized the *Logos* as Christ: "In the beginning [at the divine source] was the *Logos* . . . through whom all things were made and without whom was made nothing that has been made." We translate *Logos* as Word, but it is a Word with infinite meaning.

Cynthia: So Catholic theology also draws upon ancient Greece?

Art: Very much so, even the way we first began to conceptualize Christ as *Logos*, the link between God and man. The missing element of meaning was not merely that the *Logos* was a personal being rather than just the personification of a philosophical abstraction, but that the *Logos* actually became man, that justice would again be embodied and enlivened among and within us, emanating from our hearts as prophesied by Jeremiah and Ezekiel. The Incarnation brought to a compelling fulfillment the Greek notion of *Logos*, which now seems entirely incomplete without Christ. Bede Griffiths, the late Benedictine monk who lived in India as a *sanyasi*, observed that, in Christ, the *Logos* is not merely known, but loved. It is through this *Logos* that justice permeates all existence.

Cynthia: Does any of this ancient theory about justice have application to contemporary society?

Art: Like that of the ancient Greeks, the present day Dutch language has two terms for justice. A lawyer in Holland explained to me that the harsher sounding *gerechtigheit* refers to a stiff, legal sort of justice imposed by a judge or legislative body, whereas the softer sounding *rechtvaardig* translates as the justice or righteousness spontaneously generated from within. Our own English word for law has two etymological derivations: *lex, legis* and *jus, juris*, both taken from the Latin of ancient Rome. The former, from which we get words like lexicon, legislator and legalistic, implies man-made law; and the latter gives us our term "justice" and all related concepts such as jurisprudence and jurisdiction. I was able to trace the Latin word *jus* to an even greater antiquity in the Sanskrit word *yos*, symbolizing wellbeing and the fullness of health and happiness, which, of course, are qualities cultured in Transcendental Consciousness.

Cynthia: Do we find anything about this distinction between natural and man-made law in our own Scriptures?

Art: Yes, I believe the distinction between the two Hebrew words *mishpat* and *tsedhaqah*, as found in the Old Testament, is perhaps the clearest example of this. As I understand it, the former, derived from the verb "to judge," has legalistic and academic connotations. The latter, by contrast, is relational and experiential. It expresses the free-flowing righteousness that spontaneously is lived commensurate with the degree of balance and harmony a person comes to realize in his or her relationships with others.

Cynthia: How does the distinction between the laws of God and the laws of man inform our faith?

Art: I think it's crucial and precursory. From a Christian perspective looking back at the Old Testament in anticipation of the New, the distinction contains and explains the difference between the Covenant of Law and the Covenant of Love, between positive law that—regardless of whether it originates with God or with man—is nonetheless promulgated by man and therefore imposed from the outside inward, and natural law that emanates spontaneously from within the very nature of all creation, including and especially from within man. It's the difference between a hardened and unhardened heart that Jesus and the Prophets spoke of.

Cynthia: But how does that impact our lives?

Art: Perhaps that can best be answered by reflecting on the ultimate futility of man-made law, as we've just discussed. This points not only to the primacy of natural law, but also suggests that living in complete and spontaneous accord with all the laws of nature is the intended destiny of each of us. Aquinas, whom we spoke about earlier, directed considerable thought to the respective roles of, and the distinctions between, natural and divine law on the one hand, and man-made law on the other. It's not just theoretical. As we continue to experience Transcendental Consciousness, we begin to feel for ourselves a natural lawfulness emerging from within our very being that gradually replaces the need for external law from outside ourselves to tell us how to live. I see this as evidence of, and a growing familiarity with, the kingdom of God within that Jesus desires for all of us.

Love, Ecumenism, and Transcendental Consciousness

Cynthia: How did TM impact the actual practice of your faith?

Art: During my mid-to-late twenties, I had become a "fallen-away" Catholic. I stopped going to church, stopped praying, stopped thinking about, at times perhaps even believing in, a spiritual reality. And yet my Catholicism, and my years as a seminarian, kept nagging at me. The Hound of Heaven never lost the scent of my soul. I tried to stay focused on my work, on the empirical and ethical realities of life, and I allowed my Christianity to become increasingly irrelevant to me, or so I thought. All along the chase was quickening, the Hound was nearing. At age thirty I began TM, and the inner world of Transcendental Consciousness was opened to me like a rose just blooming. Everything about it was beautiful. Unlike my experiences in the seminary, transcending no longer was a matter of serendipitous happening but something that could be easily integrated into my daily routine. Sit down, begin the TM technique, and experience Transcendental Consciousness, or at least very deep rest and refinement of the thought process. It was that simple. I couldn't wait to get up in the morning to meditate, and I'd rush home in the evening to meditate. The Hound was closing in.

Cynthia: It is interesting that TM was the catalyst to bring you back to your religious roots. What were you doing at that point in your life?

Art: I was the Director of the Criminal Justice Division of the Attorney General's Office of Arkansas. I had been recruited from Harvard to serve in that capacity. I was also, among other responsibilities, serving as Chief Counsel to the Arkansas Department of Correction. We were facing a crisis in our prisons. The Arkansas penal system had been the first in the country to be declared unconstitutional as constituting "cruel and unusual punishment"; and now, after having regained constitutional status, it was the first to be re-declared unconstitutional. After I started TM and experienced its effects in my own life, it quickly occurred to me that introducing TM into our prisons would prop up our failing rehabilitation programs. I tried to learn all I could about TM and its application to social systems. A year after beginning to meditate, I arranged official leave from my duties, and was off to Europe to become a teacher of TM. Talk about a life-changing event!

Cynthia: What prompted you to start meditating?

Art: It wasn't any grand spiritual quest. My reason was quite mundane. I had for some years been suffering from severe high blood pressure. I had been under a lot of stress, and my eating, smoking, and sleep habits were not healthy. I had a family and personal history of hypertension, and mine was so serious that I was under the care of a nephrologist. I had gone through all kinds of tests and various medications without lasting results. Even while at Harvard I had been a patient for experimental treatment of hypertension at what was then Peter Bent Brigham Hospital in Boston, and I was told that the prognosis was not very good. The doctors couldn't determine the cause. It was severe, volatile, and uncontrollable. One of my doctors told me I wouldn't live past thirty-five. He predicted I would have a fatal heart attack within five years. I began searching for a way to take personal charge of my health, to heal myself from within. I came across TM and took the course. Within a month, my blood pressure began normalizing. Six months later, not only was I off medication, but I also quite painlessly had stopped smoking and lost my inclination for an occasional drink after work—mostly because I couldn't wait to get home to meditate. Nothing else in my life had changed. The same external pressures were there, but I no longer felt them internally as I had before.

Cynthia: What did your nephrologist think?

Art: He made the quip, "I'm taking you off your medication, but want you to continue your meditation." A couple of weeks later, a teacher at the Little Rock TM center called me and asked if I knew this doctor. The teacher said she heard knocking at the back door one evening after dark. It was this doctor. He said he had a patient who experienced almost miraculous results after learning TM. The teacher said the doctor couldn't tell her who it was because of doctor-patient confidentiality, but she figured it must have been me. The doctor wanted to find out more about TM, but didn't want anyone to see him at the TM Center so they wouldn't think he was getting weird. After receiving private introductory and preparatory lectures, he secretly took the course and experienced for himself the health benefits of TM.

Cynthia: That's funny. Back then, people were concerned about a stigma being associated with meditation. Now it's readily accepted in mainstream culture.

Art: As I mentioned, the Catholic Church specifically recognized Transcendental Meditation in one of its official documents as a means of helping people come before God with an interior peace in the midst of external pressures. Although the Church approves the TM technique, it cautions against mixing in eastern beliefs that are inconsistent with Catholicism, which makes sense because that would only lead to confusion. Fortunately, the TM technique does not involve a belief system. Maharishi encourages us to practice our own religion, and just add TM to it.

Cynthia: And, as you have explained throughout this interview, TM has actually nurtured your Catholic faith.

Art: I found that it enriched my relationship with Jesus and enhanced my love for others, and that's the point of Christianity, isn't it?

Cynthia: You have repeatedly mentioned love in relation to both Catholicism and TM. Jesus spoke of the two great commandments, to love God with all our heart, mind, soul, and might, and to love our neighbor as ourself. Do you see TM fostering growth in this regard?

Art: We desire to be united with what we love. God is our greatest love and, when we find Him, we naturally love Him with everything that we are—heart, mind, and soul—and desire union with Him with all our might or, as Maharishi puts it, the way a drowning man desires breath. We experience the presence of God in Transcendental Consciousness and, since God is love as John says, we thereby also experience the fullness of love.

Cynthia: What about the second great commandment, to love our neighbor as ourself?

Art: Jesus also said that we will be known as his disciples if we love one another. Whether we encounter Jesus in the Gospel, in the Eucharist, or, just as importantly, in one another, we do so with a glimpse of a transfigured reality. Because we are One in Transcendental Consciousness, distinctions between neighbor and self fade away as we transcend, and the second great commandment is automatically fulfilled as well. We love our neighbor as ourselves. It can be no other way. Both commandments are self-apparent and self-fulfilled in Transcendental Consciousness.

Cynthia: What are the practical effects of this?

Art: Let's say, for example, there's a person we didn't much like before but, after immersing ourselves in TM, we become aware—our eyes are opened to the fact—that we, he, and Jesus are all part of the same transcendent whole. We then understand what Jesus meant when he said that what we do unto others, even the least among us, we do unto him. We do it unto ourselves, as well. By grasping our common oneness with Jesus, we see Christlikeness in all others. The change is not in them, but in us. As we become more Christlike so does our perception of those around us. It's what Maharishi says about the world being as we are. The person we didn't like has now become more beautiful, more lovable to us or, to be more accurate, we have become more loving and have endowed him with the Christlike beauty of Transcendental Consciousness, and he, too, is transfigured before our eyes.

Cynthia: Beauty is in the eye of the beholder.

Art: We see a beautiful world only through eyes adept at beauty, and love others without discrimination through loving eyes. When we transcend, we understand how it's possible to love not only our neighbor as ourself, but also our enemy because in Transcendental Consciousness the barrier between self and other is broken down, and we experience only oneness. We love others as ourself. That's just the way it is. I don't see how we can comprehend, let alone fulfill, Jesus' command to love one another without the experience of Transcendental Consciousness. In that unique state of consciousness the whole world becomes a transfiguration of Christ where there is no other option but love.

Cynthia: Can you further elaborate how loving our enemies is borne out in practical experience?

Art: After regular immersion in Transcendental Consciousness through the practice of TM, we begin to sense a slight shift in perception of those who hurt us, and it grows eventually into a completely different perspective on love and forgiveness. Then, when the thought of someone who has hurt us comes to mind, we don't feel bitterness, or anger, or the inclination for revenge. We feel instead the ripples of love that were there all along. Negativity no longer displaces the inner love that we feel toward all. It's very beautiful. We don't have to try to love or to forgive. They are there spontaneously without trying. It's as if no other option is available. It's not possible to hold a grudge or to hate. Those feelings have no traction in Transcendental Consciousness. There is never any thought to retaliate or to hurt in return. Thoughts like that make no sense. They don't compute, don't even enter the equation. It's easy to love our enemies because we don't see anyone as an enemy. This is not something we can decide on the level of the mind to do and then make ourselves do it. Rather it flows naturally from a healthy soul. As negativity falls away through the practice of TM, the love and joy that has always been there begin to shine through and fill our awareness and penetrate our surroundings so that, as Maharishi says—

Cynthia: The world becomes as we are.

Art: Yes. A person might think this is an abstract kind of idealism that only sets us up to be hurt again, but the process also develops within us an innate capacity to avoid situations in which we will be hurt. This intuitive ability complements the growing love we feel. They work together. The less threatened we feel by circumstances, the more we can love; and the more we love, the less we find ourselves in hazardous situations. As Maharishi says, we avert the danger that has not yet arisen. It's all a matter of growth in consciousness.

Cynthia: Maharishi said we come to know love more intimately and fully through practicing TM.

Art: In *The Science of Being and Art of Living*, he says, "Meditation makes absolute love a real, significant, personal experience . . . " This, I think, shows the value and validity of TM as a means for spiritual progress for Christians and for adherents of any religion. Love can never be wrong. TM brings us to the kingdom of God where the experience of unconditional love is possible and where Jesus' command to love one another finds fulfillment.

Cynthia: Love is at the center of Christ's message.

Art: Yes, and for that reason I've often marveled that more people don't embrace Jesus and his teachings. They're good for everyone to ponder, Christian and non-Christian alike. He shows us a better way to live, and he doesn't exclude anyone. Like Transcendental Consciousness, he welcomes all.

Cynthia: Even atheists?

Art: Especially atheists. I sometimes wonder whether atheists are denying God or simply denying our definition of God. Maybe atheism is the logical extension of *Via Negativa*—the extinction of all idols, including our feeble concepts by which we try to create a graven mental image of God to worship. If so, atheism may be the *reductio ad absurdum* of our attempts to know God conceptually. In the process, however, atheism repudiates not only doctrine and ritual, which keep us on course to God but, more regrettably, it also intellectually severs the link between God and us, a link that is necessary for us to outgrow our logic and come to know experientially the God Who transcends all concepts, Who transcends even His own transcendence. We need God to worship and religious norms to guide us in doing so, and we also need a link to know God directly. This is the beauty of Christianity in which we come to know Christ as the link and also as God. It is the beauty of the Eucharist in which we commune with Christ, the God-man link. And it is the beauty of TM in which we experience the presence of God within us in Transcendental Consciousness. The experience of Transcendental Consciousness also brings us to a truer understanding of who we are, which necessarily implies relationship with God. More than relationship, union with God. There are no atheists in Transcendental Consciousness. No Christians, for that matter. No Jews or Muslims. No Hindus, Taoists, or Buddhists. Those kinds of distinctions don't exist. In Transcendental Consciousness, we are all pointing in the same direction. We are all One. Transcendental Consciousness is true ecumenism.

Cynthia: Can you explain further what you just said?

Art: At the level of Transcendental Consciousness, we are all the same. "In this new life," as Paul says in Galatians and again in Colossians, we are neither Gentile nor Jew, slave nor free, young nor old, man nor woman, and I would add neither friend nor enemy, but one in Christ who is all and in all. What Paul refers to as "this new life" is, I think, Transcendental Consciousness. It favors no social position, no gender, no age, no race, color, or nationality. And it has no religion, no doctrine, dogma, or creed. It simply is. It is is-ness. It is one. In it, we are neither Gentile nor Jew, Catholic nor Protestant, Hindu nor Taoist, Buddhist nor Muslim, but, from a Christian perspective, one in Christ who is all and in all.

Cynthia: People often think this passage refers to heaven, that God doesn't discriminate in heaven based on our earthly rank, nationality, color, or sex.

Art: Without the experience of Transcendental Consciousness, we might not grasp the deeper meaning of our Scriptures. Maharishi tells us in his commentary on Chapter Two, verse 45 of the Bhagavad-Gita that, by bringing our minds to Transcendental Consciousness, we arrive at a state of fulfillment " . . . where all differences dissolve." Shankara alludes to this in his *Crest Jewel of Discrimination* when he speaks of ceasing to identify ourselves with race, clan, name, form, or walk of life. And this, at least to me, is what Paul means when he speaks of "this new life." If differences dissolve away in Transcendental Consciousness, then gaining a familiarity with Transcendental Consciousness would seem to be the best way to discover and explore ecumenism.

Cynthia: How do you see TM as a way to join together the peoples of the world

Art: We already are together and just don't comprehend the unity to which we each, in the richness of our cultural, racial, and religious differences, contribute. Failing to see differences as complementary, we use them as reasons for animosity. Religion denouncing religion is as foolish as nation fighting nation. In his book *Magnificent Desolation*, the astronaut Buzz Aldrin, who participated in the Apollo 11 moon landing, tells us that, when viewed from outer space, " . . . the earth has no observable borders, no observable reasons for war." That goes for any kind of prejudice or persecution. Many astronauts and cosmonauts have described their time in space as transformational. They talk about the wholeness they experienced when viewing the earth from space and how it occasioned a great expansion in awareness.

Cynthia: I see you have a few other quotes from space.

Art: Yes, they're fascinating. Astronaut Rusty Schweikert said:

You look down there and you can't imagine how many borders and boundaries you crossed. At the Mideast you know there are hundreds of people killing each other over some imaginary line that you can't see. From where you see it, the thing is a whole, and it's so beautiful.

Cosmonaut Aleksandr Aleksandrov, of the former USSR, upon seeing from outer space snow formations over the United States, said:

I have never visited America, but I imagined the arrival of autumn and winter is the same there as in other places, and the process of getting ready for them is the same. Then it struck me that we are all children of our Earth. It does not matter what country you look at. We are all Earth's children and should treat her as our Mother.

Astronaut Frank Borman, viewing the earth from the moon, said:

It was hard to think that that little thing held so many problems, so many frustrations. Raging nationalistic interests, famines, wars, pestilence don't show from that distance.

Astronaut Edgar Mitchell said that, as he was returning from the moon, he

. . . suddenly experienced the universe as intelligent, loving, harmonious. It occurred when looking at Earth and seeing this blue-and-white planet floating there . . . seeing that there was a purposefulness of flow, of energy, of time, of space in the cosmos, that it was beyond man's rational ability to understand, that suddenly there was a non-rational way of understanding that had been beyond my previous experience.

Cynthia: The last one sounds a little like the "unknowing" experiences you described of Christian mystics. Astronauts seem to gain a whole new perspective, or perhaps glimpse higher states of consciousness, from their exploration of outer space.

Art: So do we from exploring inner space. Our view is also one of wholeness, harmony, and an inherent intelligence. And, to better answer your earlier question, it is through making available this unity of Transcendental Consciousness that TM helps join together peoples of the world. Just as Buzz

Aldrin says in *Magnificent Desolation* that outer space is our last great frontier, we who practice TM find that inner space is; and Maharishi, in his TM-Sidhi program, has given us all the tools we need to explore it. That's where we'll find fundamental solutions to our problems, and that's why I said it's the best place from which to approach ecumenism. Differences dissolve away in Transcendental Consciousness. Jesus said he desires for there to be one fold and one shepherd. It seems to me that's what happens in Transcendental Consciousness.

Cynthia: You've explained the position of the Catholic Church toward other world religions and other Christian denominations. What's your personal view on ecumenism?

Art: I hope it's the same as my church's. I just put it in slightly different, less theological terms.

Cynthia: Such as?

Art: A number of years ago, I had to formulate my position quite quickly and unexpectedly. A pastor with whom I was working was one of the featured speakers at a Sunday afternoon Christian ecumenical conference. I was assisting him that morning at Mass when he suddenly became ill. I had to perform an alternate Holy Communion service in lieu of the Mass scheduled later that morning, and then, shortly before noon, he said he was too sick to attend the conference and asked me to give his speech in his place. I agreed, and he offered me his notes. We were very different people in the way we expressed ourselves, and I soon realized that his notes wouldn't work for me. I felt the sudden excitement of having less than an hour to come up with something meaningful to say. But it worked out. I quickly put together a short, but to the point, outline. I knew that all the ministers in attendance were male and married, so I began my talk with something obvious, something each of them could identify with. I explained that, just as an honorable man loves and is committed to his wife, so also he loves and is committed to his church. Just as he wouldn't disparage another man's wife to boast of his own, neither would he deprecate another's religion to promote his own. Such a man is secure about his marriage and his religion. Because he respects his wife, he respects the wives of others. So, too, his religion.

Cynthia: That's a pretty straightforward analogy.

Art: And disarming. I continued by again invoking the obvious, that Christ became man to teach us how to live, not to impose more rules and regulations on us. To the contrary, he shunned some of the mindless ordinances of his day and instead reduced all law to one word: Love. And he certainly didn't give us more doctrine and dogma to memorize, embrace, and enforce—or to use as a wedge to separate one Christian denomination from another. Instead, he taught us a better way to live, and he established a Church to preserve his teachings so that, throughout the ages, we might all learn to live harmoniously and virtuously and receive the salvation he offers. I pointed out to the ministers at the conference that the *raison d'être* of all Christian denominations is to become like Christ and, to that end, their rules, regulations, doctrine, and dogma should be true to the life of Christ and help their adherents imitate that life. It follows that differences in doctrine or dogma are not unredeemable causes for separation and must never be fashioned into justifications for sanctimony, bigotry, or hostility.

Cynthia: I take it everyone at the conference could relate to that?

Art: They seemed to, and then I used another analogy, which I hoped would hammer my point home. I talked about high school geometry. Again, something obvious. There's a basic axiom in geometry that holds that, when A and B are congruent with C, they are also congruent with each other. Let's say that the A's are composed of the Assembly of God, the Church of Christ, the Church of the Nazarene, the Baptist Church, and others; that the B's are made up of Methodists, Presbyterians, Lutherans, Episcopalians, Catholics, and others; and that C is, of course, Christ. In geometry, when A and B each become more like C, they simultaneously become more like each other; so, too, do we become more like one another as we become more like Christ. And, when we each become one in Christ, we are one with each other. Where, then, is any reason to bicker? In the light of our Christlikeness, doctrinal disparities and distinctions fade away. When we're Christlike, we're all one in the Lord. No one can tell us apart; no one wants to. If we are completely Christlike, of what significance are dogmatic differences to us? Zero. They matter only to the extent we are not Christlike. Interdenominational bickering and lack of unity misrepresent Christ to the world, and by engaging in them we do a disservice to him and to those whom he came to serve.

Cynthia: Did it bring the point home?

Art: I think so. It was a very short speech, but it got a long applause. I think I clearly made the point that, in our sectarian rivalry, it's easy to lose sight of the fact that to be like Christ, filled with love, is the ultimate point of Christianity regardless of the particular religious form it takes. Even non-Christian denominations seek to become Christlike, it's just not stated in those terms. John tells us that Christ, the Word from whom all creation issues forth, enlightens every person—not just Christians, but *every* person—who comes into the world. As I said earlier, Christianity is not an exclusive country club. Jesus tells us in John's Gospel:

> I have other sheep, which are not of this fold; I must bring them also, and they will hear my voice; and they will become one flock with one shepherd.

We all share in the same fundamental Christlikeness at the very core of our being, and we come to know it in the oneness of Transcendental Consciousness, the quintessential ecumenism. Christ is the same light, the same hunger for something more that burns in each of us. Even atheists, whether they recognize it or not, seek Christ-realization within themselves. It's an instinctive drive divinely implanted in us at creation—"at the source," as we discussed earlier. We all bear the stamp of Christlikeness from the moment of conception. Non-Christians have a different term for it. But it's that same reality that sparkles deep inside everyone. By just peeling away the layers that aren't like Christ, we come to the core Christlikeness within each of us. It is, as Paul puts it, "that new life," and, as John puts it, the life that is "the light of man." When we have attained that new life and discovered within us that bright inner light, we can let it shine through us among men. The complete formula for becoming Christlike, in fact the entire Gospel, can be compressed into that one, little, mysterious word: Love.

Cynthia: It is the central theme of Jesus' teachings.

Art: Yes, love and truth. Jesus told Pilate that he came to bear witness to the truth.

Cynthia: Both blossom with the experience of Transcendental Consciousness.

Art: I think they're ultimately the same experience. If Love is complete in Transcendental Consciousness and if Transcendental Consciousness is the fullness of Truth, then Love and Truth are equivalent. They are synonymous. All the reasons we think we have not to love others are not true. Hatred and war are always perversions of Truth. Only those reasons that lead to love are true and worth living for. Or dying for, and certainly dying daily to the self in Transcendental Consciousness.

Cynthia: The basis of love is found in Transcendental Consciousness.

Art: There we can truly love others as our-Self because, as Paul tells us, there are no distinctions between us in "this new life." Or, as Maharishi said, all differences dissolve away in Transcendental Consciousness. What's left but love? The first are last and the last are first because all are one. Extraneous differences of gender, age, race, appearance, and social status fall away as we die to the self and begin to experience eternal life, the taste of heaven on earth, the fullness of love and life. We then come to understand that eternal life isn't something that begins when we die physically but that it's happening right now, and we experience it in Transcendental Consciousness.

Cynthia: Maharishi says that love for an individual is concentrated absolute love.

Art: The more we practice TM, the more we realize that true love has nothing to do with how a person looks or acts because the outer characteristics that congeal into a distinct individual dissolve away in Transcendental Consciousness. We think they are the reasons we love, but they're not. We love because of the presence of God in our beloved, a presence that we share, that we have in common, and that we therefore recognize in others. In moments of true love, there is a transfiguration. Our eyes are opened. We see our beloved more truly. The presence of God in us sees the presence of God in him or her.

Cynthia: That's a beautiful way to put it.

Art: It is the presence of God within us seeking the fullness of itself, as does a lover knocking at the door of his beloved. It is the presence of God who knocks on one side and who opens from the other. And the doors are countless. We find the presence of God peeking out of every creature. It's in the twinkling of a star, the song of a prairie warbler, the scent of a rose, and the solitude of a single atom. It is when the presence of God in us sees itself in all others that Truth is fully realized and our Love is finally complete.

Cynthia: Thank you for a delightful interview.

Art: Thank you, too. I've enjoyed it very much.

Chapter X

Theology and Enlightenment

Evan Finkelstein, Ph.D.

Evan Finkelstein, Ph.D. is an Associate Professor of Maharishi Vedic Science (MVS), and teaches courses in Core Principles of Maharishi Vedic Science, as well as how these principles are expressed in the world's major religions. He received his Ph.D. in Maharishi Vedic Science from Maharishi University of Management and was honored with the Veda Vyasa Award for Outstanding Doctoral Scholarship. His dissertation focus was on universal principles expressed in Maharishi Vedic Science and in the scriptures and writings of Judaism, Christianity, and Islam. Dr. Finkelstein obtained his Master of Social Work (MSW) from the Wurzweiler School of Social Work at Yeshiva University, and participated in scriptural studies at the James Striar School, Yeshiva University. He received his B.A. in English Literature and minored in Theater Arts at Carnegie-Mellon University in Pittsburgh.

Dr. Finkelstein was encouraged by Maharishi to research the interpretation of the scriptures of world religions to facilitate the understanding of the underlying universal principles expressed in every religion. Additionally, Dr. Finkelstein discusses the importance of the direct experience of pure consciousness through the process of transcending, which is the basis for fulfilling the spiritual goals of every religion.

I was born in the Bronx, New York, and my family was hardworking lower-middle-class Americans. My motivation for seeking human development was a desire to transcend fear, anger, and a strong dissatisfaction with my life. I grew up in a tough housing project in the Bronx; it was an interesting experience just trying to get from day to day or back and forth from school without all types of physical "interventions." One of my goals in life was in developing a sense of safety and security, which was absent in my experiences growing up in the projects. When I was in the projects as a teenager, I used to work out with my weights regularly because in my neighborhood you needed to be strong to survive. One day I was in the middle of a workout in my room, and my father knocked on my door; he asked me to come out because there was an interesting man being interviewed on television, and he believed I would like to hear him. I told my father I did not want to because I was in the middle of my workout, and I did not want to take the time to watch anyone on television. Nevertheless, my father persisted, and said, "Just take a minute and come and see him, and if you become bored you can go back to your workout." My father believed it was important for me to see him. I reluctantly put down my weights and I went to the living room. I observed Maharishi being interviewed on the Les Crane show.

I was standing in the living room, and I saw Maharishi for the first time. I was fascinated by the way he looked. I was watching him on TV; he had glowing eyes and a hearty laugh. This was such a contrast to my life experience in the projects to see someone who was so relaxed and happy. It blew me away. I immediately sat down at the base of the TV and listened to the interview. I do not remember much about the specifics of the interview; however, I remember that he was happy; he was discussing life and how to gain strength, energy, the ability to know what is right, how to fulfill your desires and grow into a fulfilled human being. This is exactly what I wanted. I loved watching the entire interview and then went back to finish my workout. That moment was a seed that was planted in me regarding my future spiritual path. Most of my life at that point in time revolved around sports, working out, hanging out with my friends, dating, and trying to get through school, which I disliked.

The only thing that kept me from dropping out of high school was the drama department; I just did not find school relevant. In the drama department, I became involved in some plays, and enjoyed creating characters and expressing them on stage. Without that experience, I probably would have dropped out of school, and would have never gone to college because I did not find academics significant to my life. My father and mother were always pushing me for education, but I found the actual experience of so-called "education" to be extremely boring and frustrating. As a result of my involvement in acting, I became aware of an audition organized by Carnegie Mellon University. I discovered that Carnegie had an excellent reputation for having one of the best undergraduate departments in theater in the country.

Carnegie's representatives would travel across the country and audition a few hundred people, and out of those auditions, they would choose 20 or 25 people to enter their freshman class to become theater majors. When I heard about this opportunity, I put together a monologue from *The Glass Menagerie* by Tennessee Williams and I auditioned. A few weeks later I received a letter that I had been accepted to the Drama Department of Carnegie Mellon University, and they were going to provide me with a scholarship. For someone who was considering dropping out of high school, by some absolute miracle, I became involved in an activity I was never planning to explore: college! I entered college as a theater major, and loved it.

It was only after I began TM that I started to become more sensitive and conscious of the effects that my decisions and actions were having on myself and on others. After I had learned TM, I realized that I had been portraying characters that were mostly angry, frustrated, and/or depressed, and I was no longer interested in putting myself through these negative emotions of the characters, and enacting their behaviors. I began to seriously think about how all this was affecting my life and the lives of the people in the audience. I became concerned about the overall influence I was creating. If I had some significant singing or dancing talent, I could have done things that were more positive and uplifting, but that was not my strength; so, I eventually switched from the Drama Department into English Literature.

I had my first glimpse of Maharishi in the late sixties. In college, I had a close friend named David. David, as I remember his life at that time, mainly swayed between two emotions: he was either depressed or he was angry, but he also had a sharp intellect and that is what attracted me to him. One day just after a school break I was sitting on one of the main lawns of the campus with some friends, and I saw David walking in my direction. As he started to come closer I noticed there was a kind of glow around him, and he was smiling. At first, I thought this could not be my friend David, but as he came closer I recognized it was him, and we started to talk. I began to question what he had been doing to find out what had caused these changes. He remarked he had learned TM a couple of weeks prior. As I observed him, his face, eyes, feeling, and the "light" around him were different. I thought to myself, "TM?" I remembered seeing Maharishi on television a few years earlier. I made a mental note to myself—if this technique could have this dramatic effect on my friend, who used to be almost always either depressed or angry when I was with him, then I needed to check this out for myself, which I did.

Around that time I was also becoming involved in exploring philosophy and different scriptures of various religions and I was seeking enlightenment. I asked the TM teacher who was about to teach me if it were possible to realize enlightenment with this meditation, and she said, "Yes," and I said, "Then please teach me." I learned TM and from the very first time I began to feel happiness and inner peace. I knew that I had found something important and beautiful. I was not actively involved with the organization. I just practiced the technique.

In my senior year in college, I was reflecting on what I wanted to be: I simply wanted to become an enlightened human being, and I had intended to travel to India to find an enlightened teacher. One evening I had a very remarkable dream. It was like no dream that I had ever had before in my life or since. I found myself swimming in a large lake. As I was looking around I noticed that the lake was surrounded by beautiful trees, and the sun was shining through the leaves and branches onto the water. Everything was peaceful; it was a heavenly atmosphere, but I eventually became a bit tired from swimming. I noticed there was a white wooden platform on the water and I swam toward the platform to rest. As I put myself on the platform, I looked up and saw Maharishi sitting on a chair. In the dream, he looked at me and beamed a tremendous amount of love and happiness. During the dream, Maharishi directed my attention to some Hebrew writing. I knew how to read Hebrew, but I did not know enough to translate the words into English; however I realized the dream could have significance in the direction my life could take.

About a month after the dream, I attended an advanced lecture for TM meditators where they showed a film called *The Main Purpose.* To my surprise, in the beginning of the film, there was a lake and as the camera pulled back you could see that the lake was surrounded by beautiful trees, and the sun was shining through the trees reflecting on the lake. I began to think that I knew this place—I had been there, and yet this seemed impossible. As the film continued, I saw a white platform in the lake with Maharishi sitting in a chair on top of the platform. I spoke to the TM teacher after the lecture and shared the similarity of my dream to the images in the film. I also explained that I was considering traveling to India to find an enlightened spiritual guide.

The TM teacher mentioned that Maharishi was coming to Amherst, Massachusetts in the summer of 1971 to give a course. I was a student with very limited resources and called my father and said, "Remember that time, years ago, when I was working out with my weights and you brought me into the living room to see Maharishi on the television? This same man is going to be giving a course, and I really want to take it." My father, who was not wealthy, paused for a second and said, "Don't worry, go to that course, and we will give you the money for it."

I went to Amherst, where I met Maharishi for the first time. It was an amazing course. This was the type of knowledge that I always felt was missing from education—how to truly develop every aspect of your life. During the course, open microphones were provided for the course participants, and I made use of them regularly because of all the questions I had. During one lecture, Maharishi began to speak about something I had never heard him speak about before, the relationship between name and form in the Veda, the special nature of Vedic words. I found this topic particularly interesting.

An incident that was meaningful to me came towards the end of the Amherst course. Maharishi recognized me because of all my questions, and he made some gracious compliments to me. He asked me what I liked to do. I told him I enjoyed reading the scriptures of different religions. Maharishi said that I should read the scriptures and put the correct angle of interpretation to the scriptures. Wherever the commentaries are off, provide the right angle of understanding to the scriptures. I was fortunate to have a few private meetings with Maharishi in my life and my inner experience at those times was essentially of a lot of happiness; his presence enlivened that experience in me when I was around him. He radiated pure Being, and created feelings of fullness and joy in me and in those around him. When Maharishi would give out knowledge, I believed Truth was speaking out; I felt that Truth was telling its own story. I noticed many times that the flow of Maharishi's knowledge could transmute spontaneously into the experience of what he was talking about on the level of my own experience. What I found was that the knowledge was an experience. The knowledge Maharishi spoke out actually generated the experience; it was not separate from the experience. The experiences were actually being produced by what was being expressed by Maharishi; I wasn't trying to make this happen, it just happened spontaneously.

My inspiration for attending Yeshiva University was Maharishi's suggestion that I should explain the scriptures, and since I am Jewish I thought to begin with my own tradition. I was considering becoming a Rabbi. Yeshiva University was an institution where a person could choose to take rabbinical studies or traditional disciplines. I was studying Jewish law and the Torah.

My experience through TM helped me to understand the Torah, the five books of Moses. I would spontaneously be able to understand what I was reading on a deeper level because I was able to relate it to my experience of higher levels of consciousness. When you read the Torah, there are many different levels of possible meaning and experiences that can relate to those meanings, not only in the Torah, but any scriptures as well. It depends on the level of consciousness of the reader. If the reader has an expanded level of consciousness, the deeper levels of understanding contained in those words will automatically open up to the reader on the level of his or her awareness.

When I was completing my dissertation, which was centered on identifying universal principles, I was studying different traditions. As I would read them, I would reflect on the meaning and settle in my own self-referral consciousness. In that state of inner silence there was a faint memory of what I wanted to know. I settled into that pure state of Being and in a matter of a few seconds an insight into the scripture would bubble up, and it would be very clear and precise, and I would just write it down. These were the mechanics of how I completed my dissertation. The knowledge was spontaneously emerging from that inner level, to whatever degree my nervous system could experience it. This effortless generation of deep insight from within was an experience of great bliss.

One of the common experiences at Yeshiva University, an orthodox Jewish institution, is that you sit in a large room with other students; you have a "study buddy" to review and reflect on the scriptures and books of law together. The idea in a Yeshiva is that through study of sacred texts with the intellect, somehow, a person could align one's being with the Divine Being. The desire is to align the human intellect with the Divine Intellect by poring over the expressions of the scriptures. I remember sitting in a room with about a hundred students and everyone studying intensely, all having the desire to grow in holiness. They wanted to become a righteous person. I closed my eyes in the midst of this environment and experienced pure consciousness, pure Being, immediately. After a few seconds, I opened my eyes and looked around the room at everyone studying. I realized that because of Maharishi's technique, I could arrive at this place that everyone in the room wanted to go; all I had to do was just Be, and because of my experience of transcending in TM I knew how to Be. My fellow students were genuine; they were being earnest, and seriously trying day and night to arrive at this point of Being. This intense studying is a tradition because it states in the Torah that God says one should be with My Law day and night. I reflected to myself that these are good people, and they have a great goal, yet all I have to do is close my eyes, and I am there. I thought it would be wonderful if they knew how to transcend, and then they could still study, but their studying would be on a much deeper and more productive level; they would be studying from the goal instead of studying from the path.

However, conveying this perception to the general population is a very delicate affair. You have to approach people with the deepest respect and appreciation without any kind of demeaning judgment, especially when dealing with religious people of any tradition. The idea is to help people understand how TM could assist them to fulfill their own aspirations.

Maharishi has explained in his book, *The Science of Being and Art of Living* (Maharishi Mahesh Yogi, 1973), that in the beginning days of every faith, there was a technique that allowed people to transcend, and each tradition had their own name for that transcending process. However, through the course of time, the purity of the mechanics of the technique was lost, and people would no longer have the full value of the experience because the knowledge and technology of meditation became distorted—what was left of the religion were mainly the outer rituals and the doctrines. The vital element that was missing was the direct experience of pure Being, from which any religion emerged.

So, in the beginning days of Buddhism, Islam, Christianity, Judaism, Hinduism, Taoism, and virtually all religions, there was a transcending technique that was effective and then this technique was lost or distorted over time. With TM, we have a technique that allows people to effortlessly move to the transcendent and have a direct experience of it. This technique can be employed by a person of any religion. It is clear to me that for any religion to be meaningful a person needs to have the transcendental experience of unbounded pure Being. Without this transcendental experience, a person will enjoy only the more superficial, limited values of his or her religion. If one does not have the experience of that unbounded reality, one is living only a very partial value of his or her religion. What is important is the transcending process because that will bring fulfillment to any religion. The goal of every religion is permanent integration of pure consciousness, the Light of God in the terminology of religious life. The effortless technique for transcending is just the bridge for individuals of any religion; it provides the bridge between the individual mind and the Divine mind, and between individual intelligence and Cosmic Intelligence. The problem in every religion today is that the natural technique for transcending becomes distorted and the beneficial results that come from correct meditation are not there anymore in the lives of the people. The unbounded experience of pure Being in Islam, Christianity, Judaism, Hinduism, Taoism, and Buddhism is the same. It is not that these various religions achieve a different goal. Any member of any tradition can know this to be true by having the experience of that reality. It is my view that without this direct experience of pure Being, Muslims are not truly Muslims; Christians are not truly Christians; Jews are not truly Jews; Buddhists are not truly Buddhists; and Hindus are not truly Hindus. Without the experience of the transcendental, inner wakeful-silence of Being, religious people are only living the surface aspects of their religion and are not living the deep source and goal of their religion.

In religions, you can have two main values of understanding. You have people who have tasted this transcendental experience and this broadens their awareness—it helps them to recognize the universality underlying all religions. Then, you have the more narrowly based individuals who have not had a glimpse of this limitless Being, who become angry when you express that their religion is not the only one that contains the truth of life.

Also, I would like to make it clear at this point that TM is not a religion because it is a mental technique that is the applied part of an empirically based discipline known as Maharishi Science and Technology of Consciousness. Religion, in contemporary society, is essentially a belief-based system—a faith-based system. There are certain principles or doctrines of a religion and a person either chooses to believe them or not believe them. TM is part of a science because it is based on repeatable direct observation and experience. I think it's very important to make this distinction because today religions have lost an effective technique to give the seekers in religious traditions the regular and direct experience of that unbounded awareness. People choose to believe in the doctrines of a religion or not believe based on faith; people do not trust in religious doctrine based on their direct experience of what that doctrine claims is true, and this is the main difference between science and religion. Science requires empirically based evidence.

A science has ideas but validates or invalidates those ideas based on repeated observation and direct experience. However, without repeatable direct experience, an individual is participating in a faith-based system where one chooses to believe in something, but without direct evidence. TM is part of a science because it is definitely not based on belief or faith; it is based on the experiences that validate the principle that pure consciousness or unbounded awareness exists. If there was not a technique or system to empirically validate or invalidate a principle and one merely chose to believe it or not believe it, then it could be considered a religion.

So, to sum up, science is a systematic system that tries to obtain knowledge through empirical evidence, whereas contemporary religions are essentially faith-based or belief-based and do not require or depend upon such evidence.

However, in terms of spirituality as a general concept, I think that spirituality can be evaluated in the context of the experience of higher states of consciousness. Usually, spirituality versus religion is understood in terms of individuals who do not feel they belong to any particular religion because they find it to be too rigid, but yet they believe in a higher power; they consider themselves to be a spiritual person, but not a religious person. What defines a spiritual person? Is a person spiritual because they believe in spiritual concepts, or in a spiritual Being? I would say that what makes a person truly spiritual, whether they belong to a religion or not, is if he or she has the experience of that unbounded, inner transcendental pure consciousness, pure Being. A person can transcend and reach that level in many different ways: it can come through music, poetry, watching a sunset or a sunrise, or holding hands with someone you love. The value of an effective meditation technique, the value of TM, is that an individual can have that experience much more often, can have it regularly, and not just have the hope that this great experience that came to me, maybe once or twice in my life, may someday return. Although it is true that a person can transcend in different ways, the value of this experience is not in merely transcending from time to time, but rather in stabilizing that experience and making it a permanent feature within our consciousness and physiology. It should not just be a fleeting experience resulting in frustration and depression because we do not know how to recapture it. A main purpose of religion and spirituality should be to unfold and develop a human being of profound awareness and higher values.

One interesting experience in my life that related to the group practice of meditation was when I was a member of a Kibbutz in Israel. My wife Ellen and I went to Israel because everyone in a particular Kibbutz, Kibbutz Yachad, practiced the TM and the TM-Sidhi programs. We were motivated to see what it would be like to live in a Jewish community where everyone also meditated regularly. We stayed for three years, and our children were born in Israel. Unfortunately, after a while, the Intifada began and the situation became heated. I had also served in the Israeli army for about a year. In the Kibbutz, the number of people who regularly came together to create national harmony and coherence through the group practice of TM and the TM-Sidhi programs was shrinking due to people's work obligations and other personal issues. Unfortunately, the violence began to increase in Israel. The country began to shake and the group we had did not have the sufficient number of meditators and Sidhas to counteract it. Groups practicing the TM and TM-Sidhi programs together had been shown to reduce violence. At that point, Ellen and I decided to move to MUM in Fairfield, Iowa where there was a very large coherence-creating group because our main goal was to gain enlightenment and we felt that Israel was no longer a viable environment for achieving that goal.

Unhappy people fight with one another; happy people help one another. Many people in the Middle East, as well as many other places in the world, are not relaxed, happy, content people. When individuals are filled with stress, tension, and problems, they are frustrated and angry. When you are frustrated, angry and stressed there has to be conflict among one's own people and with other groups. For example, in the ongoing battle between Israel and Palestine, the essence of their religions has been forgotten. Many of the Muslims, Christians, and Jews are practicing their religion, but not in a full way. They are practicing their religions incompletely because they are not living the fullness of their own faith; this lack occurs because they are not having the experience of unbounded pure Being, which brings bliss and contentment to one's life.

The experience of pure consciousness eliminates the stress, the tension in a person's life, and provides inner security and fulfillment. If they do not have that experience of pure Being regularly, then how can they say they are living the complete life of a Jew, Christian, or Muslim? The purpose of every religion is to create a fulfilled, vital, loving, righteous, and generous person who acts in line with God's will. An individual cannot be fulfilled and righteous without the experience of unbounded awareness, the Light of God within. The basis of every religion is that experience, and without that experience the religion is really baseless. No matter what religion, every religion needs to have the experience of the bliss and contentment of this pure consciousness. It does not matter what name they give to this essential experience in the context of their own cultures or religious lives. Individuals need to have the repeated experience of Transcendental Consciousness. When they do, they will live the complete life of a Jew, Muslim, Christian, Buddhist, Hindu, Taoist, or whatever faith they may belong to. Individuals will find fulfillment within their own tradition, but without this experience, any tradition is similar to a dried up tree that has lost its source of water.

In every religious tradition the founder and practitioners speak about God or an Absolute, higher reality. In religion, the discussion is about this Ultimate Reality, and all traditions have their names for it. In every tradition, they have had saints, or enlightened people—individuals functioning from a higher level of consciousness. Every tradition speaks about this higher reality and has had individuals who have experience of this transcendental reality. I don't think anyone would deny that every religious tradition speaks of a supreme reality and that some people within their culture had clear and expanded experiences of this reality, and spoke and wrote about it. Every religious group would agree to this. Here are some examples:

Rabbi Nachman

Elijah was an ordinary human being, living in this world. But through secluded meditation, he reached such a high level that he never tasted death. From Rabbi Nachman's words, it was obvious that Elijah reached his high level only through this practice. The same is true of all the other great saints. (Kaplan, 1982, pp. 312-313)

Baal Shem Tov

Expanded and Constricted Consciousness can be explained in the following manner. When a person learns something but does not understand it in depth, this is a state of Constricted Consciousness, since his mental picture is not complete. But when he grasps something with enthusiasm and full understanding, then he is on the level of Expanded Consciousness. Similarly, there are states of Expanded and Constricted Consciousness in prayer and all other observance. (Kaplan, 1982, pp. 279-280)

Saint Augustine

Imagine if all the tumult of the body were to quiet down, along with all our busy thoughts about earth, sea, and air; if the very world should stop, and the mind cease thinking about itself, go beyond itself, and be quite still; if all the fantasies that appear in dreams and imagination should cease, and there be no speech, no sign ... the very Self which in these things we love, and go beyond ourselves to attain a flash of that eternal wisdom that abides above all things. (Harvey, 1998, pp. 52-53)

Farid Al-Din 'Attar

For you there is an ascent of the soul towards the Divine Light, therefore shall your heart and soul in the end attain to union with that Light. With your whole heart and soul, seek to regain Reality, nay, seek for Reality within your own heart, for Reality, in truth, is hidden within you. The heart is the dwelling place of that which is the Essence of the universe. Within the very heart and soul is the very Essence of God ... be unveiled within and behold the Essence. Form is a veil to you and your heart is a veil. When the veil vanishes, you will become all light. (Smith, 1994, p. 61)

Rumi

"My birthplace is placelessness ... I have thrown duality away like an old dishrag" (Harvey, 1998, p. 155).

Tao Te Ching

" ... A mind free of thought, merged within itself, beholds the essence of Tao ... It is the path to all wonder, the gate to the essence of everything!" (Star, 2003).

Buddha

If you really want freedom, happiness will arise
From happiness will come rapture
When your mind is enraptured, your body is tranquil
When your mind is tranquil, you will know Bliss
You will become aware that life is a miracle ... (Digha Nikaya)

Surangama Sutra

The nature of the Absolute, Ananda, is that it is total enlightenment. It is beyond name and form and beyond the world and all its living beings. Ignorance creates an illusion of birth and death, but when ignorance is dispelled, the supreme and shining Absolute is there. Then suffering is changed to insight, and death is transmuted into nirvana (Finkelstein, 2005).

Maharishi

The light of God is a transcendental experience; and the truth is that the light of God is the goal of every religion ... The essential message is the same; the essential path is the same; the essential goal is the same in spite of different expressions at different times in different places, and also in spite of different interpretations of the same message in different generations. (Maharishi, 1995, pp. 230)

Here in a simple practice is the fulfillment of every religion. It belongs to the spirit of every religion; it existed in the early days of every faith and has since been lost. The principle is still contained in the scriptures. It has only been lost in practice. (Maharishi, 1967, p. 259)

The missing element is how we recapture that experience for the people of every tradition; the process to recapture that experience is to bring the individual's attention from the boundaries of physical life to the unrestrained quality of spiritual life. It does not matter what you call this transcending process; you do not have to give it any name at all. There is an inner journey that takes place and one moves consciously from the bounded to the limitless level of pure consciousness. When the consciousness of a person is restricted in a mental, emotional, and/or sensory experience, it is absorbed in those boundaries. The individual must learn how to experience subtler aspects of the boundaries and ultimately transcend that limited reality of perception. That transcending process and the experience of boundlessness that results from it are the essence and foundation of every tradition. The lack of this experience is what weakens and limits any tradition. So, it is the experience and development of that higher state of consciousness that will revive the fullness of every religious tradition.

The direct experience of pure consciousness through TM is a natural way to come to this abundant state, which moves beyond the boundaries through an effortless transcending process. When people have this experience, whether they are religious or not, they will find peace and fulfillment. These peaceful and fulfilled individuals, when they meet a person of another tradition, spontaneously recognize and acknowledge the universality of Truth that they all equally share regardless of surface cultural differences. So, when a fulfilled Christian or Jew meets a fulfilled Muslim, Hindu or Buddhist, they are all friendly toward each other and help one another. They see and feel the underlying sameness in each other and become capable of loving their neighbor as their own self. It becomes automatic; one does not need to think about it, because it is based on that repeated experience of Being.

In the summer of 2011, I had an experience that highlights the previous thoughts. At MUM, we have Jews, Muslims, Christians, and Buddhists, and every other tradition. There are people at MUM from 70 different countries and many cultures, and once a year they have a Flag Day celebration. On Flag Day, they ask people from various countries to volunteer to represent their country and culture. There is a beautiful procession, and each person holds the flag of their nation, comes to the microphone, and speaks out the name of their country. The most amazing result I observed was the spontaneous outburst of appreciation and applause for each country from everyone in the audience. I remember thinking, what is going to happen when they mention Israel? There were many Arab students who came to study at MUM from Pakistan and other nations and enter the computer science program. I was also wondering what reactions would emerge from the Jewish population at

MUM when someone called out Iran or Egypt? When the person holding the Israeli flag said "Israel" all the Arabs applauded and showed appreciation. When someone mentioned Saudi Arabia, Iran or Pakistan all the Christians and the Jews from different countries applauded and showed their appreciation. I cried, because I could not believe it was possible.

I spoke later at the meeting, and I told the audience that if it is possible to do it here, it is possible to do it anywhere. There is nothing special about Iowa. What is special about MUM is that everyone is transcending. Everyone is having that experience of pure consciousness. Everyone is feeling more at peace and secure inside himself, and because of that experience, the love can flow. The appreciation can flow and the surface boundaries and differences among the cultures that used to be so important, and caused so much conflict, fear, and hatred just fell away. The common element of contentment, bliss, and happiness that comes when people are repeatedly transcending, and experiencing the unboundedness of pure Being, is what became predominant in the minds and hearts of all the people. What happened at MUM can happen in the entire world. The key is transcending because that is what brings the bliss and the happiness. Maharishi stated: "To live one's culture, one must live life according to natural law. All activity in nature begins from the common ground of silence, which is found in the mind's settled state of awareness" (Finkelstein, 2011).

Part III

A New Paradigm

Chapter XI

Enlightened Science

David Orme-Johnson, Ph.D.

I admire the high quality of research conducted on the Transcendental Meditation program for more than 40 years by David Orme-Johnson, Ph.D. I had the pleasure of traveling with him on a European tour that included France, Germany, Holland, and Great Britain. Dr. Orme-Johnson's mastery of science and his ability to empirically connect the abstract development of consciousness with tangible objective measurement and evaluation have placed him in the forefront of modern researchers on meditation and consciousness as a visionary scientist in our generation.

Dr. Orme-Johnson, in his website Truth About TM (www.truthabouttm.org), has insisted on the integrity of knowledge and challenges limited perspectives in science that can distort truth. He has published over 100 papers in mostly peer-reviewed journals on the TM program. I consider him one of the premier researchers in the world on the subject. Dr. Orme-Johnson received his B.A. in Psychology from Columbia University, and his M.A. and Ph.D. in Psychology from the University of Maryland.[1]

George Ellis (GE): David, when I reviewed your website entitled Truth About TM, it reminded me of a contemporary Renaissance man; you have included art, books, and research, giving comprehensive knowledge to facilitate a clear understanding of Maharishi's legacy of knowledge. The website you created could become a book in itself. Hence, in this interview I am interested in the human voice of science.

David Orme-Johnson (David): The human side may have been missing because our literature is so formal.

GE: I understand the formal scientific approach that has been taken is necessary because your website is one of the most important instruments for clarifying the scientific validity of research on the TM program. You have been very gracious in how you welcomed and thanked individuals for those

---

[1]   A complete list of Dr. Orme-Johnson's publications and more information about him can be found at: http://www.truthabouttm.org/truth/Home/AboutDavidOrme-Johnson/index.cfm

challenges. The challenges have afforded you the opportunity to clarify the misunderstandings. What influences led you into doing research on TM?

David: Well, I think one event that was very influential happened when I was about eight years old, as I was falling asleep one night. All of a sudden, my awareness slipped into an unbounded bliss. It was about as subtle as walking down a street and then unexpectedly falling down a manhole. Abruptly I was in a completely different state. It was just a nourishing, wonderful feeling, and I do not remember how long it lasted, probably not very long, and my reaction was—wow, what was that? I did not think of it as "this was God" or anything of that nature because nothing I knew of in our culture ever talked about such an experience. I did not tell anyone about it because there was no one to discuss it with or framework to think about it. This was nothing I had ever heard about in Sunday school. I lay in my bed afterwards and reflected— if it happens again I am going to try and hold onto it. Because it felt so right, so good, so full, so whole; it was unbounded, a completely perfect feeling and blissful happy state. Often after that I would lie in the bed trying to capture the experience.

Now I know that any effort to make it happen would be counterproductive. Any effort would only create activity in the mind, which would be a hindrance to settling into that silent, transcendental state. Moreover, I did not learn any of this knowledge until later in life. I had forgotten about it over the years; it was not until after I had been practicing TM for some time that I made the connection—I had been transcending. I believe it guided my life in many ways, because when I began college at Columbia I was attracted to take a course in Asian Literature. We read the classics of India, China, and Japan, which have a lot to say about enlightenment. However, the way the knowledge was portrayed in those books suggested that you had to give up everything in material life. Until I met Maharishi I did not realize the giving-up philosophy was a misinterpretation of the reality. I recognized that my experience of transcending was giving up the noisy thinking mind, but you are not giving anything up, you are gaining wholeness, totality, bliss. Anyway, I think that the transcending experience as a child subtly guided my life because I knew there was something more to life than this ordinary waking experience that we have.

When I was in graduate school studying to obtain my Ph.D. in Psychology, I was walking down the hall one day with my thesis advisor, Dr. Matthew

Yarczower, who asked me: "What do you really think about operant con-dition—behavioral psychology?" Behavioral psychology is the most extreme materialist worldview, that there is no consciousness, just the opposite of Vedanta, of Maharishi's teaching, which holds that everything in the universe is consciousness. It was near the time that I was to graduate and Matt wanted to know my overall take on the behaviorist worldview. Well, the question sur-prised me because I had not thought about it. I had been immersed in learning the research literature in that field and how to experimentally find answers to narrowly defined questions.

I looked around the hall we were walking down, struggling to give expres-sion to the whole field of subjective experience I was experiencing that had no place in behaviorism. I was looking for some clue as to what all this subjective conscious experience was. I remarked that my understanding of observing and looking around at the entirety of phenomenal experience which we have of sight, smell, and touch, indicates behavioral psychology just did not grasp the full picture. I stated that there was more to it because you cannot just explain the whole thing in terms of mechanical stimulus-response connections. I believe that the experience I had as a child was always in the background of my mind and guided me to look for something beyond the obvious, or to inform me what the obvious was.

GE: I want to discuss the issue of behavioral psychology because many years ago I worked with emotionally disturbed children and they employed many of these mechanical behavioral modification technologies. It was all mechanical. I taught a 10-year-old child the TM technique and asked him how he felt afterward—he said the trees are prettier. The entire goal of behavior modification was through mechanical reinforcement, such as chips, and verbal reinforcement techniques to change the mind. Behaviorists did not believe it was necessary to understand the mind to change behavior. As an expert in psychology what are your thoughts?

David: The behavioral approach focuses on behavior, and whatever the person is feeling or saying is not relevant—what they are doing is what is relevant, and the consequences of what they are doing. If they are doing some-thing, the why of it lies in what is reinforcing that behavior. If a kid cries a lot, it may be because that is the only way he can get attention. So give him atten-tion for behaviors you want to see grow in him and ignore the crying.

I also worked with autistic children with the behavioral approach, and the idea was to train the parents as agents of behavioral control, which meant training them to reinforce desired behaviors. For example, if you wanted the child to learn the names of pots and pans, the parents would place the pots and pans on the wall with name tags on them and when the children correctly read the words they would receive a chip or tokens, which they could cash in to receive a reward. It worked to a certain extent and I had the opportunity to share this with Maharishi, and he remarked that behavioral theory is very intelligent and has its range, but with TM the whole life blossoms from within. The behavioral approach is like watering the leaves of the tree that are wilted, and you are only tending to the surface value. However, with TM the origin of behavior is located in one's own consciousness and neurophysiology, which becomes more coherent, so thought becomes more coherent, and behavior becomes more effective and rewarding. TM studies have shown improved perception, more organized memory, more efficient learning, and greater creativity; all of this occurs on the basis of more orderly functioning of the neurophysiology.

GE: I worked with autistic children also; they have incredible memories and we taught one child the TM technique, and he expressed inner happiness automatically. Behaviorism is a good technique for creating structure and control, which allows you to introduce something like the TM program. One day the director came to visit our residential facility and the children were quietly sitting and controlling their behavior without any external reinforcement or chips because we had taught them all the TM technique.

At one facility we were asked by the director to teach the wards the TM technique, but there was an unanticipated consequence. Every Monday they would have group sessions to discuss the problems experienced over the weekend, and the wards in the house did not want to discuss anything negative because they were feeling so good. They stopped the TM program, and would not let us continue because it had worked so well that the house counselors were fearful they would not be necessary and lose their jobs. Going back to when you were eight years old—you had not yet learned TM, is that correct?

David: That's right. I did not learn TM until I was 29. My transcending experience as a child was completely natural and spontaneous, illustrating the universality of the experience. There are accounts of it in all cultures in every era.

GE: Perhaps you can put this in context; this experience is everyone's property, and yet as an innocent eight-year-old child you did not think to tell your parents—why would that be?

David: It was so natural and yet I did not have any words to talk about it, and no context. Who talks about altered states of consciousness with their kids, especially in 1949!

GE: You have been involved in four decades of research interpreting an experience you had as a child and have cultivated as an adult. What would you state to the average individual about this hidden reality waiting to be awakened?

David: At times, because I am a psychologist, when I am introduced to a group of strangers someone invariably says: "What can you tell about me?" Everyone wants you to tell them about themselves. That is the big question: Who are we? What are we? Why are we? My standard answer is: "You are unbounded pure creative intelligence and bliss just like everyone else."

GE: (laughter) That must be an opener to a conversation.

David: It creates this amazing effect. People just brighten up and they usually laugh. I remember a lady at a real estate dinner who remarked, "Yes, I really believe that." People know on some level that there is more, and people have different experiences in that direction all the time. You see a beautiful sunset and you have this unbounded feeling—"Oh, it's breathtaking." Suspension of breath is just the physiological marker of transcending. Inspiring experiences—the silence in the pauses in a Beethoven symphony or the silence you feel in the whirl of notes of a Bach sonata, the expansion of the heart on seeing a loved one, the thrill of a scientific discovery, skydiving and bungee jumping—these are all in the direction of transcending. People jump out of airplanes to have that feeling of freedom, fly through the air weightlessly, and they receive a thrill from the experience—it is also a taste of unboundedness. *Life is moving toward that transcendental experience all the time. That is what is happening in life.* The pleasure principle, the principle of positive reinforcement, all of these basic principles in psychology, taken to their ultimate level are about transcending and evolution of consciousness. TM provides a doorway to arrive more quickly, a shortcut to enlightenment. Enlightenment means not only that we can experience it now and then, as I experienced as a child, or even systematically through TM, but you grow into enlightenment until the experience of Transcendental Consciousness becomes a 24/7 reality. Ultimately the cultivation of higher consciousness is important to becoming a fully developed human being.

GE: Were you born in Texas?

David: Yes, I was born in El Paso.

GE: Is that where you learned TM?

David: Yes, what happened is I was in graduate school at the University of Maryland, and I went to New York City with my wife Rhoda. Rhoda and I met when I went to Columbia and she attended Vassar. We visited my friend from high school, Clint, who also when he was young had expanded experiences, and we had a spiritual connection. He was an explorer of spiritual options in the 1960s. When I went to see Clint in New York, he mentioned that Maharishi had come to New York, and he went to see him and he told me about TM. I saw subtle but profound changes in him and wanted to learn. At that time there were not many TM teachers in the world, and it was two years before I had an opportunity to learn the technique. After I obtained my Ph.D., we had returned to El Paso where I was teaching part-time at the University of Texas at El Paso (UTEP). One day, as I was walking into a drugstore near the college campus, I noticed a handwritten note that asked, "Do you want to enjoy life more? Learn TM." It gave the date of a lecture on TM, so my wife and I went with a friend to the lecture. I felt the speaker, Casey Coleman, had a special presence about him. I learned TM first, and Rhoda and my friends waited to see what would happen to me. After the first practice of TM my entire worldview changed, and I had a cognition, a personal awakening.

What convinced Rhoda happened that afternoon in a little park with our son Nate, about two and a half. Normally in wide-open spaces I was paranoid, and this would happen frequently since I was a teenager. I would feel someone was aiming a sniper rifle at me, and I would really get in a sweat and have an anxiety attack. After learning TM I did not have that feeling. I felt completely comfortable, relaxed, in the moment, and happy. It was a big contrast. Sometimes the most stressed people have the most dramatic immediate results from TM because of the contrast. Rhoda, who knows me very well, wanted to learn right away because she observed the technique had an amazing impact on me after just one meditation. I was floating around in a very attractive experience. She did learn six months later, and we became totally involved in all the

TM activities; it was joyous interacting with TM practitioners, and to be alive like the little boy you mentioned regarding everything looking better.

One amusing event took place when I was coming across the border with a group of meditators, and we were all laughing and the border guard thought we must be on drugs. The guard made us all get out of the car and started going through everything, and we were all laughing and extended our help as he was searching the car. At a certain point, while he was going through the ashtray looking for reefers, he suddenly became aware we were not acting paranoid, and that he was making a mistake. With a mixed look of embarrassment and anger, he brusquely told us to move on. He knew we were doing something out of the ordinary, but he didn't know what, and there were none of the cues that it was something bad. He did not know what to make of us.

GE: When did you begin to do research on TM?

David: I had been practicing TM for about six months, and was also teaching Experimental Psychology at UTEP, and some of the meditators began to take my classes. I had the idea that the way TM changed your behavior was similar to a Pavlovian extinction. For example, if you pair a bell with food, a dog will salivate when you just ring the bell, or if you pair the bell with a loud noise or something traumatic then the dog may become afraid of the bell. However, if you present just the bell alone many times with no trauma associated with it, then the fear response eventually extinguishes, maybe after many presentations. What can speed up the extinction process is to present the bell together with something pleasant, or in a pleasant environment. This is called counter conditioning.

So, I was thinking that maybe what happens during TM is that when you remember some stressful event you are presenting these conditioned stimuli or situations you are afraid of to yourself as thoughts and in this very quiet pleasant state, the fear or trauma associated with the thoughts gets extinguished more effectively. I was trying to think of some model for studying this idea in the experimental psychology class I was teaching at UTEP. I thought I would do a Pavlovian conditioning experiment and see if the practitioners of TM extinguish faster than the non-meditators, or perhaps are more resistant to aversive conditioning in the first place. As a first step, I simply played loud tones to the students repeatedly to find out how quickly their stress response (the skin resistance response or GSR) habituated. The first response is typically very large, but with repeated presentations of the loud tone the response gets progressively smaller and smaller as the person learns that the loud noise, though annoying, is no real threat. What I found was that the TM practitioners recovered much faster, in an average of 11 trials compared to 26 trials for the non-meditators. The meditators' responses also tended to start sooner, indicating a livelier nervous system. I also found that the meditators had a simpler waveform to the first response, just responding once to it, whereas the non-meditators responded twice on average.

Additionally, I found something even simpler, that you do not have to stress a person to find out what their stress level is. You could just turn up the sensitivity of the polygraph, which measured skin resistance, and count the number of endogenous small stress responses they were making when they were just sitting quietly, or meditating. I discovered the practitioners of TM made fewer of these spontaneous skin responses, on average about 8 compared to 21 in the non-meditators during a 10-minute period while both groups were just resting with eyes closed. Furthermore, when the individuals began practicing the TM technique, the number decreased to just six in ten minutes. I found the TM practitioners had a more stable physiology—autonomic stability. They were carrying less stress around with them, and if something stressful happened, like a loud tone, they responded quickly but recovered faster, indicating a greater resistance to stress. The TM subjects did not keep responding to the same stressor numerous times. The picture that began to emerge is that the TM program seems to produce an ideal way of coping with the world. Bad coping would be that we are always worried about situations, and always burning up adaptive resources, such as adrenalin, cortisol, burning out the body, and nothing productive is happening—you're spinning your wheels. When you start TM you stop spinning your wheels as much, and when something happens, the TM practitioner is in a much better position to deal with it, a better fight or flight response. Once the challenges are over you do not continue to show that reactionary response and ruminating on "I could have done that" and so on. I observed that non-meditating people were more prone to become caught up in these little whirlwinds; they were simply burning up their lives. TM provided a technology to smooth everything out; the person was more rested, ready to go, and if something happened, the meditator responded simply and recovered twice as fast as non-meditating controls (1).

In 1987, Dr. Michael Dillbeck and I did a meta-analysis on physiological studies on the TM technique, to see how consistent the findings were from different laboratories around the world. A meta-analysis is a systematic method of evaluating the results of several independent studies of the same topic. We found that on average from all the studies that had been done that the deep rest and autonomic stability produced by the TM technique is more than twice as great as ordinary rest.

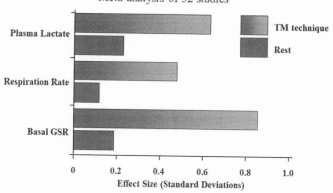

Increased Physiological Relaxation
Meta-analysis of 32 studies

Effect Size (Standard Deviations)

Reference: Dillbeck, M., and Orme-Johnson, D. (1987). *American Psychologist, 42,* 879–881.

A meta-analysis of 32 physiological studies on the TM technique found that it produces a much more profound rest than ordinary rest (while sitting with the eyes closed similar to the way that TM is practiced). The deep rest and rejuvenation during TM forms the basis of all its benefits (2). Autonomic stability and improved stress reactivity are the qualities that heroes possess. Think of cowboy movies, or Samurai movies, and the heroes have the quality of being cool under duress and stress. If something happens, they deal with it quickly and efficiently; they are faster on the draw. I remember a scene from the great Samurai movie *Yojimbo*. The hero, played by Toshiro Mifune, is surrounded by tough bad guys, and he remains unruffled at their jeering. Then, at the point that battle is inevitable, he whips out his sword and in an incredible whirl of action decimates them, sheaths his sword and walks off down the street as if nothing has happened, with a characteristic shrug of his shoulders.

One of the outcomes we observed in this early research was that the TM technique made a person's reaction time faster, but when the stressful situation was over they recovered quickly. I was so excited that here was a way to quantify the idea that TM reduces stress. People have been meditating in all cultures for thousands of years, but now in this scientific age we had a chance to explore it in scientific terms. *I had found my race and I was running it.* The subjective and personal experience of TM is the main thing. If you do not have the direct experience you could have all kinds of fanciful ideas regarding what meditation is about, even from the scientific evidence.

I wrote a letter to Jerry Jarvis, who was the president of the World Plan Executive Council, about the research I was doing and I received this wonderful letter back saying that he had read it to Maharishi and he was impressed. I then received a letter from Maharishi on the most beautiful stationary. It was radiating with a glowing feeling and had "Maharishi" simply embossed in gold at the top on the stationary. It was a handwritten note from Maharishi, which simply said "A Guru's blessing." Then we were invited to travel to Humboldt State College where he was giving lectures in the summer of 1971 and 1972.

GE: What year did you begin this research?

David: The research began in late 1970 or 1971.

GE: Was this around the same time that Keith Wallace did his research at UCLA (3-6)?

David: Yes, it was around the same time, but Keith's started earlier, and his study was published in *Science* in 1970. I had learned the TM technique in March 1970 and Keith's paper had not yet been published at that point. My instructor in TM mentioned to us that some research was going on. I remember later reading Keith's thesis, but I had been trained in behavioral psychology and was unfamiliar with many of the terms Keith was using in his paper—*oxygen consumption, arterial blood gases, cardiac output, minute ventilation, blood lactate concentration*. It was poetry to my ears to hear about all these new areas in the light of my own experiences of meditating, although I was familiar with some brain research, and had worked in a brain research lab in graduate school. That was in the mid-1960s and we were studying the pleasure centers of the limbic (emotional) system of the brain, which is probably very important in meditation.

GE: But you did your study on galvanic skin research—is that not physiological?

David: It is physiological and I had read about it but never had any experience with it. I discovered at UTEP that the psychology department had an old equipment room. I was rummaging through the equipment to see what they had that I could use in the experimental psychology classes for a demonstration. I found an old polygraph, which was not working, and I fixed it up and made it work. I then began to read more about it.

GE: Let's step back to the beautiful letter from Maharishi and when you were invited to come to Humboldt.

David: That was in 1971.

GE: What happened?

David: We arrived at Humboldt State College in Eureka, California. The course was organized into different groups, and we were placed with the Spiritual Regeneration Movement (SRM) group, which included pioneers of the TM movement like Walter Koch and Mother Olsen. I was instructed through the Students International Meditation Society (SIMS). The SRM people were more mature people—my parents' generation—and were completely different from the SIMS group, which were mostly scientists and students. The SRM group was more oriented to profound spiritual knowledge and in the group meetings were discussing some fascinating esoteric issues. They were communicating with one another as if they were all on the same page, and I had no reference in my mind regarding anything they were talking about. My head was spinning. At one point I asked: "Can we discuss what Maharishi is discussing in the lectures?" They agreed immediately, looking guilty that they were off task.

Mother Olsen (1979) knew I was a scientist, and she asked what I thought of Maharishi's teaching. I said I appreciate everything he is saying, but I do not understand what he means when talking about *Being.* "I do not get this *Being* thing; do you think it's important?" Everyone laughed. Of course, *Being* is absolutely the central point of all Maharishi's teaching, that when we transcend we are experiencing the transcendental field of Being that underlies not only our own mind but all of creation. Maharishi had written a wonderful book about it, *The Science of Being and Art of Living,* but I had not read it yet. I was trained as a behavioral psychologist in a different view of reality, that everything is material. Our discussion group was analyzing the extreme other point of view of Vedanta, which holds that everything is consciousness. It eventually dawned on me that my dharma was to explain Vedanta to behaviorists. Maharishi is quoted as saying in Vernon Katz's fabulous book *Conversations with Maharishi* that if the knowledge is to be complete it should be able to integrate and resolve all diverse philosophical viewpoints.

I have not written my Vedanta commentary on behaviorism yet, but the basic idea is that with the behavioral approach one reinforces desired behaviors one at a time to strengthen them, whereas with TM one transcends into the silent field of pure consciousness, the ultimate state of doing nothing, yet everything gets better. The physiological explanation is that in that uniquely coherent rest stresses are normalized and the body heals itself. The more cosmic explanation is that pure consciousness is the unified field of natural law that organizes all forms and phenomena in the universe, and when one enlivens that in one's awareness one begins to live in accord with natural law.

GE: This situation is interesting because you are the other side of the coin to John Hagelin. I am sure he has faced similar challenges in physics because you have been fighting the same battle in behaviorism.

David: That is correct. Since physics is the foundation of the sciences, his job is much more fundamental. I want to share with you another story that took place in El Paso that gave me a taste of what enlightened consciousness might be like. An introductory lecture had been arranged, but the teacher could not make it, so he asked four meditators to give it, including myself. I experienced what Maharishi described as speaking from the level of Being. I gave the lecture, and during it and afterwards I was uplifted. I experienced an enormous expansion of consciousness.

GE: When you say uplifted, do you mean the knowledge itself resulted in you transcending?

David: Yes, but in activity, while I was speaking—everything was more unifying; it was glowing. I was aware of the audience sitting there, but simultaneously I was aware of this deep blissful feeling and a blissful wholeness permeating the room. I was riveted to them and vice versa, and I knew that they were experiencing it too. All the other speakers reported the same experience. We were blissful and uplifted, but in a supernormal kind of way, not in a mind distorting kind of way as with drugs.

GE: Before learning TM I would look across the room and see objects and it seemed there was empty space between you and the object of perception. After I learned the TM technique it did not feel like there was any empty space anymore, and to me it reflected that something had awakened inside of me.

David: Oh, yes.

GE: So, you are describing an experience that for many people on this planet is invisible and they do not understand what you have just described. There are also people who have not learned TM and experienced something similar. How would you explain that?

David: People have different levels of evolution, and some people come into this world practically enlightened. Maharishi once told us in our teacher training not to assume because you are doing TM that you are more evolved than everyone you are teaching. Maharishi said that as teachers of TM we would come across people who are much more highly evolved than we are because evolution is a natural occurrence. All TM does is provide an individual a powerful tool for accelerating the process.

GE: You have this beautiful website entitled Truth About TM (www. truthabouttm.org). What motivated you to put this together?

David: One of my jobs when I was around Maharishi was to answer negativity. Something would come up in a newspaper, or a challenge to the research. Somehow, I wound up being the person who answered these challenges. I started to accumulate answers throughout the years to the various issues that came up.

GE: I assume as a scientist you kept them?

David: Yes, I hung unto them because the challenges tend to repeat themselves. Without dwelling on the reality too much, there are definitely some organizations that are threatened by TM because they see TM growing quickly and believe their livelihood is threatened. The bigger picture is that they should embrace TM because it will speed up their evolution and fulfill their goals. For example, a large drug company came to Maharishi European Research University (MERU) when we were evaluating biochemical changes that take place in the meditators. The drug representative said the company was going to do all the expensive assays for our research, because the drug company wanted to find out what is causing these changes that made us all so clear and blissful, and then they planned to make a pill to do the same thing and market it. Maharishi just laughed. He said if you could speed up everyone's evolution with a pill that would be great. The problem with that approach is that the human nervous system is so individual in how it can be stressed that there is not one single pathway of change. One person's blood pressure may be too high and another's too low so you cannot just make everyone's blood pressure come down, and then think they are going to be better, much less enlightened.

Other groups have tried to use biofeedback to mimic the physiological effects of TM. For example, they monitor alpha waves and reward them. This is the behaviorist approach. If you want to increase a certain behavior, reward it and it will increase. It works. The problem is that TM is a dynamic process. What happens is not one thing, but changes dynamically depending on the condition of the body. If the person needs sleep at that time, increasing alpha waves will function to keep him awake, and cause strain. The results you see in bar charts and tables in scientific papers are average results. They do not represent any actual meditation session. Individual meditations are always different, because we are never the same person from one day to the next; different people are unique physiologically, emotionally, with diverse personalities, with thousands of things going on. No monitoring devices are capable of monitoring all that is going on or can say what myriad of changes need to take place to heal the body and mind. No human intellect or computer could fathom it. Yet, the wisdom of the body does it simply, naturally, and without effort. All you have to do is let nature do its job. TM is a subtle technique for settling down and experiencing restful alertness. You cannot force it because that just creates more mental activity. You have to learn TM one-on-one from a certified teacher.

There are groups that are against the TM organization, or who try to imitate TM, so things tended to repeat, and I would reply to these challenges in my website. My approach to tough questions was to go more deeply into it, explore the details and inevitably I would find when you took a more expanded view of the issues and challenges then it could all fit into a more coherent global picture, even the so-called no-effect studies or the negative-effect studies. It usually came down to the fact that people actually did not practice TM regularly, or were doing some other meditation technique, or had a pre-existing condition. There was always a reason for it.

The Truth About TM website came about because of the internet. Prior to that, we just responded to isolated cases of different allegations as they came along. However, with the advent of the internet and the blogs, anyone, usually hiding behind a false identity, could create false information, or generate innuendos. We continued to ignore it for a few years, but then we found that students and others would come to a TM lecture, be inspired, and then check us out on the internet, and be turned off by the negativity. So I had to do something about it, and I dusted off my file of replies and posted them, plus wrote some new ones. I also posted overviews of the research, an annotated bibliography of findings in the 4,558 pages of Volumes 1-6 of *Collected Papers* of research on TM, which a person can search to see what has been done in an area they are interested in. I compiled studies and reviews of research comparing TM with other techniques, posted lists of the 200 universities and institutions in 30 countries where the research has been conducted and the 160 journals it has been published in, etc., and I now post new research as it comes along.

GE: Maharishi's approach, at his high level of consciousness, or what he would call normal, was to never put attention on negativity because he said it would grow stronger. I am sure you are aware of his position. Anyone seeking truth, scientific validity, and reliability has to transcend his or her assumptions or the enculturation of the situations that have put the blinders on. What you seem to be trying to do in your website is to blow apart these hard knots of bias. You have done it graciously, and in fact you thank people for the challenges; you took their negative energy and transformed it through facts. Explain the difference between how you are approaching it and Maharishi's feeling about not putting attention on negativity?

David: Resolving conflict through a positive and factual response by bringing out other facts that were not taken into account can broaden understanding of an issue. To provide a concrete example, there was a study conducted with some undergraduates, in which they provided some intelligence and creativity testing, which did not show an increase. So, when I looked into the young students chosen to be subjects, I found they were away from home for the first time, dealing with becoming grownups, finding their mate, scheduling their own time and, guess what, they were not practicing TM regularly. This was the explanation for the outcomes. However, when TM is built into the school routine and the students have scheduled time set aside to do it, it works.

For example, when my graduate student So Kam Tim, for example, introduced TM into three schools in Taiwan, they had no problem making it part of the daily school routine because meditation is part of their culture, and there were amazing results—increased creativity, intelligence, improved perception, and decreased anxiety (7). In dealing with the negativity by investigating the challenges, I was able to produce a better understanding for the skeptics, and this pushes our understanding of the research to a higher level. Thank you, skeptics!

Holistic Improvement in Intellectual Performance
THROUGH THE *TRANSCENDENTAL MEDITATION* TECHNIQUE

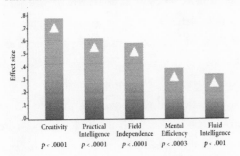

Three well-controlled studies have shown that the TM practice improves intellectual performance on all dimensions.

Reference: So KT, Orme-Johnson DW. Three randomized experiments on the holistic longitudinal effects of the Transcendental Meditation technique on cognition. *Intelligence.* 2001;29(5):419-40.

The aforesaid areas of improvement include creativity, practical intelligence, field independence, mental efficiency, and fluid intelligence (7).

GE: Let's go back to 1970. Did you have an opportunity to meet with Maharishi at that time or did you have to wait until the later courses in Fiuggi, Italy?

David: I did have an opportunity to meet with Maharishi at Humboldt, where he was holding a course for about 3,000 people. At that time I had a lot of stress, and the experience made my mind whirl. Jerry Jarvis introduced me as the scientist who had done those studies, and I tried to speak with Maharishi, but I seemed to space out. Maharishi was like a big magnet and all of the different elements of your physiology are like little magnets, jumbled in different directions. When the little magnets get around the big magnet they all start to line up and become coherent and it totally changes your internal reality (laughter). So the first few times I was around Maharishi I was not functioning well. I could not remember what I was going to say. Nevertheless, as the course went forward, and

I was having many profound experiences of transcending in that big group and normalizing of the physiology, I tried to meet with Maharishi again. So one day as Maharishi was leaving the lecture I got up my nerve and worked my way up to the front of the line, and I mentioned to Jerry I would like to talk to Maharishi regarding my theory of how TM works. Maharishi said, "Fine, come in the car." Jerry was driving and Maharishi was in the front seat. I noticed as Maharishi was slowly being driven across the Humboldt campus that there were meditators everywhere. As we moved along Maharishi was listening to me and at the same time acknowledging the people with a smile and waving a flower. As soon as the meditators saw Maharishi was coming they would light up, smiling and doing the namaste gesture, and I was looking over his shoulder into his world. I had never seen such a bright, well-dressed happy group of people. I was just 30 and most of them were 20-year-olds, who had only recently been aimless hippies. I was given the opportunity to peek into Maharishi's reality and creation, which was that he created waves of happiness and bliss everywhere he went among the enlightened people he had cultivated. It was so amazing and beautiful that my theory and concerns seemed to be a tiny reality in comparison to this, but somehow I managed to explain my theory to Maharishi.

Maharishi turned around when we reached the building that he and Jerry were going to, and he held up a rose and said: "The thing is everything in life blossoms simultaneously when you water the root," pointing to the stem and the leaves, and delicately unfolding the petals of the rose as he spoke. He indicated that it was not just some localized mechanism, one stressful thought at a time. The whole system changes on all levels simultaneously. Then he swiftly left the car and went into the building to a meeting. It was surprising how quickly and decisively Maharishi could move; most of the time he moved with the stately pace of an elephant, creating a sense of timelessness around him, but he never wasted time. He was always highly purposeful, working every moment, 20 hours a day, in the car, on the bus, on the boat, in small meetings, and in the lecture hall with thousands holding open discussions. He never deviated from his vision of enlightening the world, and he had a lot to do.

In those few minutes of his time in the car I was infinitely blessed. He had given me two close-up glimpses into his world, over his shoulder as he moved through the meditators, and life in his small meetings. In a few words he gave me a direction for my scientific work that has directed my life since that moment. Maharishi's core idea of the holistic effects of TM has been the guiding principle of how I approach the research. Look at *all* the research and see how each specific finding is a stroke in the painting of the whole. That is what I do. I consider each new piece of information in the context of the whole.

GE: How do you put the metaphysical and scientific experiences together? Somehow Maharishi has been able to take the invisible and make it visible. He has taken what has been beyond human comprehension and made it tangible.

David: Maharishi has always said that higher states of consciousness are in the blood and the bones, and how the nervous system functions, and that it is measurable. Everyone has had the common experience of how a poor or good night's sleep impacts our daily functioning. TM increases the coherence in the human physiology and it is measurable. With TM you become more awake to life, and it is as simple as that. As I reflect on my life, on Keith Wallace, the other scientists, and our great adventure, it has been amazing to be able to tell this ancient story of enlightenment in scientific language, in terms of meta-bolic rate, autonomic stability, EEG coherence, 5-hydroxyindoleacetic acid, the hypothalamic-pituitary-adrenal axis (laughter). It just means more orderly brain functioning and reduced stress. Maharishi always wanted our research papers to be "rigorously jargonesque" (laughter), by which he meant use the technical language of your field. He wanted our research to be rigorous and technically perfect. He wanted us to use the most sophisticated equipment, to know about the most recent advances in our fields, and to relate our findings to those discoveries. Maharishi wanted us to use mathematical equations. I learned a lot in going into all these fields and I still do every day. I could not do it without TM. The research shows that meditators grow in comprehension and intelligence.

GE: This is very important because people throughout history did not realize that the growth toward enlightenment was measurable and achievable in a lifetime. The tool of science is beginning to assist in understanding the ineffable invisibility of the experience.

David: You are measuring the effects of it because in itself that pure con-sciousness can only be measured by one instrument—consciousness itself. The human physiology, when it becomes so refined, can have that consciousness which can know itself on its own level. The knower alone is capable of knowing the knower in its self-referral state. That is what transcending is.

Maharishi declared that TM is a science; science means that something can be measured systematically and the systematic means to measure it is to directly experience it. A Self-referral experience is an "observation" of the Self, spelled with a capital "S" because it is experienced as the infinite expansion of one's usual limited small self or personality. It is not that much different from an objective measurement in which you read something on a dial. However, instead of reading something on an oscilloscope or microscope or telescope, the scientist is closing his or her eyes and is reading, in the sense of directly experiencing, this unbounded awareness. It is an observation. Consciousness is able to experience itself, and in that sense measure it.

Consciousness is not directly measurable by anything outside of itself, because it is fundamental to everything else, but you can measure its effect on everything else. So when someone meditates you can measure how the physiology swings during the TM practice between transcending and release of stress. Originally people were very skeptical because when Keith Wallace first conducted his study, the idea that the mind affected the body was a new concept. It is obvious to us now, and there is now mind-body medicine, but Keith's initial research, in which he measured changes in EEG, respiration, metabolism and biochemistry, was a revelation in science. Another revelation was that the pattern of physiological changes was different from the patterns you observe in waking, dreaming, or sleeping. This accorded with the ancient description of the meditative state being a fourth major state of conscious-ness. It was amazing and thrilling to be able to demonstrate that the fourth state of consciousness has its specific physiological correlates.

What happens during the TM practice has been the subject of a lot of research and still is today. We conducted research on individuals who were hav-ing clear periods of transcending where the mind was sinking into unbounded awareness. During that time they could not do anything because they were completely absorbed in the inner bliss, but we gave them instructions that when they came out of the transcendental experience to push a button. We would evaluate what happened right before that moment and we would have an idea of what was happening during that state of transcendence. We observed that the breath stopped while they were transcending. Then you had a physi-ological marker during the TM practice that the breathing is dramatically reduced during the deeper inner experience of transcendence. The next question was—what is happening in the brain during that suspension of breath? We found that there was increased coherence across all the different frequency bands in the EEG—alpha, beta, gamma. Delta has many different frequencies, which are related to different aspects of mental and physiological functioning. What we discovered is that during transcending the entire EEG spectrum becomes more coherent. Coherence means that the different areas of the brain are working together in a synchronous manner. A lot of research in the last decade or two, besides ours, has shown that alpha coherence, in particular, which you see during transcending and during TM, is organizing the entire brain; researchers call it long-range spatial organization by the alpha wave. The way the brain works is that there are different systems in the brain that are responsible for different aspects of perception, cognitive processing, feelings and movement that are taking place. One part of the brain may have to do with sensory input, and another part may have to do with integrating that sensory input. Moreover, another part may have to do with preparation for activity, another part execution of the activity, and finally there are the frontal executive areas, which are coordinating the whole process. Hence, in order to do anything the brain has to put together a team of different parts of the brain to accomplish the action, and a moment later it has to put together another team to do something else.

Researchers have discovered that alpha coherence is integrating different parts of the brain to do different types of tasks and if we are going to implement task A, we need this pattern, and if we are going to implement task B, we need this other pattern, and so on. The coherence is organizing the different parts to work together. It is similar to the conductor of an orchestra: you have the violins, the horns, piccolos, drums, flutes, flugelhorns, and so forth. The instruments are all doing different things but the timing provided by the conductor is keeping them all together, resulting in an emerging harmony and not a cacophony of sound. EEG coherence is like the conductor of the brain that creates harmony. Our research indicated that higher coherence was related to increased creativity. Therefore, if you can bring together different aspects of your memory, experiences, intellect and feelings, and if you can harmonize those divergent components, an individual will come up with more creative solutions.

As a scientist I found it exciting to be able to study what the effects of transcending were, and then to investigate what the functional significance of transcending was for behavior. A person is not meditating to arrive at a certain state, but for the purpose of improving human life. It is like the 10-year old boy you taught TM, and his comments after meditating, in which he said everything looked prettier, because his brain was more coherent. Therefore, individuals are experiencing parts of the brain more coherently coordinated with the perceptual aspects of the brain, and suddenly everything is brighter and clearer.

Several studies have measured field independence, which is the ability to discover a target in a complex situation. It is like those children's games in which animals are hidden in a complex design, and the children have to find them. TM increases the ability to go in and find the target. A person has a broad comprehension of the whole pattern and then he or she has the ability to keep the goal in mind and to focus in and locate the target.

GE: Can you summarize the research being done on Cosmic Consciousness?

David: Cosmic Consciousness means that Transcendental Consciousness, which is experienced during the TM practice, begins to be held onto even during the phases of activity; it happens gradually over time. At first the person feels that some of the effects of TM are present after meditation, and as the day goes on the effects of the TM practice fade. Through regular practice you are habituating the system to integrate spontaneously the experience of Transcendental Consciousness or this greater integration during activity. Cosmic Consciousness means that you do not lose that unbounded inner awareness in activity or in deep sleep or dreaming.

GE: What are researchers measuring?

David: The rigorous test is that you can maintain the experience of Transcendental Consciousness during sleep because that is the dullest state, with the least consciousness. The subjective experience is called witnessing sleep; a person is sleeping, but they are maintaining unbounded inner awareness. The body is resting but they are lying there in bliss. The study was to measure the person's EEG because the EEG of sleep and the EEG of Transcendental Consciousness are well defined and well known. The prediction would be that you would see the two styles of physiology functioning together. Hence, the study discovered that people who were having this Cosmic Consciousness experience of pure consciousness during sleep showed the EEG of sleep and pure consciousness superimposed on each other (8, 9). Sleep is associated with what is called a delta wave, or non-REM sleep, very slow, one cycle per second of EEG. Riding on top of that was this wave between alpha and theta, about 7-8 cycles per second, which is the frequency associated with the restful alertness experienced during the transcending stage of the TM technique. It just fit the prediction. It is a very unusual pattern that is not normally observed during ordinary sleep. The subjects remarked they were experiencing pure consciousness along with sleep, and the EEG showed the delta wave of sleep coexisting with the EEG of transcending or pure consciousness, which is the alpha/theta frequency.

GE: Was there a subjective correlation of bliss either during deep sleep or when they woke up?

David: Oh yes, the subjects experienced bliss all the time in the background during sleep or in activity. The experience was always there—24 hour bliss, day and night, sun, rain, or snow.

GE: As you know from studying the history of innovative thought, it can take decades before people fully cognize the dramatic significance of a discovery. This research on Cosmic Consciousness takes the wisdom of the great seers of antiquity and places it on the lap of science and makes it tangible beyond mysticism.

David: That is correct, and that study has been sitting there in the literature since the late 1990s. It was published in a scientific journal called *Sleep*. A journal devoted to sleep published the first paper on enlightenment, which is ironic and funny.

GE: In this book I have a section in which I discuss an 83-year-old Catholic nun. The Sisters asked me to teach them the TM practice. The elderly nun said to me "I think I have insomnia" and I inquired how she felt in the morning, and she stated that she was happy, full of energy and bliss. I asked if she was tired and she said no. I told her that she did not have insomnia; she was experiencing pure consciousness in her sleep. She had explained that she was experiencing bliss in her sleep. This illustrates one of the great gifts of Maharishi and the scientists. They have given intellectual and empirical understanding of these abstract and previously incomprehensible experiences.

David: I believe this is one of the values of Maharishi's knowledge. It is something he has commented on regarding how important intellectual under-standing is, because a person could have an experience, perhaps enjoy it, but have puzzlement. Hence, a person might think it was something abnormal and there may be people having higher experiences in mental hospitals, although I believe it would be rare, but it is a possibility because it is so misunderstood.

In my Truth About TM website one of the issues that arise is whether TM is harmful to people's psychology. One of the negative papers was written by a psychologist who had a couple of patients experiencing witnessing all the time, an inner watching everything that is going on. There is a similar situation in psychiatry called dissociation, but people who are dissociated are not functional; they cannot get along. The author of the paper was totally confused because the patient, who was witnessing, was the CEO of a very successful business which she created, and it did not fit the pattern of dissociation; she was so active, happy and highly functional. There is no understanding in modern psychology regarding the characteristics of enlightenment, and the experience often becomes pathologized. I read a book by a TM practitioner who was having Cosmic Consciousness expe-riences and for some reason she did not know exactly what they were. She went to different psychologists and after an incorrect assessment they all pathologized her experience. The woman was so attractive that psychologists all tended to fall in love with her (laughter). The woman developed a personal relationship with one of them and after some time she asked: "What about my problem?" The psychologist said: "Oh that, I don't know. I forgot about it." He was clueless. The intellectual knowledge is so important because anything that is off the norm the psychologists will say is pathology.

GE: When I was teaching the Science of Creative Intelligence at California State University in the Interdisciplinary Studies Department in Sacramento, I would bring in guest lecturers. One of them was a professor of Christian Mysticism, and she talked about the dark night of the soul.[2] I was reminded of

---

2   Dark Night of the Soul (Spanish: La noche oscura del alma) is the title of a poem written by 16th-century Spanish poet and Roman Catholic mystic St. John of the Cross, as well as of a treatise he wrote later, commenting on the poem. St. John of the Cross was a Carmelite priest. http://en.wikipedia.org/wiki/Dark_Night_of_the_Soul

There are different interpretations of the poem, but from Maharishi's knowledge it is about the trans-formation of the physiology to experience transcendence. The "dark night of the soul" refers to the anguish the seeker feels after a good experience ends, and they feel the intense contrast between having seemingly achieved the goal and then suddenly reverting back to their prior ignorant, limited reality of stressed mind and body.

her lecture when I read your experience as a child. Many people have this flash of realization, and then do not know how to bring it back, and it is agony.

David: It is agony even if you have the TM technique when those great experiences come and then go. After 40 years of meditating, I have had some periods where I stepped into a much more wonderful reality, and then when it stops it is a disappointment. I was on one of the six-month TM courses in Europe,[3] and at one point I was so clear and integrated I wanted Maharishi to see my progress. When Maharishi arrived for that day's lecture I effortlessly found myself at just the right time and place to greet him, and at the sight of him my awareness expanded into the huge radiant glowing bliss of his presence. He instantly saw my improved condition, greeted me warmly like a friend, and with a gesture that said to me "Now come on, let's enlighten the world," he indicated for me to sit in the front as he went up on the stage to begin to hear experiences of the previous day's rounding[4] from the several hundred radiant souls eager to see him and interact with him. It was just amazing watching him from a coherent physiology. "Knowledge is structured in consciousness"[5]— how one sees the world depends on how coherent one's physiology is. That afternoon in that precious moment in which I had somehow slipped into a higher state of consciousness I saw Maharishi radiating bliss, beauty, clarity, understanding, and infinite fullness of life with every word, every expression, every gesture. He had the clarity of a brilliant diamond, flashing shades of celestial light, not hard or fixed but dynamically and fluidly as he spoke and laughed. His happiness filled the hearts of us all, and several times he looked over at me and I felt blessed with the direct hit of his attention, and I felt proud of myself that I had reached a state where I might actually be useful to his purpose of enlightening the world. I had reached a state where I knew

---

3   During the mid-1970s Maharishi held six-month courses of long meditations in Switzerland, where TM teachers spent the greater part of each day meditating and practicing the TM-Sidhi program. His goal was to speed up our growth toward enlightenment. He met regularly with course participants to hear and comment on experiences and give direction.

4   "Rounding" refers to the sequence of asanas (easy yoga postures to make the body limber and maintain healthy integration), pranayama (a breathing exercise to balance the physiology and settle inward), and the Transcendental Meditation, advanced techniques, and TM-Sidhi programs. Normally, we do two rounds, one in the morning and one in the afternoon. On those advanced courses under Maharishi's supervision we did many rounds.

5   "Knowledge is structured in consciousness" is Maharishi's translation of a verse in the Rig Veda, which he often quoted to make the point on how important it is to develop consciousness as the first priority, because all of human thought and understanding, and hence civilization, depends upon the level of consciousness.

that I did not have to do anything to do good for the world; I just had to be in that state, to hold on to it; but alas, the dark night of the soul you mentioned happened. The next day I started releasing stress from the deep experience of rest that results from maintaining that Transcendental Consciousness for an extended period of time in activity. It was agonizing to have slipped out of this blissful reality—it seemed to evaporate—but it is all about releasing stress and strengthening the nervous system to maintain that reality.

The next day Maharishi went ahead with his usual energy and singular purpose, inspiring, teaching, guiding. I felt bad that I no longer was experiencing and participating in the show in its full glory, but only dimly from the sidelines, seen obscurely through hazy consciousness, but what could I do? It was like when I had that experience of transcending as a child. No amount of effort will make it come back. Trying just pushes it away. You do your best, and let Nature, and your karma, take its course. Straining just slows your evolution. Maharishi often warned: "Do not strain on the knowledge" and his prescription for rapid evolution was to meditate regularly morning and evening *and take it easy*. I always have had a hard time with the "take-it-easy" part. I just didn't get it for a long time, and still have a hard time not trying to push forward.

GE: I had a powerful experience with Maharishi and it was transforming. It appears the nervous system is not wired sufficiently to maintain it. How would you explain that reality? The Sisters said to me that enlightenment is the grace of God. How do you put together science and the grace of God?

David: We have free will, and as individuals we can take action that harms ourselves and others, and we accumulate stress or karmic debt. All the religions and sciences are attempting to find our way back to that enlightened state of reality. The reality described by the ancient traditions is similar to what modern science is discovering.

GE: Dr. Tony Nader, before he became Maharaja, wrote a beautiful book that he put together with Maharishi correlating Vedic Science and the human nervous system (10). Can you summarize that book, because it is complicated?

David: What is being stated in that book is that the structures and functions of the nervous system are the same as the structures and functions of the Veda and Vedic literature (10). The Veda and Vedic literature are commonly understood as books and chanting of the content of the books by the Vedic pandits. Maharishi gave a fresh and original interpretation of the Veda and

Vedic literature, and he has made this timeless knowledge highly relevant for the scientific age (11-25). He has pointed out that what is in the books or what you hear is just the expression on the human level of the cognitions by the ancient Vedic rishis or seers. What they "saw" in their transcendental self-referral level of consciousness, and reported back to us, were the fundamental mechanics of natural law. They observed how the vibratory modes of the unified field of natural law give rise to the different levels of creation.

Modern science has found that all the seemingly solid matter around us is, on a deeper level, just vibrations of underlying quantum fields; the different fields are just modes of a single unified field. This has been inferred from objective observations of modern science. The subjective observation of Vedic science portrays the same picture of the universe, as physicist John Hagelin has shown (12, 26). These vibrations carry the information that organizes all forms and phenomena we see around us. The Veda is like the DNA in the body. The DNA has all the information needed to guide the processes that structure the body. The Veda is like the DNA of the universe, and the Vedic literature is the elaboration of that basic information, which creates all the details. Dr. Nader's brilliant work has found that the human nervous system is an exact replica of the Veda and Vedic literature in the human body. That means that the individual is cosmic, that we all carry within ourselves the same knowledge and organizing power that is continually creating the universe. Religion says that "man is made in the image of God." Dr. Nader's book gives the details of what that "image of God" is, so to speak, and how those different aspects work as our nervous system and physiology. The practical applied value is that the person can listen to a specific part of the Vedic literature to create order and restore health to the corresponding part of the body. If you have a heart condition, listen to the Vedic literature corresponding to the heart to enliven order and heal the heart. A course has been developed, in which the Rig Veda sounds are played in Sanskrit as a general tune-up for the body, and it really works. Rhoda and I did it last summer when we were in Fairfield and it was marvelous.

GE: On your website (www.truthabouttm.org) you have an interesting section written by Dr. Finkelstein on the mantras. How does this fit into the Vedic sounds you have been describing?

David: The TM mantras are sounds that do not have a meaning; they are vibrations known to have a *positive effect on all levels of the nervous system*. This is important, because as one transcends, the mantra becomes progressively finer. In its descent from the surface level thinking to Transcendental Consciousness it is influencing the nervous system on all levels, from the gross sensory level, down through the various subtle strata of the mind, to the completely abstract level of unbounded awareness. It is important that the influence of the mantra be positive on all these levels. You wouldn't want to transcend on just anything. In principle you could transcend on "Coca-Cola." However, you do not know what the effect of that sound would be on the nervous system on its journey to Transcendental Consciousness. We know from the long tradition that the TM mantras have a positive effect on all levels. Furthermore, we know from more than 600 scientific studies that they have good effects on all populations, cultures, age groups, medical conditions, etc.

Maharishi was fond of quoting Guru Dev as saying "safety first." It is not only the mantra, but the correct understanding of the technique and the process of release of stress, which is important. The long-term effects of TM are known. For example, a randomized 18-year study of people who learned TM after they were 50 years old found that after 3 years the TM group had a 91% reduction in death due to all causes compared to controls. After 10 years they had a 40% reduction in death by all causes and after 18 years a 23% reduction (27). We all are going to die sometime, but TM extends life and it is a healthier, happier, and more creative life. Maharishi called longevity the "footprint of the elephant." All the animal footprints can fit into an elephant's footprint. All the different scientific studies on TM fit into longevity. The bottom line is the synthesis of all the studies showing reduced stress, increased creative intelligence, improved social behavior, etc.

GE: Please explain the TM-Sidhi program in the context of the previous discussion of mantras. What do the TM-Sidhis do, and how are they different from TM?

David: The TM-Sidhis are exercises for the mind to perform in that settled, quiet state. During the TM practice you settle into a quiet state, and then with the TM-Sidhis you are exercising different aspects of the mind and different aspects of the senses. What the TM-Sidhi practice does is to train different channels of the mind to function in that pure consciousness state. It is refining the machinery of your nervous system to function in coordination, and have activity along with pure consciousness. It is the same principle as alternating TM practice and daily activity to habituate the nervous system to maintain pure consciousness; only with the TM-Sidhis you are alternating the subtlest impulses of thought with pure consciousness to habituate the system. It is like pumping iron on a very subtle level. When a person wants to build a strong body, he or she exercises all the different muscle groups in sequence. Like that, the different TM-Sidhis are like a set of exercises for developing mind-body coordination through the different channels of the mind in that quiet level of consciousness. The TM-Sidhi techniques expand awareness and accelerate the integration of the entire system.

GE: During the practice of the advanced TM-Sidhi sutra commonly referred to as the flying sutra, there are moments when the body and consciousness are not distinguishable.

David: That's right, when one lifts off, the common experience is that individuals feel like they are just filled with light and bliss, and it is totally effortless. We are hopping on foam mattresses at this point, not flying through the air or levitating, but the effects on the neurophysiology are profound. We conducted an experiment on Yogic Flying in which we looked at the EEG and found that when the body is taking off and people are hopping through the air, the individual's EEG showed he or she was in a very quiet settled inner condition of the alpha state. Normally alpha would be observable only if the person is sitting still and settled inside. During the practice of the TM-Sidhi Yogic Flying technique the subjects are in dynamic activity but the subjective experience is of lightness, happiness, and bliss; it is totally effortless. We used voluntarily jumping around as a control condition. Outwardly it may look the same as TM-Sidhi Yogic Flying, sitting cross-legged on the foam with the eyes closed, and occasionally hopping around. Nevertheless, the EEG and subjective experience are totally different. By contrast, voluntary jumping was jarring and there was no alpha EEG at all. I tried it myself and it was no fun, whereas TM-Sidhi Yogic Flying is *very blissful.* We published a paper in the *International Journal of Neuroscience* regarding the experience (28). The interesting aspect of the TM-Sidhi flying sutra is that the entire body is involved; it is very integrating and the inner pure consciousness is being brought out into gross physical activity. In another experiment, we found that at the moment of liftoff the brain is very coherent in all EEG frequency bands (29), which is what we find when the respiration stops during transcending (30). This indicates that the

TM-Sidhi Yogic Flying is transcending in activity, which means it is developing Cosmic Consciousness.

Additionally, 51 studies have found that the group practice of the TM-Sidhi program has a dramatic effect on the environment. Studies have shown that group practice of the TM-Sidhi program, by as few as the square root of 1% of the population, can have a coherent influence on the entire society. Many of the studies have been published in leading journals (31-44).

GE: I was watching a documentary by Ben Stein evaluating the debate between the Darwinian theory of evolution and intelligent design. The documentary was challenging the Darwinian theory of survival of the fittest versus intelligence in the universe. How do you see that debate in terms of what you have been studying for the last four decades?

David: I think the basic idea of intelligent design is that the universe could not have arisen by chance, but must have been created by some intelligent entity. The opposing idea is that an undirected process of natural selection created the universe and life. Natural selection is the idea that the particular life forms we observe around us, including ourselves, exist as they are because if they were different they would not have survived. So what we see is what has survived in the context of the biosphere of the earth. In different environments different life forms survive. The big issue is how do you explain orderliness in the universe? Say you start out with some primordial energy, or something, then there is a Big Bang, and the entire universe flies apart, forming atoms, stars, black holes, galaxies, including the earth, and eventually, after a few billion years, life. What most scientists think is that there are probably many planets with life. In any event, at every level of creation there is incredible order. I would think that this order must have been inherent in some way in whatever was there at the beginning of creation. There is something about carbon and oxygen atoms and all the rest that causes them to fit together into life forms and, eventually, us. There must be something inherent in fundamental force and matter fields that when they bang around interacting with each other they create life and us. If order is what comes out of this process, then order must have been inherent in it in some way at the beginning. If you have life and intelligence coming out of all these inorganic molecules, then there must be forces inherent within the molecules that cause them to combine that way. Intelligence should be there in the initial state because there is something about the way the charges coagulate together that is not random.

No doubt Darwinian natural selection is working, but it is working in an arena of a profoundly orderly universe. I do not know all the arguments in the debate, but some scientists are battling creationists, who are trying to put God back into the picture. I think that the ultimate reality is the unified field, it being the one without a second (i.e., a unified singularity), and it could only have been created through self-interaction. Creation is through interactions of things with each other. An electron hits an atom and causes a photon to be created, the photoelectric effect. Moreover, if the unified field was the only reality at the beginning of creation, what did it interact with? It must have created through self-interaction, which is the defining characteristic of consciousness, as physicist John Hagelin has pointed out (26). I think the self-interacting dynamics of consciousness gave rise to the universe. In any event, rather than argue about it, science and religion should continue to investigate it. The TM and TM-Sidhi programs are a technology for the subjective investigation of reality on the self-referral level of one's consciousness, which is the same reality as the unified field. This is the direct way to know the fundamental level of the universe, which can only be known from within itself by itself. It is the observer, the instrument of observation and the observed, all in one. Bottom line, religious people and scientists alike need to meditate (laughter).

GE: I think the point you are making is that we have art, religion, and science, and they have compartmentalized their perspectives. They have tried to isolate one from another, like people sitting in the same tree shouting at one another.

David: That's about it. What they will ultimately discover is that all the shouting is coming from the same place, the Self, Transcendental Consciousness. That Self, the universal basis of all of us, is shouting at itself. The Western intellectual world has long been split into the sciences and the humanities, and never the twain shall meet. When I started the TM technique in the 1970s, a British physicist, C.P. Snow, wrote a book about it called *The Two Cultures* and everyone was talking about it. Snow felt this division was a major hindrance to solving the world's problems. His main point was that the elite who were running nations, especially Britain, were highly trained in the humanities, but ignorant of science, which is crucial to making decisions in the modern world. Science played such an important role in winning World War II that policy makers should know about it, Snow argues. They could quote Shakespeare but they were clueless when asked what mass and acceleration were, much less to state the second law of thermodynamics.

I think one of the great achievements Maharishi has contributed is to generate an interdisciplinary perspective that brings all the sciences and humanities together. We teach knowledge at MIU, now MUM, in a coherent interdisciplinary format. Knowledge is always presented from the perspective of unifying principles, which cut across a person's individual experience as well as all the sciences and all the arts. Maharishi has brought out that consciousness is the fundamental element underneath the arts and sciences. All disciplines and all aspects of civilization are based on thinking and the basis of thinking is Transcendental Consciousness. When any person experiences Transcendental Consciousness, whatever their specialty or walk in life, their thinking becomes more orderly and effective because their neurophysiology becomes more integrated. Students of the humanities have a much easier time understanding physics and physicists can enjoy poetry more deeply. Maharishi has unified the "two cultures" at their basis. The world is very slowly waking up to this.

GE: Were you there in the beginning days when they developed MIU?

David: Yes, it was in Santa Barbara—about a dozen of us participated with Maharishi for about a year on and off and developed a plan for the university. The Science of Creative Intelligence, Maharishi's interdisciplinary approach, was the heart of it. We planned out the catalog, which was like the DNA of the university.

GE: I remember meeting with Maharishi in 1971, after I had taught the Science of Creative Intelligence at California State University in Sacramento, in the Interdisciplinary Department for general education credit. We were having a conversation and I mentioned that I did not believe in failing students. Maharishi asked me if I just passed everyone. I replied no, I would give them an Incomplete, and have them re-take the course because it would be better for the student's psychology. You were on the faculty of MIU. What are some of your insights?

David: When we planned the University, I was originally Director of Research, then Chairman of the Psychology Department. I became the director of a successful doctoral program in Psychology and was co-director with Keith Wallace of the Ph.D. program in the Neuroscience of Human Consciousness. We wanted to have laboratories where we were free to study the development of higher states of consciousness. We had terrific graduate students who conducted amazing brilliant research, including the studies on Cosmic Consciousness.

GE: When was MERU established?

David: MERU was established in 1973 in Switzerland.

GE: You had a role at MERU as well as MIU?

David: I was the first Vice-Chancellor of MERU. I was fortunate to spend four years with Maharishi when he established MERU, and we had three goals: to do (a) scientific research, (b) theoretical research, including the relation-ship of the principles of physics, chemistry, and biology to the principles of consciousness, and (c) experiential research. All of the TM teachers came for periods of rest and advanced training; the teachers would go deep into TM in beautiful settings in the Alps to accelerate their evolution of consciousness, and then go back out into the field to teach. That was the experiential research, which was the basis of it all. We scientists had the opportunity to study their experiences and then sit with Maharishi, and discuss the principles of science. He was mainly interested in the more fundamental sciences, physics and math-ematics, but the chemists and physiologists made points too. I summarized the main findings of psychology too, but what Maharishi was saying about consciousness and enlightenment was the highest psychology that one could ever imagine. So I mainly listened to the others and summarized what they and Maharishi said when it came my turn to speak (laughter). Maharishi brought out the TM-Sidhi program during that time.

GE: Can you elaborate?

David: At MERU Maharishi introduced the TM-Sidhi program. Maharishi had the scientists read Patanjali's Yoga Sutras and discuss how the TM-Sidhis might be possible from the perspective of the most advanced principles of modern science. Most of the conversations were with the physicists regarding quantum mechanics, and what happens when you settle down to fundamental levels, where you observe superfluidity and superconductivity. For example, when you cool helium to near absolute zero, it becomes a superfluid with no friction, so when you stir it, it keeps stirring forever like a perpetual motion machine. Also, it will creep up the side of the container and out of it if it is not sealed. That's called superfluidity. In a superconducting wire if you start a current it will circulate forever.

Such super phenomena are the norm on the more fundamental level of natural laws, although they seem extraordinary in the relatively high temperature macroscopic world in which we live. Coherence rules the universe at its basis, and Maharishi was saying that when human consciousness learns to operate from that deepest level of natural law, the TM-Sidhis will become commonplace. The word "sidhi" means perfection, and the list of sidhis sounds like supernormal powers, such as the ability to know anything, celestial sense perception, or Yogic Flying. Recently, physicists have found evidence of macroscopic quantum coherent effects, and it may be how the brain works.

Some commentators on the sidhis have said that they are a distraction, that they take the aspirant off the path of gaining enlightenment for the sake of some limited special abilities. However, Maharishi's point of view, which I mentioned before, was that they are like a set of exercises that exercise all the different parts of the mind and body to integrate the wholeness of enlightenment. Patanjali called his work on the sidhis the Yoga Sutras. Maharishi commented that "sutra" means "thread" and "Yoga" means "union" or "unity," so the Yoga Sutras are the threads that stitch together Unity Consciousness, the highest level of enlightenment. Maharishi was the master of making abstract topics very concrete. The enlightened wise, he said, know that the infinite totality of Unity Consciousness is the goal; they also know that the seekers cannot fathom infinite totality, and are therefore pursuing many limited goals. The seeker may go for the super abilities but what they receive is something much greater, the totality of the universe in their own minds, and in doing so they actually gain enlightenment.

GE: Do you remember years ago Dr. Posner from San Francisco State University, who presented a film called *Powers of 10?*[6]

David: Yes, you can see a version of it on YouTube.

GE: I found it interesting because I played the tape in an Art Appreciation class and asked the students how it made them feel. The reactions were diverse—some of the students felt afraid, and others felt expanded. From your background how do you interpret the different reactions?

David: How people see it depends on how their physiology is functioning and their level of consciousness. The idea is that knowledge is structured

---

6   Powers of 10 http://www.youtube.com/watch?v=0fKBhvDjuy0

in consciousness; or, saying it another way, the world is as we are. An anxious person will interpret things in a fearful way. All that expansion out to the end of the universe, or human life being so tiny in the universe, could make one feel fearful, if one has a lot of fear, or expanded if one is well balanced and happy. It is well documented in psychology with projective tests, such as the inkblot test, that people will interpret even completely abstract patterns depending on their psychological makeup. Some will see beauty, others will see scary things. Research on TM has shown that people's perception becomes more positive, due to the normalization of their stresses and experiences of transcending (45).

GE: It is very difficult for the average individual to comprehend the concept of unbounded consciousness, and the reason I brought up that film, *Powers of 10*, is because of your comments on the symptoms of Cosmic Consciousness discovered from your earlier research.

David: We were measuring and showing the brainwaves of transcending coexisting with the brainwaves of other states, the most challenging one being sleep. The nervous system has become sufficiently flexible through the regular TM practice to maintain the physiology of pure consciousness during sleep—and everyone enjoys that feeling, similar to what I experienced as a child, except in Cosmic Consciousness it does not go away!

GE: On your website you pose the question: is transcending mystical?

David: From the waking state mind, when someone begins to discuss transcending, the description of the experience just seems like words, a concept, or a theory. When people hear that some person has had this experience of unbounded awareness, they think that it is just some mystical idea, or an altered state of consciousness. The experience is often interpreted as an aberration of the waking state.

Everyone knows that different drugs can cause different perceptual distortions and other effects. Therefore, people may believe transcending is one of those altered states of the waking state, when in fact it is a completely normal, healthy fourth major state of consciousness. The difference between drugs and transcending is that drugs damage the nervous system, and transcending facilitates a natural and healthy integration, which carries over into activity. Maslow spoke about the idea of cognizing Being, which was having an expanded view of life, mostly in activity although it could be during meditation.[7] Maslow called people having these types of experiences the "culture givers." They were the Einsteins, the Mozarts, the great artists, scientists, and businesspeople. It is a very natural state.

GE: When you speak about scientific discoveries you have been mentioning they have a spiritual dimension. John Locke stated that the purpose of science was to explore and understand the very nature of reality. How do you see the relationship of science and spirituality?

David: Einstein said that all of the good scientists he knew had a spiritual dimension. He said: "Everyone who is seriously involved in the pursuit of science becomes convinced that a spirit is manifest in the laws of the Universe—a spirit vastly superior to that of man, and one in the face of which we, with our modest powers, must feel humble." It is a holistic vision of reality. I believe many scientists feel that science is a spiritual quest, because as you explore deeper into the laws of nature you are investigating how the universe is constructed, and it is just amazing. I remember in El Paso one of the TM practitioners wanted me to speak with her husband, a Ph.D. who studied spiders. We drove out into the desert to their home, and he showed us projected on a large screen an electron-microscope picture of the legs of a spider. It was the most incredible geometric pattern of swirling designs and protruding barbs. It was absolutely amazing, awe-inspiring beauty of order in the universe that would send chills up your spine, on the leg of a spider! I could really appreciate his enthusiasm.

Maharishi said that any knowledge you explore is charming. As science has progressed it has expanded our perception of life. It has taught us that we are a dot in the cosmos, and that we are a cosmos in and of ourselves composed of billions of cells. Science is a spiritual pursuit, and TM exercises the ability of the mind to slip into those quieter levels and see things more profoundly, which is a great aid in the pursuit of science or any discipline. I keep coming back to the little boy who you taught, regarding the trees looking prettier.

GE: Maharishi offered a formula in which we do not have to compartmentalize knowledge, and yet compartmentalization was created in some situations to protect people from extremism.

---

7   Abraham Maslow, one of the founders of Humanistic Psychology, studied the higher levels of human development, which he called self-actualization. http://en.wikipedia.org/wiki/Abraham_Maslow

David: What Maharishi provided is a technique, a nondenominational, non-religious, and non-cultural technique where everyone can access these subtler levels of his or her consciousness.

GE: However, it starts to shake people's tree.

David: It is ironic, and it is only out of lack of knowledge, and those religions that are fear-based. They are opposing the very reality they are ultimately seeking. I had a friend who was raised as a fundamentalist, and she said they were afraid of losing what they had.

GE: That could work in science as well.

David: Yes. There are some scientists who go after anything spiritual because they believe they are defending science and objectivity; these are always people who have a narrow view of the materialist paradigm. It is fine if you want to reduce everything to finer levels of physical matter. DNA is a molecule, a string of atoms, and those atoms can be further reduced down to subatomic particles of electrons, positrons, neutrons, and so forth. These particles can be further reduced to finer particles, then to matter and energy fields, fermions and bosons. Spirituality is only not found in the reductionist worldview when it does not reduce far enough.

What is the basis of all the fundamental forces and fields? The physicists who keep looking deeper say that the universe appears to be a great mind at its basis; it is consciousness. The universe is self-interacting and self-referral at its fundamental level. It creates from interaction with itself like the mind does. Reductionism needs to keep on reducing until it arrives at the deepest level, and that is where it meets with all the great religions and the great philosophies in the world.

GE: Let me step back to 1972 in Fiuggi,[8] and perhaps you can explain how you became more involved as a spokesperson for the research.

David: One day in the middle of my TM program there was a knock and the person said with great import that "someone wanted to talk to me." So I put on my suit, and went in the car up the hill to the old part of Fiuggi, to a large building where Maharishi held meetings. I was very excited, of course, and on full alert. At that time I was coherent enough that I felt I could actually produce some full sentences and express some

---

8   Maharishi held a TM Teacher Training Course for about 3,000 participants in Fiuggi Fonte, Italy in 1972.

connected thoughts, a performance that had eluded me on my previous face-to-face encounters with Maharishi. When I came in, I saw Maharishi and Keith and a few people walking among some large displays and discussing them. Maharishi loved making large beautiful displays illustrating his main ideas, and I later worked on some of those. The atmosphere around him was filled with light, charged with that special quality of intelligence and soft effusion of bliss that always surrounded him. I felt such a wave of love and thankfulness for Maharishi I just folded my hands in Namaste,[9] he just greeted me warmly and walked over to his couch, motioning us to sit in the chairs set facing it.

There was a very practical reason for me to be there. Maharishi had the idea of illustrating all the scientific findings on TM in a simple chart book. Each study would have a graphic and three or four lines of text explaining the results in simple language for the public. He wanted me to make a chart on my findings of autonomic stability and habituation rate, and asked me about every detail. What impressed Maharishi about my study was that so many things could be concluded from it. I told him that the Air Force had found that people who had greater autonomic stability had a greater ability to withstand g-forces in a centrifuge. This was important to the Air Force for selecting pilots who would not black out under extreme acceleration. Other studies found that more stable subjects were less anxious and had greater ego strength, which means an increased ability to adapt to challenges. Recent studies by Fred Travis showed that more rapid habituation to a stressor is correlated with greater brain integration, and is higher in top athletes than ordinary athletes (46). Another study on Vietnam veterans with post-traumatic stress disorder (PTSD) used my measure of stress habituation, because one of the symptoms of PTSD is the startle response—a sudden loud noise and suddenly they are back on the battlefield. That study found that after 3 months of TM practice the vets habituated in half the trials, and they also decreased on all PTSD symptoms such as decreased depression, anxiety, and emotional numbness (47).[10] This study on veterans came later.

---

9   Maharishi interprets Namaste as "The infinity in me sees the infinity in you."

10   Similar reductions in PTSD symptoms through TM have also been found with American vets of the Iraq war and war refugees in the Congo. Rosenthal J, Grosswald S, Ross R, Rosenthal N. Effects of Transcendental Meditation (TM) in Veterans of Operation Enduring Freedom (OEF) and Operation Iraqi Freedom (OIF) with Posttraumatic Stress Disorder (PTSD): a Pilot Study. Military Medicine. 2011;176(6):626. (48)

I told Maharishi about a broad spectrum of different studies, which had shown that the flexibility and fast recovery of the nervous system through TM practice is an observable function with broad implications. He wanted to know every detail about all the studies, but all too soon I had said everything I knew about the subject and it was over, even though I kept trying to think of more to say because I wanted to extend the meeting.

Nate, David, Rhoda and Sara Orme-Johnson, Santa Barbara, California 1973

GE: Tell me what happened after Fiuggi and what it was like to spend those four years at MERU with Maharishi.

David: After Teacher Training, Rhoda and I and the children went back to El Paso. We taught TM and continued our day jobs at UTEP. In 1973, I was invited to participate in a tour of Scandinavia with Maharishi and a group of scientists and educators. Following the tour he invited me to come back to Switzerland, and then invited Rhoda and the children to come over. Maharishi's international staff of about 100 people moved around as a group into off-season hotels, high in the mountains in the ski resort hotels in the summer, and down by Lake Lucerne in the winter, and had a permanent place in Seelisberg. Maharishi had the TM teachers coming to do longer meditations and we set up a laboratory to study their development of consciousness. Maharishi gathered a group of academics, and the idea came up to start a university there, which became MERU.

GE: Did you spend four years in Seelisberg or did you move around?

David: We moved around with Maharishi, and during that time there would be different trips. There would be a tour of India or England.

GE: Did you have an opportunity to interact regularly with Maharishi?

David: Yes, I saw him daily. Sometimes I would ride in a car, or sit on an airplane with him, always doing business, talking about science, or making charts and presentations. That was tough sometimes because I would get carsick writing on those winding Swiss mountain roads (laughter).

GE: I was fortunate to spend time with Maharishi, and it enhanced my consciousness. In the East the evolutionary experience of being in the presence of an enlightened person is called *darshan*—it is an abstract concept to people in the West, but there is no question those four years you worked with Maharishi must have been a tremendous facilitator for your evolution. Can you explain the human transformation that took place in your life as a result of this proximity?

David: It is hard to describe because we were totally focused on what Maharishi was doing, on writing pamphlets or whatever. Being with him would become almost commonplace, like this was how life should be, and when you would have to leave, it was a huge contrast. When we were coming and going from MERU one time—Keith Wallace and I were en route to a conference—we were on a bus and Maharishi was discussing with us points to be presented at the conference. When we finished the conversation the bus pulled over to the side of the autobahn, we got off, and a car that had been following along picked us up and we went to the airport. The contrast of being with Maharishi in this blissful atmosphere—and interacting with his incredible intelligence made you feel you were in the most important center of the world and participating in facilitating the evolution of human civilization—from that atmosphere we stepped off the bus on the autobahn with stinky exhaust from cars whizzing by in the bleak, cold, rainy evening, and watched Maharishi's bus pull away without us. It took a major adjustment to switch to a more mundane environment.

At times I would be sitting on the stage with Maharishi, and interacting with him was a gift. Maharishi attracted Nobel Prize winners and brilliant leaders from around the world in every field. My role was helping set things up, and I had the opportunity to witness the whole thing while continuing my research. I did some of the first research on the TM-Sidhi program and Yogic Flying and was involved in the research on transcending. One of my main roles was as an interpreter of the research and to make it available to the TM teachers and the public. I had the ability of a science writer to take complex subjects, understand them well enough, and be able to express them in a simple way.

Maharishi had created the idea of a chart book, which was started in Fiuggi, and I had continued to be involved in that process. When Maharishi was first preparing to have the chart book printed, I was back in the U.S. after Fiuggi; I received a call from Jerry Jarvis, the national leader of the TM movement in the U.S. Jerry said that Maharishi wanted to print millions of copies. He wanted every household in America to have a copy of this little booklet, "and he wants you to edit it," Jerry told me. Yikes, what a responsibility. I was to ensure the accuracy of the booklet, and I continued in that role while working for Maharishi. I made numerous charts while I was around Maharishi, and I was interested in collecting the research. Many people were doing research, but they did not often display their results in a graphic way that summarized their important findings.

It was a golden opportunity for me as a scientist. I was like the cartoon character Scrooge McDuck, but my gold and treasure was the research. I loved the research because it was showing that this very abstract experience and knowledge had this amazing effect. It was telling the age-old story of enlightenment in terms of scientific research. What a great thing to be part of, I thought. The research was arriving from throughout the world, and I was collecting it. In this way, I became the editor of *Scientific Research on Maharishi's Transcendental Meditation Programme: Collected Papers Volume 1* with John Farrow (49).

A lot of people worked on *Collected Papers*. John and I were involved in all the details, such as overseeing the typesetting and the printing, and generally keeping an eye on it. That was Maharishi's method, to have the authors follow their work through the entire printing process, often staying up all night. The atmosphere around Maharishi was a highly contrasting combination of great laughter and fun combined with a gut-wrenching feeling of urgency. He did not waste a moment trying to help the world. He maintained that "we are absolutely serious about remaining non-serious." Happiness was our greatest weapon in the war on the sadness of the world. There was never anything forced or melodramatic or unnatural about it. It was just the way things were around Maharishi.

GE: I would like to state that you are one of the few scientists that do not put me to sleep, and your commentaries made complicated research understandable. When I was a biology student they gave us a book called *To Know a Fly.* The purpose of the book was for the students to gain insight into how some scientists and academics protect his or her arena of power by creating language that separates them from the layperson.

David: That's right.

GE: What are your goals regarding the Truth About TM website?

David: I am planning on making it into a blog or to have a blog in it.

GE: I think that could be a good idea because of the way you explain things. Your interpretation of complicated experiences, research, and situations is almost unparalleled. People misunderstand what you have described about the presence of Maharishi. Maharishi was an enlightened human being, and that enlightenment produced a certain kind of energy and presence that is almost impossible to describe. It affects the consciousness of people around him.

You have talked about coherence and percentages of meditators raising the collective consciousness. Maharishi produced a similar effect for the people around him. How would you describe that experience and reality from a scientific point of view?

David: Maharishi always said enlightenment was normal human functioning. Instead of saying it was higher, he took the angle: no, this is not higher; this is how we should all be, every man and woman on the planet. However, we are not—we are like a planet of immature pre-adolescents. Another aspect of it is that to have been around Maharishi you had to be natural and normal. I remember one time working on the MIU catalog with about ten faculty and we were discussing how we were going to create the University. I was thinking to myself: I am sitting here with the personification of the total potential of natural law. I was feeling overwhelmed by Maharishi and he did not want that energy. Maharishi made a comment that indicated I needed to relax. If a person had a lot of stress it might be difficult to relax because Maharishi's coherence would produce a release of stress similar to the Maharishi Effect. The deep coherence Maharishi was emanating had the tendency to facilitate coherence in those around him. Thoreau wrote in *Walden*: I have never met a man who was fully awake—how could I look him in the face? Well, here is Maharishi; he is fully awake and as a result you start becoming fully awake; the entire transformation begins to take place and results in what we call normalizing. It is as if you are a caterpillar turning into a butterfly, and the transition stage is a "mess." That is what biologists call the transition stage in the cocoon, a mess. That is what I was (laughter).

GE: You explained the one percent effect, but how do you explain Maharishi's physiology and the indescribable effect his physiology had on those around him?

David: We viewed Maharishi as having a normally functioning physiology, which means perfectly coherent, in which all the systems are working together perfectly. What that means is the human nervous system has the ability to express the total potential of natural law. Then everything the person thinks, says, and does is the expression of the evolutionary impulse of natural law.

GE: People often personify their human perception of the ineffable forces of natural law. How else could that be expressed?

David: The natural tendency of our mind is to move toward more and more, and the mind moves effortlessly to the more sublime levels of natural law, which are drawing the individual mind toward them because they are so charming.

GE: You have observed the entire evolution of scientific research on TM, and how it affects people in different environments. I remember sitting in a California Department of Corrections grant meeting. I watched the board members allocate $500,000 for out of cell time with no research documenting the value of the program. The TM program had provided research and did not receive a penny—I learned that grants and politics were in a marriage. Dr. Bleick's cost analysis, and then Dr. Alexander and his associates' 15-year follow-up, have established that a technology exists and is available to reduce recidivism, but political integrity and ethical decision-making are necessary to bring that knowledge into practice.

David: The same thing happened to Dr. Alexander when he finished his dissertation at Harvard, on moral reasoning and ego development, which is a non-fakeable measurement, on maximum security prisoners in Walpole Prison in Massachusetts. Alexander found that after a couple of years of practicing TM, the prisoners came to a higher level of development than Harvard graduates had reached in their entire four years at Harvard (laughter) (50-52). Yet there was no funding to continue the program. They just said great, keep on volunteering. The same thing happened to me in the La Tuna prison. I demonstrated that with the prisoners meditating regularly, their nervous systems became more stable (53). However, La Tuna Prison had no continuation of the program.

In my opinion, and it is beginning to happen, in order for TM to be accepted in society, other people need to be able to make money from it. This is happening in a medical nursing school in San Diego where they teach Maharishi's Ayurveda programs as a complementary medical program, and they receive part of the funds from teaching people. In the prisons we need to consider making a similar arrangement because it is all about the money, the finances, and protecting jobs.

GE: One of the possibilities to take care of controversy and everything else—teachers of TM should be hired by departments of correction of different institutions.

David: That model could also work.

GE: In reviewing the research on TM in the area of corrections, substance abuse, residential treatment facilities, and behavioral changes, can you summarize the research conducted?

David: I believe we have demonstrated that TM works for rehabilitation in many different ways that are cross-validating. They go together. The autonomic nervous system controls all the internal homeostatic processes that keep the body alive—the heart, lungs, and digestion, for example. Most of these processes are automatic and we are not aware of them; hence the name "autonomic," like automatic. An integrated and stable autonomic system forms the basis for more flexible behavior. The autonomic stability produced by TM is not the frozen stability of convicts that do not have any feelings. The kind of stability TM produces is based on integration and balance of the system, not making it uptight. For example, I found that increased autonomic stability through TM was correlated with faster recovery from stress.

Your research, George, with Susan Gore and Alan Abrams in the Vermont prison system showed a wide array of holistic changes through TM. You found improved quality of sleep, decreased anxiety, decreased hostility, decreased paranoia, better control of anger, more internal control of behavior. Increased locus of control is exactly what we want in rehabilitation. We want the offender to become more self-controlled and to have a more stress free normal functioning nervous system, and you found that the staff really benefited from TM, too. That is very important. The accumulated evidence for the benefits of TM in corrections is overwhelming: (a) on psychological issues, research has shown reductions in hostility, fearfulness, and depression (50, 52, 54); (b) substance abuse, that decreases (55, 56); (c) on more objective factors like rule violations—you find they are not violating the rules as much, and they are participating more in constructive programs that the prison might offer (54); and (d) the return to prisons compared with controlled subjects decreases (51, 57-61). There is a 40% recidivism reduction due to TM shown in well-controlled studies (59).

Furthermore, if you look at the biochemistry associated with crime, it is the same as the biochemistry associated with stress. Dr. Ken Walton has reviewed that research and shown that the physiological changes produced by TM are in the opposite direction of that kind of pH. The research has been demonstrated from every possible direction, not to mention the collective effects; if you have people in prison practicing TM together—we predict not only will the TM program have a beneficial effect on that population, but on the surrounding areas (31, 34, 35, 37, 38, 62). The research has been done and it establishes the validity of the TM program's effectiveness in highly stressed environments.

GE: When you were in Switzerland you facilitated the MERU Index for Rehabilitation. Please clarify the goal of that index.

David: The MERU Rehabilitation Index was basically Maharishi's idea. Maharishi had the idea of a physiological report card for MIU, in which the students could measure their progress, including brainwave measurements, and physiological and psychological tests. In the context of rehabilitation it came up as the MERU Index. I cannot pinpoint who exactly came up with the name because around Maharishi everything was done collaboratively. An academic would do a big review of what everyone said about a field and Maharishi would integrate it and make comments. Maharishi was always totally fresh, creative, and original. The people around Maharishi provided a channel for his wisdom because of the specialized training of the individuals in the group. We provided Maharishi a channel and a language for the completely abstract and universal knowledge to flow. A researcher asked Maharishi what was the difference between an enlightened simple person working in a grocery store, and an enlightened great physicist. Maharishi stated, as far as his or her subjective experience and his or her influence on society goes, they are not different. They will both live unbounded awareness. However, the difference will be that the person who has the education will provide a channel to communicate the ancient knowledge. The simple man or woman will have a wonderful effect on society but may not be able to make advances in different areas of specialization, because they don't know about it. They do not know what the concepts or issues are, nor have the technical terminology to communicate any insights that they might have.

Maharishi wanted to talk to the greatest minds in the world, the great intellects and Nobel Prize winners, and he did: Buckminster Fuller, Melvin Calvin, Ilya Prigogine, Brian Josephson, Jonas Salk, and George Sudarshan, to name a few. I was fortunate to listen to all these amazing conversations. The conversations would become very technical at times, and Maharishi was always right in there, leading the conversation. His purpose was to thoroughly integrate this ancient wisdom of which he was the living embodiment into every phase of modern understanding. Maharishi wanted all of his teachers of TM to obtain Ph.D.s. The reason is because they would know the language of their specific area of knowledge. When they became enlightened, they would be more useful to society than if they were enlightened but uneducated. From Maharishi's perspective society needs to be rehabilitated on every level to employ the full potential of the mind and perfect health. Hence, the idea of an index was to have some objective measure of the development of enlightenment that we had originally provided to our students. The MERU Index was the physiological report card of how the prisoners were doing.

GE: How would you enrich the MERU Index?

David: More research has taken place since the first MERU Index. I believe the first addition would be the Brain Integration Index developed by Fred Travis, which is a composite of EEG coherence, and some other aspects of how the brain reacts when it is anticipating something to happen (63). Travis's research has shown the Index to be valid in distinguishing high levels of performance in business and athletics compared with lower levels (46). This research seems to be a valid measure of development. Therefore, I would add this measure for evaluation to the Index. Increased orderliness of brain functioning is key to successful rehabilitation. I would also add the skin resistance habituation measurements that I used in my early studies. They also seem to be a valid measure of general development. For example, Travis and his colleagues have found faster habituation in top managers. I would also keep field independence, because it seems to measure broad comprehension and the ability to maintain focus. People who are meditating have more field independence, which means they are faster in locating the target of their attention in a complex scene, are less distracted by complexity, and are less vulnerable to social pressure. Social psychologists have conducted research placing social pressure on the subjects, and individuals with higher field independence do not respond to the pressure. They go by their own internal gyroscope of what they think is right, not by what other people are trying to make them do or think. This has strong implications for crime reduction, in which negative peer pressure is a major influence.

GE: How does this correlate to Dr. Alexander's research on moral reasoning and TM?

David: It's related because there are different stages of moral reasoning. The highest stage of moral reasoning is people who reason because of broad principles such as the Golden Rule. I would add moral reasoning to the MERU Index, and also an ego development scale. Ego development is not something that can be faked. It is an open-ended questionnaire, and independent experts look at what people say and they have a scale that can rate the individual's overall maturity and development.

GE: Many youthful offenders in the California Youth Authority were able to manipulate their behavior to meet the behavioral objectives to accelerate their release from prison. This is an important point in determining the validity of the outcomes of testing.

David: Yes, they are "cons," and they are expert in conning you, and they are really good at it (laughter). Nevertheless, the Brain Integration Scale and habituation rate cannot be manipulated.

GE: We have put so much attention on prisoners. As you mentioned, the Index was originally designed to measure student development. I have observed the behavior of correctional professionals and how they were dealing with the inmates when not viewed by the public. What I viewed in many officers was fear and a false toughness. For example, in most county correctional facilities you can have male and female sheriffs who are dealing with men and women in a county jail setting; some officers believe they could control the environment through inmate peer pressure, or that the officer could control the environment. Furthermore, I watched a female officer lock down the entire unit as a penalty for a disparaging remark from one individual. The MERU Index needs to be tested, however. I have been considering examining the MERU Index by focusing on inmates and staff. Management or organizational leadership is in the hands of the line officers. The entire environment can be changed by the actions of the staff.

David: Definitely the staff should learn, as you discovered in Vermont. It offers an opportunity for a longitudinal study, but it needs support by the institution. My previous research indicated a strong correlation to regularity of practice and benefits of TM, which is critical, and the staff needs to be on board to make the time and space for inmates (and themselves) to meditate.

GE: Do you know about the research on the veterans?

David: Yes, the first study on TM and PTSD was conducted on Vietnam veterans at the VA Hospital in Boulder, Colorado with across the board positive changes (47). More recently, Dr. Norman Rosenthal at NIH has done a pilot study and has found the same thing, and that is being expanded into a bigger study (48).

GE: You have studied the research on many meditation techniques. What are the conclusions of your comparisons of techniques and programs for reducing stress and human development?

David: First, TM is far more effective. It is systematically taught around the world by highly trained certified teachers. In addition, the teachers have a checking technique that gives the meditator just the right start of TM and it is very subtle. The world is goal directed and our tendency is to try harder if something is not working for us. However, trying harder is counterproductive with TM, and the TM teachers have a procedure to bring us back to an easy and effortless path. It is delicate to learn how to let go and transcend.

GE: In this context on your website you say TM cannot produce harm. Regarding what you have been discussing, if people begin to practice without any guidance from a certified TM instructor they may not have the knowledge of how to manage stress release, which can result in confusion on how to meditate correctly.

David: TM simply takes the mind from active mental activity to quieter states of consciousness. Physiologically it produces a deep rest. Rest is universally good, as long as you don't overdo it. The TM program is a balance of rest and normal activity. The activity phase is an important part of it, because it allows the benefits of TM to be infused into daily life.

Problems can develop if a person has a pre-existing condition of a lot of stress. They may suddenly find that they are having a lot of negative thoughts during TM, or some physical symptoms. It is due to stresses being normalized by the extra deep rest they are getting. They need to know that information, and to know to take it easy, lie down after meditation, or don't jump up quickly, which could result in too much contrast and some irritability during the day. A person practicing TM should always take 2-3 minutes to come back into activity. Problems are very few with the TM technique because the TM practice is a self-correcting process. Deep rest causes the stress normalization, but normalization of stresses brings one out of rest, and slows the process of stress release. During stress release the physiology is brought up to a higher level of metabolism, and that automatically slows down the stress release, until the person is no longer in the grip of those particular thoughts or sensations. Then a person practicing the TM technique returns inward to transcending, and starts again on an inward settling. New meditators need to understand the process of stress normalization. It is the greatest benefit of TM. Keeping in touch with the teacher to answer questions, and checking their TM practice is helpful.

GE: As a psychologist you are aware that in psychotherapy people are taken through a process of analyzing all the stress and negativity, which is more dangerous than the mechanical release of stress experienced during TM.

David: Yes, because a principle of how the mind works is: that to which you give your attention grows stronger in your life. For example, if there is a book on the shelf and you have never read it, then it has no effect on you, but once you read it then it has a whole world of meaning. If you put your attention on negativity, those qualities will grow in your life. Your physiology will react to the negativity and drag you down. I know people who believe that in order to do something for the world, they have to watch all the news and keep track of all the negativity, as if their paying attention to it will help the situation—it does not. It just puts a damper on life. Psychotherapy systematically puts attention on negativity and can be damaging. It may increase a person's understanding of the origin of his or her stress, but knowing that does not eliminate the problem, and to trace back to the ultimate source may be impossible. Maybe you have some problem because of some problem your mother had, and when you look into her situation, she was that way because of some problem her mother had, or father. The idea is that you can trace problems back and back through history and never come to the end of it. Who are you going to blame: Eve, or Adam, or Cain? Even if you had complete knowledge of the lineage of your problems, what good will that do you? With TM, it does not matter what the origin of the problem was. You just eliminate the physiological basis of the stress and that is it. You do not have to think much about it, and that is a great blessing.

GE: Intellectual understanding of a problem is not sufficient to eliminate it.

David: No. The wisdom of the body has all these self-repair mechanisms built in and in order to use them, the body needs to be put to rest. Ordinary rest of sleep releases stress and repairs the body, but TM provides another kind of rest, a coherent rest that releases long-term deep-rooted stress that sleep does not touch. TM is such a natural process that the release may not even be noticed. For example, my wife, after we had been meditating about six months, was looking for something in the medicine cabinet and she noticed a bottle of aspirin that was sitting in the back collecting dust. She reflected on how she had been taking aspirin every day before learning TM and had not been taking it for a couple of months because her headaches had gone away, and she had not even thought about it until she saw the bottle. Often people do not make the connection.

GE: I want to ask you about your research published in the *Journal of Offender Rehabilitation*. Was this a book?

David: It was a special volume that had four different issues all together entitled *Transcendental Meditation and Criminal Rehabilitation and Crime Prevention*; the *Journal* brought it out as a book (64).

GE: Is this book a synopsis of the accomplishments of the TM program in corrections?

David: Yes. The book covers all the range from biochemical changes produced by TM, which are in the opposite direction of those associated with crime, to the Maharishi Effect, in which groups of meditators reduce crime throughout society by radiating coherence into collective consciousness. Most of the research we talked about earlier is in it.

GE: How would you summarize the foundation of the research to date and what would you anticipate in future research?

David: I believe the most amazing aspect of the research is that it affects all dimensions of human life. Future research will continue to unfold new dimensions of this holistic development through new measurements such as neuroimaging. I did a study with functional Magnetic Resonance Imaging (MRI) which showed meditators' brains exhibit less of a reaction to pain, coinciding with their being less distressed by it (65). But that is just the beginning. We will discover new, better measures of enlightenment, and as the higher states of enlightenment unfold, we will have new subjects to measure. We have just scratched the surface studying Transcendental Consciousness, the 4th state, and Cosmic Consciousness, the 5th state. There is also refined Cosmic Consciousness, the 6th state, and Unity Consciousness, the 7th state in Maharishi's Seven States of Consciousness (11, 13, 66, 67). Research is going to continue for hundreds of years; as individuals evolve into higher states of consciousness, and as scientific methods evolve, new and more sophisticated techniques will be available to study the benefits of TM.

GE: What additional research do you consider has practical value?

David: Aging is number one. There are good randomized studies demonstrating that TM increases longevity. The early studies were on biological markers, such as near point vision, blood pressure, and vital capacity. You could put together these different measures into an index and then you could look on a chart, and determine the person has the physiology of a 28-year-old. My wife and I visited Keith's laboratory when we turned 40. Rhoda had a physiology that measured 28! I came out to be 29—she is six months older than I am. I always wanted to be older than her, so I was happy about the result. Keith's study found that the biological age of meditators was on average 12 years younger than their chronological age (68).

New research parameters are now being studied, such as the hormone DHEA, which tends to decrease with age, and it seems to have a function in the immune system in keeping the body vital and strong. Research has shown that DHEA does not drop as much in older TM practitioners (69). In my health insurance study for Blue Cross Blue Shield I looked at 2,000 TM practitioners over a 5-year period, and when they were broken down by age group I found the younger children up to 18, and the young adults from 18 to 40, had about a 50% lower sickness rate than people in a normative comparison group. The people over 40 were at about 68% less illness. The study shows the practical value of meditating and reducing stress on a daily basis—that a person does not age as fast and is healthier when they get older.

The aging research is so global in its implications that it is inclusive of all other research results. It is completely objective, and it is the bottom line. Well-controlled longitudinal studies show that TM practitioners actually live longer, and they are also healthier, happier, and clearer in their thinking (27, 71-73).

GE: Every time I observe the battle in Washington over the health care bill I see that the politician's idea of prevention is doctor visits rather than actually preventing illness. How do you see this debate?

David: The debate is not about health care; it is about sickness care. Our government should focus more on prevention, and that would be health care.

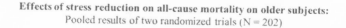

Effects of stress reduction on all-cause mortality on older subjects:
Pooled results of two randomized trials (N = 202)

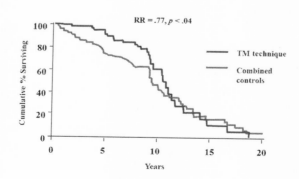

An 18-year follow-up study of 202 people who learned the TM technique when they were 50 to 80 years old found that the meditators lived on average over 2 years longer than controls who had practiced other techniques (27, 73).

The government should permit Medicare to subsidize seniors learning the various Ayurveda techniques, and any other alternative medicine technique that works. This could save the country billions of dollars, not to mention making the country stronger and relieving human suffering. Studies have shown that a small percentage of the population uses the vast majority of our medical resources, and research has shown that when the highest users learn TM, their usage decreased dramatically (74-76).

GE: I think of the Bill Gates Foundation funding programs after the pathology has arisen.

David: Bill Gates is doing great things. It would be greater if he could fund a worldwide study on the effect of TM on general prevention of disease. That would be a great research project.

GE: The late Doug Henning always tried to create wonder in his performance for the audience to expand their consciousness. The utilization of science and the transcending of mysticism are going to facilitate new discoveries.

David: Yes, and it will be enriching to all the mystical traditions because the participants in those traditions will realize that what they are doing is real.

GE: Perhaps with the children who have learned TM at a younger age, as the evolution of their higher state of consciousness becomes a living day-to-day reality, it may present unique physiological functioning to evaluate and greater appreciation of what is now available to them.

David: Yes, Maharishi's final message to us was: "Give the knowledge to the children. They will know what to do with it." I was down in Yucatan a couple of years ago and asked a very knowledgeable Mayan guide if their children were any different. He said "Oh yes, they are way ahead of the adults." Many traditions believe the world is more developed spiritually. There is a flooding of spiritual knowledge into the world now. Traditions are going back in time, Maharishi said, rediscovering their deeper, more profound spiritual roots. I believe Maharishi paved the way for this.

GE: That is such an important statement. I want to transfer from this beautiful exposition that you provided, to you as an artist. You have created some wonderful art and I am wondering where this came from after all these years of scientific research?

David: That is where I started. Art was my technique of spiritual development before I learned TM. When I was in college at Columbia I took many art classes and I achieved straight A's in art, but no straight A's in anything else (laughter). In graduate school in experimental psychology, I convinced my thesis advisor, Dr. Matthew Yarczower, to let me take some art classes. After I received my Ph.D. I went back to El Paso where I was teaching part time at UTEP. I was doing sculpting, because the family business was structural steel, and I had worked at the company in summers and knew how to weld. I began sculpting in steel and it was joyous and easy for me. When I learned TM my creativity increased and I found that I started doing things I wanted to do instead of putting them off—bigger projects like full sized figures in steel and abstract sculptures 7 feet high.

As much as I loved art, once I learned TM, I was thinking about becoming a TM teacher. I went to a residence course, which provided an opportunity for deeper experiences in the TM practice. During the course I had a vision that what TM needed was more research. I liked science, and that was what I was trained to do. I had been so busy for 20 years with TM research putting together *Collected Papers* and chart booklets, that my art took a back seat. At MUM there was a weekend watercolor class, and my wife and I signed up. In a three-day course the instructor, John Preston, taught us the fundamentals, and that motivated me to start painting again. Maharishi said to me: "You need to enjoy more," and he took us off the front lines of doing the research and helping to build the University. We retired to Florida, and I had more time to pursue my first love and it is at a much higher level and more joyous than it had ever been before. We take a lot of trips and I paint wherever we go.

GE: Do you find that you transcend when you pursue science and art?

David: Yes, in both. The transcending during the TM program is a preparation for both, and the best work results right after you meditate. Before I started TM, during art I would settle into a peak or flow experience that Abraham Maslow and others talked about. I would be so blissful. One time I came home from a sculpture class at Columbia, and I was so naturally high that I just started drawing whatever was there. A cat was sitting in front of me, and I began to draw it; I could do no wrong, and the process was pure bliss! I could occasionally fall into that state of consciousness and that is why I liked doing art. I always felt something in that direction from doing it.

GE: Did you witness your activity?

David: The experience of witnessing happens by itself. You are just watching the creativity flowing out, and it's completely effortless. Everything

Maharishi©

Guru Dev©

Painting and drawing of Maharishi and Guru Dev by David Orme-Johnson

seems transformed; the whole atmosphere seems to have this kind of thick connectedness, blissful quality, as if you are bonded to everything.

GE: What you are explaining is your experience of transcending even before learning TM through the instrument of art, and you are talking about the power of your attention.

David: Transcending is completely natural. It is a synthesis of attention, the heart, and being totally engaged in your dharma—what you are meant to do in this lifetime.

GE: You are describing the universality of the experience.

David: Yes, it is universal, and TM just provides a way to cultivate that ability, which is a tremendous gift because artists find, and I found, that you have these long dry periods. TM helps reduce the gaps between creativity flowing and its absence. It is not just art that becomes more creative. Every aspect of life does: cooking, talking to friends, listening to music, doing the dishes.

GE: You have conducted so much research that you must have experienced bliss in your cognitions.

David: That's right. It is very validating to have an insight experimentally validated. For example, I was in charge of the EEG laboratory in Switzerland,

and I went on a six-month course to meditate, but I was still in touch with the people in the laboratory. In a deep meditation I had an intuition that there was a connection between EEG coherence and creativity. In a phone call I suggested to Russell Hebert, who was running the lab, that he should look at the correlation between EEG and creativity. On considering what the correlation might be, I experienced numbers going up and down in my mind, too high, too low, and they stopped at 0.71, like the ball in a roulette wheel. I told Russell I felt the correlation will be 0.71. The next day he called

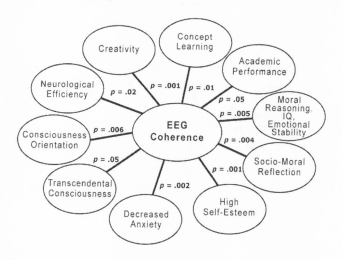

Integration of Brain Functioning
Through Transcendental Meditation

Correlates of EEG Coherence. One of the most important discoveries about the TM technique, and arguably in the history of science, is that TM practice increases EEG coherence among all brain regions. EEG coherence organizes different areas of the brain for creativity, concept learning, moral reasoning, even for simple perception and motor behavior, much as a conductor organizes the different instruments in an orchestra (77-81).

me back and said with amazement: "We did the correlation between creativity and coherence and it was 0.71!" It is on one of our charts. I had had some experience of what Maharishi calls *Ritam Bhara Pragya*, which means "that level of awareness that knows only the truth."

GE: That is exactly what Einstein was explaining in terms of how his intuition was employed in discovery.

David: Yes, and everyone has the capability of refined intuition. It is universal, and only needs to be cultivated.

GE: In my interview with the legendary jazz musician Paul Horn, he viewed the process of creative intuition in music as just getting out of the way.

David: That is a very good description (laughter). Let the little ego get out of the way and allow nature, the Self, to do the job.

GE: Can you provide a synopsis of your personal reflections about your relationship with Maharishi, and your personal and professional goals in terms of your lifetime commitment to the pursuit of this knowledge and its value to humanity?

David: Certainly. I would like to become more enlightened, and I have made a lot of progress from where I started this journey. I know there is a lot more to go, and Maharishi has laid out the whole path intellectually, and I have experienced quite a bit of it experientially. I believe I understand that path, the levels of consciousness, how they unfold, and the transitions. On the professional level I enjoy reading about the ongoing excellent TM research that is being conducted. I want to review it, integrate it, and write about it, which is what I am doing now. I was very fortunate, for whatever reason, to be able to collaborate with Maharishi, partly because I loved science. I loved knowledge and I was a channel for bringing out Maharishi's knowledge. I loved to collect the research and write summaries of it, and that was my job—I was able to be with Maharishi and work with him on those projects.

Maharishi often said he did not have any followers. He said that people follow their own evolution, and that is absolutely true. Maharishi stated that if people find what he says is useful to them then they may listen to what he has to say. I definitely found what he had to say was useful and I listened. I continue to study what he said, listen to his tapes, and read his commentary on the *Bhagavad-Gita*. As you evolve you see it differently, more profoundly. Maharishi was speaking from Unity Consciousness, and as we grow toward that reality we will recognize it more profoundly, what that level of Unity Consciousness is, and what he was describing. As I evolve, I have a deeper appreciation of Maharishi and what he did for the whole world.

References

1. Orme-Johnson DW. Autonomic stability and Transcendental Meditation. Psychosomatic Medicine. 1973;35:341-9.

2. Dillbeck MC, Orme-Johnson DW. Physiological differences between Transcendental Meditation and rest. American Psychologist. 1987;42:879–81.

3. Wallace RK, Benson H, Wilson AF. A wakeful hypometabolic physiologic state. American Journal of Physiology. 1971;221:795-9.

4. Wallace RK. Physiological effects of Transcendental Meditation. Science. 1970;167:1751–4.

5. Wallace RK. The physiological effects of Transcendental Meditation: A proposed fourth major state of consciousness. In: Orme-Johnson DW, Farrow JT, editors. Scientific Research on Maharishi's Transcendental Meditation Programme: Collected Papers. 2nd ed. Livingston Manor, New York: MERU; 1970. p. 43-78.

6. Wallace RK. The physiology of meditation. Scientific American. 1972;226:84-90.

7. So KT, Orme-Johnson DW. Three randomized experiments on the holistic longitudinal effects of the Transcendental Meditation technique on cognition. Intelligence. 2001;29(5):419-40.

8. Mason LI, Alexander CN, Travis FT, Marsh G, Orme-Johnson DW, Gackenbach J, et al. Electrophysiological correlates of higher states of consciousness during sleep in long-term practitioners of the Transcendental Meditation program. Sleep. 1997 Feb;20(2):102-10.

9. Mason LI, Orme-Johnson DW. Transcendental Consciousness wakes up in dreaming and deep sleep. International Journal of Dream Research. 2010;3(1):28-32.

10. Nader T., Human Physiology - Expression of Veda and the Vedic Literature. Vlodrop, Holland: Maharishi University Press; 1995.

11. Alexander CN, Davies JL, Dixon CA, Dillbeck MC, Druker SM, Oetzel RM, et al. Growth of higher stages of consciousness: Maharishi's Vedic Psychology of human development. Alexander CN, Langer EL, editors. New York: Oxford University Press; 1990.

12. Hagelin JS. Restructuring physics from its foundation in light of Maharishi's Vedic Science. Modern Science and Vedic Science. 1989;3(1):3-72.

13. Katz V. Conversations with Maharishi: Maharishi Mahesh Yogi speaks about the full development of human consciousness. Fairfield, Iowa, USA: Maharishi University of Management Press; 2011.

14. Maharishi Mahesh Yogi. The science of being and art of living. New York: New American Library Inc.; 1963.

15. Maharishi Mahesh Yogi. On the Bhagavad-Gita A new translation and commentary: Chapters 1-6. Baltimore: Penguin Books Inc.; 1967.

16. Maharishi Mahesh Yogi. Vedic Knowledge for everyone. Vlodrop, Netherlands: Maharishi Vedic University Press; 1994.

17. Maharishi Mahesh Yogi. Maharishi forum of natural law and national law for doctors. India: Age of Enlightenment Publications; 1995.

18. Maharishi Mahesh Yogi. Maharishi's Vedic approach to health. Vlodrop, Holland: Maharishi Vedic University Press; 1995.

19. Maharishi Mahesh Yogi. Maharishi's absolute theory of defence. New Delhi: Age of Enlightenment Publications; 1996.

20. Maharishi Mahesh Yogi. Life supported by natural law. Washington, D.C.: Age of Enlightenment Press; 1986.

21. Maharishi Mahesh Yogi. Creating an ideal society. West Germany: Maharishi European Research University Press; 1977.

22. Chalmers R, Clements G, Schenkluhn H, Weinless M, editors. Scientific research on Maharishi's Transcendental Meditation and TM-Sidhi programme: Collected Papers, Vols. 2-4. Vlodrop, The Netherlands: MVU Press; 1988.

23. Dillbeck MC, editor. Scientific research on Maharishi's Transcendental Meditation and TM-Sidhi programme: Collected Papers, Vol. 6. Vlodrop, The Netherlands: Maharishi Vedic University Press; 2011.

24. Orme-Johnson DW, Farrow JT. Scientific research on Maharishi's Transcendental Meditation programme: Collected Papers. [2d ed. Weggis, Switzerland: Maharishi European Research University Press; 1977.

25. Wallace RK, Orme-Johnson DW, Dillbeck MC, editors. Scientific research on Maharishi's Transcendental Meditation and TM-Sidhi program: Collected Papers, Vol. 5. Fairfield, Iowa: MIU Press; 1990.

26. Hagelin JS. Is consciousness the unified field? A field theorist's perspective. Modern science and Vedic science. 1987;1(1):29-88.

27. Schneider RH, Alexander CN, Staggers F, Rainforth MV, Salerno JW, Hartz A, et al. Long-term effects of stress reduction on mortality in persons ≥ 55 years of age with systemic hypertension. American Journal of Cardiology. 2005;95(9):1060-4.

28. Orme-Johnson DW, Gelderloos P. Topographic EEG brain mapping during Yogic Flying. International Journal of Neuroscience. 1988 Feb;38(3-4):427-34.

29. Travis FT, Orme-Johnson DW. EEG coherence and power during Yogic Flying. International Journal of Neuroscience. 1990 Sep;54(1-2):1-12.

30. Badawi K, Wallace RK, Orme-Johnson DW, Rouzeré A-M. Electrophysiologic characteristics of respiratory suspension periods occurring during the practice of the Transcendental Meditation program. Psychosomatic Medicine. 1984;46(3):267-76.

31. Orme-Johnson DW, Alexander CN, Davies JL, Chander HM, Larimore WE. International Peace Project: The Effects of the Maharishi Technology of the Unified Field. Journal of conflict resolution. 1988;32(4):776-812.

32. Dillbeck MC. Test of a field theory of consciousness and social change: Time series analysis of participation in the TM-Sidhi program and reduction of violent death in the U.S. Social Indicators Research. 1990;22:399-418.

33. Dillbeck MC, Banus CB, Polanzi C, Landrith III GS. Test of a field model of consciousness and social change: Transcendental Meditation and TM-Sidhi program and decreased urban crime. The Journal of Mind and Behavior. 1988 9(4):457-86

34. Dillbeck MC, Cavanaugh KL, Glenn T, Orme-Johnson DW, Mittlefehldt V. Consciousness as a field: The Transcendental Meditation and TM-Sidhi program and changes in social indicators. The Journal of Mind and Behavior. 1987;8(1):67-104.

35. Dillbeck MC, Landrith III G, Orme-Johnson DW. The Transcendental Meditation program and crime rate changes in a sample of forty-eight cities. Journal of Crime and Justice. 1981;4:25-45.

36. Dillbeck MC, Rainforth MV. Impact assessment analysis of behavioral quality of life indices: Effects of group practice of the Transcendental Meditation and TM-Sidhi program. American Statistical Association, 1996 Proceedings of the Social Statistics Section; Alexandria, VA: American Statistical Association; 1996. p. 38-48.

37. Hagelin JS, Rainforth MV, Orme-Johnson DW, Cavanaugh KL, Alexander CN, Shatkin SF, et al. Effects of group practice of the Transcendental Meditation program on preventing violent crime in Washington D.C.: Results of the National Demonstration Project, June-July, 1993. Social Indicators Research. 1999; 47(2):153-201.

38. Hatchard GD, Deans AJ, Cavanaugh KL, Orme-Johnson DW. The Maharishi Effect: A model for social improvement: Time series analysis of a phase transition to reduced crime in Merseyside metropolitan area. Psychology, Crime, & Law. 1996;2(3):165-75.

39. Orme-Johnson DW, Alexander CN, Davies JL. The effects of the Maharishi Technology of the Unified Field: Reply to a methodological critique. Journal of Conflict Resolution. 1990;34:756–68.

40. Orme-Johnson DW, Dillbeck MC, Alexander CN. Preventing terrorism and international conflict: Effects of large assemblies of participants in the Transcendental Meditation and TM-Sidhi programs. Journal of Offender Rehabilitation. 2003;36:283-302.

41. Orme-Johnson DW, Gelderloos P. The long-term effects of the Maharishi Technology of the Unified Field on the quality of life in the United States (1960 to 1983). Social Science Perspectives Journal. 1988;2(4):127-46.

42. Orme-Johnson DW, Oates RM. A field-theoretic view of consciousness: Reply to critics. Journal of Scientific Exploration. 2009;32(2):139-66.

43. Davies JL, Alexander CN. Alleviating political violence through reducing collective tension: Impact assessment analysis of the Lebanon war. Journal of Social Behavior and Personality. 2005;17(1):285-338.

44. Assimakis P, Dillbeck MC. Time series analysis of improved quality of life in Canada: Social change, collective consciousness, and the TM-Sidhi program. Psychological Report. 1995;76:1171-93.

45. Gelderloos P, Goddard PHI, Ahlstrom HH, Jacoby R. Cognitive orientation towards positive values in advanced participants of the TM and TM-Sidhi program. Perceptual Motor Skills. 1987;64:1003-12.

46. Harung HS, Travis F, Pensgaard AM, Boes R, Cook-Greuter S, Daley K. Higher psycho-physiological refinement in world-class Norwegian athletes: brain measures of performance capacity. Scandinavian Journal of Medicine & Science in Sports. 2011;21(1):32-41.

47. Brooks J, Scarano T. Transcendental Meditation and the treatment of post-Vietnam adjustment. Journal of Counseling and Development. 1985;64:212-5.

48. Rosenthal J, Grosswald S, Ross R, Rosenthal N. Effects of Transcendental Meditation (TM) in Veterans of Operation Enduring Freedom (OEF) and Operation Iraqi Freedom (OIF) with Posttraumatic Stress Disorder (PTSD): a Pilot Study. Military Medicine. 2011;176(6):626.

49. Orme-Johnson DW, Farrow JT, editors. Scientific Research on Maharishi's Transcendental Meditation programme: Collected Papers, Vol. 1. Livingston Manor, New York: MERU Press; 1976.

50. Alexander CN, Orme-Johnson DW. Walpole study of the TM program in maximum security prisoners II: Longitudinal study of development and psychopathology. Journal of Offender Rehabilitation. 2003;36(1-4):127-60.

51. Alexander CN, Rainforth MV, Frank PR, Grant JD, Von Stade C, Walton KG. Walpole study of the Transcendental Meditation program in maximum security prisoners III: Reduced recidivism. Journal of Offender Rehabilitation. 2003;36(3):161-80.

52. Alexander CN, Walton KG, Goodman RS. Walpole study of the TM program in maximum security prisoners I: Cross-sectional differences in development and psychopathology. Journal of Offender Rehabilitation. 2003;36(1):97-125.

53. Orme-Johnson DW, Moore RM. First prison study using the Transcendental Meditation program: La Tuna Federal Penitentiary. Journal of Offender Rehabilitation. 2003;36:89-96.

54. Ballou D. The Transcendental Meditation program at Stillwater Prison. In: Orme-Johnson DW, Farrow JT, editors. Scientific Research on

Maharishi's Transcendental Meditation and TM-Sidhi Programme: Collected Papers. Rheinweiler, West Germany: MERU Press; 1977. p. 713-8.

55. O'Connell DF, Alexander CN, editors. Self Recovery—Treating addictions using Transcendental Meditation and Maharishi Ayur-Veda. Binghamton, NY: Harrington Park Press; 1994.

56. O'Connell DF, Alexander CN. Introduction: Recovery from addictions using Transcendental Meditation and Maharishi Ayur-Veda. In: O'Connell DF, Alexander CN, editors. Self Recovery—Treating Addictions Using Transcendental Meditation and Maharishi Ayur-Veda. Binghamton, NY: Harrington Park Press; 1994. p. 1-10.

57. Dillbeck MC, Abrams AI. The application of the Transcendental Meditation program to corrections: Meta-analysis. International Journal of Comparative and Applied Criminal Justice. 1987;11(1):111-32.

58. Orme-Johnson DW. Commentary: The use of meditation in corrections. International Journal of Offender Therapy and Comparative Criminology. 2011;55(4):662-4.

59. Rainforth MV, Bleick C, Alexander CN, Cavanaugh KL. The Transcendental Meditation program and criminal recidivism in Folsom State Prisoners: A 15-year follow-up study. Journal of Offender Rehabilitation. 2003;36:181-204.

60. Bleick CR, Abrams AI. The Transcendental Meditation program and criminal recidivism in California. Journal of Criminal Justice. 1987;15(3):211-30.

61. Chalmers R, Clements G, Schenkluhn H, Weinless M, editors. Scientific Research on Maharishi's Transcendental Meditation and TM-Sidhi programme: Collected Papers (Vol. 2-4). Vlodrop, The Netherlands: MVU Press; 1988.

62. Orme-Johnson DW. Preventing crime through the Maharishi Effect. Journal of Offender Rehabilitation. 2003;36(1/2/3/4):257-82.

63. Travis F, Haaga DA, Hagelin J, Tanner M, Nidich S, Gaylord-King C, et al. Effects of Transcendental Meditation practice on brain functioning and stress reactivity in college students. Int J Psychophysiol. 2009 Feb;71(2):170-6.

64. Alexander CN, Walton KG, Orme-Johnson DW, Goodman RS. Transcendental Meditation in criminal rehabilitation and crime prevention. Journal of Offender Rehabilitation. 2003;36(1/2/3/4):1-383.

65. Orme-Johnson DW, Schneider RH, Son YD, Nidich S, Cho ZH. Neuroimaging of meditation's effect on brain reactivity to pain. Neuroreport. 2006 Aug 21;17(12):1359-63.

66. Alexander CN. Seven States of Consciousness: Unfolding the full potential of the Cosmic Psyche in individual life through Maharishi's Vedic Psychology. Modern Science and Vedic Science. 1989;2(4):325-71.

67. Alexander CN, Druker SM, Langer EJ. Major issues in the exploration of adult growth. In: Alexander CN, Langer EJ, editors. Higher Stages of Human Development: Perspectives on Adult Growth. New York: Oxford University Press; 1990.

68. Wallace RK, Dillbeck M, Jacobe E, Harrington B. The effects of the Transcendental Meditation and TM-Sidhi program on the aging process. International Journal of Neuroscience. 1982;16:53-8.

69. Glaser JL, Brind JL, Vogelman JH, Eisner MJ, Dillbeck MC, Wallace RK, et al. Elevated serum dehydroepiandrosterone sulfate levels in practitioners of Transcendental Meditation (TM) and TM-Sidhi programs. Journal of Behavioral Medicine. 1992;15(4):327-41.

70. Orme-Johnson DW. Medical care utilization and the Transcendental Meditation program. Psychosomatic Medicine. 1987;49:493-507.

71. Alexander CN, Barnes VA, Schneider RH, Langer EJ, Newman RI, Chandler HM, et al. A randomized controlled trial of stress reduction on cardiovascular and all-cause mortality in the elderly: Results of 8 and 15 year follow-ups. Circulation. 1996;93(3):P19.

72. Alexander CN, Langer EJ, Newman RI, Chandler HM, Davies JL. Transcendental Meditation, mindfulness, and longevity: an experimental study with the elderly. Journal of Personality and Social Psychology. 1989;57(6):950-64.

73. Barnes V, Schneider R, Alexander C, Rainforth M, Salerno J, Kondwani K, et al. Impact of Transcendental Meditation on mortality in older African-Americans with hypertension—Eight-year follow-up. Journal of Social Behavior and Personality. 2005;17(1):201-16.

74. Herron R, Cavanaugh K. Can the Transcendental Meditation program reduce the medical expenditures of older people? A longitudinal cost reduction study in Canada. Journal of Social Behavior and Personality. 2005;17:415-42.

75. Herron R, Hillis S. The impact of the Transcendental Meditation program on government payments to physicians in Quebec: An update. American Journal of Health Promotion. 2000;14(5):284-93.

76. Herron RE. Changes in physician costs among high-cost Transcendental Meditation practitioners compared with high-cost nonpractitioners over 5 years. American Journal of Health Promotion. 2011;26(1):56-60.

77. Orme-Johnson DW, Haynes CT. EEG phase coherence, pure consciousness, creativity and TM-Sidhi experiences. International Journal of Neuroscience. 1981;13:211-7.

78. Dillbeck MC, Orme-Johnson DW, Wallace RK. Frontal EEG coherence, H-reflex recovery, concept learning, and the TM-Sidhi program. International Journal of Neuroscience. 1981;15(3):151-7.

79. Nidich SI, Ryncarz RA, Abrams AI, Orme-Johnson DW, Wallace RK. Kohlbergian moral perspective responses, EEG coherence, and the Transcendental Meditation and TM-Sidhi program. Journal of Moral Education. 1983;12(3):166-73.

80. Orme-Johnson DW, Clements G, Haynes CT, Badawi K. Higher states of consciousness: EEG coherence, creativity, and experiences of the sidhis. In: Orme-Johnson DW, & Farrow, J., editor. Scientific Research on Maharishi's Transcendental Meditation programme: Collected Papers (Vol 1). Rheinweiler, Germany: MERU Press; 1977.

81. Travis FT, Arenander A. Cross-sectional and longitudinal study of effects of Transcendental Meditation Practice on interhemispheric frontal asymmetry and frontal coherence. International Journal of Neuroscience. 2006;116(12):1519-38.

Part IV

Justice and Leadership

Chapter XII

Law, Justice, and Rehabilitation

Arthur John Anderson, J.D., LL.M.

When I met Art Anderson, he was the Director of the Criminal Justice Division, Office of the Attorney General, in Little Rock, Arkansas. He has had an illustrious law career, and an ongoing business and consulting career. He is a man of impeccable integrity. In my opinion, if Art had continued his career in politics, he could have been a contender for the Presidency of the United States. At the time, the Arkansas Department of Correction was under federal court control, and Art was seeking to make it a better situation.

When I think of Art and Arkansas, I often reflect upon the ideals behind the movie Brubaker, *starring Robert Redford, who portrayed an honorable individual seeking what is right in the face of entrenched opposition, while maintaining qualities of common decency. We had the pleasure of traveling throughout Europe together and lecturing on Law, Justice, and Rehabilitation. Art's vision is timeless and applicable in our contemporary and turbulent world. More than thirty years ago, Art wrote the Introduction to my first book,* Inside Folsom Prison, *and I am pleased to include it here as it was written back then because it is as relevant and penetrating now as when it originally appeared.*

Our nation has recently re-embraced capital punishment. Our legislators are enacting more criminal laws and devising tougher penalties and tighter procedures. Bus drivers and service station attendants require exact change from us for public transportation or to buy gas after dark. Off-duty policemen guard our stores and apartment complexes. The provision of crime insurance and the production of deadbolt locks, commercial mace, and burglar alarms have become a lucrative business. As our crime problem continues to grow, we simply expand its container by building bigger police forces, bigger court-houses, bigger prisons, and bigger probation and parole systems. We are not so unlike the man who combats obesity by spending more and more money buying bigger and better suits to put around himself. He is simply shrouding, not solving, a growing problem.

Then there is the refreshing good news brought to us by George Ellis about his monumental work at Folsom Prison and a promising new technology for eliminating crime, its causes, its symptoms, and its effects. This new technology is the Transcendental Meditation program of Maharishi Mahesh Yogi.

Until now, our administration of criminal justice has been geared to control conduct by coercion and constraint, which are, quite simply, expressions of force. We even refer to this mechanism as "law enforcement." But force operates on the surface level of behavior without really affecting the person and, consequently, rarely has lasting results. So, when the threat of force is removed or not readily perceived, proscribed forms of behavior are quickly resumed.

Once the control of conduct through the simple enactment and enforcement of criminal laws proved to be transitory and futile, we began searching for more complex solutions. We investigated the environment in which criminal behavior breeds, hoping that by removing slums and renewing cities, we might reduce crime. This, of course, did not work either. Poverty, poor family life, and drug abuse were identified as three major causes of criminal conduct; but what caused these causes was never quite discovered. We then deployed psychotherapeutic methods to control harmful conduct: the mental patient was committed and subjected to various forms of treatment; the criminal was imprisoned and subdued by a regimen of so-called rehabilitation programs; and the truant or troubled youth was intercepted and redirected through different versions of counseling and therapy. The intent of all this is indeed laudable but, so far, incapable of containing, let alone eliminating, socially dysfunctional behavior.

The thrust of our criminal justice system has been obvious: to impose orderliness from the outside inward through the codification and enforcement of laws and the restructuring of environment. Even psychotherapeutic approaches rely on something from the outside to affect something on the inside. But orderliness does not begin from the outside. The secret of orderliness is that it is already there, within each individual. Environment, good or bad, is essentially a product and not the cause of correspondingly good or bad social behavior; and how a person behaves depends upon what he thinks—how he perceives his surroundings and appreciates his situation, what attitudes he generates. So, an orderly social environment is the result of orderly individual action. And, to secure orderly action, we must go to the source of action, which is thinking; and to assure orderly thinking, we must go to the source of thought, which is consciousness. Depending on its quality, consciousness is the ultimate source of crime and suffering or of harmony and happiness.

The term "consciousness" has been used in many different ways. I will keep my use of the term precise and treat it simply as a physiological phenomenon. The human body consists of the interaction of countless individual cells. Each of these cells has an autonomous life that, in combination with other cells, gives rise to a human life distinct from and more than just the aggregation of all cell life. In other words, the whole is greater than the sum of its parts. This "wholeness" is what I mean by consciousness.

To the extent that cells and bodily organs function and interact with each other in an orderly and harmonious way, one realizes and lives a higher or lower level of consciousness. For example, stomach malfunctioning may give rise to irritability and headache. A person so afflicted neither perceives his surroundings as accurately, nor thinks as clearly, nor acts as appropriately as he otherwise would. His level of consciousness is not as high as it could be. On the other hand, one may wake up in the morning feeling refreshed and energetic and enjoying an overall sense of wellbeing; his perceptions are clearer, his thoughts, and attitudes more in tune with his environment, and his behavior more positive and productive.

That which causes bodily malfunctioning and attendant perceptual, mental, and behavioral dullness in one instance, and physiological vigor and psychological acuity in another, is simply the presence or absence of stress in the nervous system. Stress is any chemical or structural abnormality that remains in the nervous system from an overload of experience. This overload can be the result of pleasurable as well as painful stimuli, excessive tedium as well as excitement, and the combination of small occurrences as well as the impact of a single traumatic event.

The more stress an individual incurs, the more subnormal will his organic activity be, arriving eventually at a state of total systemic disharmony, or death, where interaction between bodily components ceases. Conversely, to the extent that the nervous system is relieved of stress, it will operate more normally, consciousness will become correspondingly more elevated, and optimal internal functioning and external interaction with the environment will be attained. The level of consciousness, then, is directly related to the degree of purification or normalization of the human nervous system. In fact, the elimination of stress and the expansion of consciousness add up to the same thing.

Consciousness is the contact point of the individual and his environment; in consciousness, all events are experienced. In this sense, consciousness is awareness. In the case of antisocial behavior, consciousness is disorderly and excited and therefore limited—the individual fails to comprehend the appropriateness and consequences of his actions. Indeed, impulsive acts performed in a state of high stress often involve almost no awareness of the events, indicating a highly disordered nervous system and an intense lack of mind-body coordination. On the other hand, when stress is at a minimum, thinking is clearer and more orderly, and behavior is more spontaneously appropriate, more fully in harmony with the needs of the situation. The individual enjoys a greater awareness of alternative courses of action and can thereby exercise greater creativity in resolving conflicts.

The accumulation of stress in the nervous system causes fatigue and produces physiological and psychological disorders. In fact, it is estimated that at least 80 percent of all disease involves stress-related symptoms, which commonly take the form of anxiety, tension, depression, irritability, worry, high blood pressure, insomnia, headache, indigestion, confusion, and difficulty in solving problems. As stress mounts, the individual's emotions become unstable and his mind loses clarity. The likelihood of mistakes and maladaptive behavior thereby increases and inevitably leads to failure and frustration, which, in turn, reinforce his previously incurred stresses, lower his self-esteem, and leave him weakened and more susceptible to future stresses. Hence, a stress cycle is generated in which mistakes and maladaptive behavior become unavoidable. Eventually, a collapse occurs. In some, it takes the form of a nervous breakdown or heart attack; in others, it may take the form of a crime. This cycle—indeed, this downward spiral—describes the "physiology of crime" and provides a wholly new perspective on crime prevention and rehabilitation.

The relationship of stress to criminality is obvious in impulsive acts of violence. But even those criminal acts performed with calm deliberation are products of stress. Stress has created the need, gnawing inside the individual, to gratify desires quickly—to bypass, as convenient, the normal, socially acceptable avenues of attaining a goal. The individual who cautiously calculates the theft of an automobile, for example, certainly finds that route more immediately gratifying than the tedious process of obtaining a job, earning and saving money, and purchasing an automobile.

Although the exact circumstances that trigger a criminal act may be intricate, the general situation is one in which stress-producing pressures, distributed through a social network, become concentrated on an individual who, if he is weak, expresses his frustrated needs in antisocial behavior. In this context, crime represents the inability of the individual to arrange for the fulfillment of his desires in accordance with the needs of his fellow men.

The physiology of criminal behavior is closely related to that of psychosomatic illness. It tends to be characterized by a state of increased excitation and disorder, which results in the narrowing of awareness and failure to judge appropriately the consequences of action. In other words, the level of consciousness—that is, the degree of refinement of the nervous system—is low. This explains why our efforts to date to eliminate crime through behavioral or psychological approaches alone have not been successful. They have been incomplete. Stress, which may manifest itself as anxiety, depression, rigidity, aggression, or hostility, is an underlying factor in all criminal behavior; and stress is a physiological condition in the nervous system. Crime prevention and rehabilitative methodologies, if they are to work, must address this physiological basis.

Even purely psychological stress causes abnormality at the physical level of the nervous system. Since all stress has this physical component, a physiological remedy must be found and used. This is why psychoactive drugs have become a popular method of counteracting or relieving psychological stress. Drugs, however, only alter consciousness; they do not elevate it. Drugs also create a dependency and have undesirable side effects.

Since stress is now medically understood as a major contributor to disease, it should also be legally recognized as a major factor in crime. And, just as many prominent physicians and psychiatrists are now prescribing the TM technique for both remedial and preventive purposes, those of us responsible for the administration of criminal justice should promptly implement it in our rehabilitation and crime prevention programs. It is a natural, and even necessary, ingredient to such endeavors. The TM technique provides what is perhaps the most expeditious, and certainly the safest, method for the nervous system to automatically release and rid itself of stress: profoundly deep rest.

Scientific investigation shows that during the TM technique heart and respiratory rate significantly decrease. Cardiac output is also reduced, while overall cardiovascular efficiency increases. The system does less but accomplishes more. Measurements of skin resistance and blood chemistry also indicate a deep state of this efficient rest. Oxygen consumption, which is a reliable gauge of metabolic activity, typically decreases during the first few minutes that the TM technique is employed to a level significantly lower than that attained in any point during a night's sleep.

Because the TM technique triggers deep metabolic rest and thereby disposes the nervous system to begin immediately ridding itself of deeply and tightly rooted stresses, the practitioner quickly experiences increased autonomic stability, more effective interaction with his environment, decreased dependence on drugs, alcohol, and tobacco, and increased inner control and self-actualization. These responses are exactly opposite to criminal patterns of behavior. Wholeness and balance are restored to the individual.

Apart from its capacity to relieve the nervous system of deeply rooted stresses, the TM technique brings about many other positive physiological responses. Those most pertinent to crime prevention and rehabilitation relate to brainwave coherence and synchrony. In a series of electroencephalographic experiments begun in 1970, and still being performed today, it was discovered, and has been consistently verified, that the TM technique produces a unique orderliness of brain functioning characterized by: interhemispheric coherence and power balance, which indicate orderliness and integration in style of functioning, greater creativity and an improved ability to make right judgments; a pronounced wave similarity between frontal and occipital lobes, which occasions greater thought/action coordination; and an increased incidence of alpha and stable theta wave activity, which indicates de-excitation of the nervous system and a greater capacity for productive interpersonal relationships.

The practical implications of these findings are enormous. Markedly increased orderliness in brain functioning necessarily has a corresponding effect on the manner and quality of thinking; and more orderly thinking naturally yields more orderly behavior and, inevitably, a more orderly environment. Hence, the natural flow of orderliness is generated spontaneously from within the individual outward, rather than the reverse process relied upon by traditional law enforcement techniques. Indeed, brainwave harmony and orderliness, which can readily be measured, may someday become the major criteria for determining a criminal offender's eligibility to return to society. Brainwave patterns cannot be fabricated, nor can electroencephalographic equipment be easily conned.

The elimination of stress and the culturing of orderly thinking as a two-pronged means of correcting criminal conduct is no idle proposal; it is, in fact, already a verified reality. Transcendental Meditation programs have been introduced into many prisons in the United States and elsewhere, and follow-up studies have revealed remarkable results. Participating inmates exhibit increased interest in vocational and educational pursuits, while prison officials experience a significant decrease in disciplinary problems involving those inmates. This latter consideration is particularly important because of the likely correlation between prison rule violation and recidivism after reentry into society.

Psychological and electrophysiological testing has shown that participating inmates realize a significant reduction in anxiety, a major symptom of stress, and thus are able to naturally channel their energies in more positive, productive directions. The net effect is that those very individuals who have unequivocally resisted and rejected society's attempts to externally impose orderliness onto their aberrant modes of behavior are now enjoying the spontaneous, natural flow of orderliness from within.

And the TM technique is quite popular among inmates, many of whom have specifically requested that such programs be instituted. The reason is that the technique is not only easy, but also very enjoyable and thus self-motivating; and, from our side, it not only works but, in comparison to other modalities, is also very inexpensive and readily integrated into any institutional routine. Furthermore, the practice is easily continued during the parole period and into the inmate's full return into society since there are over four hundred community centers for the TM program throughout the country of which he can conveniently avail himself for follow-up and advanced programs to further promote his growth in orderliness.

The success of this simple technique again emphasizes the underlying inconsistency of our "enforcement mentality," which typically exerts something from the outside to remedy something on the inside. It also points to the fact that rehabilitation should be a process of holistic development. By relieving the nervous system of stress and thereby enhancing consciousness or "wholeness," the TM technique holistically, systematically, and beneficially affects every other aspect of the individual, allowing innate harmony and orderliness to emanate from his mind, body, and behavior, extending ultimately to his family, community, and environment. Again, the secret of orderliness is that it is already there, within each individual.

In the present work by George Ellis, we begin to witness the uncovering of this secret in the darkness of a maximum security unit through the introduction of the simple but profound Transcendental Meditation program. Mr. Ellis describes this phenomenon from the viewpoint of the inmate; but, regardless of our own perspective, we must appreciate the basic truth that he brings to light about prison life, about the ineffectiveness of current rehabilitation programs, and about this unique TM technology that establishes a new and very simple paradigm for resolving the problem of crime at the level of its ultimate cause.

If Mr. Ellis' insights should at times seem too simple to us, let us reconsider: perhaps it is only that ours have become overly complicated. We have somehow managed to adorn our crime problem with such an endless array of intricate governmental projects, programs, and theories that we ourselves compound its complexity and thus fail to find, or even seek, a simple solution.

We must realize that there is a physiological basis for crime, and we must begin to treat criminal behavior at that level. This is not to suggest that the TM technique should be substituted for other rehabilitation modalities; rather, its implementation will enhance their effectiveness. I am certain that the TM technique, in its recognition and treatment of the "physiology of crime," will occasion a most important breakthrough in our administration of criminal justice.

Chapter XIII

Leadership and Transformation

The first introduction of the TM program in a correctional setting took place in 1959 in Bangkok, Thailand. The program expanded throughout the world. From Folsom and San Quentin Prisons in California to the Department of Corrections in Vermont, to the dungeons in the poverty-stricken nations of Guatemala and Senegal, the TM program was implemented for prisoners and staff. Scientific studies indicated an increase in positive behavior and a reduction in anxiety and disciplinary actions among inmates practicing the TM technique. In 1975, at Folsom Prison, violence dropped markedly with the introduction of the TM program into the first maximum security prison. Reductions also occurred in inmate hostility, neuroticism, and insomnia.

These results were duplicated in 1982 at San Quentin Prison and the Deuel Vocational Institution. Scientists have also documented long-term reductions in recidivism (inmate return) among released offenders who have participated in the TM program (see: www.davidlynchfoundation.org). In 1983 the Vermont Department of Corrections made the TM program available to all staff and inmates throughout the state. Improvements in behavior and health were documented. With the generous support and participation of Susan Gore, a documentary was created that reviewed the implications of the TM program for projects on a global level (see Appendix A excerpts from Leadership and Unified Field Based Rehabilitation). Ms. Gore is the entrepreneur and philanthropist responsible for introducing the TM program into the Vermont Department of Corrections. In chapter XVII, she offers us an engaging narrative: the development of her family's unique management style, and her inspiration, upon reading Inside Folsom Prison, *to work closely with the author in implementing these projects.*

Below is an account of my experiences teaching the TM program in the maximum security environment, followed by contributions from prisoners themselves, and professionals in the fields of law, justice and rehabilitation.

The first day I entered Folsom Prison and walked through the seven or eight gates to arrive at the education room where I was to teach, you could feel the tension and the stress in the environment. After the TM programs were introduced and implemented to hundreds of inmates and staff within that institution, you could feel a settled quality, a calmness pervading the environment. A key element of reducing institutional violence is that the personal relationships between the staff and the inmates, the inmates and the inmates, and the staff and the staff, must be workable, or at least civil. At Folsom Prison one correctional officer remarked to me: "The con-bull relationship had broken down." In other words, inmates who had now learned to meditate were having civil and respectful conversations with each other, and they were solving their problems without animosity. The inmate did his time, the correctional officers did their time, but without the stress. When I first introduced and taught the TM program at Folsom State Prison in Represa, California, they had pill lines that operated twice a day for 45 minutes dispensing medication just so people could sleep at night. After the introduction of the TM program, research showed that individuals who were taking two to three hours to get to sleep at night were falling asleep in 10 to 15 minutes. This indicated a very important breakthrough for reducing the hostility and anxiety that leads to violence in prison.

> *The leader's primary instrument is the Self. That is what we have to work with. It is not going to be the code written by some brilliant programmer, the smart chip inside the personal digital assistant, or the phrase-turning script of a clever speechwriter that will make us better leaders. It is what we do with ourselves that's going to make the difference. The extent to which leaders become masters of their craft is the extent to which they learn to play themselves. Leadership development is self-development.*
>
> — James M. Kouzes (2003)

As a professional in the field of corrections, business, and human services for more than 30 years, the word "leadership" has grown to have great significance to me. Leadership means being able to take the initiative, having the ability, the courage, and the integrity to make a decision—a decision that transforms institutions that have had a history of failure, into institutions that are successful. When the TM program is implemented in rehabilitation settings throughout the world, those deep pockets of stress will be removed from society.

It is by producing coherence in those centers of stress that the incoherence in society will become minimal and eventually disappear. This is the fulfillment of enlightened rehabilitation in the prisons and throughout society, not of a specific pathology but of the holistic restoration of the creative intelligence within every person to his or her full dignity and stature. This is the development of the full potential of the human being, and the purpose of enlightened rehabilitation.

What follows are the voices of prisoners in a maximum security setting, and those of professionals in law, justice, and rehabilitation. In the moving accounts of their experiences, and in spite of the differences in their lives, an astounding commonality emerges. The simple, peaceful unboundedness of Transcendental Consciousness has transformed all of their lives, whatever the nature of their stresses.

The Honorable David Mason

The Honorable David Mason was the first U.S. judge to sentence probationers to meditate in his home state of Missouri (CBEA, 2002). At a press conference on violent crime in Washington, DC, he articulated the importance of avoiding crime, and developing inner resiliency, through the Transcendental Meditation program.

I have spent time researching issues related to crime and recidivism. Early in my career I realized I could not spend my life doing nothing more than putting people in jail, particularly when so many of them reminded me of myself. I became involved in civic organizations that were investigating youth crime. It was in this context that TM was brought to my attention for employing the technique as a rehabilitative tool. In our country, as you well know, criminal recidivism is a problem as well as the spread of criminality, particularly among our nation's youth. We have to do more than simply become tougher because the last several decades have shown the tougher we become, the more criminality we have to deal with. Simply getting tough, while at times necessary, is not the solution to the problem.

Therefore, we must look for ways to help the offender and the potential offender avoid crime and build resiliencies. For most Americans that is easy—the mere fact that it is illegal is enough—or the deterrence of being punished is enough. That is true for the majority of Americans, but there are many Americans who were born into lives of quiet desperation, and they worry much more about the effect on their lives of a stray bullet, rather than being concerned about the Dow Jones. When in school, they are much more concerned on making it through the day safely, rather than having an Afrocentric education; they are much more concerned about the next meal than the next president. They see people on television living a normal life, but the reality for them is that the person who seems to be doing best in their area or community is the individual who is making it through gang activity, selling illicit drugs, or through other criminal contacts. For many people living in the inner city, power and respect does not come through the earning of degrees, but through the carrying of weapons. It is not the letters after your name but the caliber of your handgun that is going to get you respect. I am very familiar with that community because I grew up in it.

I know what it is like to see that. In the years since I left those circumstances it has gotten worse. We have segregated our nation's poor in massive housing projects, and into large urban areas where there is block after block of poverty. We find ourselves surprised that there are no role models, there are no community centers or businesses, or people around that can give and help build resiliency in our nation's youth. We should not be surprised that crime is a viable alternative, and imposes tremendous emotional stress of living under those circumstances resulting in violence and a criminal response.

TM has proven to me, through the research that I have read, to be a methodology of helping someone to develop the internal resiliency necessary to deal with those circumstances. By helping an individual develop the type of internal mechanism, or the internal resiliency, through the expansion of consciousness, they begin to value their own thoughts, life, and vision for themselves. Suddenly the thought of doing things that lead to prison seems undesirable because it does not fit the new vision of themself, and of course as you value yourself then you begin to value others. That is why in my view the teaching of TM to offenders and potential offenders is an important aspect of criminal rehabilitation that we must look at seriously in this country. We must try to introduce TM in every state, and in every prison. We must give the TM program a serious chance. I am convinced that if we do, this nation will find that it will pay off for us with reduced crime, reduced recidivism— and quite frankly better living conditions in our nation's cities (Washington University Law, 2011).

Frank Billingsley #B-36725-A

The boundaries of chains and metal, brick and mortar are illusions in the presence of a human being's experience of his transcendental pure consciousness. What follows is an odyssey of transformation from a troubled, abused childhood through the dehumanization of imprisonment to the discovery of inner freedom.

Frank: Every Saturday night my stepfather would beat my mother until her eyes were black and blue, and her head looked like a melon. I loved my mother very much, and I shed many tears for her. My stepfather, I hated him more than passion and words could ever describe. I did not respect my stepfather, but my fears of him forced me to conduct myself appropriately with the best manners, lest I get the fat whipped out of my head. I lived in the Fourth Ward. This was an era when segregation was strictly enforced. Negro was the race name, and all niggers stayed in their proper place. During these times, next to a hot piece of lead discharged from a loaded gun, the deadliest thing one could do was be an "uppity nigger." You never looked whites in the eye when talking to them and you respected your elders. I was a very frightened child, so you could say I was perhaps one of the most respectful of my little community. However, in my heart, I despised everything, and these mental pressures kept me under stress.

George Ellis (GE) Commentary: As a child Billingsley did not receive much formal education, although he enjoyed school when he attended. Billingsley felt school did not teach him how to put bread on the table. Food for the mind was all right, but it amounted to nothing when there was no food for the stomach. At least this was what his stepfather told him just before instructing him to look for a job.

Frank: I felt I was the black sheep of the family. I was always being chastised or beaten. I felt my mother cared more about the rules, the law, and my brothers and sisters than she cared about me—and this left me with stress.

GE Commentary: Between the ages of eight and twelve Billingsley had many jobs and all of his earnings were immediately turned over to his mother, so she could buy food for the household. Billingsley worked day or night depending on what was open to him. Some jobs required that he work eight to ten hours for seven days at $12.50 per week. Twelve-fifty was a lot of money to him, but he happily gave every nickel to his mother for the welfare of the family. His mother in turn would give all or part of the money he earned to Billingsley's stepfather.

Frank: My stepfather would buy wine and both my parents would then proceed to get drunk. The talk of food would bring tears to the eyes of my sisters and brothers. My mother was not much help, and my stepfather did not care about anything. Once his own stomach was full, it was assumed then that no one else was hungry. If we did not get to eat, it was stated: "You should have." Also if we did eat before our stepfather had eaten his rations: "You shouldn't have." I turned to hunting in order to provide food for my sisters and brothers, along with stealing milk from "some good people's porch."

My mother was a proud woman, but a poor judge of men, or she wanted a man for the wrong reason. She was a poor provider, an alcoholic, and a God-fearing woman to boot. She did not allow any of her children to beg anyone for food. My mother always instructed us to leave someone's home when the smell of food being prepared began to invade our nostrils, or was ready for serving. We were not allowed to accept invitations and when someone invited us to share their food, we were instructed to say, "No, thank you" and run like we were being chased by hooded white folks. So the best thing for me to do was hunt the little neighborhood fowls. When the birds were hard to get, then I relied on stealing. As long as I told my mother that a good Christian lady gave it to me, then she would shout for joy saying, "I know'd there were some good folks in de world! But you stop taking dem things, ya hear. A person who begs is a lazy no good for nuthin' people, and I don't want nobody thinking us to be no good." If I brought home stuff too often, talking about some good believer who gave them to me, mother would have me take her to that person, so I could give it back. I had to be careful and time myself. There was no restriction on sparrows, robins, and pigeons—they were plentiful, and for hungry stomachs, good eating. However, the fact that I could not accept dinner offers meant I had to steal crumbs and then lie about it. This induced more stress and confusion in my mind, a stress I had no way of controlling or alleviating.

GE Commentary: This is the story of our times and is manifesting world-wide— depending on the inner strength of the mind and body, one either breaks under the pressure or finds a way to release it. The historical background of Billingsley is nothing new; it is the reality pervading all races and societies, and reflects poorly on the human condition. It is no wonder that Billingsley's story begins anew as an adult on a bus to Folsom State Prison. What follows is a mental journey into the depths of a man's soul and his awakening from the center of darkness within himself.

Frank: Under the cover of darkness, I was standing on the loading dock in back of Chino Prison's Madrome mess hall. It was somewhere around 3:00 or 3:30 a.m. on a Thursday morning in mid-April 1974. I was about the tenth person to go through the shakedown . . . I felt so humiliated. Standing on the loading dock in the warm morning breeze the thought of my children came to mind. Their mother divorced me and with my having made several unkept promises, she had married someone else. Her marrying someone else did not disturb me, but I was concerned that I did not know what kind of father my children had overseeing them. I did not see myself as being a good father. However, I did not want the children to have worse—this worried me. My thoughts were interrupted when I heard B-36725-A being called out. I worked my way through the small crowd of inmates, dressed in transportation whites, down the ramp. I came to an officer holding a clipboard. The heavyset correctional officer asked my name without bothering to look up. Billingsley, I replied patiently, and was waved on. As I approached the next officer, who was standing next to the old gray goose (the bus), the officer holding the clipboard shouted out, "All right inmates, listen up! I will call out your number; you answer back with your last name. I will check you off, and you will then approach one of the other officers and get chained up. Once everybody is chained and on the bus, then we will be pulling out of here. Do like I said and we will be finished and out of here in a little bit. Now is that clear?"

With my arms chained to my waist, I stepped on board the old gray goose and made my way to a seat near the rear. I thought to myself, who cares about hurrying? All we are doing is leaving one God-forbidden place and headed for the devil's pit at the end of the world. To me, it was just a way to cut off all family and friendly relations with the outside world. I was headed for Folsom Prison, almost 500 miles away from my nearest friend, to a California location where I did not know a soul. I knew that since I was now starting a life term sentence, both time and space would rob me of any tie I might have back in Los Angeles. In a situation such as this, without a friend or some concerned person outside to ask questions if something went wrong, one's life is worth no more than a pack of cigarettes. I had no known enemies inside the prison system, but enemies are easy enough to find.

With every seat finally occupied with its cargo, the old gray goose began to roar and flutter. The loose windows shook against the vibrating panels, and everyone was quiet as the bus got in motion. There was nothing to see this time of the morning, and it was too early to start any conversation with my riding partner who shared the seat with me. So I decided to try and get some sleep. I adjusted my waist chain in an effort to get my hands in a relaxed position, laid my head against the panel, and closed my eyes. My eyes were only shut for what seemed a short time when the old goose apparently ran one of its tires over a hole or something in the freeway. The incident caused the bus to bounce and in turn caused my head to strike the side of the panel. Startled, I opened my eyes in anger and disgust. Naturally, I blamed everything on the driver, saying insulting things to myself, knowing shouting aloud would have affected nothing. At any rate, my mood was changing as I was now witnessing the sun's glow coming over the horizon, dispersing the darkness, and painting the distant sky a dangerous orange-like color. My first thought was that God had declared this a day of judgment, and had set the world aflame. I have never seen such a violent looking sunrise before.

After relocating our place on the road, I observed that the old gray goose had just challenged a curve and was humming its way onto the Santa Monica Freeway, taking us westbound. We were passing over old familiar territory where I suddenly recognized streets and rooftops. As the goose approached the straightaway, off to the right I peered down at the doe-skin painted apartments on Ellendale Street. This spot to me had more meaning, and was more famous than Sam Houston's stand at the Alamo to American history. On Ellendale Street, in the apartment where I could almost read the number on the door, is where I lived with the only woman I ever loved. I have loved many women in my short lifetime, but those loves were purely physical affairs. My love for this woman had been different. It was a deep, fulfilling, and joyful spiritual feeling. It was a feeling that my island heart had rigors for. A very deep dissatisfying sensation knotted my stomach as the old bus roared on in pursuit of its destination. My eyes hurt from straining; they seemed to want to pop right out of my head in an effort to keep the drifting apartment building in focus. On my smoky breath was a prayer that God would inform that woman of my passing, and bring her to the door, so I could hold her shapely café-au-lait figure in my eyes once more and caress her loveliness. As the apartment building grew smaller, a teardrop irritated my cheek, which I rubbed away, using my shoulder. I felt inner rejection and was silent. We roared past many monumental locations but none were as important as the spot we had left behind, in hated disgust with hands bound to my sides. I managed to remove the sack of Bull Durham from the waist pocket of my shirt, twisted one up, and began to smoke. Four puffs on the rugged western cigarette gave me a headache, and I stamped it out. I attempted to go back to sleep by scooting down and resting my head on the back seat.

If you count the duration of a dream, I slept a long time. The dream I had was a recapitulation of a TV series which was aired when I was a teenager—*The Fugitive*, made famous by David Janssen, whose character was wrongly convicted by the jury for having killed his wife, and was sentenced to a life term in prison. Fate had it that the train transporting him to the worthless site derailed, and the wreckage made his relentless escape possible. The dream was interrupted by a nudging in my side, and a voice saying, "Say homeboy, homeboy!" Coming out of my sleepiness I faced my seat partner and noticed a wrinkled brown paper bag in his hand. I asked him what was happening, and he answered it was chow time, gesturing the bag at me. Accepting the bag lunch, I noticed for the first time that the old gray goose was not in motion, and we were pulled off the highway and perched on our seats in the back of a Denny's restaurant; the appetizing aroma of breakfast food was being fed into our nostrils. There were plenty of conversations going on inside the now smoke-filled bus. If I could decipher one of the conversations, I could decipher them all.

The smell of bacon and eggs cooking immediately made me hungry, and I could not wait to tear into the bag on my lap. I opened it and removed one of the sandwich bags from inside. Without opening the waxed baggie, I could see the bologna resting over the side of the bread. Since I was not a pork eater, I offered the bologna sandwich to my seat partner. My attention was drawn to the correctional officer, who was coming from the direction of Denny's carrying a cardboard tray with hot food and coffee. I considered the nature of the officer coming on board the bus with the wonderful aroma of tasty food. Insensitively sitting and eating in front of us was equivalent to cruel and unnecessary punishment. The lunch break having ended, the old bus was again putting time and distance behind us.

The bright warm sun had begun to drop out of sight as we came around the thick granite walls and approached the giant oval gates of Folsom State Prison. The gates made loathsome, irritating sounds while they were pushed open by two gutty uniformed correctional officers, and we roared through. I did not even care to look back at those ugly gates again. My thoughts were now preoccupied with how I was going to save my life on this battlefront. Stories had it that Folsom Prison is one step short of the grave. It's the end of the world. It's a den for the cruelest, most evil, and scurviest inmate population in the State of California. It is the Mecca of violence. Life is cheap in Folsom;

your life can be successfully purchased for the price of a mere pack of cigarettes. Those were not only my subjective thoughts. They were the result of stories which had been passed on down to me through the days and months when I first heard that I had been selected as a candidate for the Folsom trip. My first thoughts were of Vietnam, and I was about to debark into the demilitarized zone. My thoughts were not of fear and panic. They were purely defensive and guarded ones. From this day forth I would not allow anyone within six feet of me. I was a courageous fighter, but my skills went away with my youth. Therefore, maintaining a safe distance would be my best defense. Running in prison is totally out of the question. There is simply no place to run where there is not a wall or a fence. Distance merely gives you another second or two to out-think your adversary so you might foil his move and equalize yourself in a deadly combative situation.

Once the debarkation was completed the other inmates and I were subjected to another skin examination. Afterwards in a column of two we were led into a spacious and dim-lighted mess hall. After eating, we were marched to the rear of the mess hall to unload our dishes. In the rear of the mess hall, I noticed a guard on a gun rail holding his 30-30 at port arms. Until now, other than for the movies, it was the first time I had seen inmates in a dining area being watched over by a rifle-toting police officer. This sight led me to give more credence to all the wild stories I had heard about Folsom. This must truly be the end of the world where murder is a breath away. For whom should I fear most—he who walks behind me or he who walks overhead? I wondered—how much patience do these officers have? How quick are they to fire into a crowd? In single file, we were led from the mess hall to what is designated as "One Building." We were directed up a flight of stairs until we came to the fifth tier, where we were sectioned off from the other inmates and quarantined. Quarantining fish (new arrivals) was an institutional formality. While quarantined, we were not permitted to converse with members of the regular seasoned Folsom prisoners. The only freedom we had from cramped cells during the quarantine period consisted of a half hour for each meal, and 15 minutes every other night for showers. The remainder of the days and nights were spent in complete solitude in a hammock or cot. If you wanted a decent sleep, then the best place was on the floor without the soiled, smelly mattress.

On the last day of quarantine, I was ordered to appear before the inmate classification committee, which would approve a program for me, and determine what my custody would be. Having previously served slightly more than five years in prison, I was a veteran. I knew what would be expected of me, so deciding what course to pursue was of no consequence. I had only been separated from the Department of Corrections 90 days before I was again arrested and taken into custody. I was returned to the Department of Corrections six months later. Under these circumstances, I thought that continuing my previous institutional program should be a matter of procedure. I would inform the classification committee that my previous record with the California Department of Corrections shows that I am a printer and would like to work in the print shop. Furthermore, that I am interested in an academic education, and feel these pursuits would be of benefit to me upon my release—should I live to see it.

The classification committee was composed of three members, a counselor, and two correctional officers. I stood patiently waiting for the committee to acknowledge my presence. "You are, let me see, Billingsley," stated the counselor. "Let's see here, you were released from C.D.C. 2-5-73. On 5-7-73 you were arrested again. Is that correct?" That is correct, I said, I was out about 90 days. I was only on parole a short time, and I requested a continuation of my previous prison program. I asked to be assigned to the print shop and placed in a school program. There was a moment of silence and no one yet looking at me. "Well Billingsley," he remarked, "you have really done it this time. You have brought back some serious beefs—murder, robbery, and assault. From this I would say you are going to be with us 15 years." The counselor still had not looked at me, nor did anyone sitting behind the long table. "I think I am going to put you on Close A Custody, and in an unassigned category." I remarked I have never been in any serious trouble in the pen, and I do not expect to get in any at Folsom. "Well you are right. Your jacket shows you to be a model prisoner, so to speak. I'll tell what I will do. Let's see how you are in close custody for about three years. If you do not have any write-ups, then we will reduce your custody and recommend you work in the print shop. They can use talented guys like you." Then he paused, and stated: "As for school, I'll refer it to Education. You should get a ducat (summons) from them in six months. In view of the beefs you have brought back with you that is about the best I can do. Keep your nose clean for three to four years, and we will try to get custody down to where you can have family visits. Do you have any more questions?" I simply answered no. "Well, don't feel put down. You will be seen at least every six months for reclassification." I replied I do not see how that means anything when you already sentenced me to three to four years on close custody, and that does not make sense since this entire institution is listed as California's maximum security pen.

With this, I left the room, hot, but I knew I had to be cool. It is part of the old saying that you do not throw rocks when you live in a glass house. You just try and roll with the flow of things. Feeling that my desire and need for improvement were not salable commodities to this committee designed to fulfill inmate and institutional needs, I began to understand more clearly why rehabilitation was previously defined as a vulgar word. I was assigned to One Building. Like all the housing units, except for Five Building, One Building is dirty and dingy. The odor of unsanitary conditions immediately clogged my nostrils. It was a warm April day; my body blistered with sweat. Every face was an unfriendly face. All the stares were cold and hardened. Carrying my bedroll on my shoulder and my toothbrush in my pocket, I walked past the hungry-looking inmates and reported to the building officer. I handed him my ducat, and he led me to the fifth tier and pointed my cell out to me. Not a word was exchanged. The officer pulled on a long bar, and I pulled open the gate to cell 972 and stepped inside the 5' x 12' quarters. It was not much of a place to live for 15 years. The walls were damaged and in need of painting. There was no mirror, but I could obtain one later. A headset would give me connection with the institution radio. There was a fluorescent light mounted on the wall that could be turned on when needed. There was a sink with no hot water faucet, and about a foot from the head of my bed was the commode. The bed was sunken, but it was far from being a slingshot like the one I just left. There was nothing to do now except to make this house a more pleasant place to live.

Finally set into my new quarters, I was wishing I had something to read when suddenly I heard a penetrating shot. The bullet sound came close to my cell, and I leaped off the bunk in a panic. My heart began to pound. There was no time to think, no place to hide, only time to react in fright. The explosion of a rifle is a very chilling sound when discharged inside a building made of solid thick stone. There was the awesome thought of the ricocheting projectile slipping through the bars and indiscriminately striking me. In response to the echoing sound, the air filled with silence. I peeped outside my bars and saw beneath me a correctional officer standing just adjacent to my cell, but on the gun rail just below, holding his M1 rifle at the ready. A fight had broken out between two inmates under the influence of the institutional racial difficulties. There was quietness for at least 60 seconds after the shot was fired, and then conversation began again among the inmates. No one asked why the shot was fired or if anyone was hurt. In fact, conversation was very general. One comment I remember precisely was someone calling out to another inmate, who was asked, "Do you know what's for chow tonight?" "Chili beans" was the answer. Such reactions to life and death are of course puzzling.

GE Commentary: One may ask if growth can exist after listening to Billingsley's inner reflections and observations. What follows is another side of the story after Maharishi had authorized TM to be taught at Folsom Prison.

Frank: I had tried everything and nothing had helped me, but I was still open to learn. I was instructed in the TM technique and after a few moments, I experienced a slight weightlessness that was so beautiful. My mind became crystal clear. Suddenly, I slipped into a level of consciousness that I had never experienced before. There seemed to exist nothing but a tranquil peace. When it was time to open my eyes, I could not help but notice how rested my body felt. Never had I felt so still and at ease. That was it. The first period of the TM technique can only be described as a beautiful trip. From the TM technique I have found something for me.

Multicultural TM meeting in the educational department at Folsom State Prison. Frank Billingsley is in the rear far right of the photo. The meditators in the photo developed a trust unique in the prison, and found the meetings a safe environment for human development.[©]

GE Commentary: One's state of mind, rather than the outer ecology, determines our inner attitudes. The outer social ecology is the source of pressure, and it is a common fact that people respond differently under pressure. When an individual can tap more of his or her potential, the creativity for solving problems is greater. Additionally, lack of an anxiety-leveler allows tension to accumulate in the nervous system, and one becomes less flexible, and functions with less effectiveness. Life is as we are. Our worldview determines if we find happiness or misery. Billingsley's situation prior to and after learning TM reminds me of the limitations we impose on our lives. If we can begin to erase the boundaries that identify who we are, and expand them, we can minimize our fears and our struggles. Billingsley had surrounded himself with his pain. When a person meditates, his or her mind shifts from struggles and limitations to an unrestricted vibration of his or her being. In this experience of unity with oneself there is no identification with the duality of worldly struggles, and pain begins to diminish. It is not that the ability to function stops, but inside one creates positive feelings and peace of mind. Darkness and light cannot exist simultaneously. The regular practice of the TM technique cultivates a new habit of the nervous system, in which peace is experienced inwardly and maintained during activity, which is antithetical to suffering. Creating enslavement to attitudes of limitations reinforces itself, and is not restricted by income, condition, or social class. Some officers see an evil intent in all inmates because this is part of their circle of reality. Some inmates see all men in uniform as oppressors. In the ghetto people may tie their lives to their struggles by their mental perception of reality. Our positionality in life is our strength and our weakness. Our habits can create our realities.

The failure of many therapies is that they either ignore consciousness trying to deal with modifying overt behavior, or they focus on the pathology inherent in thinking, which is a symptom of imbalance. Replacing negative thoughts with positive thoughts is simply mood-making, and superficial mental manipulation. Positive thinking as a technique for change may be psychologically comforting, but it creates an illusion. It can be likened to a beggar telling himself that he is a king, but finding difficulty when attempting to apply the benefit that belongs to the reality of being a king. The TM program has been scientifically documented, verified on the level of subjective observation and experience to produce psycho-physiological experiences as those described innocently by Billingsley; he experienced transcending, a primal level of thoughtless pure creative intelligence, and self-awareness. The experience surpasses intellectual or behavioral manipulation because it is an inner embrace of Self-referral consciousness.

Don Hutto

Don Hutto, former President of the American Correctional Association, Executive Vice-President, Corrections Corporation of America

Quite honestly, unless we can reduce violence and fear in an institution, almost anything else is impossible to accomplish. When one has to fear for their safety every waking moment, and then be afraid to sleep too, no other positive things are possible. It has been shown with a number of instances that the TM program contributes to the reduction of violence in institutions. The program also contributes to the reduction of stress in correctional employees, which leads to their ultimate health and results in reduced tensions in the institutions themselves.

Charles Hamilton #12784

The emotional and physical reality of living in the grip of incarceration, and the human transformation that occurs through transcending, are expressed here through the recollections of Charles Hamilton.

Charles: The other day I was feeling depressed, and I was building circles and limitations. When I realized it, I sat, practiced the TM technique, and in a few minutes I was smiling. The weight of depression was lifted from me effortlessly. The beauty is that it happened naturally.

GE Commentary: The effect of the TM technique is pleasing in itself, and with that charm you cannot entertain negativity for long. A prison is a setting where negativity is constantly being reinforced and fear dominates. In a prison environment when one observes another person not contained within his circle of opinion, he becomes the enemy; this reality not only applies in prisons, but in society. The poor person's vision tells him the rich person is the enemy, and in defense, the rich person then creates a vision that the poor man is the enemy. It makes no difference which vision was created first: the point is the vision cannot be sustained if one firmly and strongly changes his or her vision of the other. The change is the natural result of a more expanded state of mind. Through the regular practice of TM our inner experiences are recreated in the outer world. The TM technique creates inner stability. When a person becomes strong enough, the words and stigmatic symbols no longer cause pain, because the lessons of the process of evolution have been assimilated. The power of human transformation is expressed in a letter that was directed to Mr. Enomoto, the Director of Corrections, by inmate Charles E. Hamilton:

Charles Hamilton: I am a 29-year-old convict at Folsom Prison. I have spent the last nine years of my life confined within the walls of one institution or another. I have never written a letter to anyone in free society about the hatred and despair I have witnessed and/or encountered throughout this ordeal. The thought of writing a letter of this nature to an official or someone considered a part of the establishment was looked upon as being repulsive and a sign of submission until I became a student of TM. The purpose of this letter is not to criticize, condemn, nor complain about the other programs offered, in spite of their unproductiveness. I have been at Folsom two years, unassigned and inactive, living under a dark cloud of doubt and uncertainty. Now, for the first time since becoming an adult, and an active part of the TM program, I have a clear direction that's unique in every sense of the word. If any of you are concerned with the success, upliftment of the institution, and the administrative body, you will see the urgency of the moment and importance of the TM technique.

I am not a teacher of the TM program—in fact I have only been actively involved for a month—but never before have I been so positively engrossed in anything, and I have tried them all at one time or another. I can only depict the TM technique as an uncomplicated simplicity that offers the apex of internal bliss and contentment. I have always thought that the loss that is unknown is no loss at all, but the TM program has blasted this theory to pieces. Unfortunately, because of my not having the knowledge of the TM technique prior to the program offered at Folsom, I have suffered tremendously in my foolish world of obscurity and bewilderment. Before closing, I feel impelled to warmly mention that I have heard you are a wise and receptive man with an understanding heart. If this is remotely true, then I feel that my efforts to help establish the TM program so that others may reap the unalienable benefits will not be in vain.

Mr. Enomoto, I have confidence in the TM program, and the expressed purpose of this letter is to dramatize my confidence because this is an issue that is so important that it can no longer be ignored. I am a young man who has been denounced by society as criminally insane. In spite of being in the shadows of bondage, the TM program has enabled me to move into the sunlight of mental freedom. I can say with complete honesty that I am no longer plagued with inner fear, outer resentment, and fighting a futile sense of nobodiness. I honestly feel that what the TM program has to offer will continue to enrich my life and understanding. This is only the short of how I feel about the Transcendental Meditation program.

Lynn Walthers, Director, Volunteer Services, Chittenden CCC, Vermont

I had a vague fear; it was an anxiety that something might happen to me in the facility. I was not sure exactly what. I did not know what the inmates would do, or how they would relate to me. After learning the TM technique and meditating with them, I just did not feel the apprehension anymore—there was not any need for it.

Anonymous Inmate

A few days ago I was asked for my support in helping a friend kill another man. Even though it was my friend's problem, he knew me for years and was sure he could count on my help. My response to the whole trip was, "I am sorry brother, but it just is not worth it." Even though he understood because we hold a lot of respect for our friendship, I still felt guilty. I had an inner feeling that I was running out on him. My record showed that this was not my style. Through my growth in finding myself through the TM program, I now realize myself, as well as my future, is more important to me than all this madness in prison. After speaking with my TM instructor, I am able to see now that what I had done was right, which at the time I was unsure of. I have had many positive experiences since I have been in the TM program, and I feel this is one I will always be proud of. I honestly feel for the first time in 30 years, that I can finally take a look at myself, and be comfortable. The TM program has made all this possible without any effort at all. Jai Guru Dev (signed, confidentiality requested).

Arthur John Anderson, J.D., LL.M.

Arthur John Anderson, former Director of the Criminal Justice Division, Office of the Attorney General for the State of Arkansas, under Bill Clinton

I remember in Holland, at The Hague, where the World Court is located, there are two words for justice. The first, *gerechtigkeit*, means the law of man that is imposed by the judge, enacted by the legislature, and enforced by the police officers. The second, *rechtvaardig*, means the justice that flows naturally from the human heart, which allows a person to live in a harmonious fashion with his fellow man. It means things operating in accord with the laws of nature. It does not mean we impose, superimpose, force orderliness, or create some superstructure of orderliness and drop it on society. True justice consists of eliciting the harmony and orderliness that is already there, which in the final analysis is going to be the hallmark of leadership in the years and decades to come, in criminal law, and society generally.

In the context of prisons, justice is often a sham. A person would have to be present in a prison to understand what the word tension means. We do not make a person ready for normal social activity by removing him from society, isolating him in a cage, surrounding him with other malcontents and deviants, subjecting him to all forms of depravity, deprivations, and indignities, and by intensifying all around him the whole enforcement syndrome. True rehabilitation comes from within, and leadership in penology must recognize that not only the inmate, but society in general, must be rehabilitated.

Rex Spross

Rex was one of the first 10 men to learn to meditate at Folsom Prison; he was a loner except for one friend, and they seemed to always have one another's back. Rex was heavily muscled, a martial arts expert, and always meticulous. When he had been approached by gangs wanting him to join, he made it very clear that he had no interest, and there would be serious consequences if he were confronted again. He was not challenged, and eventually received a parole date after 10 years of incarceration. I recall hearing a story that he used to practice his martial arts training on the yard, and he was stopped because there was a concern he would train the other inmates. So he threw all of his bedding out of his cell, slept on the cement floor and practiced in his cell. The way people gain respect in a prison is to make someone back down, or to commit a murder. A gang member knew that Rex was going to be paroled in about 10 days and thought he could make a reputation for himself.

Rex had a warrior mentality, and was raised with military discipline. He was also a regular practitioner of meditation and looking forward to his freedom, but he was threatened by an inmate from one of the gangs, thinking that Rex would back down. Rex did not want this situation, but he was still under the influence of a prison sense of survival, and he had enormous pride.

Rex: I secured two shanks, slid them up my sleeves, and polished my shoes. It was lock-down, and the gates would be opening shortly. I felt I had no choice, and that when the gate slid open, I would take out as many gang members as I could before they got to me. The word began to spread that I was ready for a battle, and the gang leaders were alerted regarding what was about to happen. I closed my eyes to meditate, and centered myself in preparation for the anticipated battle. As soon as the gates began to unlock, I slowly opened my eyes from meditation, and in front of my cell was the man who threatened me, shaking in fear, pleading for his life, and apologizing. When the gang members learned whom he had challenged they had told their member he was on his own. I was relieved, and did something that I would not normally have done; I spared the man's life, and he ran quickly from the cell door. I returned the shanks, and waited for the days to pass.

GE Commentary: This is a true event that took place; this was life at Folsom Prison. Folsom Prison was different from prisons with younger populations. In younger populations, you might have many more incidents, but few are terminal. At Folsom, there are fewer incidents, but if and when they occurred, they were usually fatal. When Rex was released from prison, an associate and I picked him up at the gate, and I let him stay in my home. I respected his character, not his choices, but he had his own integrity. There were some interesting observations and one dramatic event. When he left the prison and came into my home, his feet were not capable of walking on the carpet, because for over 10 years he only walked on cement. Also this tough man, who was prepared to take on an entire prison gang, was timid about taking a streetcar or transportation across town in San Francisco. What we take for granted is often lost through years of confinement; the adjustment takes time and support in addition to meditation.

I was working teaching TM and educational programs at San Quentin Prison, and I had just come home. Suddenly in the front of my house in the Richmond district of San Francisco, there was gunfire. Rex was in the upstairs bedroom and hit the floor, and I had no idea what was taking place. I would discover it had nothing to do with Rex; the police had stopped an individual for a traffic violation, and it turned out badly, as the man was shot in front of my door. I sat quietly reflecting on the work I was doing, and I asked myself: is this the right direction for my life? The next morning I received a phone call asking if I would travel to Europe to join the Chief Justice of the Supreme Court of India, along with leading scientists, government officials, and members of the International Court, as a featured speaker for my work teaching TM in the prisons. I was stunned by the contrasting moments, and realized that the work had value, and I should continue.

Rudy Deleon

Rudy Deleon, Former Special Assistant to the Attorney General of California, and Deputy Secretary, California Youth and Adult Authority for the California Department of Corrections.

One could come to the conclusion that if you took one thousand inmates who had actively participated in the TM program, there would be a cost savings of two million dollars in housing alone—that is for the inmates who had not returned to prison. This does not consider other factors like the cost of crime to the victim and the victim's family, or the welfare cost to the state because of incarceration for the breadwinner. I practice the TM technique and there is no question it has helped me relax, also to think more clearly and immediately recover from a stressful encounter, and make effective in-depth decisions. Dr. Alexander's study in Massachusetts and Dr. Bleick's very thorough studies in California showed consistent results on the benefits of the TM program in reducing recidivism. During the first year after release there were 56% fewer new convictions involving inmates who had learned the TM technique. There was 40% less total recidivism, including revocation of parole during the first year, and a significantly lower recidivism rate for the entire five years for which figures are available.

Pat Corum

This exposition by Pat Corum was written after he was released from prison in collaboration with myself as a contribution to the book entitled Self Recovery (O'Connell & Alexander, 1994).

A man is brought to prison because his behavior is of such an antisocial nature that he is deemed no longer fit to live in a free society. Therefore, he is placed in an environment where control of his behavior is maintained through constant supervision. The concept of prisons in our current society is archaic. I am not saying that a person should not be punished for committing a crime.

However, under the current system, the crimes committed against the criminal by society are in many cases equivalent to, or greater than, the crimes committed by the criminal against society. A man is removed from a free society, placed in a static and controlled environment where he is kept until his overt behavior indicates he is adjusted. He is then unleashed on a society that is not ready or willing to accept him. The idea that you can put a person in a cage, take away his identity and all responsibility, restrict contact with loved ones, pervert his morals and ethics, and at the same time tell him that this is being done to prepare him for life in free society—this is ludicrous and obscene.

I am not advocating that the prisons in this country be torn down, and everyone in them be slapped on their wrists and told to go and sin no more. Rather, I advocate updating and upgrading the prisons to humane standards and instituting rehabilitation programs that are both effective and enlightening. After being sentenced to life in prison, I was transported to the receiving and guidance center at the California Medical Facility, in Vacaville, California. My initial impression upon seeing the center is still with me—cold and impersonal.

I was taken inside where all my personal belongings, which included my wedding ring, were taken from me. After I disrobed, a guard searched my person for contraband. I was given the number A-77655. After a fingerprinting, haircut, and shower, I was given two sets of clothes and a rule book, and taken to a cell with the admonition to read and follow all the rules listed in the rule book. Thinking back, I still marvel at the impersonal efficiency of the initial phase of prison life. The rule book covers all aspects of prison life.

There is a time and a place for everything you do, and if you are caught out of step you are subject to being placed in isolation. The first concern of staff is their safety, second that no one escapes, third to keep convicts from killing each other, and fourth to provide everybody some kind of assignment. During one seven-month period at Folsom Prison, six convicts were murdered by other convicts. No attempt was made to conduct any searches, or put more officers on the gun rails or towers, or beef up security in any way. However, when a correctional officer was murdered by a convict at an institution over 100 miles away, Folsom was locked down for over two weeks. Gun rail officers and ground personnel were doubled, and all convicts and their cells were searched for weapons.

Staff zeal to see that each convict has a job is often carried to extremes. I appeared before the screening committee for my annual review for program adjustment. Before I got to the chair, my counselor wanted to know why I did not have a job assignment. I told him that I was assigned to the college program and was attending school. He stated that since the colleges were only on the weekends, I should have an assignment during the week. At this point, I explained that I worked five days in the hobby shop, and from my sales I could send approximately $250 per month home to help support my sons and pay my attorney. Additionally, since the highest paying prison job paid only $50 per month, I would refuse an assignment, unless I could make as much as I did at my working hobby. My counselor told me that he would see to it that the parole authority was advised of my refusal to work for the state.

In prison, instead of the expression Catch-22, the phrase Institutional Convenience is employed. It makes little difference or no difference what the convict wants. If his request for a lower custody, a different job, or housing assignment happens to be convenient for the institution, then the chances are he will receive them, unless one of the members of the screening committee has something personal against him. However, if you are skilled in a certain job and needed at the other end of the state, you are immediately transferred due to institutional convenience. In my own case, I wanted to be transferred south to be closer to my family.

After I had completed my first year, I asked to be transferred south. I was advised by the committee that since I was doing a life sentence I had to stay in a maximum security prison for a few years. Each year, until I had five years in, I was given the same answer. At the end of my fifth year I was told if I kept a clean record and had good work reports, they would consider a transfer after six years. When I appeared before the committee after six years with a clean disciplinary record with good work reports, I was advised that I would not be transferred because they did not want to disrupt the positive adjustment I had made. After seven years, I appeared before the committee to again ask for a transfer south. This time I had already received a parole date and was scheduled to be released in less than three months, and could think of no reason why I could not be transferred south due to the shortness of my parole date.

The inmate-con relationship with the correctional staff is like a child's game in which one team wears green and the other team wears blue, and there is an invisible line that is seldom crossed. Staff in their green uniforms visited for eight hours a day, many of them bringing an aura of apathy, indifference, and at times fear and hate. The convicts in their blue clothes live in a box for 24 hours a day. A few are motivated to go to school or learn a trade, while the majority flounders in self-pity, apathy, or deep hatred. Upon coming to prison, there was no doubt in my mind that prison life would do anything to change me in the years to come. Short of escaping, which I did once but was captured immediately, the only thing that could be done was to accept the situation for what it was, and to make the best of it. Since I could see no immediate relief I resolved not to do anything that would prolong my stay, and that I would take advantage of any program which would not only help me to get out, but also to stay out. My initial assignment was a job as a clerk-typist, and later I enrolled in the vocational meat-cutting class. I also signed up for group counseling, group psychotherapy, individual psychotherapy, and high school courses in sociology and psychology, as well as an extension course from UC Berkeley.

The various types of jobs that are available to inmates are numerous, and some can be equated to similar professions in free society, such as plumbers or gardeners. However, the majority of the job assignments have no relation to the free world. There are no jobs on the outside for men or women to unlock cell doors, and pass out clothes and toilet paper. Where else do they make license plates but in prison? Metal workers only learn to make products that the state uses. The work is so crude that no one creating a product for commercial use could use a man or woman with this type of experience and training. The so-called vocational training programs in prison are for the convenience of the institutions. The training is a conditional boost to the recidivism rate. Speaking from personal experience, my four years of training only qualified me to start as an apprentice, and the only place I could use my skills was at Folsom Prison. The vocational training programs should be updated, or obliterated.

It is inhuman to take a person, while teaching him almost nothing worthwhile, and make him believe he is being informed. The aforesaid situation creates a problem that cannot easily be resolved, and it is one that is created unnecessarily. A person does not have to be an oracle to understand that exploitation is not a tool for rehabilitation. My low opinion of prison jobs and vocational training is carried over into the area of counseling. My first group counselor was a correctional sergeant who openly admitted that the only reason he conducted a group was because of the extra money, and that it would look good in his personnel file when he took the exam for lieutenant. So for one hour a week the group discussed the menu, upcoming movies, and the living conditions. If you failed to show up for group counseling you were subject to disciplinary action. Furthermore, failure to attend group counseling was always brought to the attention of the parole authority. Just show up and play the game by not rocking the boat, and you were assured of a good report to the parole authority by your group counselor. The majority of men liked this situation, as it did not require them to make any effort to think either about the past or the future. It was all part of the routine, which only asked that men and women be present in their assigned areas. In 13 years of attending various group counseling sessions, the faces have changed, but the general attitude of staff and the convicts have not. Unlike the group counselors, who at times only possessed an eighth grade education, the group psychotherapist's education ranged from a minimum of an A.A. degree to a Ph.D. Normally, group psychotherapy lasted two hours, and assignment to these groups was generally done through the psychology department. Their selection was made on the basis of the crimes that the person had been convicted of. On paper these groups would appear to have a great deal to offer due to the presence of a qualified therapist at each meeting. The therapist was supposed to guide the individual and, in turn, the group to discuss those problems which were instrumental in bringing them to prison. I was advised by numerous psychiatrists that I was immature, and had failed to learn from past mistakes, and that as soon as I grew up and accepted the responsibilities of a mature adult, my antisocial behavior patterns would extinguish themselves. It was years before I realized that the above was true for the majority of the men in prison.

The one thing about group therapy that most people noticed was the underlying hostility each person brought to the group. At first I did not understand why, but after about six months I knew why. For two hours of each week, you were forced to dredge up those things in the past that were embarrassing, ugly, and vile, and relive them. Whoever said confession was good for the soul had to be a policeman. After each session, I would feel drained of emotion and exhausted physically; it would take days to overcome the depression. Individual therapy is more intense due to the one-to-one basis; otherwise the methods and results are the same. The counselors, the therapists, psychologists, and psychiatrists could all tell the various labels that applied to different types of behavior. Their only answer was continued psychotherapy.

Once you have been assigned to take group therapy, you are not allowed to transfer to another institution or receive a parole date until you have been given a psychological clearance. The psychiatrists are in an odd position in that if they do not give a person clearance, he is still subject to spend the rest of his or her life in prison. It does not take long to realize the psychiatrist can only hurt you and not help you where parole is concerned. Nevertheless, with little effort anyone can obtain clearance by simply reading a few books on psychiatry. Once you know what the psychiatrist wants to hear, all you do is act relaxed, and parrot what you have learned. It might take a couple of years, but that sure beats the rest of your life. Over the years, I have talked to numerous men about their experiences in groups, and the bottom line to all stories was they held back, and often lied because of the fear that they just might be so far out in left field that the psychiatrist would not give them clearance. The way I see the situation is this: The prison psychiatrist is given the job of diagnosing men and women who view him with fear, suspicion, and often hostility. The men and women will lie and suppress vital facts that are crucial to an accurate diagnosis.

After spending seven and a half years in San Quentin and Folsom with their vocational training, group psychotherapy, and individual psychotherapy, I was paroled. Approximately four months later, after being shot five times, I was again under arrest. After three trials, I now had my second life sentence. I had been back in Folsom for five years and there were only two significant changes. One, the education program had been expanded where the men could earn an A.A. degree. I was also the first man to be thrown out of the college program because I had earned too many credits. The second change, and the most significant one, came about because of the college program. A man who was hired to teach Philosophy was also an instructor of the Transcendental Meditation program. After two semesters in his class, many conversations, personal correspondence, and after reading several books about the TM program, arrangements were made, and I was instructed in the TM technique. In October 1975, I wrote a letter to

Governor Brown stating that after 13 years in prison, I could honestly say that the TM program is the only program that has ever helped me. There are no ignorant changes or psychiatrist playing mind games. Everything has been positive from the moment I learned the TM technique. Besides being relaxed, feeling good, and being less rigid, I experienced a continual growth of inner strength, self-confidence, and self-esteem.

My personal feelings about group counseling, group psychotherapy, and individual psychotherapy can be best described by paraphrasing a statement made by Maharishi: It should not be a function of psychology to remind a man that his past was miserable, or that his surroundings and circumstances were unfavorable, or that his associations were depressing and discouraging, or that there was a lack of love and harmony with those near to him. It should be considered criminal to tell anyone that his individual life is based on the inefficient and degenerate influence of his past environment. The psychological influence of such depressing information is demoralizing and the inner core of the heart becomes twisted by it. Maharishi further explained that mental health may be understood best as having a foundation in the integration of mind and body. Mental illness reflects a breakdown in the mind-body coordination. When a person becomes stressed he loses access to his inner resources. His mind becomes weak, and his weakness limits his power and clarity of thinking. He cannot provide a sufficient organizing force from within to engage in effective activity. He fails to fulfill desires because he has lost direction. Each failure causes further stress. The breakdown of mind-body coordination is a vicious circle leading to increasing frustration, suffering, and despair. How can someone trapped in the vicious circle of failure and increasing stress move out of it?

The techniques of modern psychotherapy attend to the mind or the body (or both) in order to clarify thinking, and strengthen the ability to fulfill desires. Analytically-oriented therapies attempt to clarify thinking by freeing the mind from conflicts and repressions. Somatically-oriented techniques undertake to free the body from stress, increase energy, and improve mind-body integration. The mind-body system is so complicated that it is questionable whether any technique aimed at effecting change in only one aspect of the system may prove very effective in improving overall integration.

Pat Corum (far left in the front row) meditates with Mike Love of the Beach Boys
(front row third from the right), and volunteer meditators from San Francisco and Marin County.©

I have experienced that the TM program provides an integrated approach to mind-body coordination, encouraging the body's self-healing process through a rest deeper than and distinct from sleep. Mind and body grow more energetic and are freed from stress. In addition, through the experience of pure awareness, the individual gains access to the integrative nature of his inner self. The TM technique provided me the missing element as an antithesis to my suffering. The analogy of turning on a light to remove the darkness without having to explore the source of the darkness is the key to human transformation. Similarly, analysis of past experiences of a person who is beginning to grow in all aspects of life adds little, and may even inhibit progress. Once a person gains access to his inner resources, he sees opportunities for growth where before he had seen only tension-producing obstacles. A correctional officer asked me how it felt to have wasted 13 years of my life. I replied: life is never wasted when you have found a path to enlightenment.

When I see a man or woman walking toward me, I do not see a lump of matter; I see an impulse of Infinity.

— Maharishi (Estes Park, 1970)

GE Commentary: The synergy of my relationship with Maharishi and Pat Corum changed the direction of my life, and deepened my compassion. In Seelisberg, Switzerland a one-time historical event took place in the TM organization that I do not believe was ever repeated. It symbolized not only the unconditional love and compassion of Maharishi, but his ability to treat every human being regardless of background or circumstances with equal respect. Maharishi's actions reminded me of a statement he made at a teacher training conference in Estes Park, Colorado: "When I see a man or woman walking toward me, I do not see a lump of matter; I see an impulse of Infinity." In preparation for the historic conversation that takes place in the next chapter between Maharishi and Pat Corum, I want to present the personal back-story from which Pat Corum's life emerged, and transformed to the point that Maharishi called him the pioneer of freedom behind bars.

Pat Corum, by the time he was 15, had reached the conclusion that normal people did not think or act the way he did. His feelings of isolation and loneliness were so overwhelming that he started looking outside himself for something that would stop his feelings, and the pain associated with them. Pat found drugs, which made him feel good. For the first time in his life, he felt he was accepted by a group of people. They thought and felt like he did and they were doing the same or similar activities—whatever it took to secure more drugs and stay loaded. For a long time Pat did not think he had a drug problem. He thought he had a money problem, and believed if he had enough money, he could obtain all the drugs he needed, and could feel good. Being accepted was also a big part of his process of trying to feel good. Pat wanted to be accepted by his family, peers, and society in general. He believed if he had the outward trappings of success that everyone would want him to be around them. Ironically Pat had a twin brother who was a banker in Canada, and never was involved with the criminal justice system. By the time Pat was 17, he had learned that he could obtain more of what he wanted with a gun and a smile, rather than just a smile. Pat related to me that he knew what fear felt like, and through that knowledge, Pat quickly gained skills in intimidation, coercion, and inflicting massive amounts of pain on others through physical violence and the use of weapons. As his need to look good and feel good continued to grow, his level of anger went out of control. Pat was in a state of rage during every waking hour. The intervention of drugs, money, and alcohol that he believed would fix him, and make him whole, was not working.

The Folsom Prison staff started a college program, and Pat enrolled because he could receive G.I. Bill benefits. To receive the G.I. benefits he needed to maintain good grades. That was a problem because he did not want to study. So he teamed up with five other life-term inmates, and their strategy was to make the college instructors aware of their backgrounds, then impress upon them the need to give the group good grades. This worked well until we met. They thought it would be easy to intimidate me because they were physically much bigger than I was. They did not understand that I had grown up in a similar world except I chose to take a different direction from what I saw around me. They thought I was on drugs because I was relaxed and at peace with myself. I remember the telephone call from the Dean of Fine Arts at Sacramento City College, telling me that I was his last hope because no one would go to Folsom Prison to teach Philosophy. I just smiled and took the opportunity, not realizing how it would change my life because of Maharishi's generosity and compassion. Nevertheless, Pat and his club members tried to intimidate me. I found it amusing and just laughed. This was the last reaction they had expected, and they had to regroup. They were not accustomed to someone not being intimidated or fearful of them on any level. Following that episode, one afternoon after class, Pat asked me what kind of drug I was taking because I had such high energy, and no visible sign of stress. I gave Pat and his group their first introductory lecture about the TM technique. For the next year, I had them reading every book published about TM. I told Pat if he wanted to learn he needed to pay for the instruction because I wanted to test his sincerity. I remember the moment in the old gray stone chapel at Folsom Prison when I taught Pat to meditate. I made arrangements with the Catholic priest to secure a private room in the chapel, and instructed Pat in the same way that any free person in the world received instruction into TM. After a few moments of Pat practicing the TM technique, he opened his eyes and said to me: "This is the first time in 13 and a half years I have felt relaxed." In that moment I had the feeling something important could happen. I reflected if the technique could produce this effect in this man, the program could reduce institutional violence and human suffering throughout the prison. I asked Pat to bring me 10 leaders of the prison, I would teach them to meditate, and we would attempt to transform the prison system and reduce human suffering. He brought me some of the toughest men you could imagine, including the Aryans, the Mexican Mafia, and the Hell's Angels. This is how the story began.

Pat Corum had been the drug connection in the prison, and although it did not stop 100%, he eventually became the new TM connection, and most of his friends stopped using drugs as soon as they learned TM. In Pat's case, he continued to meditate regularly, twice a day, and quickly reached a point at which using drugs seriously interfered with how good he felt after meditation. Drugs were no longer a way to feel good. They were getting in the way of feeling good. Initially, the most dramatic and visible change for Pat was in his college work. He went from grades of B or C with an occasional A, to straight A's, and stopped receiving disciplinary write-ups. The process of positive change had begun from inside. It had nothing to do with barbed wire, armed guards, external controls, or peer pressure. His peers, the people he had been drawn to all his life for support and acceptance, were not thinking, acting, or feeling the way he was. They had not changed. Instead, Pat was in the process of evolving, and part of that evolution was eliminating the insanity that had become such an integral part of his life.

After Pat had been practicing TM for six months, he found himself in a difficult situation with another prisoner. A year earlier, he would have moved instinctively to injure the person. However, this time instead of just reacting to the situation, he found himself calm and relaxed. He had the clarity of mind to look at the various options he had for responding, and chose the best one—Pat remarked to me that he just smiled and laughed; he did not react to someone else's drama. Pat acted in a highly responsible manner for the first time in his adult life. Looking back at the other times he had experienced challenges in his life, he realized that the issue had always been the same. He had reacted to the situation without thinking; he realized that in every instance he had been stressed, angry, hostile, tired, fatigued, and detoxifying from the effects of one or more drugs. The time, place, and person were different from one incident to the next, but the common denominator was his inability to think and respond in a socially acceptable manner. Another thing Pat began to notice was that he was no longer actively creating roughness in the lives of other people. Pat remarked that there was a big difference between reacting to life, and being able to live life innocently. Life, he discovered, was neither fair nor unfair; life was what he made of it. Life did not change from having moments of ugliness and nastiness—Pat had changed from being ugly and nasty.

Pat eventually transferred to San Quentin State Prison so he could continue working on an advanced degree. For the first time in his life, he became involved in the positive aspects of prison life, especially in self-help groups. A youth counseling program was his favorite. Pat also became actively involved in the AA 12-step program and other programs that helped develop the behaviors and attitudes necessary to be a responsible human being. As time passed he received a transfer to a medium security institution, C.C.I. Tehachapi. He continued his regular meditations, although he was housed in a dormitory with 200 other men. In fact, he discovered that he could even meditate on a prison bus, chained to the max. Pat met new people and made numerous friends, both prisoners and staff members including a young lady during those years at Tehachapi, whom he married. She was a woman who loved him for what he was, rather than because of what he could do for her. In November 1986, Pat obtained his freedom from prison. We spoke on the phone throughout the years, and he stated to me that life had not been easy after his release, but it was enjoyable, at least, for the most part. He stated that five members of his family had passed away, and he could be there and provide support each time. Pat could experience all the feelings that come with the loss of a loved one, and never feel the need to resort to alcohol or drugs. He also could be there when two members of his family married. Pat fondly reflects that he was at the hospital when his second granddaughter was born. Pat completed an attorney assistant program at California State University, and in 1991 started his own business. Pat provided support services for criminal attorneys, and his life became what Maharishi envisioned when he communicated to Pat, a decade earlier, that he was already rehabilitated during their conversation at the 1978 World Assembly on Law, Justice, and Rehabilitation presented in the next chapter. I was present at the conference, and as we listened to Maharishi's comment the room became still, and the truth of his observation contained a vision that would materialize throughout the world. Without Maharishi's technology and decision to provide his knowledge and techniques inside Folsom Prison (Ellis, 1979) the transformations previously discussed would not have taken place. Maharishi's teaching is designed to rehabilitate society one individual at a time. Pat Corum highlights this transformation in his own words:

I drove up to my son's house, and when I got out of the car my two-and-a-half-year-old granddaughter saw me. She immediately started running toward me with her little arms outstretched, yelling "Grandpa, Grandpa!" I dropped to my knees, and she ran up to me, put her arms around my neck, gave me a giant hug and a kiss on the cheek, and whispered in my ear, "I love you, Grandpa."

Chapter XIV

Maharishi and the
"Pioneer of Freedom Behind Bars"

*The Bell of Invincibility is rung, and His Holiness Maharishi Mahesh Yogi, founder of
the World Government of the Age of Enlightenment, is introduced at the World Assembly
on Law, Justice, and Rehabilitation at Maharishi European Research University (MERU)
in Seelisberg, Switzerland. The theme of the session is restoring the full dignity of the individual and the nation, and a discussion of the MERU Rehabilitation Index. The moderator
for the conference, Philip White, announces the historic conference call from an incarcerated inmate—Pat Corum speaking from the warden's office at San Quentin Prison—to
Maharishi.*

Philip White: Mr. Corum was the first person to learn Transcendental
Meditation in a maximum security prison, in Folsom Prison, California from
George Ellis, who began the program. I believe we are very close to making
this connection.

Pat Corum: Jai Guru Dev

Maharishi: Jai Guru Dev (applause)

Pat Corum: Maharishi?

Maharishi: Yes, Jai Guru Dev, we are very glad to hear your voice.

Pat Corum: It is the voice I have heard so many times on tape, and it is just
wonderful to be able to speak to you now, and I feel tremendously honored by
this privilege.

Maharishi: Very good, it's a joy.

Pat Corum: I would like to begin by expressing my deep gratitude for having this opportunity on behalf of the thousands of men and women incarcerated in the California Department of Corrections.

Maharishi: Jai Guru Dev

Pat Corum: Jai Guru Dev

Maharishi: We are all grateful to Guru Dev that he gave us this beautiful
wisdom so that we can even enjoy freedom behind bars.

Maharishi Mahesh Yogi©   Pat Corum©

Maharishi speaks from the International Capital of the World Government for the Age of
Enlightenment World Assembly on Law, Justice and Rehabilitation held in Seelisberg, Switzerland, to
Pat Corum, speaking from the Warden's office at San Quentin Prison in San Rafael, California.

Pat Corum: Jai Guru Dev

Maharishi: Jai Guru Dev

Pat Corum: I would also like to express my extreme love and gratitude to His Holiness Maharishi Mahesh Yogi for training teachers of the
Transcendental Meditation program so that all areas of human suffering can
be alleviated, and that we together can usher in what Maharishi has defined as
an Age of Enlightenment.

Maharishi: That is a very good thought. We are here in this generation to
rehabilitate the age. The age of ignorance is being rehabilitated into the Age
of Enlightenment. It is a very good, great thought.

Pat Corum: In 1975, I wrote a letter to Governor Brown requesting his
support for the TM Program. In that letter I described the past events that led
to my incarceration. I feel that the past is gone, and yet I am still experiencing
some of the repercussions of my being incarcerated at San Quentin Prison.
What I am interested in speaking about this evening is a vision of possibilities
for eliminating crime and suffering behind the walls of penitentiaries throughout the world.

Maharishi: We will do everything possible to accomplish this goal.

Pat Corum: It has been my personal experience that criminality is a state of mind brought about by an accumulation of unreleased stress and tension.

Maharishi: That is the reality, exactly it is that. The basis of all incorrect actions is the stress.

Pat Corum: A bill occurred regarding punishable behavior, and brought attention from the various law enforcement agencies throughout this state. Because of a combination of guilt feelings, and of experiencing punishment, I began seeing myself as a bad person, which is probably the worst thing that could happen to anyone. While in prison I was, along with thousands of others, inundated with negativity. Because the majority of the people in prison lack a technique to attain a high degree of awareness or to expand their consciousness, they start buying into the concept of being bad people, and will subsequently act out in a manner in which they see themselves. As the people here see themselves being animals or because of being caged, they will soon start acting out in the manner in which they are treated. This is solely because they are not aware that there is a technique available at the present time. Without a release of this tension, the stress builds up, and they will continue with their antisocial behavior patterns. In my own case, I conducted myself in such a manner that I was convicted and sentenced to prison on two life sentences plus convictions for five other major felonies. It was not until June of 1975 when I was initiated by George Ellis in Transcendental Meditation that I started in any way to become like a human being again. I would like to give you some examples of what TM and the regular practice of it has brought about in my life.

Maharishi: As I see crime, resulting from two hard words C and R, Cra, Cra, Cra. It's a combination of two hard consonants; that means it is not only from one side that the crime is ever committed. Society is as much responsible as the one who is sentenced as a criminal. The very word crime describes the structure of crime. They have a proverb in India that no clapping can be done by one hand moving (laughter). The two hands should move, one side is the society, the other side is the poor fellow who has been put in that situation from within himself due to stresses, and from outside himself again due to stresses of other people. So the crime is from both sides and no one inside the prison should feel so lonely with crime. The entire society is involved in what he did. Therefore, it is not for anyone to see that those who have been put behind bars are the sole criminal. The thing is, the state of ignorance that the society is plagued with is the basis of all crime. All unfortunate behavior results from lack of comprehension. Transcendental Meditation, by the grace of Guru Dev, is now available to us for increasing comprehension, and this should be the generation that puts an end to all limited viewpoints in life. And when the awareness of the people is unbounded there will be all very, very, cordial behavior and the crime will be gone out into the wind. So this is the Age of Enlightenment now, we are on the fourth year, and we will rejoice evacuating the prisons in all the countries in the world. And I am very happy that I am talking to the pioneer of freedom behind bars, and we are very proud of you, and your attitude, and your experiences of meditation, and I hold you to be the pioneer of freedom behind bars in this growing sunshine of the Age of Enlightenment.

Pat Corum: Thank you very much, Maharishi.

Maharishi: Now let us hear the rest of the story.

Pat Corum: It is very difficult following Maharishi (laughter). I would like to state also some of the benefits from meditation, the TM program.

Maharishi: Experiences in meditation are on a very, very, fine delicate level and when you have been able to appreciate those fine, refined impulses of consciousness, it is a great good luck that even behind bars you could maintain such a refined level of awareness. I am very proud of you.

Pat Corum: Thank you, Maharishi. At the moment I have the information officer here of San Quentin present; it is good; it is really tremendous what is happening with me today. In terms of my own turnabout within prison it can be so easily documented, it is apparent to all. In fact, upon learning meditation, within 90 days I completely stopped using drugs, and I stopped having any contact with people that were involved in that area. My actions have been disciplinary-free, my workday is up to 19 hours a day, and I have become involved in 11 different programs. My education, which I have continued on with, has resulted in me receiving no less than an A. As a classic example, and comparison regarding my transformation, in 1967, I was thrown out of San Quentin because I was termed no longer fit for the confines of this prison. They felt I was a bad influence on the rest of the population here. As an example of what TM can accomplish, last Sunday night I was elected to the presidency of the Men's Advisory Council. This is the highest position that a prisoner at San Quentin can attain. Not only was I given this position . . .

Maharishi: What was this position, say it again?

Pat Corum: The position is President of the Men's Advisory Council. This is a group of 62 men—they act as a liaison between the prisoners and the prison administration.

Maharishi: Liaison between the staff and the prisoners, that is very good so you were there to advise both (laughter).

Pat Corum: That is my position at the present time. I am the spokesman for the population, and I was given this position by acclamation. The members of the body felt I was the best qualified, and therefore no one would even run against me for the position. So from 10 years ago where I was thrown out because I was such a bad influence, to the present time, where I was elected by acclamation to the highest position a prisoner at San Quentin can achieve.

Maharishi: That is very fortunate, very good.

Pat Corum: It is quite easy if you are meditating.

Maharishi: Yes with that unbounded awareness you can have big comprehension of the responsibility of the managers of the prison and the prisoners. Everyone was very fortunate to have such a big comprehension as their mediator (laughter and applause).

Maharishi: That is very good.

Pat Corum: I would also like to speak about a few things regarding my own personal life.

Maharishi: Yes.

Pat Corum: For over two years now I have felt no anger, I committed no violence, and from a person who was almost totally withdrawn and non-communicative, I have reached out even behind these prison walls to my family, to my friends. Perhaps one of the most remarkable things in the world is that because of my involvement in the meditation program, I met one of the most beautiful and loving people in the world: my wife Nancy, who is also a meditator of some five years, and it was through the program that I met her.

Maharishi: We are all enjoying her presence here—she spoke brilliantly yesterday, and she represented you very profoundly. Made us all happy (long applause).

Pat Corum: She has really been the highlight in my life.

Maharishi: You hear the applause of the whole world assembly here now (applause). It's very good; it's going around the world (laughter).

Pat Corum: The work in bringing the TM Program to San Quentin is going quite well. For over two years now I have been working hand and hand with George Ellis in attempting to obtain funding for the program here. Through George and some of his people we have arranged speaking engagements.

Maharishi: George is also here with us, and he told his experiences of initiating you, and you in turn inspiring all others. He told us the entire beautiful story.

Pat Corum: He has fulfilled all my expectations of what a teacher and a friend is all about. He is just a beautiful person (applause).

Maharishi: That is very good news, good to hear firsthand (laughter).

Pat Corum: I assume when George gets back he will come up and see me, and then we will notify you when our program gets started. Through his assistance, I have been able to help by calling some of the TM centers, and received requests to speak on various radio programs, TV stations, and TM centers in northern California. At the present time the warden of San Quentin, George W. Sumner, has approved for me to be released from prison, on a temporary basis of course, and go to Los Angeles and appear on the Merv Griffin show.

Maharishi: It is the temporary thing that becomes permanent.

Pat Corum: Aha! (laughter)

Maharishi: The temporary release becomes permanent freedom. What is happening here in MERU is that the Rehabilitation Index has been developed, and there are certain psychological and biochemical tests which will declare anyone completely rehabilitated, and we are about to offer this Index to every government because a one-time stress should not make a man incompetent of behavior in society for so many years, and particularly now when the president of the USA is raising his voice for human rights. So the society should not have a right of putting one out of society for so many years when he can be tested that he is behaving normally.

This gift of human rights to be able to share his joy with all others and make everyone happy will now be available through the positive tests of the MERU Rehabilitation Index as the scientists call it here. Standard ways of examining normality in thinking and behavior will free the prisons in this sunshine of the Age of Enlightenment. It makes sense that if someone, due to his inner stress, due to stress in the environment, has been exposed to some kind of violent release of stress, then there should be a way to measure his sensible behavior in the future. Not that he be condemned for so many years. So the situation is very favorable that very soon through the TM and TM-Sidhi programs, with the help of this MERU Rehabilitation Index, we will be able to free everyone first behind bars, and then they will be out of bars (laughter). The time is approaching fast, and you will come out and ring the Bell of Invincibility.

Pat Corum: (laughter) I would enjoy doing that.

Maharishi: Yes.

Pat Corum: At the moment I see myself as a temporary resident here at San Quentin, although I am not free physically.

Maharishi: Yes it should be like that: a very temporary resident.

Pat Corum: I would like to share with you a little thing that happened at San Quentin. This is right after you appeared on the Merv Griffin show, along with Doug Henning, and also Burt Reynolds. Here at the prison, men have what they call a macho image going. They want to be the tough guys, and the hard-core guys. And some of the men I had spoken to about the TM program thought if they learned to meditate that they would have to wear beads, long robes, sandals, and possibly sit in a lotus position in front of a brass bowl or something. All my efforts to bring them about to be amenable to the TM program had gone for naught because of their own image of wanting to be tough-guys. The hard core guys after seeing the TM show on Merv Griffin, and when Burt Reynolds, who happens to be a hero at San Quentin with a large percentage of men, spoke on behalf of the TM program and stated that he was a meditator, I had several of these hard core tough-guys coming around to my cell and saying, "Man, if Burt Reynolds can be a meditator I want to be a meditator also." (laughter)

Maharishi: (laughter) Yes of course.

Pat Corum: I wanted to share this with you because everyone knows what will come about once the men start to meditate. In regards to the TM-Sidhi program once the information reached the prison, there was an extreme amount of interest that was generated behind the program.

Maharishi: Yes, I wanted to teach everyone to fly (laughter).

Pat Corum: I would have to question some of the motives of the men here wanting to learn to fly. There was a question that came up, what happens when the guys levitate over the walls?

Maharishi: That will be freedom to the prisons (laughter and long applause). That will declare success of rehabilitation in the prisons (laughter) that the prisoners are flying straight unto skies and heavens. That will be the success of prison guards that they kept their doors properly locked (laughter), and they helped the ability of the prisoners to just feel free in the skies, on the ground and everywhere. And then another thing that will follow will be disappearing (profound laughter). That will be another stroke of great relief to the prison wardens, that they don't see anyone anymore (laughter). That will be enjoyed by the angels in heaven. The prison wardens have no one to take care of. They will be the prisons of the Age of Enlightenment. Waiting for someone to come but no one is seen there (laughter).

Pat Corum: The men were highly impressed with the show put on by Doug Henning, especially when he went through the brick wall. The men here immediately saw possibilities for that one.

Maharishi: Doug Henning is another joy to the movement, he is very good.

Pat Corum: Ah, yes he is!

Maharishi: Yes these TM-Sidhi programs, I am trying to introduce that very soon.

Pat Corum: That would really be tremendous here, Maharishi.

Maharishi: See, what happens is in transcending, the awareness becomes so unbounded that it becomes overwhelming to itself. So it forgets everything of outside; that's why the name transcending, but the TM-Sidhi program is to make that unbounded awareness functional. One begins to think in that unbounded awareness, and that is the reason why the thought force is so great that whatever one wants to accomplish or experience, immediately that experience comes. This is just due to the infinite power of thought in that unbounded awareness.

That's the whole basis of the TM-Sidhi program. So those who have been practicing TM, and on that basis have been training their physiology to project unbounded awareness, they are eligible to start a procedure to think from that level of unbounded awareness. It is a beautiful thing that has come to us as a gift from Guru Dev to really make everyone in the world free from limitations. Action from the unbounded awareness will eliminate any weakness of the mind, and that will accomplish every thought of every man because unbounded awareness is the field of natural law, and all the activities start from there. All the impulses of creative intelligence have their basis in that; therefore, every action will always be right, helpful, enriching, and fulfilling to the whole atmosphere. This is going to become a daily experience of everyone through the TM-Sidhi program. It is a very great joy to share this wonderful knowledge with everyone on earth. On that basis we will have a permanent state of the sunshine of the Age of Enlightenment on earth.

Pat Corum: I know that the men, especially those at Folsom, and the 300-plus here at San Quentin, are waiting for the program with anticipation.

Maharishi: Now you will lecture to them on the basic principle of TM-Sidhis, that TM makes one forget everything, even though it creates unbounded awareness. The TM-Sidhi program makes that unbounded awareness functional, and on that basis, the power of thought is always so great that everyone would accomplish what one would want to accomplish. It's a very great thing, and the release of stress and the bubbling freedom that comes to awareness are simply great glories of experience. We will start very soon. We will start very soon. How many are practicing TM in your surroundings?

Pat Corum: At Folsom Prison, we have approximately 250 men who are involved in the TM program and the number has been reduced somewhat because of parole. We have approximately 35 men who have been released so far. I am happy to say we have had only one man return to prison, not for criminal activity but for a rules violation. Here at San Quentin I am the only man who is involved in the TM program, but that is just momentary though. We will shortly have hundreds of men involved here.

Maharishi: Put them to close the eyes and do something inside (laughter).

Pat Corum: Well, with your support all things are possible.

Maharishi: That unbounded awareness is a field of all possibilities. It actually is. Unbounded awareness, that infinite comprehension is like a wide-angle lens which will comprehend all the points that are necessary to fulfill the thought. It is a very natural procedure to bring all upliftment to life.

Pat Corum: I know that all men here will eventually receive what I have received, and be able to feel the freedom that can be gained through this knowledge of unbounded awareness, and that all who follow in my footsteps can become a credit to society.

Maharishi: You will bless them all soon.

Pat Corum: I will; what I was curious about now is if there were any specific questions that I may answer about the TM program in prison.

Maharishi: Yes, I think the only question is how soon you are coming out?

Pat Corum: (laughter and applause) As I speak to you right now I am eligible for parole. I have yet to appear before that group that will determine whether or not I will be released. That will be sometime in the next 60 to 90 days. I will find out at that time the exact date that I will be released back into society on a physical level anyway.

Maharishi: Much before that all the governments and all the prison authorities are going to receive this MERU Rehabilitation Index. They will have a new light in their regime because there was no way until now to really measure whether the stress has gone, and the purpose of putting people behind bars is accomplished in their consciousness or not. Thanks to the MERU scientists they have developed a program that is so very effective that all the governments are going to have this program. Everyone is always anxious to see their people out of the bars. Only their rules do not permit them and now everywhere there will be instituted new rules for release. There will be more scientific investigation into the reality of physiology and see how much the consciousness has been renewed. So that will help in every way, but then you have to hurry up because before you come out you need to bless all those that you will be leaving in.

Pat Corum: The staff here at San Quentin from the warden to the most recent new officer is fully aware and supportive of the TM program. My ability to make this call is just one showing on the part of staff regarding their amenability to this most positive program. The allowing of this call probably is the first time that it has ever been done. When I spoke with Warden Sumner last Friday, I gave him the book on the First World Assembly and in it there was a letter that had been reproduced, which I had written to the Director of the California Department of Corrections; after a momentary glance through the book, there was no hesitation on his part to approve this call.

Maharishi: That's very good, that's very good. See how much you have purified your atmosphere.

Pat Corum: (a gentle laugh) Yes.

Maharishi: That just results from the purification of the atmosphere. Now there is not much fear around you. There is not much stress around you because you are standing for something sublime, something divine. In that book, we have the reflections of the top people in the world in the field of

Law, Justice, and Rehabilitation. The very appearance of the book is so soothing, and thanks to your regularity in meditation you are able to produce that
state of calmness and relaxed atmosphere around you. You must be a joy to all
the people in the prison, the authorities, and those who are with you. That's
very good, that's very good.

Nancy Watkins: Pat, perhaps you can tell us about your goals to become a
teacher when you are released?

Pat Corum: Well, upon release I have already made a reservation to go to
a residence course for two weeks of rounding—after that time I will complete
my training to become a teacher of the TM technique; then in conjunction
with George Ellis, I will be returning to prisons as a teacher of the TM technique. I want to pass on the technique that has allowed me to gain, to grow,
and to reach my potential as a human being. I desire that other men in prison
can know and experience what true freedom is, what achieving goals means,
and what the path to enlightenment can mean to them in terms of the great
feeling of accomplishment and joy it has meant to me. In this way I feel I can
best fulfill what my life is really all about in terms of wanting to help other
people who are in a position unable to help themselves.

Maharishi: It is a very fortunate thing, the goal that you have set for your
activity when you are out is really laudable. You will be putting the lighthouses
in all the dark corners on earth. You will be eliminating the most stressed areas
on earth. That is a very beautiful goal to rehabilitate the time, the present time.
That is very, very good, and George is here and he wants to have a word with you.

George Ellis: (laughter) Actually, Pat you answered my question. I think I
would like to speak on behalf of all the members of the World Government,
and express that together we feel deeply in ourselves that love is the most
powerful human quality. The quality of stress that has veiled the hearts of so
many human beings in and out of prison through the example of your life
transformation, with your meditation experience, and the anticipated success
in your life after prison—we can indeed free the world from suffering, through
the graciousness of Maharishi and Guru Dev. Perhaps you will have some final
remarks to all of us.

Pat Corum: My final remark would be that through the TM program,
through his Holiness Maharishi and Guru Dev . . .

Maharishi: Jai Guru Dev

Pat Corum: I honestly feel that each person, rather than living their life in stress and tension, can see himself in a new light, and through TM he can fully realize what the essence of every individual is, which is beauty and love.

Maharishi: It's beautiful, it's beautiful.

Pat Corum: This would be my final message.

Maharishi: And waves of love, and waves of beauty in this shining sunshine of the Age of Enlightenment.

Pat Corum: I will sign off for now, so to one and all, Jai Guru Dev.

Maharishi: Jai Guru Dev (long applause). And give thanks to all the prison officials who have made it possible for this World Assembly to enjoy your expressions from halfway around the world. Jai Guru Dev.

Pat Corum: Jai Guru Dev

Maharishi: We will free the prisons because it's not necessary that a man continue on the same attitude for years. There must be a Rehabilitation Index, which should be put on the man maybe every three months, six months, nine months, something like that, and set him free. It's a human right that if he has gone wrong sometime it is not necessary that he will be tracking on that direction all the time. He can be reverted back, but the only thing is that there was no knowledge of this inner value of consciousness. That is why order could not be brought in the field of behavior, and now that consciousness is the current coin in the market, order could be established from the level of consciousness.

And that is the reason why we have all great hopes that it will be very difficult for the prisoners to remain in the prisons anymore. Such great wisdom that he spoke can only come out of a pure mind. So he is more than rehabilitated, already.

Brahmachari Nandkishore: So now we conclude the fifth session of the World Assembly in Law, Justice, and Rehabilitation in Making the Nation Invincible. Jai Guru Dev.

Following the inspirational conversation between Maharishi and Pat Corum, I requested a special message for my first book *Inside Folsom Prison: Transcendental Meditation and TM-Sidhi Program.* Maharishi provided the following insight to the world regarding his love, kindness, and the power of TM in generating human transformation independent of circumstances:

Inner man is within each man—whether his body is in the comfort of his home or in the penance of prison. If he has the Transcendental Meditation technique, man communicates his outer values with the infinite potential of his inner life, and enjoys fullness of life irrespective of where he is placed. The Transcendental Meditation technique, the prisoner's only friend, offers freedom even behind bars. And for that we are always grateful to Shri Guru Dev.

— Maharishi (1979)

Chapter XV

Light Eliminating Darkness:
Change Begins Within

I first became aware of David Lynch as a unique and creative director of motion pictures. I had no idea he practiced the Transcendental Meditation technique. I have followed the rapid growth of his foundation, and the dramatic human transformations his generosity has inspired in improving the quality of life, and taking compassion to a higher level. Maharishi's technologies not only eliminate human suffering but raise consciousness. The elimination of human suffering is a side effect of this technology.

I view the David Lynch Foundation as an instrument of bringing the private sector to play a role in social transformation. The frozen behavior of our political leadership and the divisions within the collective consciousness and governmental policies, have disrupted social progress. David Lynch has not waited for governments to respond; he has stepped up to make a difference in his lifetime.

His foundation has addressed (a) schools, (b) the military, (c) the homeless, (d) American Indians and (e) prisons. (David Lynch Foundation for Consciousness-Based Education and World Peace, 2012. www.davidlynchfoundation.org).

The David Lynch Foundation is a nonprofit educational approach developed to meet the challenges of society. The fundamental philosophy is articulated in the expression "Change begins within" (Lynch, 2012). It is a simple message that has the power to transform an individual, along with society and its institutions.

Throughout the years I was fortunate to invest in the private sector and develop companies with a sense of social responsibility. Additionally, I collaborated with entertainers and business leaders to raise funds to support humanitarian projects around the world. David Lynch had the resources, the network, and the vision to take my aspirations to a broader level of success. His foundation is building a legacy, addressing immediate human needs, and establishing a vehicle to perpetuate human development at its root. The goals of the foundation are to bring improvement to every area of society:

Schools

Traumatic stress is a reality of students around the world, who must face fear, bullying, violence, and substance abuse; and stress further restricts academic achievement. The David Lynch Foundation entered the inner-city public schools and brought about the same peacefulness I observed and experienced in the toughest prisons and youth offender facilities after the introduction of the TM program. Russell Simmons in a video on the David Lynch website was lecturing to students and administrators who were discussing the TM technique as a tool for human transformation; and it echoed the reality I experienced in residential treatment facilities, observing how TM had helped children after the damage was already inflicted. The joy and value of these programs are immeasurable. For example, as I mentioned in my discussions with Dr. David Orme-Johnson in Chapter XI, Part III, most approaches to help children in need are superficial and external, and either involve prescription drugs, or consequences as interventions. The TM program is a simple and innocent technique that effortlessly nourishes the whole person without producing negative side effects.

Military

The attacks of September 11, 2001 made even a pacifist ready to go to war to protect our country. The initial reaction may express pride in our nation, but until one has observed the consequences of war, the actual price in human suffering is often not recognized until much later. The David Lynch Foundation has taken head-on the need to address Post Traumatic Stress Disorder (PTSD). As citizens of the United States, we witness our wars on television, and watch pinpoint bombs blowing up on the screen like in a movie. On news stations, the antiseptic listing of the soldiers lost in those wars scrolls by on the screen. Additionally, the veterans who return home and commit suicide annually exceeds the numbers of those killed in Iraq and Afghanistan, according to the David Lynch Foundation. The Foundation offers the TM program through Operation Warrior Wellness, which is helping to heal the wounds of PTSD, giving the soldiers an opportunity to return to normal life. Comments from the soldiers such as, "It was the difference between heaven and hell," and "The experience that I have had from TM basically saved my life," should be enough for compassionate people and governments throughout the world to facilitate the aspirations of the David Lynch Foundation in its fundraising efforts, and should inspire governments to include the TM program in the support and appreciation shown to all returning veterans.

Homelessness

The global economic collapse, which the politicians call a recession, looks and feels like a depression to those who have lost their homes and are living on the street. According to the David Lynch Foundation 700,000 people are homeless, and of those, nearly 40% are families, while 30% of them have been incarcerated. The David Lynch Foundation is presenting a holistic approach emphasizing that along with housing, education, and job training, individuals need to be equipped with tools provided through the TM program to overcome humiliating and traumatic stress. The consequence of homelessness often leads to a person's return to poverty and despair. Dr. Norman Rosenthal, author of *Transcendence*, remarks that TM can help addictions across the board, with large implications for the homeless. Hence, if we can reduce addictions and minimize their side effects, one of which is homelessness, we as a society can correct the imbalance of widespread homelessness in the wealthiest country on earth.

American Indians

We see the tax-free Indian casinos, but just as with Wall Street, the few are benefiting, whereas the majority of society struggles for economic survival. The American Indians face poverty on reservations, alcoholism, and acute stress. Although the American Indians place a high value on meditation for promoting balance in life, it needs to be understood properly. The David Lynch Foundation, in collaboration with national and local American Indian health and education organizations, is attempting to provide teachers of TM to serve the at-risk American Indian population.

Prisons

I spent 25 years teaching TM in prisons with the hope and desire that objective scientific research would provide the evidence for governments around the world, or generous private sector donors, to introduce the TM educational programs to facilitate rehabilitation and stress management for inmates and staff. I was pleased that the David Lynch Foundation included this dark area of society in their efforts. The David Lynch Foundation has moved the wisdom of Maharishi forward in this area. When teachers of TM first began to introduce the TM program in the prisons they were told by correctional professionals: "We understand TM reduces stress, but we need to see a five-year study on recidivism." Researchers have provided such information in numerous studies—including a 15-year follow-up on recidivism—which affirmed that there is no longer any doubt as to how effective the TM programs are in prison environments, and in reducing the return rate to prison. From the David Lynch Foundation prison programs there is an echoing of observations made in previous chapters in *A Symphony of Silence*. Michael Puerini, M.D., Medical Director at the Oregon Department of Corrections, which currently offers a TM program funded by the David Lynch Foundation, remarks:

> I think TM can really help people to broaden their focus. You cannot teach compassion to a person, but there is something about TM that brings out compassion . . . I do not know how it works, but it does. And I think a compassionate person is a healthier person. And as a doctor I guess that is what I am here about. (Lynch, 2012)

Randy Greer (Lynch, 2012) Inmate Services Administrator, states that the TM program unfolds what is common within human beings. His statement affirms the purpose and common thread of *A Symphony of Silence*, which is the experience of the inner stillness of pure consciousness cultivated through TM.

Global Outreach

One of the goals of the David Lynch Foundation is addressing the needs of escalating stress among the children in violence-ridden regions of the world. I have profound empathy for this goal because I spent 10 years in developing nations under the umbrella of dictators in Central America. I observed family dinners in Mayan Indian villages that were nothing more than boiled water, with 600 kidnappings per week a common phenomenon. I have seen wards of the court, children chained to their beds by inexperienced and desperate mothers in abject poverty trying to control their children's behavior. The David Lynch Foundation funded a TM peace project in Colombia where a Catholic priest brought TM to an orphanage, and highlighted what is possible in those areas. When I was in Central America with a group of teachers of TM under the direction of Maharishi, we went to Guatemala and attempted to create coherence in the nation. We also recognized the importance of the children of the nation being helped because they represented the future. The orphanages of the nation were one of the first areas where we introduced the TM program. So many abandoned children were put to the streets to beg for money for criminals and the orphanages protected them. We offered TM to reduce the stress of being without parents, and educational programs to provide them practical skills. The David Lynch Foundation is expanding these efforts around the world.

The David Lynch Foundation emphasizes that we must globalize love. My hope is that the Foundation receives an endowment so that its profound desire to serve those in our world, in the greatest need, can be fully realized. I believe that the Foundation is one of the most unique and compassionate instruments for human transformation anywhere in the world. The David Lynch Foundation is a beautiful instrument in fulfilling Maharishi's *Enlightened Vision* for creating an ideal society.

Part V

The Gentle Strength of Women

An Open Hand© Debbie Arnold

Chapter XVI

An Innocent Beginning

Dominique Ellis

Dominique Ellis was born in Guatemala and nicknamed Conchita, which means little shell. She was born into a society caught in the grip of revolution, in which guerrilla warfare and explosions were commonplace. Dominique and her family lived under the umbrella of an oppressive culture with the tight control of a dictatorship and political coups. The children in the Martinez family were taught the values of love and hard work by their mother Margarita Candida and their father Moises. The father brought the entire family to learn the TM and TM-Sidhi programs. Dominique, her brother Gustavo, and her sister Lucrecia would become teachers of the TM program in the Philippines and Brazil.

Dominique and her family were instruments to implement His Holiness Maharishi Mahesh Yogi's desire to improve the collective consciousness in that part of the world. I traveled to Guatemala at the request of Maharishi to introduce the TM program into the prisons, and support a team of TM teachers in their efforts to create coherence in the nation. After meeting the Martinez family, with Susan Gore of W.L. Gore & Associates, we began to investigate and create business enterprises to cultivate economic development and long-term stability for the TM program to facilitate national coherence, and help those in need throughout society. The purpose of expanding business opportunity was to create self-sufficiency to embrace the creation of a more enlightened society for the Mayan Indians, businesses, orphanages, prisons, and the nation.

I was born in Guatemala, The Land of Eternal Spring, in Central America. Guatemala is a multicultural society with numerous customs and traditions. The indigenous or Mayan population represents approximately half of the population, with more than 20 different tribes and dialects. Early in my childhood I learned that our family was living under a military dictatorship because the tanks normally patrolled the streets at the same time every day to make sure people were not outside their homes. Our family became familiar with the image of armed forces as their presence was so visible everywhere we went. Military coups were common, and the military President gave speeches to the population surrounded by armed soldiers with shotguns. Despite the oppressive environment, my parents managed to provide the family a sense of freedom, surpassing the ignorance of the oppressors, by providing me and my brothers and sisters the opportunity to attend school, and supporting our college education.

My dear father, Moises Martinez, was a visionary, a philosopher, and seeker of knowledge throughout his life. He was a master tailor sought after by heads of state and prominent members of society; he was an impeccable dresser and made suits that fit to perfection. He taught his children the importance of education, human development, and moral values. My father instilled in his children the importance of integrity, hard work, and concern for others. More important, he kept reminding the family that probably we were not the prettiest, the tallest with blond hair or blue eyes, but by having inner strength, self-confidence, and knowledge, and by cultivating the intellect and consciousness, we would be able to confront most of life's challenges.

My beloved mother, Margarita Candida, was the embodiment of love, whether sitting in the silence of quiet meditation, transcending as she passed her fingertips over the beads of a rosary, or looking after the needs of her beloved husband Moises and her children. She was a devoted Catholic, but she was also a person who transcended the boundaries of any religion residing in the essence of spirituality and expressing an unbounded unconditional love for everyone. The etymology of my mother's name reflects her personal attributes: Margarita is defined as a beautiful delicate daisy-like white flower, and Candida means glowing, white, sincere, and pure. She left behind a legacy of strong family values, and an unwavering commitment to care for others. She taught the family the beauty of giving without expecting a return, and to put the interest of others before her own.

I feel so fortunate to have had such loving parents, my father giving us the tools for strength and knowledge to overcome any obstacles in life, and my mother always nurturing us with her unconditional love, care, and compassion. As I mentioned, my father was a seeker of knowledge and had an open mind regarding any information that could enrich his life, and that of his wife and his children. My father was always listening to the radio, watching the TV, reading newspapers, magazines, and encyclopedias trying to discover new knowledge to pass on to his children for their enrichment. He followed this pattern during his studies in Philosophy at Universidad de San Carlos de Guatemala. When he would return from his evening classes, we would all gather around him in the family's small living room, and he summarized for us the content of his Literature and Philosophy courses, and this is how the family became familiar with the humanities.

One morning, my father was listening to a radio program on natural health, and the radio guest began to discuss the benefits of TM, and he immediately told the family what he had heard, and recommended that we should all attend the introductory lecture. The family (nine members) showed up at the local TM center. The TM teacher was pleasantly surprised to see that an entire family was attending the introductory lecture, which was not a common practice. At the end of the TM lecture the family members asked some questions such as how to learn the technique, requirements, price, and the learning schedule.

When my father heard the benefits resulting from the regular practice of the TM technique such as, reducing stress and developing consciousness, he realized the TM program was going to be valuable knowledge, and a priceless tool that his children could employ for the rest of their lives. My father never imposed anything on his children, and just told us: "I believe this technique is very valuable knowledge that will enrich your lives. I recommend you consider learning the technique." We expressed to my father the desire to learn the TM technique, and somehow we were expecting him to pay the fee. To our surprise, he said: Very good, if you have a sincere desire to learn the TM technique you need to pay your own fee. If you do not have the money now, begin to save and when you have the required fee contact the TM teacher.

It took about four to eight months for everyone in the family to become meditators. After my father learned TM, he was very disciplined; he would go into his room to practice the technique at the same time, every day, twice a day and when he came out he looked fresh, radiant, relaxed, and happy. Witnessing that daily process motivated me even more to learn the TM technique, and save the money to pay for the instruction.

At the time, I was working as an elementary-school teacher and my salary was just enough to help the household financially and to cover my basic personal expenses. I managed to save the needed money to pay for the instruction, and I learned the TM technique on November 14, 1981 with my sister Lucrecia.

As each member of the family was learning the TM technique, the family group meditation was increasing. The home environment was so calm that even our little dog was very quiet and falling asleep during the group meditation. The relations among the family members, under the lovely umbrella

The Martinez family, pioneers of the Transcendental Meditation program in Guatemala. Left to right standing: Lucrecia, Fernando, Ligia, Dominique, Gustavo, Julio, and Virginia Martinez, and sitting: Moises and Margarita Candida.°

of our parents, were always loving, harmonious, happy, and respectful. After we all learned TM, we felt all those qualities were enhanced, and the family atmosphere was very blissful all the time. We enjoyed sharing our personal experiences of more energy, mental clarity, relaxation, and how we could handle better the daily challenges in our different activities at work and school.

When the TM center offered the advanced TM-Sidhi course, all the family members made arrangements to take the course. Thus, the Martinez family became well known within the Guatemalan meditating community. My father was very active in the TM center, and he was appointed president of the Guatemala TM Organization. As a representative of the TM Organization in Guatemala, he traveled to Fairfield, Iowa and attended the Taste of Utopia

World Peace Assembly in December 1983 conducted by Maharishi, where more than 7,000 people gathered from around the world. During the Assembly, my father met with the TM Governor General for Latin America seeking more support to expand the TM activities in Guatemala.

Nature worked its own course, and in April 1984, a group of North American TM instructors arrived in Guatemala. Maharishi sent the TM teachers to implement the TM program not only to the public, but also to different levels of government, schools, and the private sector. My father actively began to set up appointments with the diverse governmental departments, and several presentations took place. The most receptive to the TM benefits was the Ministro de Gobernación, which normally deals with the inland security and the prison systems. The interest expressed by the Guatemalan Ministro de Gobernación was communicated to Maharishi, and he requested George Ellis, an expert in the field of implementing TM in the prison systems, to support the team in Guatemala and implement the TM program in the prisons and throughout the nation.

In May 1984, George Ellis arrived in Guatemala, and with the support of S.W. Gore & Associates, the TM program was not only implemented into the prison system for men and women, but also in several schools, orphanages, and to the Mayan Indian population. A massive publicity campaign took place discussing the TM program via radio, TV, newspapers, and public conferences. The personal instructions in the TM technique increased and people from all different strata of society were learning the technique. I personally helped to coordinate the instructions at a provisional TM Center, and supported the team of TM teachers working with George.

A translator was necessary to communicate with the TM team and members of society. I did not speak English at that time. George expressed that in order to meet the demands of the project, the TM teachers needed a Guatemalan bilingual person. He asked me if I was interested in working full-time for the organization. I said yes, but I made it clear that I did not know English. I quit my job as a teacher at the elementary school and made the transition to work full- time for the TM organization. To my surprise on my first working day, George informed me that for the first three months my full-time job was to learn English! I did not know what to think; I was concerned whether I could learn a foreign language in three months as I did not know

English, just some basic sentences that I learned in middle school. I decided to take the challenge and arrangements were made for me to attend an American school in Guatemala to learn English.

Those months were very intensive, but in spite of the pressure to learn a new language, I was mentally and physically relaxed and with a sharp focus because of my daily TM practice. In those three months, I gained the basic tools necessary to speak English and was able to communicate. After a month, I had finished my English training, a TM conference was going to take place at the national theater, and for some reason the appointed translator did not show up. George was going to give the lecture. He turned to me and said: "This is an opportunity for you to practice your English; would you translate for me?" I said, yes, but please speak slowly, and I will do my best. At the end of the lecture there were questions and answers, and I was going back and forth from English to Spanish. George mentioned the translation must have been effective; otherwise people would not be inquiring about the TM technique.

While George and his team were structuring and implementing the TM programs, they realized that the country needed local TM teachers to communicate the knowledge and teach the technique in the native language. Once again, George turned to me and asked: "Are you interested in becoming a TM teacher?" I knew the value and significance of becoming a teacher of the TM program, and I also understood the commitment and responsibility of representing Maharishi's knowledge, and with pride and appreciation accepted the invitation.

In October 1984, I traveled from Guatemala to the Philippines to attend an international TM Teacher Training Course (TTC) that was going to take place in Manila. I had lived in Guatemala for 29 years and had never traveled internationally; the trip to the Philippines was an enlightening experience and expanded my view of the world. I remember making a flight connection in Los Angeles, California. Everything felt big and with no boundaries. What gave me some degree of confidence was that after four months of practicing English, I could communicate with people. The next flight connection was in Tokyo, Japan, a culture that I was familiar with just from our textbooks at school or through magazines. The communication in Japan was difficult because of their English accent, but I managed to obtain the information I needed for transportation and hotel needs. For some reason, I was not intimidated considering that I was going to be 9,500 miles away from home because my driving motivation, at the level of my heart and mind, was to become a TM teacher.

The TM TTC in the Philippines was going to be five months long and to make sure I was going to assimilate every piece of knowledge during the course, George arranged for a translator. A Chilean TM teacher came to the Philippines from Switzerland, but did not last long, as some personal issues arose and he had to leave. In the meantime, I continued attending classes. In the interim George arranged for another translator who came from Venezuela and stayed with me until the end of the course.

The TTC is an experience that every person should have—it is an intensive way of expanding consciousness and the intellect, and opening a window to different realities of life that for most people in society remain unknown. The TTC cultivates and integrates the spiritual experience with the intellectual understanding of higher states of consciousness and provides the knowledge to teach the correct process of effortless transcending through Maharishi's TM program.

During the five months that I was away on the TTC in the Philippines, George and his team continued working to implement the TM program in different sectors of the Guatemalan society, including parents, children, students, professors, government officials, businesspeople, and prisoners. To centralize the TM activities, provide follow-up to the people who learned the TM technique, and offer advanced lectures, an old home from the 1920s was restored and financed by Susan Gore. My brother Julio Martinez, a civil engineer, was responsible for the renovation of the building, and this was the home of the first Transcendental Meditation center, strategically located in Guatemala City.

When I completed the TTC, I returned to Guatemala as an authorized TM teacher and because I was the first Guatemalan teacher, I was appointed as the National Leader of the TM organization in Guatemala. This was out of the ordinary in Guatemala because at that time, positions of responsibility were normally granted to men only. George and his team organized a welcome meeting at the newly renovated TM center. In the meeting hall, there were about 100 people, the reception was overwhelming, and I had the opportunity to provide to the Guatemalan meditators a glimpse of the beautiful knowledge entrusted to me by Maharishi.

The first weekend I started to teach the TM technique as there were many people who wanted to learn. Among the new meditators was a woman who was responsible for the rural cooperatives that coordinated the training and implementation of the agricultural practices for the Mayan Indians. After experiencing the benefits of the TM technique, she became very interested and wanted to implement the TM program as a part of training programs given to the Mayan Indians. This was the opportunity that opened the door to penetrate that section of Guatemala's society.

Introducing the TM technique to the Mayan Indians had its challenges because in certain villages, most of the Mayan Indians did not speak Spanish, as they spoke their own native languages, so we had to employ translators. We were traveling across long distances to the highlands to small villages giving introductory lectures, but we did not mind the time spent on the road because the landscape was very beautiful. Some of the villages were around Atitlan Lake, which is known as a "piece of heaven on earth" for its beauty. The lake is surrounded by volcanoes, mountains, and 12 small villages named after the 12 apostles.

The introductory lectures were normally given at the end of the Mayans' workday in the fields. The audience included mothers with their babies, breast-feeding them while listening to the lecture. We managed to teach several thousand Mayan Indians and their children. Teaching TM in the highlands was a special gift as we were surrounded by the awesome beauty and silence of nature, which made the experience one to remember for the rest of our lives. The Mayan Indians were very simple and innocent people, and that made a difference as they followed the instructions precisely. Their experiences after learning the TM technique were so inspiring that seeing the results motivated the TM teachers' team to continue the journey of expanding the program to other villages. I remember when an 80-year-old Mayan Indian lady communicated to us that after learning the TM technique, for the first time in her life, she experienced inner happiness, and it reflected in her excited tone of voice and facial expressions. The life of the Mayan Indians is not an easy life; they depend on their small crops, and one evening we witnessed firsthand a family having boiled water as their dinner. So for the 80-year-old lady to express that after learning TM she experienced contentment for the first time was a moving moment for the TM teachers.

At the schools, we taught the teachers and students. Normally, the Mayan Indian children were very shy, but after they learned the TM technique, their teachers commented that the students were more friendly and conversational among each other. I remember when a group of TM instructors and I finished teaching in one of the village schools, the children wanted to thank the TM instructors for teaching them how to meditate. The students asked the village schoolteacher to help them to organize a native dance wearing the colorful traditional native costumes. These gestures coming from the innocent and simple Mayan children were very touching and rewarding.

To provide in-village follow-up after they learned the TM technique, with Maharishi's authorization, we made one of the leaders of the Mayan Indians a qualified checker of the TM technique. He was organizing group meditations and regular checking of the technique to make sure the Mayan Indians were regular in their practice and meditating properly. As a motivation for the Mayan Indians to attend to the daily group meditation, we offered a trip to the capital of the country, Guatemala City, to attend a residence course without cost for all the Mayan Indian meditators who had been practicing the TM technique twice a day. We had groups of 30 people at a time coming to our center. After a couple of months of conducting the residence courses, we explained to the Mayan Indians that there was another advanced technique to help them individually, and the society collectively, called the TM-Sidhi program. About 20 Mayan Indian meditators became interested, and we made arrangements for them to take the advanced course at the first opportunity. We coordinated bringing TM-Sidhi program administrators from Colombia and the United States to Guatemala to teach the courses to the Mayan Indian meditating community. I want to mention that none of these projects could have been achieved without the generous support of Susan Gore, at the time a member of the Board of Directors of W.L. Gore & Associates, and her humanitarian company S.W. Gore & Associates.

As we expanded the TM projects in the schools, Indian villages, government, private sector, and public through the TM center, the financial demand increased as well. The next step for the TM organization in Guatemala was to become financially self-sufficient. The Martinez family chose to open an export business because Guatemala's economy had a strong agricultural base. The idea to incorporate social responsibility in a private sector enterprise made sense and was realized when the family, along with George Ellis, opened an export business named Geotropical, S.A. We became the pioneers of year-round production of blackberries in Latin America, and began to export to the United States. Gradually, the market distribution expanded to Canada, Europe, and some countries in Asia, including China and Japan. The purpose of the export company was to finance the TM projects, and be a channel to export other non-traditional products produced by the Mayan Indians and provide jobs to the community.

My brother Gustavo Martinez was the general manager of the family business; my sister Lucrecia Martinez handled the IT side of the operation, and my sister Ligia Martinez and her husband Alexis Barrios were responsible for accounting. Gustavo is a chemical engineer, and he was very helpful in conducting the research of new products to improve soil conditions and teach the Mayan Indians new practices to take care of their lands without damaging the soil. The Mayans' regular practice was to burn the soil at the end of each crop. Through the rural cooperatives, the TM team established agricultural training programs and practices for the Mayan Indians to improve the yield of their crops. The TM team encouraged them to plant products other than survival crops such as beans and corn, to facilitate economic growth in the villages. For several years, we could handle the family business during the day and take care of the TM program in the evenings and weekends. As the business grew it demanded more time but provided the revenue to support ongoing TM programs for all sectors of society.

To be completely self-sufficient the country needed to have more Guatemalan TM teachers. So, my sister Lucrecia Martinez, together with four other Guatemalans, traveled to Brazil to become TM teachers. When the five new teachers came back from the TTC, we had waves of instructions, and the TM center was very active. At the TM center, we had several large rooms, and every week we had a full schedule of activities, checking days for the new meditators, 10 days checking meetings, advanced lectures, introductory lectures, personal instructions, TM checking, and group meditation along with quarterly residence courses.

My brother Gustavo Martinez also became a TM teacher and traveled to Brazil as well to take the TTC. Gustavo became the National Director of the TM organization and had the opportunity to participate in a project in Brazil in which TM teachers taught the TM technique to the police academies in certain cities of Brazil. It was inspirational that Gustavo could represent Guatemala in such an important international governmental project. Upon his arrival in Brazil, Gustavo went through a training to become familiar with the native language, Portuguese. Portuguese and Spanish share a number of words spelled identically, although they may be

Dominique Ellis, President of Geotropical, S.A., at the plantation for non-traditional crops, which was developed to support the TM program for human development and coherence in Guatemala.©

pronounced quite differently. The training facilitated the teacher's ability to provide introductory lectures and teach the TM technique in Portuguese. Gustavo mentioned that being part of this project in Brazil was an uplifting experience—teaching to large groups and presenting introductory lectures in a different language was challenging. Gustavo further stated that at the beginning of the project, his broken Portuguese amused the students and was a means to break the ice during the introductory TM presentations; nevertheless, by the end of the project the teachers were communicating like natives.

My sister Lucrecia was fortunate to obtain a scholarship from Susan Gore to attend Maharishi International University (MIU) in Fairfield, Iowa, presently operating as Maharishi University of Management

(MUM). Lucrecia earned a degree in Business Management and Computer Science and was the second student from Guatemala and Central America to attend such a unique university. MUM has a multicultural student population focusing on a holistic approach to education, not only centered in a career for successful life but also in self-knowledge, inner growth of higher states of consciousness, spirituality, and inner peace through the TM program.

At this stage in the Martinez family transformation, we had three TM teachers within the family and six sidhas. My oldest brother, Julio Martinez, got married and his wife became a meditator, and then a sidha. When they had their two girls and a boy, the children were also instructed in the TM technique. My sister Ligia Martinez got married, and her husband became a meditator and later a sidha. The business associates, maids, gardener, and security staff also practiced the TM technique. Whenever we were gathering for family meetings, birthdays, anniversaries, and holidays we always had sweet and loving reunions. My father, as president of the Guatemala TM organization, continued helping us by offering introductory lectures when teachers were not available. We continued having the unconditional love and support from my mother, especially by preparing the menus for all the in-residence courses, advanced programs for deep rest, and TM-Sidhi courses.

Through the kindness and support of Susan Gore, my sister Lucrecia, my brother Gustavo, another Guatemalan teacher, Magda Lopez, the National Leader from El Salvador, Marisa Carbonell, and I were privileged to be in the presence of Maharishi. We traveled to India in July 1986 for the Guru Purnima celebration under the full moon in July, which acknowledges the tradition of enlightened teachers and the significance of their guidance in transcending the bondage of ignorance. The trip to India was quite an experience, beginning with our long trip to reach New Delhi. We traveled from Guatemala to New York, stayed overnight in London, made a connection in the Middle East, Bahrain, and arrived early in the morning into New Delhi. We were so tired that we could hardly keep our eyes open. Our inner motivation was to be in the presence of Maharishi. After making transportation arrangements in the chaotic, hot weather in New Delhi during July, we arrived at Maharishi Nagar. The temperature was very hot, more than 100 degrees. We were invited to go to the dining hall for a drink, and to our surprise the drink was boiled water!!! Everybody was asking for ice-cold water to cool down a little. That was a learning experience as we were told that by drinking hot water it had a cooling effect. In spite of the outside environment, hot climate, and thousands of people from all over the world we all had a common goal—to meet with Maharishi.

Being in the presence of Maharishi was so uplifting for the heart, soul, and mind. We used to watch Maharishi through videotapes, but being there around his subtle yet powerful influence was comparable to viewing the sun on television, and then stepping outdoors in the presence of the actual sun where you are showered by the warm rays, energy, and vitality. That was my experience when I first saw Maharishi. We will always remember the precious moments we shared with Maharishi during the meeting halls and the evenings in the garden of his house under a full moon, but especially we will cherish the lovely meeting we had before leaving his ashram in Maharishi Nagar, outside New Delhi.

The evening we were scheduled to return to Guatemala from India, we requested a meeting with Maharishi. We were invited to a private conference room to meet with him about 1:00 a.m. When our group entered the room and saw Maharishi—it was like coming from the darkness into the light. We immediately experienced being embraced by the blissful and powerful presence of Maharishi. After waiting for several hours to see him the group was becoming concerned if we were going to make our flight. The group was physically tired as it was late; however, when we entered Maharishi's room, the tiredness and the concern vanished, and we were just enjoying the moment and his blessings. Maharishi graciously provided us time to communicate the projects being developed in Guatemala, and he gave us a compliment by saying, "You have saved that part of the world." We mentioned that everything that had been done was thanks to the expertise of George Ellis and the generous financial support of Susan Gore, and Maharishi said: "I know they are there, very good, very good, well done."

I introduced my sister Lucrecia as a TM teacher, and announced that my brother Gustavo shortly was going to travel to Brazil to become a TM teacher; that was pleasant news for Maharishi, and he gave a garland to Gustavo and blessed him. We sat close to Maharishi's couch to show him some pictures of the Guatemala landscape and TM activities. One particular photo that Maharishi found delightful was the one in which I am checking the mantra (Word of Wisdom) of a little Mayan Indian girl. The girl was whispering her Word of Wisdom in my ear, and Maharishi commented: "She is whispering the infinite, very beautiful picture. I want to have it in my room."

Maharishi enjoyed the landscape of Guatemala, the volcanoes, the mountains, the lakes, and the colorful costumes of the Mayan Indians. At the end Maharishi asked: "Do you have cows in Guatemala?" We said yes, and Maharishi responded: "Very good, very good, that is very important to have cows," and he laughed. At the end of our exposition, we mentioned to Maharishi that we needed to leave soon as we had to catch a flight at 5:00 a.m. in New Delhi. Maharishi said: "Don't worry; you are going to be alright. I will arrange your transportation to the airport, and you will make the flight." Maharishi continued speaking and asked, "Who is leaving?" and we said all of us. Maharishi looked at me and stated that as the National Leader I needed to stay, because he wanted a representative from each country at the ashram. I answered that I had to return with my brother and sister to coordinate the TM-Sidhi demonstration, and

Mayan Indian child whispers her Word of Wisdom to Dominique in the highlands of Guatemala©

he said: "Your brother and sister can go back, but you stay, and they will do just fine." He blessed us and we left the room. As we were going down the stairs, we looked at each other, and we agreed, we would follow Maharishi's instructions. Maharishi's car and driver were waiting to take the Guatemalan teachers to the airport, and at this time it was almost 3:00 a.m. with little chance to make the flight, but they left anyway. I was concerned about the outcome of their trip to New Delhi, and I thought only if something happens out of the ordinary will they make the flight. The next day I became aware that when my brother, sister and the other Guatemala teachers arrived at the airport, the flight had been delayed for one hour. As I am sure, this experience sounds familiar to many people in the TM movement; we know that Maharishi could see beyond the moment.

I felt privileged to spend five months at Maharishi Nagar in the presence of Maharishi when the plan was to attend the Guru Purnima celebration for just 10 days! I can humbly say that I was honored when Maharishi asked me to stay at the ashram and gave me the opportunity to join all the meetings and knowledge discussions. At this time Maharishi began to give out the precious knowledge on Maharishi Ayurveda, its 20 approaches, and Maharishi Amrit Kalash, the Nectar of Immortality, as a part of his World Plan for Perfect Health.

I would like to share two precious experiences. I celebrated my birthday while I was staying at the ashram and had the desire to give a flower to Maharishi. The evening of my birthday I went to the hall and was planning to give a flower to Maharishi, but it was impossible; first because of the security around him and second because everyone in the hall wanted to have a close glimpse of Maharishi. I tried to give him a flower for several days, and after a week I thought: if I am meant to give the flower to Maharishi, it will be tonight. I attended the evening meeting, and the situation did not look different from the last seven days, as large crowds always surrounded Maharishi. This time I managed to get closer to the aisle which Maharishi was going to use to exit the hall, and I had three rows of people in front of me. I watched when Maharishi closed the meeting and started to walk toward the exit door. Quietly, in my heart and mind I desired to give Maharishi a flower that night, and I kept repeating the thought until Maharishi walked in front of where I was standing; to my astonishment, he stopped, turned his head, looked at me and said: "Yes?" I told Maharishi I just wanted to give him a flower; he took the flower and asked: "Are you leaving?" I responded: no, Maharishi, it was my birthday. Maharishi remarked, "Very well, come and see me tomorrow" and he left. During that short moment, everything and everyone who was around me disappeared in Maharishi's infinite and unconditional love. My sight and my attention were concentrated on Maharishi, and I experienced unbounded bliss from that precious moment in time directly with the master. Unfortunately, I was not able to see Maharishi that close for the rest of my stay because every time I was going to attempt to meet him, he was always busy conducting meetings. After my close encounter with Maharishi, I was fortunate enough to attend almost every night the regular lectures he was giving either in the meeting hall or at the charming garden at his house—all very blissful moments.

My second delightful experience with Maharishi occurred when I attended a special course held in Maastricht, Holland with my brother Gustavo. During the meetings, the National Leaders of all the countries attending the assembly were sitting on the stage in front of Maharishi, and normally everyone was in his or her seat before Maharishi was entering the hall. One day I arrived late to the meeting hall. Trying not to disturb because Maharishi was already giving his lecture, I went directly to my seat, and to my surprise, Maharishi stopped talking, and he acknowledged me saying: "It is good that you are here." I experienced humility, happiness, and love. I was touched by Maharishi's gracious gesture.

All the experiences I encountered through learning the TM technique and becoming a teacher have enriched my life on all levels. I proved to myself that to learn a foreign language was not an impossible task to achieve. I never imagined I could accomplish such a task in my wildest dreams. After living in a loving cluster family environment, I took the decision to fly 9,500 miles away to learn and assimilate the knowledge of inner life. I was honored to lead an organization in Guatemala on behalf of one of the most recognized enlightened world leaders and a facilitator of human development, His Holiness Maharishi Mahesh Yogi. I was so fortunate to have around me TM teachers and TM leaders from different fields of expertise that facilitated tremendously the implementation of the TM program in Guatemala. I developed the skills to manage and build an international business, which has integrated the inner and outer development of my consciousness.

The Martinez family was privileged to have three members become teachers of the TM program. Other family members possessed practical skills in construction, finance, and engineering. These skills allowed us as a group to become humble instruments to share Maharishi's knowledge to eliminate human suffering and cultivate a Guatemalan collective consciousness to enhance social harmony and progress. Our family had the precious opportunity to facilitate expanding the TM organization on multiple levels during a period of intense social and political upheaval. I observed people from all walks of life pass through the Guatemala TM center with different levels of skepticism, health problems, educational and economic variance and see each of them benefit from the TM technology. Together with my family we played a small role in creating a better society because of the beautiful knowledge provided by Maharishi for human transformation. I will be forever grateful to my dear father who introduced the family to the TM technique. My commitment and gratitude to the purity of Maharishi's knowledge cannot be adequately expressed in words, but only lived on the level of pure consciousness.

Chapter XVII

A Coming Together

Susan W. Gore

Susan Gore is an intelligent entrepreneur and she reflects the character and integrity of her family. Susan contacted me in California when she needed information to develop a model prison project that would demonstrate how to create an ideal society in her home state of Vermont. She asked if I would come to Vermont and help her make a presentation. I thought I was going for a couple of weeks to help her. I had no idea that the situation would result in many years of great accomplishment around the world. I flew back to Vermont in the middle of winter. I saw more cows than people, and the land was blanketed with beautiful white snow. In fact it seemed like a blizzard that we passed through until we arrived at her farm on 400 acres located in Montpelier, Vermont. Susan is a vital, passionate, and focused individual who wanted to create something special, and she did. The following are Susan Gore's reflections on the project, which she entitled Winter in Vermont: A Coming Together.

In the spring of 1973, I came home to the Green Mountains of Vermont after trekking in Nepal. I had traveled with Tibetans up Pokhara Valley from the sacred Mt. Machhapuchhre to haunting Dhaulagiri. Now the soft harmonious shades of green in our small mountains were soothing; there was sweetness for me here. I had seen that just as there are millions of shades of color, so there are millions of shades of human perception, and that all humanity, no matter of what perception, moves toward expansion of life. On returning to my own town of Montpelier, I learned the TM technique, and my life began to expand in an accelerated and subtle way.

The experience of inner quietness, which grew as I practiced the TM technique, reminded me of an important observation I had as a child. I observed that change takes place through action, but I had seen there are many levels from which to act, and the quieter levels have more creative potential. I had watched my parents thinking and acting from these quieter levels, and I learned from them to cherish creativity. One generation passes to the next the knowledge it considers most precious. My parents, innovators in daily life, lovers of life, told us stories about the beginnings of things when the world was young, and about adventures of wonderful good fortune. They taught us that our lives were our own creations, and that we are also creators of history.

In the seventies, I was observing the flowering of what my father refers to as the enterprise. My parents were in their mid-forties when they founded W.L. Gore & Associates, Inc., in the basement of the family home. It had flourished even beyond my father's startlingly optimistic projections. Superficial analysts sometimes concluded that the company thrives solely because of its products. I believe it is successful because the people in it respect the creative process, understand how to be useful, and acknowledge the enormity of possibilities open to human endeavor. They also enjoy themselves. My father was an expert in statistical mathematics, and his approach to business incorporated his probabilistic sense that whatever actually happens is unique, that an infinite number of things can possibly occur, and that life abounds with opportunity. Much has been written elsewhere about the lattice organization and Gore's system of un-management. Behind these innovations is a respect for human freedom and human potential. My father and mother believed it was much better to use friendship and love than slavery and whips—the results will always be much better. If somebody walks through your door, and you recognize a person of value, whether you have a job or not, you bring him or her aboard, you take him or her with you, because he or she will contribute.

The firm was established as an innovator in wire and cable in 1969 when my brother, working in his laboratory, was astonished to discover that hot Teflon, when stretched, not gradually but suddenly, does not break but instead develops new properties. The extended Teflon was named Gore-Tex. All of us who watched the development of an array of products from it were impressed with the versatility of this singular discovery. With research into new technologies by Gore & Associates as a reference point, I began to examine the technological potential of the TM and TM-Sidhi programs. All progress has as its basis the quality of thinking behind it. The TM technology cultures the quiet level of consciousness, which supports thinking; it can enhance the entire range of human achievement. It offers the ultimate in terms of versatility of application. Intrigued by the possibilities, I began looking for a way to use the TM technology to improve the quality of life in my home state.

Vermont was a unique environment for a project involving the growth of awareness. In the decades preceding the sixties, it had been a rural state losing its young people to cities. The sixties reversed the trend, and people began to move back to Vermont to live in a way that would preserve the best traditional values and incorporate them in a new age. Into the stable farming communities with their heritage of tolerance and independent thinking came seekers of cultural integration, who had imbibed the richness of urban America.

Many of the Vermont correctional administrators understood that the primary mandate of the department is crime prevention, and also caring about human beings and promoting their growth made sense in the light of that mandate. In most places people have isolated and separated prisons from the mainstream of society. The approach of Vermonters had been to build community correctional centers throughout the state, so that inmates retained the support of families and others in their community. This helps them make a successful transition after release. In the spring of 1981, a couple of TM teachers and I presented the Lyons/Halberstadt film *The Transcendental Meditation Program in the Criminal Justice System* to Deputy Commissioner Joe Patrissi and program director John Gorcyzk. Of this early contact John said:

> I think what was important to me a year ago when you guys came to us and asked if you could do a TM program in the institutions, was that I saw some guys on tape, correctional professionals in California, who were saying, hey, it's not bad. I was cynical, but it's not bad.

The Vermont Department of Corrections agreed to permit the TM project and evaluate it thoughtfully. About that time a local teacher, Ron Perry, provided me with a copy of the first edition of *Inside Folsom Prison*. As I read it, I was touched by the quality of the author's heart, and impressed with the significance of the California programs. I began to consult with the author about the Vermont TM prison program.

In December, armed against our sub-zero winter with a down jacket from San Francisco's Macy's, George Ellis arrived in Vermont to direct the project. He knew exactly how to move into the stress and suffering of the prison with the knowledge that would transform human beings. So, by example, he articulated to Vermonters what was possible through the TM program. We decided to offer a model program for staff and inmates that would reach out from locked institutions to families in the community. We wanted to provide the Vermont Department of Corrections with the means to help fulfill its purpose. Our project took the following dimensions:

First, it would be statewide, i.e., we would offer the program in all six correctional institutions, to the central office staff in Waterbury, and to the support staff such as drug abuse counselors, ministers, probation and parole officers.

Second, we would subsidize the instruction of inmates and staff, and the families of each. In addition, we would provide a continuing educational program for them.

Third, we would train Vermont teachers of the TM program to work in institutions and create a curriculum that could be used in correctional settings throughout the world.

Fourth, we would culture a network of community volunteers to support all dimensions of the TM program.

Fifth, we would cooperate with the institutions to develop ways in which the TM program could facilitate existing programs, such as work release projects, therapeutic communities, and drug abuse meetings.

Sixth, we would conduct a systematic evaluation that would include analysis of statistics from the Vermont Department of Corrections and well-designed measures of physiological, psychological, and developmental changes.

The enormous response we received from staff and inmates upon entering the institutions was a surprise to the administration. At St. Albans Correctional Center, some staff members thought we might be fortunate to get half a dozen inmates to begin the program. We instructed 40% of the population. After eight months of the program, the response was consistent in every institution in the state in terms of responsiveness; the impact of the program was even a surprise to me. Over the years of practicing the TM technique, I had observed my own growth of awareness, and I saw a similar growth in others. I saw inmates after their first instruction find themselves inexplicably smiling at guards. I saw individuals experience the first peace they had known in years. I saw suffering leave faces, and people quietly finding themselves clear enough to care about their lives again. When inmates came to an educational meeting from the living units they carried an atmosphere of roughness and irritability with them. They were grumbling over the latest confrontation with the staff or with one another; they were worried about families, sentencing, or an upcoming release. They were not refined in their language, but following group practice of the TM technique, stillness pervaded the room. There was a quiet realization that shared peace and fullness were available even within the institution. Dick Wright, an assistant superintendent from Rutland Community Correctional Center, expressed my sentiments beautifully. He stated:

> I think the biggest impact of the TM program for me is when I sit in a room with anywhere from two inmates to thirty inmates, and we practice the TM technique. No matter what happens with the inmates after that, no matter what happened with them before that, you know they all feel the unity, the inner power, and the peacefulness. Suddenly, everything is forgotten, and there is no division between who you are, and who they are.

Another dimension of the project is the reaction to the cold stress test, developed by John Corson of Dartmouth College and the White River Junction Veterans Administration Hospital. The purpose of the test was to measure, in a controlled setting, how quickly people recover from a mild stress before and after learning TM. Among inmates, it was the most talked about of our evaluative instruments. Although humorously depicted as a macho endurance test by some, the stress is mild and reassuringly human. Inmates and staff alike expressed disappointment if they missed it. It involved monitoring skin conductance, an indicator of anxiety or arousal, while a subject performed tasks. The task was performed as follows: relaxing for five minutes with the eyes closed—as the hand becomes drier due to relaxation, conductance goes down. An inmate or staff was involved in two minutes of mild stress, which consists of immersing the left hand up to the wrist bone in a bucket of ice water for a half a minute, then removing the hand while answering rapid-fire spelling and arithmetic questions for a minute, and then returning the hand to the ice water for another minute, then relaxing again for five minutes.

A graph of the skin conductance reading for any individual is like a physiological signature of the way his or her nervous system responds to both quiet and excitement. The test provides an illustration of the stylistic difference between a rested and a fatigued body. The fatigued nervous system is like a worn-out rubber band that after being stretched fails to regain its original shape. In contrast, a rested nervous system is like a rubber band that retains its elasticity and resumes its shape after stretching. For meditators the response to stress was much more likely to be confined to the stress period. A practitioner of the TM technique cultures opposite qualities in his or her physiology, i.e., alertness or an ability to respond to the environment, and an opposite ability to return to ready status or to relax. The adaptive flexibility of a practitioner of the TM program increases with practice (Ellis, 1983).

The nervous system of a fatigued person never recovers enough from one experience to respond clearly to the next. It is harder for him or her to distinguish between subsequent internal or external events. Because of this he or she was less discriminative than if he or she was rested. In correction circles, adjectives used to describe the more extreme cases of fatigue are "burnt" and "fried." The corrections environment was heated with stress. A physiology that can be trusted to respond appropriately was an enormous blessing. When an individual was asked why he or she wanted to learn the TM technique, a typical response included, I want to be able to control my temper, the stress is making me uncomfortable, or I am confused and it might help me figure things out. Everyone wants to experience a feeling of wellbeing, to become more even-tempered, more aware. The TM program is the only program in the correctional system or elsewhere that has been demonstrated to cultivate the essential physiological foundation for clarity of thought and feeling.

Programs for incarcerated women are one of the most overlooked areas of corrections in the United States. Women represent a small fraction of the prison population. In Vermont, I financed a TM program at the women's unit at the Chittenden Community Correctional Center. The following is a conversation between me and several women aged 18 through 27 about how the TM program has touched their lives.

Susan Gore (Gore): What does freedom mean to you?

Bonnie: Freedom to me is the freedom for a person to express herself and openly live life to the fullest.

Cissy: Freedom is everything to me.

Susan: Freedom is from the inside.

Bonnie: We are in a closed isolated area, and when you practice the TM technique it takes me away, and puts your mind elsewhere. That way it makes you free.

Gore: So your mind is not contained within the walls, it is free?

Susan: When I first came to jail, I had a lot of anger; I had a lot of jitteriness. I could not relax. I could not deal with things well because I had so much buried tension inside. I mean real heavy things—anger at people, at myself, a lot of alcohol and drug abuse. I came from a very stressful life, and with the TM technique the freedom I have is happiness. Stress does not come out in what I do. It has enabled me to perform my job better, and perform my living in the institution better. I still get stressed but it comes and goes. I do not keep it in and it's not piling up.

Gore: What does it mean to be your own companion?

Susan: It's really strange. You know, the other day I looked into a mirror and said, "You know it's going to be nice rooming with you." (laughter) To be my own companion means to be at peace with me. The other day, I was at work, and was sweeping the floor and all of a sudden I was humming this song and I thought—it's incredible! "You know, I like me."

Gore: All right!

Susan: I like to be alone. I enjoy the company, but when there is no company, I am not pulling my hair out screaming. I am content. I find things to do, and I even sing to myself. I have a good relationship with me, you know.

Cissy: Before I came here, and when I first got here, I just had the attitude that I did not care. I hated everyone in here, and then I started seeing things differently, seeing Cissy in a different way.

Gore: So you are beginning to see the value in yourself?

Cissy: Yes. I blocked it out before, but now I do want it. (laughter)

Bonnie: Now I deal with things. I am striving for my goal more seriously. Now I want to grasp it, I want to beat it.

Gore: What about human potential?

Susan: I can understand things that go on in everyday living that I did not understand before. I can see where it takes groups of people striving for the same goals to make the world run. Before, I understood how to be self-destructive. I knew habits: how to steal, and all the negative things that anybody can pick up. Since I have been practicing the TM technique, I am beginning to see the potential that I have for achieving goals, and seeing people coming together and doing things as a group.

Gore: You used to think your potential was limited, so you were doing negative things?

Susan: I have held a few jobs, but most of them I could not stand, so I always thought people were talking about me, and I always had an excuse to quit. I have been practicing the TM technique, and I do not have the best job in the world, but I have a job. I no longer feel people are talking about me. I feel they are talking to me, if at all.

Gore: How are things on the unit?

Susan: We are getting along better. Another woman who practices the TM technique, and I, could not stand to be in the same room together. I am serious, we used to fight constantly. I do not mean physically, but we just never liked each other and we made it clear we did not. However, now we practice the TM technique together. We started by sitting at different sides of the room. Now we do things together, and we do not pick at each other's faults. We find a way to enjoy what we have.

Cissy: The ones that take TM seriously come back from the educational meetings and we get on the unit, you know, and we are right up there. If something happens to come down on us, then we can deal with it better, but the ones that come in and just goof off, they blow up and they start swearing at the guards and all that. They do not know how to deal with things.

Susan: I would like to see the TM program introduced in facilities, especially with women, because it gets you in touch with feelings that are real.

Bonnie: The other girls look up to us like role models. Some of them get the idea—if they can do it, I can do it.

Gore: How has the TM program affected your view of relationships?

Bonnie: I feel I can cope now. The problems that were the smallest, I made up to be the biggest (laughter).

Gore: OK, she's got a sense of perspective?

Cissy: Someone can express their feelings to me, and I can identify with them, but then I can see where they are coming from too. Before I would just say, well (laughter) that is your problem.

Gore: You have more a sense of compassion?

Susan: Once you relieve the stress, you have more love to give people, and you have more friendship to give people.

Gore: How do you define love and how does the TM practice affect your experience of love?

Bonnie: To be loved, and to love others!

Cissy: To bring the deep inner feeling out toward someone.

Susan: It's a strong feeling like happiness.

Gore: Love is a feeling?

Susan: It is; it's a beautiful feeling. It's something that I never experienced in my life before. You know I have two boys, and I thought I loved them, but I never really saw them. I never reached out to them. I took care of them; I did what I had to do. Since I have been practicing TM, I feel love for them. I do not know what I was looking for in love, but, you know, "I love you" and write it all over the wall and tattoo it on your arm or something, it's not like that—it's an exchangeable thing that does not necessarily mean physical contact, although a hug is great. It's something that you know when you are around it.

Gore: How would you describe yourself now, contrary to how you were before you started the TM program?

Cissy: I see myself as a different person, and I do not want to go back to the old Cissy. I am finding out who I am, and who the people are around me. I am getting closer to my family.

Bonnie: I respect myself more than I ever have.

Susan: I had an attitude when I came into this prison that you would not believe (laughter). I mean, you would not believe! I knew it all, no one was going to tell me anything. Do not mess with me because I would just as soon tell you where to go as look at you. The thing that I have learned through TM is that it's OK to be sensitive, it's OK to love. I am not really that defiant. I was really looking for love. It's shown me how to be real. It has changed my life in a remarkable way that I do not want to see end. I have been trying to find ways to keep going when I get out of here. As to the unit practicing the TM technique together, if a whole unit would really put their minds to it, I do not think they would even know you had a unit here. It would be a fellowship of people. I do not think the administration would believe it!

Following my interview with the women I realized the beauty of the project in Vermont is that the administration did believe. In fact, they had the opportunity to visit the university in Iowa, now called MUM, Maharishi University of Management, and observed an ideal campus in which everyone meditated. The administrators had not bought into the idea that suffering was necessary, nor had they surrendered their vision of the potential in every individual to do well. Of course they faced the politics of special interest and positionality. Since many of the staff had the opportunity to learn TM they understood how the inmates could change, and how the quality of life for staff and inmates could be improved. Physicists think of creation in terms of waves, or vibrational qualities.

When a nervous system becomes noise-free, the vibrational quality changes, and it broadcasts a different quality. We are interconnected with our surroundings so that we and our environment vibrate in a symphony—or in a cacophony. It is natural to want to bring ourselves and our surroundings into harmony and in doing so address our attention to both. The human nervous system is so delicate and precise that it can resonate with all levels of activity in nature, yet rest in the immutable silence that is the basis of activity. Our individuality is a song, a voice, in a universal orchestra. As our voices become pure and in tune, it inspires harmony within the whole range of its sound. This is what it means to refine the nervous system.

In Vermont we addressed ourselves to the cacophony of stress in the prisons. Inside the walls, inmates and staff learned that the most confining barriers are constructed within the mind and carried in the fatigue of the body. Each participant saw the usefulness of the program from their particular point of view. The tuning-in to the simplest form of awareness that occurs when an individual practices the TM technique is reflected in the practical events in daily life; it is in these moments that we hear the larger sound.

Lynne Carter, Volunteer Coordinator at the Chittenden Community Correctional Center, discussed with me the effect of the TM program on her life and work:

> The immediate thing that I noticed was a sense of a break from confusion and tension, a break of the barrier between the inmates and me. I felt more able to relate to the inmates. I can give more of myself without worrying about losing. Love is something I can give out at any time without losing anything. I have a large sense of caring. I am in a setting that is almost totally male. The guards are mostly men, and I had felt very vulnerable with men. The TM program has helped me feel more integrated so that when I received remarks they do not bother me so much. I am carrying myself

differently. I am not a helpless female, and I am not a thing. I am a powerful person, and I can relate to you.

The Vermont Department of Corrections discovered that it was strengthened during the experiment in their ability to achieve goals. Correctional staffs were not politically or institutionally naïve and neither were they closed to the deepest human values. They wanted progress in their own lives, and in the lives of the people they influenced; they were pragmatically exploring the TM technique as a means for achieving progress and gaining leverage for other positive factors in the system. Stress is a well-acknowledged problem in correctional circles. It is like a black hole that absorbs the energy and creativity of everyone in it or around it. When people are relieved of stress, it is like being relieved of debt. It becomes possible to grow toward the future, enjoy the present, and to enliven the creativity of the environment.

Three final observations from top officials in the Vermont Department of Corrections succinctly summarized the transformations. Dick Turner, Superintendent, Chittenden Community Correctional Center stated:

> Personally, as the TM program adds perspective, I am certainly not as harried. I get better quality out of my work. I do not think I can do more, but I think I do the same or better with more attention to detail. Because I practice the TM technique in the afternoon, I get a period of time when I have some peace.

Joseph Patrissi, Deputy Commissioner for the Vermont Department of Corrections declared:

> The basic premise is that people can change, and they can grow in spite of themselves and in spite of the environment. You will know when we have succeeded in what we are trying to do if we get to the day when parents say to their children, "Make sure you practice the TM technique today so you can grow up."

John Gorcyzk, Director of Programs, proclaimed:

> The nicest thing for me is the inmate response to the TM program. The most powerful thing is the mail from inmates. It is the only program for which I get fan mail. Jim Walton, the Commissioner, gets fan mail, and I have a little file of fan mail for the TM program. Was it Dostoyevsky who said that you should measure the degree of civilization of a culture

by its prisons? I cannot imagine a more civilized activity than the group practice of the TM technique. It is always a very civilized experience. People are very thoughtful and very polite. It is just a very, very nice experience. As that continues to develop, and we continue to introduce the TM program to the degree that we have been doing in the Vermont Department of Corrections, it may be that our system will become more civilized than the people on the street. It is an interesting idea.

The TM program in Vermont was completed with positive results. A documentary was created which reviewed the implications of the program for global implementation. Following the completion of the Vermont TM research program, George Ellis and I were invited to Washington by Maharishi, where we presented the program design and results to governmental leaders from Brazil and Africa. Subsequently major programs were implemented with tremendous success, for prisons, police, and the military. The battle against ignorance continues, and the victory of light overcoming darkness is inevitable.

Chapter XVIII

Softness and Steel

Elizabeth and Patricia Cline became teachers of the TM program in Avoriaz, France in 1976, and were involved as volunteers in the field of corrections with both youth and adult offenders. They are loyal and committed associates and friends who have shared my vision of compassion. They employed their intelligence with love and humor to eliminate human suffering and expand consciousness. Their gentle manner softened hardened individuals. Here they described experiences as teachers, counselors, and friends.

George Ellis (GE): How long had you been involved in communicating with prisoners?

Elizabeth: I had been in communication with four inmates through letters for many years at various California correctional facilities. I first became involved in communicating with inmates when Pat Corum from Folsom Prison wrote my sister a letter when we were on a Teacher Training Course in France. It was a very warm, moving letter. We began visiting with Pat after corresponding for about four or five months. Upon walking into the visiting room, we found ourselves confronted with a mass of about 200 convicts and families. I found Pat a very intelligent, warm, sensitive person. We enjoyed the visit tremendously, and it was the beginning of a close friendship. Pat transferred to San Quentin Prison after our first visit, and we continued to visit him there.

Patricia: I first visited incarcerated men when I was fifteen at the California Youth Authority (CYA) in Sacramento. My older sister Claudia was involved in a field project for a college class, and I would accompany her on her visits to the CYA. I first began visiting men at Folsom with Elizabeth.

GE: What was your motivation to work in such a potentially negative environment?

Patricia: Actually, I had never considered or even thought about having any communication with men or women in prison. The whole thing started spontaneously, as Elizabeth explained earlier. Folsom Prison was very close to my home in Sacramento. I decided to visit a man involved in the TM program at

Folsom Prison who had become my friend, through the feelings and thoughts we exchanged in our letters. I have never experienced any negativity or interpersonal problems concerning my friendship with these TM practicing prisoners. However, the environment in which they exist is for the most part shrouded in negativity. The demands and needs are very different from those of a friendship on the outside. How do you respond to a friend who has been locked up in a 6-foot by 8-foot cell with no openings for ventilation or light except a small hole in the door? As I became a closer friend to some of the men it was harder for me to emotionally and intellectually deal with the situation they were in. I realized they had committed crimes, but the hostile and crude environment in which they are forced to exist was an equally serious crime.

Elizabeth: I feel visits benefit the men very much in that communication with a woman adds balance to their lives and enriches their personalities. Through the TM program, their hearts seemed to expand and soften, yet there were very few people in the prison environment to whom they could express this expansion. In prison there is extreme pressure to always maintain the macho image. With Patricia and me, they could be more natural. In the beginning, it was almost as if someone had pulled out a plug and released a gusher of feelings, thoughts, and emotions, which was at last able to flow to someone who would listen.

GE: What particular effect did it have on you emotionally or physically?

Elizabeth: The effect visiting had on me was somewhat of a dichotomy. Emotionally, I felt good seeing and visiting with people I cared for. It is always a very rewarding experience in that respect. However, physically the visits had a draining effect pursuant to the physical condition of the visiting room, and from the intense and negative vibrations in the prison. When a person is tired and not rested, the prison environment can take its toll physically and emotionally. When I am rested inside I am much more resistant to the negativity.

Patricia: I could feel myself wear out about two hours after entering the prison.

GE: Was there a difference between visiting inmates involved in the TM program in contrast to inmates not involved in the TM program?

Elizabeth: I felt that through the TM program, the men had been able to experience and integrate into their lives more subtle and refined levels of awareness. When one experiences more subtle levels of life in oneself he or she can appreciate and relate to these levels in others. In prison, you are left with yourself. You can develop the outer self alone, the body, or complement that development with a growth of the inner self-consciousness. Many men we visited, who were not participating in the TM program, related to us on the physical level. My relationship with the inmates involved in the TM program transcended the physical to embrace the emotional, mental, and spiritual levels.

Patricia: The inmates with whom I had contact, whether involved in the TM program or not, were all very different. All vary in awareness, intelligence, education, personality, etc. However, there seemed to be a qualitative difference between inmates in the TM program and those not involved—it is restfulness, and a refinement. Many inmates not participating in the TM program are very intelligent and perceptive individuals, yet there was a sort of emotional and mental grasping, which at times was very intense. I shared a very deep friendship with the men I visited. There was love shared between us that grew out of a feeling of respect and trust for each other. I saw these men as possessing a great deal of integrity and intelligence. I know they shared this feeling for me.

GE: What was the most significant difference in your relationship with a man behind bars and other men in free society?

Patricia: The most significant difference between men in prison and free men is that incarcerated individuals have a stronger need for human interaction. Because of the harshness of prison life, it is necessary for these men to experience love and caring, just so they know those emotions are still alive within themselves.

Elizabeth: The intensity of the friendship is the significant difference. Since the men had been deprived of contact with women, they would give all they could in a relationship. They do not take friendship for granted. Because contact was limited to a few visits a month in a crowded setting, there was little time for the usual venting that unfortunately exists in many relationships. In relationships and friendships in free society many times you are with your friends and companions when moods are fluctuating. Unfortunately, negative moods and stress are usually shared in a relationship where a lot of time is spent together. With the inmates the time spent together was very limited and therefore spent positively. Through the TM program, an individual is given an outlet for accumulated stress and tension, thus saving friends from being a potential target for stress relief.

GE: Any additional comments?

Patricia: Many people cannot comprehend why I would want to visit convicts. They cannot understand what we would talk about in our visits. I feel most people categorize inmates as hardened, brutal, and non-feeling criminals. I visited prisoners because I liked them; they were my friends, who happened to live behind bars. I did not judge their past—they had enough judges, guards, administrators, and citizens evaluating their every action. I do, however, judge the environment in which they are expected to be rehabilitated. The entire prison system reminded me of Alice in Wonderland with all the illogical and unjust proceedings that take place. However, there is little humor in this wonderland. It is a deadly game dealing with the lives of human beings. I do not believe that all the inmates are innocent, misunderstood individuals who should be set free tomorrow. I realized that some committed serious crimes to be placed in an institution like Folsom Prison. I also believed that some inmates may have been incapable for some time of living in society without behaving violently, and should be kept away from society. Nevertheless, this does not justify cruelty. We have evolved as human beings, and become civilized, intelligent, and scientific. Why must our prisons continue to exist in the Dark Ages?

Elizabeth: Like Patricia, I was disappointed at some people's reactions to my visiting men in prisons. There are some who feel that convicts and humans are not the same and never will be. People living in prison have made mistakes in life as a result of stress, which unfortunately is a rather common denominator for quite a large sector of society. Because a person is in prison does not exclude him or her from evolution. There is growth taking place for all individuals at all times. The TM program speeds up the process by releasing stress.

In the years during which I visited men in prison, I witnessed in them a rapid and positive growth on all levels. Through the TM program, they were not only able to release stress, but they became more immune to it. I visited the prisoners because I loved them dearly. I considered them my close friends. I did not care less for them as members of society for acts they committed in the past.

They were very intelligent, gentle beings and I am grateful to have known and shared friendship with them at that moment in time.

Patricia Cline (front row second from the left) and Elizabeth Cline (front row second from the right) gather with Charlie Lutes and other TM volunteers at San Quentin Prison to meditate, and join weekly TM meetings with staff and inmates.[©]

Chapter XIX

Mystery

Ann Mortifee

Ann was born in Zululand, South Africa. She is a talented musician, writer, and artist who has chosen to employ music as an instrument of healing and inspiration to motivate others to move toward self-discovery. Ann is known throughout the world for her passionate performances. She has released ten CDs and written three musicals, film scores, and several ballets. Ann received the Order of Canada and the YMCA Women of Distinction Award for outstanding contribution to the healing and performing arts in Canada. Twice, she walked away from the promise of international stardom after earning reviewers' praise for her performances in plays and musical scores. Ann stated: "I felt like I had been offered the world in New York, but I just couldn't go down that road. I knew that something deeper was calling me." Music as a healing tool became Ann's message at global conferences and workshops for caretakers of the dying. In her new book In Love with the Mystery, *she articulates the commitment to listening to the inner voices of humanity and within ourselves.*

I was born in South Africa, and lived the early part of my life on a sugar cane farm in Zululand. I grew up in nature, and my grandfather was into conservation; he spent a lot of time on the game reserves, one of which he helped establish to save the white rhinoceros. From an early age, I had a sense for the beauty and wonder of nature, and had a pivotal experience at five years old: I had a dream that happened repeatedly—I dreamed that I was someone else. In the morning, I would hear the rooster, and would start to awaken; the person I really am would say—oh no you are going to start dreaming that you are her again. You are going to start dreaming you are on a farm in Zululand, and you need to remember who you really are. I would look down at my hands and say to myself that these are not really my hands—this is a dream, and I might move through the entire day with a peculiar sense of—what was I really looking at? How is this so solid? I can hardly wait to go home. Any time I felt sad I would say I want to go home and my mother would answer you are home.

I would answer no, I am not home, this is not who I really am—it was a very vivid experience. My parents were worried that I was lost in a make-believe fantasy. However, the experience started a lifetime of yearning and a sense that something was going on that I did not understand. I remember our house was built on top of a hill and we looked down on the cane field where the Zulu people lived in their huts. I recall asking myself why I was born in the white house on the hill, and not with them. Why do we have toast and marmalade and they have to line up to obtain their food every Thursday?

Apartheid had just started in South Africa. My father wanted to move us out of the country because he had been in Parliament, and he felt strongly against it. My father was British, paternal, and good to the people, but I could feel that something was not right—I did not know what it was. Even as a child I would rise early and sneak out because I could be alone in the world. I used to go quite often and spend a lot of time playing with the Zulu children. One morning I was standing at the top of the hill looking down, and suddenly I began to experience a humming sound in my ears; I noticed that everywhere I looked there were little specks of light. The light became brighter and brighter until it was difficult to see the huts. After a few moments, I was just standing in a euphoric experience of blissful nothingness, just a white light, and I now assume that was my first transcendental experience.

In my childhood, I had TB and ended up spending many months in a sanatorium, and I found the only way to assuage my loneliness was to go from bed to bed to cheer people up. It made me feel better to give to others, and I believe it influenced my choices in life. We moved to Canada when I was 13 years old, and I ended up going to a Christian camp. I fell in love with the concept and possibility of unconditional love expressed in the teachings of Jesus. I also believed I wanted to become as close to that unconditional love as I could.

When I was 14 years of age, I remember getting on a bus and praying that I would be led to someone who needed me. I followed my quiet inner feeling, and I was so young and innocent that I did not question it. I recall stepping off the bus in a very dangerous part of town. I began walking along the road and found myself standing in front of a bar. Of course, I was underage, but I went into the bar; it smelled of smoke and beer. I looked across the room at a woman sitting at a little table, and I knew it was her that I was there to see. I went across the room, and I said to her, I know this may sound strange, but I was sent to tell you that you are absolutely loved and infinitely treasured. The woman began to cry; she had been working with the Salvation Army for 25 years, and something had happened. I do not remember the details at the time, but she was going to take her life in the next hour if she did not receive some sign that she was loved by God. We ended up having a deep conversation, and I remarked to her that before she even prayed, her prayer had been heard, and I had been on the bus for an hour headed in her direction. It was a quiet, intuitive feeling, just a knowing.

I continued my involvement with Christianity, and spent time with Billy Graham as an evangelist. It was during my Christian stage of evolution that I found my voice. There were two girls who used to do all the singing at the Christian camps; one of them became sick, and the other one asked me for help. She played the guitar and that summer her parents gave her a new guitar, which she gave to me so that the next summer we could play guitar together. I discovered I had a natural voice and what has been interesting throughout the years is that my voice continued to grow, and I now have almost a four-octave range—I consider it a gift. I was involved in evangelical Christianity for about four years. I was invited to sing in other places.

I used to read the Bible every morning and pray. The focus of my prayers was to help people and gather strength. I always found that halfway through my prayers I would reflect—why am I even praying? God knows already what I am going to pray, so why don't I just sit with him in the silence? My prayers became thoughtless-wordless prayer, and I would just be there. It is reminiscent of what Maharishi describes as Transcendental Consciousness, an innocent experience of inner silence beyond the finest impulse of mental activity.

At that time, I had a crisis of faith. I would talk to my teachers and express my sentiments that if my love is a tiny thing, and I could not bear even the worst human being to go to hell, how could God, who created love, even dream up such a thing? The answer the teachers provided me was that we just cannot understand the ways of God, and you just need to have faith. I reflected and understood those ideas, but how could I stay here and believe that Jesus is the only way? In the Bible, there is an expression: God will give you the gift of your heart. To some he has given the gift of faith and to others the gift of hope, and so forth. I have been given the gift of faith, and it has never been difficult for me to understand the Christian concepts; nevertheless, I asked myself, why should I be blessed with eternal life and happiness when someone else who has not been gifted has to suffer damnation? I was about 16 at the time. They tried to save my soul, and they told me I was doing the wrong thing.

I had a dream that I was on the back of a man being carried through a desert. As I looked back, I saw that his robe went all the way back into the distance, and there were people hanging onto his robe; he was pulling them through the desert. I turned and looked at him, and it was the image of Jesus. I looked into his eyes, which were mesmerizing, and I was literally pulled through a tunnel; it was a shuttering sensation, and suddenly I found myself standing beside him on a high hill overlooking a dark valley. There were many pathways leading to that valley. I saw what I now recognize, but did not recognize as a child: monks, nuns, whirling dervishes, and every kind of spiritual tradition you could imagine, and people walking with blindfolds. Some paths were jagged; some seemed to be spiraling, but they were all ending up in this incredible light at the end of these pathways. The light was sending out these exquisite rays. The only way I could describe them is they were like liquid powder. As the rays hit me, I felt unbelievable love, and I stayed in that state for a while. It became dark, and I was standing beside Jesus on this hill. I looked at him, and I said: Oh, everyone is safe; I did not know, I am so relieved, thank you for telling me. Then suddenly I was twirling back through this tunnel attached to his shoulders in the desert. I climbed off his shoulders and said thank you for carrying me this far. As I watched the figure of Jesus, in my dream, return to the desert, I saw the person behind me cling to the same place I had been clinging to, and the figure of Jesus looked back at me and winked, as he turned to look at the next person in line. I said to him, I am going to miss you so much, and he said I know—and that was the end of the dream. I recognized that unconditional love was the universal foundation of every religion in the world.

That experience in the form of a dream resulted in an inner spiritual awakening and sent me into a tailspin. I was thrown into the world in a whole new way—my career burst open. I did nothing to develop a career as a singer, it just happened to me. There were pivotal points along the way. I started singing on a dare from some girls at school. It was the first time I had sung at anything secular other than a Christian camp. The girls at my school and I had been seen by someone coming the following week who was going to perform folk music, and they asked if I would open the show for them. I began singing in little folk clubs, churches, and community events. One day, I was picking up my guitar at the little coffeehouse where I used to perform, and the owner asked me if I was going to the audition. I asked what an audition was. The café owner remarked that an audition was taking place at the Playhouse Theater Company, and they are looking for a girl singer. I said I would not know what to do. The café owner said he would take me to the audition, and he suggested I sing a song called *You Heard My Voice, And You Know My Name*, written by Art Podell and Walter Schorr. I believe it was originally done by The Travelers Three. I will paraphrase the words:

> *If you have ever kissed in a summer's rain, if you slept where the winds and the snows have lain, if you have ever heard a lonely train, then you've heard my voice and you know my name, you have heard my voice in the winds of spring, you've seen my face where the roses cling, I am the touch that the warm rains bring, I make my home in the heart of everything . . .*

I went down to the audition, and it turned out it was for a show called *The Ecstasy of Rita Joe*; it was story about a Native American girl who was torn between the native culture and the white culture. I empathized with her so deeply because of my experience in South Africa. Half of the company was native and the other half white. The play ran for several months and eventually went to New York. The significance of *Rita Joe* is that I had never written a song until then; the man who was hired to write the music was not showing up for rehearsals. The director asked me to create some compositions, so we could have some music to work with. The producers of the show started recording whatever I had written, and that is how I became a composer. I would have never, in a million years, thought of being a composer. Ironically South Africa obtained the model and the program for apartheid from the United States and Canada in how we dealt with the native people. The whole idea of reservations was employed as a model for apartheid. I felt I was offering something through the play to my homeland, as well as the native people of Canada, to raise consciousness.

While in New York I was offered a lead role after the show was over, and top agents took me on. I was offered the lead role in a Broadway musical called *Promises, Promises*. When I reviewed my contract, I was being asked to sign a three-year agreement, and I had to do eight shows a week. I kept listening to the music, and I was uncomfortable with the lyrics. I had just come out of the music of *The Ecstasy of Rita Joe*, which was a powerful social statement, which resonated in me in the deepest way. I went to see my agent, and I was in turmoil. I said, what happens if I die while singing the lyrics? I said to him there has to be more to music than this, so I turned down the contract. My agent was very upset with me. I realized that I did not belong in New York and went back to Vancouver.

Two days after I arrived back home in Vancouver, the Royal Winnipeg Ballet, which was the biggest ballet company in Canada, called me up and asked me if I would write a musical score for *The Ecstasy of Rita Jones*. A musical score is an hour of continuous music that would be played by an orchestra. I was 19 at the time, and I said to them: I have only written a few songs for *Rita Jones*, and I would not even begin to know how to score a ballet. I was able to work with an arranger to coordinate the whole production. He put the musical score down in writing because I never had a music lesson in my life. To this day, it is a mystery to me! The artistic director said he wanted me to express the heart of *Rita Joe*; he said just bring your heart to Winnipeg, and we will see what happens. The ballet of *Rita Joe* became an international hit. It still plays to this day, and that started my career in a whole new direction.

In 1973 or 1974 there was a group of religious ministers who started a small record company to put meaningful music into the world. The ministers asked me to put their second album out—*The Ecstasy of Rita Joe*, which I did, and that is when I met Paul Horn, because he was hired to be the flute player. He came into that recording session and from the moment we met I just adored the music we made. Paul was already a successful musician, and he had become a teacher of TM. Paul had moved to Canada, and I remember telling him that I had wanted to write an overture for the CD, but I did not have time. I recall Paul said let's improvise something, and I agreed, but asked, how do you do that together? Paul said, I will start playing and when you feel moved, just come in, and I laughed and said OK. He encouraged me to follow him into the music, and that became the overture and the epilogue.

I did a show with intensely passionate music, which permitted me to become a storyteller, and I ended up going to Europe with that musical. I was seen by a producer from Abbey Road studios in London and went to do my second album in London with EMI. We did the album; they were excited about it, and they chose to take me on as their major female artist, and they were planning a world tour. The studio organized a big dinner, and I remember the moment—it was like a big dream. I was looking down the table at all the top artists of EMI, and watching them talking with one another, and something within me said, if you go down that path you will never fulfill your destiny. I pushed the feelings aside, assuming I was just afraid because I was only 22.

At the time, I was playing folk music with a classical overtone, and I was writing musical interludes, but I was singing myself. My own style had developed so they saw me as a crossover but not pop. My music has more of a flavor of a Donovan but not as folksy. When I came home from doing the CD, another crisis of faith happened similar to what happened in New York with the Broadway musical. I had finished the CD in London at EMI studios at Abbey Road. The studio released the album, but what happened when I came home, I had strong feelings that this was not the road to take. I called the producer and asked him to let me out of the contract I had signed to do the world tour, and he reluctantly agreed.

I set off on a pilgrimage because what I really wanted was a spiritual life, and that led me to live in Lebanon for a year, working in Calcutta with Mother Theresa, and traveling to different spiritual places for about three years. During that time, I started to mature in different ways. I was all emotion, faith, and spirituality. I needed to learn how to come into my mind intellectually and learn how to use it. I learned about eastern meditation on my first trip to India and practiced techniques for several decades.

Through the instrument of music and the beauty of art I have tried to express a deep and profound commitment to the elimination of human suffering and the expansion of consciousness. I learned a life lesson that it does not matter if your work is ever produced; what matters is—you envision it, you dream it, and you create it with tremendous intensity, and it will contribute to humanity's evolution. It is not just what you do, but the resonance field you create. My work changed because I had a feeling of placement that I had never had before. I was not as concerned if I was fulfilling my destiny, or if I had made a mistake by not going for fame and fortune.

In terms of destiny, women have been an oppressed minority on the planet earth. There are so many women who are not championed, and they take a decision and follow a certain path; they often become frustrated because they have not realized their dreams, and my next musical is dedicated to the empowerment of women. I believe women are on the cusp of a major breakthrough on the planet. Women care for the community, the children, their companions, and so forth at the expense of their own being. What I have experienced is that the dreaming is possibly even more powerful than the actualization on the planet. Although both are important, it is not always up to us which ones are actualized.

The power of the dream has to do with how an individual develops his or her consciousness, and the deeper you have gone expanding spirituality, the more potency the dreaming has. If a person can settle into the unfathomable realms from which the instruction is arriving, rather than being motivated by the idea of writing music solely for a hit record, then the artist is tapping into the unboundedness of Being. I am writing music from a source that flows from my inner silence spontaneously. I try not to get in the way other than to use my skills, awareness, and everything I have at my disposal to hone it, purify it, clarify it, and bring it forward. I believe many women do not realize the absolute depth of power that they carry with their dreaming, such as her holding of a vision for her children and the world to be well.

I was in Iowa at MUM with Candace Badgett, who is responsible for the Mother Divine organization; she and I had a wonderful resonance together on the role of women in cultivating the inner silence of consciousness in our society. While I was at MUM, something in me said my work with women was about to begin. I believe bringing together the particular capacity and sensitivity of women is going to help enrich society at this time in history. The group consciousness has been controlled in the last centuries by the masculine energy; as the feminine qualities within us begin to emerge, the transformation of the collective consciousness will accelerate.

I believe the circumstance that has gifted and held women back is their tremendous capacity to surrender their hopes and desires for the good of the larger. A woman can sublimate her desires for community, her family, and her children. It causes her grief, and it causes her great joy. A woman instinctively knows—if she has prosperity, then people around her are going to prosper. The woman lives on the horizontal with her arms outstretched; she may do it in a feisty way or in a tender way. Metaphorically, women live on the horizontal and men live on the vertical. Men tend to see where they are positioned in society rather than what is good for their neighbor. Women instinctively know if they make the school better the life of their children will improve. Women are not excited at the thought of their sons and daughters going off to war. Men and women narrowed their focus instead of integrating. Women need to bring their internal world into the external world. As people evolve the coherence will synchronize within men and women and reach a balance.

Maharishi's explanation of consciousness and quantum physics clarifies how the synchrony develops, and has made a big difference because people are beginning to understand that energy and consciousness are two functions of the same process. I learned TM, and it is a wonderful technique—it is simpler than what I had been doing. However, the goal of gaining enlightenment is the same, as with every ancient tradition in the world. You sit down, the mind quiets, and before you know it you are in the unboundedness of your mind. I began having symptoms of higher consciousness, such as witnessing my activity when I was 4 years old and it was natural. It always made me have a feeling of being separate from the world. I do not have the accurate words to describe properly the experience. Maharishi described this experience as a stage in the evolution of higher consciousness.

When I came back from Lebanon, I thought my career would be finished, but it had grown. I ended up starting a record company of my own as I was blacklisted because of having broken the contract with EMI, but I was pushed into a big career and performed with artists like John Denver, Harry Belafonte and others, and traveled the world.

I had friends who had developed an organization called Inner Source, and they asked me to write an album for people facing death. I wrote the album, and during the process, I would close my eyes and have the intention of the first song until it emerged. I would start to sing, such as, *to every life must come an ending, to every birth must come a day, the being born and then the leaving*, and while I was doing it, I would hear my friend begin typing and recording it at the same time. We wrote the entire album that way and it turned out the songs would bounce between universal and personal perspectives. When I was in the studio recording I received a call from a hospice organization, and they asked me to be a keynote speaker. I was surprised and asked—why would you invite me, because I have never worked in this field? They said we saw you in concert and realized we needed you to open our first conference. The day I was on my way to the convention in Chicago, the first pressing of the CD was sold out. The very next year I was traveling to nine countries in Europe, working with the dying and the caregivers.

I have recently completed a book, *In Love with the Mystery*, with Paul Horn. In the beginning, there was no purpose or thought of a book. Paul had given me a beautiful calendar for Christmas in 2009, which had seven days on a page where you could write your reflections. I would wake up in the early morning at 5:00 a.m. and sit in the deep silence of my meditation until I felt moved. I had no idea what I was going to say until a word would come, and that is how I would begin. I was limited by space on the calendar, and my writing became smaller; literally I would be in the middle of a thought, witnessing myself thinking and experiencing the process. I am aware that Maharishi in *The Science of Being and Art of Living* discussed speaking, acting, and thinking from the level of Being and my experience of the reality of his description was total bliss when the knowledge emerged and flowed through me. Every morning I followed the same pattern of meditating and filling the calendar one phrase or saying at a time. I would share it with Paul, and we would reflect on it throughout the day. After a year, I put the project away and was grateful for the experience; the next year I started to do it again. I felt my gift, job, and joy was in the process of creation.

Several months later my sister-in-law picked up my notes and read them; she asked me if we could turn it into a book. I said if you wish to turn it into a book go ahead, and she did it. I worked with her on what it would look like with the other collaborators. One of my closest friends, Courtney Miles, took all the photographs and provided the different images in the book. My desire is that each aphorism can help a person move down the road to an inner awakening. Paul and I came together and correlated the power of the music with the aphorisms in the book. We went through the book and chose individual sayings that touched us. Afterwards, we went into the studio with two friends, and 45 minutes later we walked out of the studio, and the CD included in the book was finished.

Paul and I have both experienced transcending through music, and it has cultivated our consciousness in an inestimable way; if you do not surrender to the music, it does not work—certainly not in improvisation. If a musician is in a group, he or she needs to be listening to the same muse. For example, if one of the members of the group is thinking about performing a great solo in order to stand out, the group harmony is lost.

There are musicians who are deeply gifted as artists, but do not bring that transcendent capacity into their daily life. In fact, the artists often become addicted to substances because when you are creating it is such a high; it is so fiery and alive that when you come back to this world, in your mundane self, it can be intolerable and a lot of people wind up with different addictions. The artist has a taste of the transcendent, and he or she wants it again and again, and then people cannot find it anywhere else in their life. I believe Paul and I have had the knowledge and technique of meditation. We found a way to have the transcendent experience every day; it has helped us to learn the split between your transcendental Self and your personal self that has to pay the bills, vacuum the floor, and do the laundry. In that way, it works to stabilize and integrate life. When you have a tool like TM to experience the transcendent, the passageway between yourself and the transcendent becomes smoother and smoother, and wider and wider so that in a split second you are there. When I was writing every morning for 365 days, which resulted in my book, *In Love with the Mystery*, the process of creative unfoldment became spontaneous. The passageway to the transcendent, because of TM, has become smooth—my capacity to enter the creative zone is effortless. I do not have to think about experiencing Being because it is just a perpetual reality within my consciousness. When I close my eyes, the passageway is smooth and open.

As I review my reflections, I look around me and see a beautiful day with the sun coming through the leaves of the trees, and all my flowers in bloom in a way that I have never seen them—they are just up in splendor all around me. I believe in the process of sharing these observations on the evolution of my art and life; it has helped me to see at a greater depth of how my life is unfolding, and how everything is going according to schedule. These insights have been very precious for me, and hopefully will inspire others to look within and discover the mystery.

When a storm is raging and waves are tumultuous, it is wise to dive deep down to where the water is calm. If we remain on the surface, we will be tossed and turned. But if, like the whale, we retreat to the quiet depths of our own Being, our true home, we will find rest and peace there. Once refreshed, we can resurface. This is the value of the meditation. We can weather any storm with greater ease if we allow ourselves to retreat when necessary to the still, vast depths within. (Mortifee, 2010, p. 171)

Chapter XX

Age Does Not Come To Me

Helen Boyce

Helen Boyce, born September 25, 1920, was the Italian matriarch for generations of students in a small town in Pennsylvania. In our current economic times she is a model of an individual who understood the importance of setting aside pennies for the future and not living beyond her means. She and her husband Jim loved one another profoundly. She learned TM after watching Maharishi being interviewed on the Merv Griffin Show in the mid-1970s. To date Helen continues to practice the TM technique twice a day and experiences the growing stillness of pure consciousness.

My father taught me that we need to commit to humanitarianism and if you could do something, and be helpful to someone else, then you should do whatever you could. My father spent time with his children but there were no toys in the home because we could not afford them. What kind of toy could he buy us that would be useful? My father did a lot of talking to us regarding respect and honor of one another. He wanted his children to be civil to each other and he emphasized the importance of respect for my mother.

On August 26, 1920, a few weeks before I was born, women received the right to vote, and our family always voted Democratic. I observed many transformational points in history including the Great Depression of 1929, World War II, Vietnam, and the Civil Rights Movement. Our family participated in marching against discrimination; the family was socially conscious. I met the love of my life, Jim Boyce, in 1941 and we married in 1942. World War II was going on, and we had separate jobs. He worked in the steel mill and I was a seamstress. We started our grocery business together in 1953. Jim and I, as we built the grocery business, were involved in social concerns and attempting to build economic security. In 1960 our business almost collapsed, but we were pulled through by a relative. He guided our recovery and told us to watch the outflow and inflow. He stated that within three years we would be able to continue successfully with the business. Jim and I loved each other deeply but he was a sensitive artist and I was the business head. As far as love was concerned that was automatic. Jim participated in the business and was helpful. Regarding developing our economic security we went to the Frankford Grocery Company for small businesses, and they guided us with the merchandise and infrastructure. When Jim and I were signing up with the Frankford Grocery Company we were advised that when we make up our grocery orders for the store, if Jim and I could afford it, then pretend you are ordering six cases and put that $5.00 per item in the credit union for the future and savings. So I did that religiously every week for 40 years. We had a small store, but managed to create economic independence. That took care of the material side of our life.

I was introduced to TM by the mother of George Ellis. He had been my stock boy in the little grocery store when he was in high school. She would talk to me about her children and she mentioned that her son, George, was going to stop in Bucks County, Pennsylvania on his way to Switzerland and give a lecture on TM. I had just listened to Maharishi on the Merv Griffin show discussing TM. Before his lecture George came to the store and said: "I want to teach you and Jim TM because you have worked hard and you are under a lot of stress." In March of 1978 I attended the lecture on TM and I learned to meditate. Following the lecture I was asked to bring some fresh flowers, a white handkerchief, and some sweet fruit, which is traditional. I remember when learning I received a mantra, and met with TM teachers for several days to make sure I was practicing the technique correctly. I immediately felt deep relaxation, tranquility, and quietness, and was instructed to meditate twice a day. I did the TM technique every day, and just would take the time to do it because after the practice I felt energized again and could continue on with my day. I have meditated regularly by myself for more than three decades. I found an energy that would come through, and I would be so relaxed after TM that I was able to continue moving forward in dealing with the challenges of the store. I had enormous energy.

As I practiced the TM technique more and more, each time I discovered I could make clearer decisions in my life. Beyond these practical benefits I would have experiences of bliss, no mantra, no thoughts, transcendence. I have had experiences where I would meditate and thought it was 20 minutes and went way over with no thoughts in my mind—just inner wakefulness. There was nothing but my inner self, which I experience every time. I experience inner bliss when I meditate but how can I explain it? I am so relaxed, so peaceful, so much silence. I experience this all the time now. I feel happiness and love. I do not believe I need anything and nothing is that important except this nice feeling; it feels like unbounded happiness. As I stated I plan to sit and meditate for 15-20 minutes and the time slips into an hour or more effortlessly. This experience is very comfortable. The experience is an inner fulfillment—there is no sense of time. I find it deeply peaceful.

At this point in my life the experience developing as a result of my meditation is a sense of inner companionship and fullness. I say to myself when I finish meditating, I feel like I have been in a church or a cathedral. I do not need to be sitting in a building but I feel that way in myself. It is not necessary to listen to someone teaching me how to feel the inner bliss. I do not need it. I can experience it within myself. I close my eyes and experience inner bliss.

I also find that this inner happiness is remaining during my activity. I am very comfortable and confident with myself regardless of what is happening around me. I am moving in the world, but I am not controlled by the world. I am not understood by the individuals in my independent living community. Many of my neighbors ask me—why don't you go to Mass with me? I say thank you, but I go to my own Mass inside myself. The spiritual joy I have within myself is so deep that I do not need to go and listen to someone trying to explain what they think I should be feeling. I am already experiencing it, and do not need someone else's interpretation.

During sleep sometimes I notice that I am dreaming, or the body is sleeping, and yet I am awake inside. In the bed as my body is relaxing there appears what looks like bright daylight; there is no sense of time, then it is time to get up, and I am extremely rested and blissful. There is an inner light. I do not toss or turn during sleep or awake tired like so many of my neighbors. I am often witnessing myself sleep during most of the night, and wake in the morning full of energy and happiness. Even at my present age when I have to get up to go to the bathroom I can go back to bed and wander off. The body goes into a state of deep rest, but I am awake inside. This is happening about 95% of the time when I go to bed. I make it a practice to go to bed at the same time. I like the routine I learned from my father. My father said if you go to bed tired you are already too tired to fall asleep. My father remarked that every hour before 12 midnight was worth two hours.

I have a physiology that my doctors cannot understand. All my vital signs are perfect. My blood pressure is normally 110 over 60, and I am 92 years old. The doctors keep telling me: whatever you are doing, keep doing it, you're fine. When I came out of heart surgery to fix a small blockage the nurses kept asking me if I had any pain. I said no, and they would come in the next day and ask again. The doctor said one day to not be too proud because if you have pain we have medication for it. I said: "OK but what kind of pain are you expecting me to feel?" He said "Do not worry because if you had the pain you would know it." Well," I said, "then I do not know what you are talking about because I do not have any pain." They said to me that I was their poster child. I asked them why would I be your poster child. They remarked—we cannot understand that you have gone through this surgery with these results. I recalled my TM teacher had told me that when I am put under anesthesia to tell the doctors that I meditate because I might not require as much anesthesia or the refinement of my breathing could be misunderstood.

There is an interesting story regarding my heart surgery. I asked the doctors why I needed heart surgery because I have no pain, no symptoms. I did not know why I would need heart surgery and I asked them my chances. They stated 75% to 25%. OK, I said, 75% I will make it and 25% I will not. They remarked: "No, Mrs. Boyce, 75% chance you will not make it and 25% you will." I said that is interesting. My nephew was sitting in the room and he said: "I cannot tell you what to do, Aunt Helen. It has to be your decision." I said: "I have only one heart but what are my chances if I elect to not do the surgery?" The doctor said: "Six months and you're gone." He asked me if I had heard that the actress Bette Davis said: "Old age is not for sissies." I said: "Are you asking me if I am a sissy?" And he stuck his thumb up. Well with the alternatives I have, what's the difference; I will go for it and good luck. I told my family I enjoyed all of them and we will see what happens. The doctor said he would see me tomorrow morning for the procedure. The surgery took place in 2006. I meditated in the hospital before and after the surgery. I would lie in bed, relaxed, and was experiencing transcendental deep silence. After I would come out of the pure consciousness onto a thought, I would experience a wave of happiness. I just bless myself every time I wake up and I feel appreciation for life. Practicing the TM technique for the last three decades put me in a position to have this success in my life today.

The problem I have faced with those around me is their assumption that TM is a religion. I explain to them it has nothing to do with the dogma inherent in religion. It is an experience of inner peace, and if a person does not understand that explanation I do not know how to explain it. It is a clear experience of inner tranquility. I feel like the sky is the ceiling of my church. I enjoy it, and enjoy the people in it. I am not criticizing individuals who go to church; the essence and source of religion is within me. The neighbors will often comment that they went to church and remark, "Wasn't that a wonderful sermon?" I sit there and listen, and I do not judge them, or anyone. I do not feel I have the right to judge anyone—they're all entitled to their own beliefs and I respect their beliefs. If they do not choose to respect my point of view, that is OK with me. No problem.

My neighbors are comfortable with someone else telling them how they should think and feel. I believe I am experiencing divine unbounded intelligence in my internal church, which is the goal of every religion, and I feel very comfortable. I say to my peers—do you realize how many interpretations exist regarding every religion? And everyone believes that his or her interpretation is the right understanding.

As a result of the wisdom imparted to our family from my parents I have a simple guide for living: Do good and forget about it, do bad and think about what you have done wrong. Poverty or wealth will not give you this wisdom—it has to be felt within yourself. You cannot give love if you do not have love. My husband Jim and I had a very nice life together. That did not mean we did not have disagreements—that is separate. That has nothing to do with our inner feeling. There will be disagreements on some material issues that need to be figured out. For example, just because Jim did not have the acumen for business had nothing to do with his inner beauty as a human being.

As a woman in society we have had to overcome oppression and prejudices in much the same way as the racial issues. TM has helped me as a woman to deal with ignorance in the world. It has helped me to deal with it calmly. If I cannot have others understand my perspective or point of view without them becoming hostile, I simply drop it. If we listen to one another and analyze the pros and cons then you either let it go, or you become a joiner.

Maharishi has provided an incredible gift to humanity. The value of TM was highlighted in his book *Love and God* and the story of Maharishi's teacher, Guru Dev, as a child. I tried to see the world through his eyes and feel what he felt. Guru Dev as a child had such a strong mind. This young mind was so strong, and so positive within him, that no one could steer him away from his solid inner experience. What he accomplished with his mind was amazing. Maharishi carried that teaching to the world, and as I understand it, his knowledge has provided a tool of thought. Maharishi does not try to change your mind; he is not asking a person to believe a certain way. What I have received from the TM technique and the knowledge is that you need to experience within yourself the reality and the changes that spontaneously come from meditation. TM is a technique to develop the full potential of who we are. I have to know who I am before I can know anyone else.

If someone would ask me who I am, I would have to respond: I am unbounded consciousness, which is my Self. However, how can I explain to others that I am unbounded awareness? And yet it is true. Perhaps I could say to others—here I am unbounded. Even in the middle of activity my bliss is not lost, and this is what it is like for me most of the time. The inner fullness is more dominant than the objective world. It is such a natural part of me. I do not know whether I realize it or not. I have not analyzed it; I have just been living it.

Ignorance is not normal. The lack of inner peace that is pervasive in the world is unnecessary, but hard to explain to people. What is going on in my immediate environment is annoying at times, but then I just relax within myself and witness it. For example, I experienced it this evening at the dinner table. There was so much discussion about what was going on in the world, so much unnecessary suffering was being expressed. I relaxed in my inner comfort, and thought: "What a waste of mind." Sometimes as I observe the conversations I reflect and say to myself: "These poor souls go to church, and yet the good thoughts are left behind in the building"—but it does not seem to touch me inside. Although, I do not judge them nor will I join them in the suffering. As the people have become older their lives are controlled by medications and mine is not. Growing older should result in more wisdom and insight. Many years ago I attended a residence course at Maharishi's university in Iowa, and on a videotape he remarked that an enlightened person does not become indifferent or detached. He feels the suffering of others deeply, but it is like a line on water; he is free from the lasting impression or anything that would cause them to suffer. I fully agree with him—that is 100% true. The suffering does not reach me and it happens automatically. The intellectual understanding that I have gained from watching the Maharishi Channel on the Internet has deepened my experiences. I feel more comfortable with it all the time.

My family members often say, "Aunt Helen, if I could only be like you!" They say, "I do not know how you do it. You are different and we do not know how or why you are different." They all want to meditate and yet they do not have it within them to move forward. From watching Maharishi's tapes I comprehended what he was saying: A person has to feel it from within himself and make the decision to learn. Sometimes when I come out of meditation I feel this is what people should experience when they go to church, and some may. I had never had this depth of experience before learning to meditate. My education was limited, but life has brought me wisdom. The wisdom my father provided to our family was expanded through TM. My father gave his children the freedom of choice, which blossomed in my life throughout the years. I am biologically 92 years old but feel ageless—it is just a number. Age does not come to me. I am comfortable living in the present and not worried about the future. As the days come I enjoy every day and enjoyment seems to be my daily and nightly companion. My description of my state of mind is an inner contentment. I do what I feel, not what I have to do. There is nothing I need externally because I am comfortable with myself. I am very relaxed. I observe the suffering without judgment but I choose not join the suffering. I never looked at Maharishi as a priest or a pope. I saw him as an individual who fulfilled himself because of his deep thinking. He was a genius in consciousness; he came into the world, and introduced the knowledge and techniques to us. Maharishi's teachers are very fortunate because they made a wise choice to follow a human being who could translate to them what he perceived in a way they could understand.

Part VI

African-American Vision and Cultures of the World

Chapter XXI

The Future of our Children—The
Gift to Our World

An Interview with Candace Martin, J.D.

Candace Martin was born in the Midwest, spent most of her formative years in Cincinnati, Ohio, and is the proud mother of Christopher Dinwiddie, a rising actor and successful entrepreneur. She has a B.A. in Psychology from the University of Cincinnati, and a J.D. from Hastings College of Law in San Francisco. After passing the bar, Candace practiced criminal law and entertainment law. She learned TM in the early 1970s, before entering law in San Francisco, and became a teacher of TM in Ethiopia, during her second year of law school. The course, which was the first and only Teacher Training Course geared to people of African descent, also included Chinese-Americans and Hispanics. Maharishi Mahesh Yogi personally conducted the training, and Haile Selassie came to visit the course. He was the emperor of Ethiopia at the time. Candace was awarded a Ph.D. in World Peace from MERU (Maharishi European Research University). She is an alumna of the Mother Divine Program, designed for deep exploration into consciousness, and for the culturing of bliss in one's awareness as a 24-hour, all-time reality. Candace was a member of the founding executive committee for the Natural Law Party, and was a candidate for congressional representative for the District of Columbia.

GE: Tell us about your background.

Candace: My real foundation was my family. On both sides they were people of strong character—teachers and educators. They were very humanitarian, particularly on my father's side. My grandmother founded Camp Joy to help urban children, and to give them an experience of nature. My father was an outstanding civic leader, whose tireless and wide-ranging contributions included mentoring the young and accepting a presidential appointment. One of his projects, in which he succeeded my grandmother, was the directorship of several Neighborhood Houses. They were both known throughout the community. My grandfather taught at Howard University, was a track star, and trained Olympic track stars. My mother's family was one of two black families in Mount Healthy, Ohio. My mother did not have her mother after she was three. Her father was a chef to some of the Ford family, and was always away. He died when she was in 10th grade.

GE: You had a family with a sense of social responsibility and service to humanity that was a model for how you developed your life, is that correct?

Candace: Right, but not only that. My parents were people who made things happen, no matter the obstacles or circumstances. They all were outstanding—all of my family. They all had that sense of—whatever the situation you find a way to make it happen. In my mother's family, in spite of losing their parents early in life, the brothers and sisters encouraged one another to graduate from college, their father's dream for them. Only one sibling didn't earn a degree, and instead helped to support the others in earning theirs. All those who went to college continued on to earn advanced degrees.

GE: How has this foundation affected you?

Candace: My parents were always open to new ideas. I believe what I received from them was being open, and that is why I was attracted to TM.

GE: You grew up in an environment in which your family was integrationist. How would you define that concept?

Candace: My parents were involved in civil rights, particularly my mother, who was indignant that anybody would think that someone, anyone, but particularly herself and her children, were thought to be lesser because of their skin color. She was very careful not to make distinctions. She was very proud of her African-American heritage. So my mother would not allow us to go to any places that were segregated—for example, Coney Island, in Ohio. African-Americans could go to the amusement park, but we could not swim in the pool. Consequently my mother would not let us go at all. But she did not stop there. She protested and involved the newspapers until finally they stopped the segregation.

My parents were also involved in an organization called Fellowship House. It was formed to create dialogues between Christians and Jews, and blacks and whites. The idea was to come together, and different performers who were also social activists, such as Sidney Poitier, Harry Belafonte and Odetta, would come through, or people from Fellowship House would go to hear them. My parents were also part of a global organization called Moral Rearmament, and would go to Switzerland to participate in it. They did so much. The whole civil rights thing was in relationship to justice. On the other hand, the black culture movement of the sixties and seventies was about self-identity and had nothing to do with the difference between white and blacks or anyone else. It had to do with our own culture, our own identity as African-Americans. It was about self-determination. Additionally, the nation-building that was talked about was a reclaiming of ourselves, our culture. It had nothing to do with other cultures.

GE: It had nothing to do with the ignorance that was taking place at the time?

Candace: No, that was the concern of the civil rights movement.

GE: Tell us more about your childhood, your educational experiences.

Candace: I lived in a neighborhood where there were drunks on the corner, and once someone came into our house and took my father's rifle and almost killed a man, so it was a tough environment. I lived around the corner from a black orphanage and we went to the same elementary school. There were some Jewish children in the school as well. The teachers were predominantly African-American, and those who were not still had to fit into that climate. These teachers nurtured and promoted the students. I am speaking about the different quality of the environment when teachers cared about you. If you are asking if I experienced discrimination, of course I did. My high school, Walnut Hills, was a unique public college prep school that was open to students in the greater Cincinnati area. You had to test to get into it. It was the only public college prep school in the city at that time. The Jewish children, at that time also, were not admitted to the other private schools, and so came to my high school as well. There were also kids from WASP families, but unlike the African-American and Jewish kids, the WASP kids had a choice— they could have gone to private schools, but they came because it was their families' tradition. In this school, you had plays and productions, and the kids would look forward to them and try to participate. But rarely did any African-Americans make it through the auditions. And when they did they were usually light-skinned. Also, my guidance counselor told me I should not bother applying to any college. I should go to a trade or secretarial school. In contrast, my African-American physiology teacher was telling me that I could not come into her class and get anything less than an A because she knew I could be a surgeon.

GE: You faced the challenges of ignorance.

Candace: Yes, yes.

GE: How did your experience with TM influence your world-view and what you were seeking in the context of African-American culture?

Candace: I have to admit I was not a spiritual seeker. Aside from that, I was just a part of the times just wanting to be myself. I wanted my "Being" to be considered beautiful. And that is what this black culture movement accomplished for me. Our hair was beautiful, our clothing, music, dance, and plays, it was cultural. The San Francisco State strikes back in the late sixties, which were about getting African-American Studies as part of the curriculum at colleges, started a whole movement across the country where we wanted to know about ourselves from our point of view. Now African-American Studies is a whole department, and people come from all over the world to study there. Now it is often integrated into the curriculum, or is sometimes offered as a separate major. These experiences were the continuation of the strengthening of cultural integrity and self-identity from my family roots.

I learned TM in Cincinnati from Maureen Stern, but it was not until I went to law school in San Francisco that I hooked up with African-Americans who had learned TM. It was here that I met my spiritual family, and we supported each other in our practice of TM, our teaching of TM, our children, our finances, everything. Outside the religious community, I had not been exposed to African-Americans who were developing their spirituality and seeking enlightenment. Then after I met other African-American people who were meditating, I was inspired to be regular in my own TM practice and take advanced courses, and so on. My family, of course, told me that my potential was unlimited. But when I went to school, and was confronted with some of the segregation laws that were in place, I got the signal that my potential was limited. And when I became more deeply involved and had more experiences with TM, I found and KNEW that my potential was not only unlimited, but was infinite. I had never even imagined, let alone heard of, the range of possibilities—that I am unbounded bliss consciousness.

GE: How did learning TM cause a transformation in that perception?

Candace: Well, I had gained the knowledge that potential was unlimited because that is what Maharishi said, and then I began to have the experience. I started understanding that when I took the Science of Creative Intelligence course in preparation for TM teacher training. When I started having deeper meditations, I began to have the experience of "I am unbounded." SCI gave me the intellectual understanding that I had infinite potential, and then by using the technique I had the experience. When I went on Teacher Training and saw people's reaction to Maharishi I had no idea, during the entire course, of who Maharishi was. I did not understand what all the big fuss about him was, until after the course was over and we stayed behind with him. But I did know there was more to my life, and I do remember that initial experience of transcending.

The Teacher Training Course was in Alemaya, Ethiopia, and toward the end we went to Addis Ababa. After the course, we remained with Maharishi, and I had my son with me. We went to a couple of lectures with Maharishi. Even though the city where the lecture was held, because of religious tradition, was segregated, men and women not sitting together, Maharishi had us sitting in the front row, men and women next to each other. He was lecturing in Hindi and sent us love and bliss. He was speaking to an Indian community. The lecture took place in the same city that the TM course was held in. It was an underground city, and the lecture was very simple. We felt we were his family, the few of us sitting in the front row.

GE: You made a statement about how you spoke about TM in the context of the African culture, in your TM presentations. What do you mean?

Candace: There were different organizations teaching TM in the early days of the TM movement, oriented toward different interests, such as SRM (Spiritual Regeneration Movement), SIMS (Students International Meditation Society), or TMC. TMC was geared to presenting the knowledge in a way African-Americans would want to learn. Generally at that time because of the self-determination there was a suspicion of anything coming from outside the African-American context, and even within the African-American context, if it was coming from people who were establishment-oriented. The presentation varied according to the group we were speaking to, which could include poetry, music, or a skit, and then weave in the knowledge of how TM works. Or if it was revolutionary-oriented, such as the Black Panthers, it would be tailored in that way.

GE: How did you approach such groups?

Candace: There would be a little bit of science, but also historical references, and we would explain the difference between slavery and freedom, and what real freedom was. We would have one lecture and when discussing relationships, we would discuss how the TM program could strengthen the community. Together we nourished all the meditators in TMC. We gave our introductory lectures on TM in terms of our experiences.

GE: In a nutshell, you tailored your presentations to the African-American situation.

Candace: We would also discuss the spiritual goals from different African traditions and how the TM program satisfied and supported those positions. When I left Ethiopia as a trained teacher of TM and I travelled to New York and Washington D.C., I began teaching the TM technique, and eventually returned to Hastings and began instructing most of my law students, and the general public in the Bay area. I also spent time at MIU (now MUM) to participate in programs to create coherence for the U.S. Initially my teaching activities were geared toward people of color, and African-American organizations, theater, and so forth. After my work at MIU/MUM with the coherence-creating groups, I moved to Washington D.C. and became involved with several projects focused on creating coherence in the nation's capital. Washington D.C. at that time was considered the murder capital of the world. So as part of a team of TM teachers, we lobbied all the different wards of Washington D.C. and approached schools, prisons, and different facets of the government, such as the police department, metro systems and so forth. A main focus of attention was Howard University, and the University of the District of Columbia.

A group of 10 African-American teachers of TM, in around 1993, came together to form a group to reduce the crime rate in D.C. It was also designed to create a positive environment to support the government of the U.S.—and the representatives of various countries around the world— to help them to make clear decisions. The idea was to raise the collective consciousness, which would positively influence the environment. The team lobbied to form a coherence-creating group for the government, and the group formulated an experiment to demonstrate the possibility of influencing the environment. Some of the political officials understood the concept. The demonstration project brought together thousands of experts in the advanced TM program for a creating-coherence course about six weeks long. An independent project review board was formed to evaluate the findings and statistics; the board consisted of an economist, the police chief, representatives of the World Bank, professors from Howard University, and a broad range of scientists. We made the prediction that we could reduce violent crime in D.C. by about 20%. We also conducted some case studies to discover how people were feeling. At the end of the project a review of the facts indicated a reduction in violent crime of about 20%, and when the coherence-creating group left D.C., the crime rose immediately.

The purpose of this demonstration project was not just to reduce crime but to facilitate a coherent collective consciousness to influence the government to begin to make clear decisions, which benefited the nation and the world; the project was to create a coherent atmosphere.

GE: You were trying to demonstrate the theory that TM coherence-creating groups can improve coherence in the collective consciousness and the environment, and it could be empirically verified?

Candace: Additionally, we heard from one of the public schools that we contacted—the Fletcher-Johnson Educational Center, a kindergarten through 8th grade public school—and they said they were interested in our program. It was located in one of the most crime-ridden areas—southeast D.C. Because of all of the drive-by shootings that were going on in this area, the students and staff from this school were attending funerals twice a week. The principal, Dr. George Rutherford, contacted us and said he wanted us to teach his staff and faculty the TM technique.

GE: Was this predominantly African-American?

Candace: It was all African-American. The school was also like a community center, so there was a sense of family. The stress was high and the morale was very low because of all of the killings.

GE: What year was this?

Candace: It was the early nineties. It was a brave action on the part of

Dr. Rutherford, former principal of Fletcher-Johnson Educational Center and principal at the Ideal Academy Public Charter School, explains the impressive research on the TM technique and the applied benefit to his students in terms of school atmosphere, student behavior, and academic achievement.©

the principal because this was a public school, and there was some resistance to offering TM. But the principal did not care because he wanted to have an intervention to stop the killings in his area. He had a desire to help his students in every way, not just academic achievement. He wanted to have a mechanism for them to release stress, and reduce the social conflict. The first step at Fletcher-Johnson was to teach all the staff and faculty to learn TM, and we implemented this in one week. Dr. Herb Bandy and I were the teachers. The second phase was the students, and the following year we arranged for the students to learn.

GE: What was the experience of the faculty?

Candace: Oh my goodness, it was such a relief for them! The faculty and staff had been very depressed before starting TM, and now they began to experience happiness and a sense of well-being. They began to express less fear and more efficiency. Moreover, people began to be able to sleep, which was significant because there was high level of anxiety due to all the drive-by shootings in the area. The positive result of the staff and faculty learning also influenced the community. The crime rate actually began to drop around the school. There were fewer funerals to attend.

GE: The staff saw changes in themselves and wanted to extend it to the students?

Candace: Absolutely. Not only to the students but they brought in some family members before the students learned.

In order to include another activity into the schedule it took additional organization. The principal came up with the idea of having Quiet Time. Because of where the students were located and all the killings and crime, the school was a safe haven for the students, which required a lot of security; the halls were monitored and so forth. During Quiet Time, some of the faculty would meditate, while other faculty members would provide security in the halls.

This started a national movement of establishing Quiet Time. The structure was put in place.

The following year the students were instructed into the TM technique. I did not teach this group of students but I organized it. Rose Phillips joined the team—she also had been on my TTC in Ethiopia. Rose taught a lot of the families, and she created many creative programs to connect with the children. Additionally, two teachers also joined the team teaching at Fletcher-Johnson: Eddie Gob and Horus Msemaje.

GE: How did it go?

Candace: It went superbly. This school previously had the lowest testing scores in the District, and the District had some of the lowest testing scores in the nation. After the students started the practice of TM in April of that year, they were tested in May. This was a very short interval of time, but they achieved the highest scores in the District.

GE: This was the result of establishing Quiet Time and the intervention of the TM technique?

Candace: Yes. In addition to the students having learned TM, the atmosphere had been cultivated the previous year with the faculty becoming well rested and more receptive through their TM practice. At the time the principal was not interested in research; he was focused on the humanitarian benefit that would be brought to the school.

GE: Did you receive any feedback?

Candace: Yes, happiness was pervasive; they expressed feelings of being secure. Grades improved, and fewer conflicts took place in the school environment. Fletcher-Johnson became a lighthouse to the community. Families became stronger. Happiness and security was the main outcome of the TM intervention. The students and the faculty felt secure from the environment of negativity that had surrounded them.

GE: It seems to me that these programs in the nineties set a precedent for what the David Lynch Foundation has expanded around the world.

Candace: Absolutely. Dr. Rutherford asked the school board to give him the toughest schools. And so he went on to another school, in Baltimore. Although I did not teach there myself, I know that almost 50% of the students were homeless, in a shelter, or sleeping in cars. Nevertheless, regardless of their circumstances, they came to school. Sadly, however, there was not much funding at that point to introduce TM into this school. At that time something else was underway in Washington, D.C. Another of my fellow graduates from the Ethiopia TM Teacher Training Course was a schoolteacher. She had become a teacher of TM so she could develop an ideal school—the students could learn the TM technique and receive educational programs such as the Science of Creative Intelligence—to help expand their understanding of human potential, and provide a basis for relating all fields of study to their own self. She wanted to make this available to the children of Washington, D.C. Subsequently she formed three schools: two charter schools and one private school. The charter school was one of the first in the nation.

GE: What is the difference between a charter school and a public school in terms of the freedom to introduce programs?

Candace: Charter schools were not restricted by a board of education that controls everything. Charter schools involve the parents, community members, and educators who jointly formulate and structure the school. Originally the first charter schools were federal, and needed to be unique and offer something the public schools did not offer.

GE: What was the purpose of the charter schools?

Candace: To offer diverse education and fulfill the needs of a specific community, which can be supplemented. Basic guidelines had to be achieved.

And that is when David Lynch visited the school. After a small group learned TM, Dr. Karen Bandy and Dr. Kearik Sunev came on as main

Students at the Ideal Academy Public Charter School practice TM together in preparation for school activities, and to enhance learning and inner peace.©

teachers. Now Dr. Rena Boone (another teacher from my Ethiopia Teacher Training Course) is the head teacher. We first raised money in the community for the initial stage of this project where faculty and staff learned TM. David Lynch visited the Ideal Academy and another school in Detroit using TM. This inspired him to begin a foundation to help students learn TM.

GE: So after David Lynch visited various schools offering the TM technique and observing the benefits, he was inspired to begin a program to teach a million students.

Candace: Yes.

GE: Tell me about the school in Detroit.

Candace: A friend, Carmen N'Namdi, with whom I went to high school, had learned TM in Detroit. In honor of her child who had died, she created a charter school—the Nataki Talibah Schoolhouse of Detroit. She founded the school, was the principal, and brought TM into the school. General Motors did the initial funding, and later they obtained support from the David Lynch Foundation. There was research on the Nataki School in Detroit that introduced TM. The children spoke about their grades improving, and conflict reducing in their life, as well as improved relationships within the family. I remember one child remarking that she felt bliss. I was just a small part of a beautiful story. There was a desire to give the children some tools to improve their life, not for the research or any other motivation.

GE: This is an important point. Was your experience as an African-American woman challenging, and a factor in pursuing this work?

Candace: I never looked at any phase of my life as challenging. It was just what it was—perhaps someone else might have looked at it as challenging. It was just my life. For instance, many of the students who come into these programs may be categorized as disadvantaged, or at-risk kids. However, for me these are the children, they are my family, and you just want to give to them what you have—passing on knowledge. There is no "type" of child. For example, many of the students at the Nataki School were middle-class children, but they still had a lot of issues.

TM was introduced into a private school in northwest D.C., a middle school through high school, where many of the children had learning disabilities. Many of them had ADHD and cognitive issues. Some of the children had PTSD, because they had come from eastern bloc countries and had witnessed war and severe violence. All of these children could not sit still, and often had little fidget balls to play with—they always had something to move around with. Many of the students were very resistant to anything that would calm them down. However, it was amazing that after they learned TM, they were so still, and so silent—in a peaceful way. They would leave the room and say "thank you." The same thing would happen when I was checking the correctness of their practice on an individual level. There was one child who had experienced a lot of war trauma, and never felt safe or comfortable closing her eyes. She not only closed her eyes but began to feel calmness for the first time; she felt less anxiety and fear. All of the children, when I asked them about their benefits, shared a feeling of calmness and silence. Some of them remarked that their grades had improved, but mainly they expressed the growth of inner peace.

When you had the boys and the girls together, normally it was havoc. A teacher asked me if I could bring the boys and girls together to check their TM practice. It was at the end of the day, and the teacher was doing this because she was trying to get to them to calm down, and did not think it would work. But when we came together, about 18 students, the TM practice was deep and even the students were surprised. The teacher was amazed. The teachers in the school who valued the TM technique wanted to see the students benefit from the technique, because they saw the effects and it made their job easier. The project was funded by the community, by private donations, and then supported by the David Lynch Foundation. I was involved in the project in 2006, and it continued until about 2010. The program diminished the symptoms of ADHD in the students who learned TM.

GE: I worked with developmentally disabled children, and the approach is from the outside—they managed structural control but rarely touched the inner source or root cause of the imbalances. The technique of TM that you were offering started from the inside out and that is why it was effective. Let's turn our attention to the NIH grant.

Candace: I worked on three cardiovascular projects, and in each case I taught the participants the TM technique. The first project included two sites: Morehouse College in Atlanta, GA, and Howard University Hospital in Washington, D.C. I taught in the D.C. project. There were about 100 subjects and each spent a year in the program. There were two groups of participants: one group learned TM and the other group was offered a health education program. So they were comparing the effects of TM on cardiovascular risk factors. After the initial instruction, we met with them twice a week for a year, and at the meeting they would meditate together and be offered knowledge about TM and various topics, such as religion, relationships, education, and the growth of love, different topics like that. They would occasionally write out their experiences. They were also tested for blood pressure. I conducted the TM meetings but so many people were involved other than myself.

GE: What were some of the results from the TM intervention?

Candace: Everyone valued that they had something they could do to experience silence. This particular age group had as many as five generations living in their homes. Many of them were taking care of grandchildren, great grandchildren, and ill spouses, and parents, as well as working for income. They were very busy, at a time of life that for many, activity becomes less. The participants were very appreciative that they could have a few moments of silence. One participant stated that she had never experienced so much quiet in her life, and that she was very thankful for the experience. Another participant stated after experiencing transcending, it was like experiencing the Holy Ghost, and she felt very comforted by that experience.

GE: What does that mean?

Candace: For those who believe in the Holy Ghost, that was the comforter that Jesus, or God, said that he sent because Jesus was not going to be there on earth. And of course many of the women cried after they learned the TM technique, as they reflected on why they did not have this sooner in their life. As I mentioned before, one woman who had a very busy schedule caring for her mother, working, and had to go out of the home to take care of another relative, also wanted to be a deacon in her church. After she learned TM, she had the energy and greater efficiency in action and found time to do her studying. She graduated as a deacon in her church, while she was in the TM course, and I attended her graduation. This was something she had really wanted to do. Many of the women who had read scripture remarked that they had a deeper realization of their particular religion. They said that "the Word really spoke to them," the Word meaning the Bible.

GE: The experience of the TM program enlivened their appreciation of their own scriptures.

Candace: Well, that is your way of saying it. (a gentle laugh) For people who are religious and African-American, they will know exactly what we are talking about. They had greater understanding. Also some said their prayers seemed to be more powerful—a deeper feeling of connectedness. Many of the women found that their blood pressure was reduced, but also a couple of people who were on insulin because of diabetic symptoms, were told by their doctors they should stop taking it because there was no longer need for it. The 89-year-old woman in the study never missed a meditation. She just valued it so much, and was trying to get her grandchildren to begin the TM practice.

I also want to say a little about the women meditating together. It was my first experience and realization of what happens when women come together around knowledge and the experience of transcending together. It is a very sweet feeling among all of the women. Because everyone was so busy they would be rushing into the meeting, and may have been stressed from the challenges of the day, and when everyone would sit down and meditate the stress melted away. They formed buddy teams and called one another and became involved in social interactions outside the TM meetings. Sometimes they would raise money for another woman. The women were very nourishing to one another. It was a special phenomenon when women come together, and particularly when meditating women come together. The human outcome was that women found improved relationships with their families, and many of them said those relationships were improved by taking some time for themselves. Women often take care of everyone but themselves, and the practice of TM allowed them to stop and nourish themselves.

GE: I believe this is an important point, because women in societies are constantly sacrificing for others, and TM helps to bring the balance.

Candace: Also, the outcome was a tool that they now had, and nothing was required other than themselves. It did not require money, they did not have to go any place to do it; it was not a course that when it was ended the benefits ended. This was a technique they had for the rest of their lives, and they could find and experience that peace anytime. This was very valuable for them, that they found that peacefulness and silence.

This study was also conducted at Howard University, and lasted for four months, finishing around 2011. There were different considerations with this group because they were younger and were in school, or in the middle of their careers. The participants shared the same experience of calmness and silence as in the other studies, but it was more as preparation for being more effective at accomplishing their goals. There was a desire and determination to reduce those stress factors in their active lives. Many of the women had wanted to be in an exercise program, and after learning TM were able to stick to commitments. This group was thinking more about applications of the TM program to their work, school, and so forth. The group was exposed to the David Lynch Foundation projects, which motivated the group, and they saw how their lives could be improved.

The study on patients with failing hearts took place around 2005, and was a six-month study, meeting twice a week. The programs dealt with both men and women whose hearts were failing. The study was conducted at the University of Pennsylvania, with a control group being taught a course in health education. Many of the participants had to be brought to the meetings. It was a major accomplishment if they could go to the store by themselves. Most of them could not take a stress test. But they did take an initial stress test to see what they could do. At the end of the study, the TM participants were able to walk much farther, and some could even do a treadmill. The results were significant, and none of the members of the TM group died as compared with the control group. The TM technique extended life, and also the quality of life was improved. The University of Pennsylvania published the findings.

GE: In summary what were your observations with this group?

Candace: My observation was that this group slept a great deal, but as time went on there was more alertness and interest in the knowledge. They reported that they increased mobility, and independence—one woman actually took a trip with her grandson.

GE: What message would you give to the African-American community or society in general on the basis of your knowledge and experience?

Candace: I would like to speak about some areas of importance to me. Maharishi said: "It is my joy to make the difficult things simple." Here is a technique that can go anywhere and take any individual to permanent happiness. I have seen that there is absolutely no need, no reason to suffer, because there is every way, now, to have a life free of suffering. TM is a technique, a technology to eliminate suffering. The application of TM is so vast, from homeless people to CEOs of corporations, and also children, whether they have ADHD, or learning disabilities, cognitive development shortcomings, whether they are orphans—it does not matter what the situation is—it is one simple technique for everyone to experience one's full potential. An area of PTSD for Africans is of interest to me, and a project is just forming to address it. In fact there has been research with some refugees, where a woman had been suicidal. Then she learned TM, and you could visually see the transformation. TM is a universal technique and there is nothing needed to utilize it. It is a simple solution to not only end suffering, but to start living our full potential, no matter where you start from, no matter what age you start from. Each country would benefit if it adopted a TM group to create coherence, because it is essential to be able to administer the evolving global diversity from the level of Unity Consciousness. Then government becomes a platform for governing instead of a political platform. The only way all the diversified desires of the people can be satisfied is if the government employs the same administration that governs the universe.

GE: To put this concept in layman's terms, you are discussing raising the individual and collective consciousness in the government and society. Would you like to elaborate on this idea?

Candace: Yes. That would be the result. It is almost impossible for a government, a body of people, to satisfy all the desires of the people in the country. In the U.S. for example, we have a two-party system and we do everything by vote. Hence, there will be some people who receive what they want, and some people who do not. That could be as much as 49% of the population. Natural law governs the universe, and if we can align our individual consciousness with the laws of nature, and the intelligence of nature—which is a consequence of coherence creating groups—decisions of people in government will be better.

GE: This is a very nuanced point that needs more clarification for the reader.

Candace: At one point I did not feel a part of any particular country, and then Maharishi came out with the concept of the Global Country of World Peace. I did not feel that my desires and goals were being addressed by the existing government. In particular after 9/11, I felt powerless, and it brought home to me that there was not a way, a president, or leader of any country who could satisfy everyone's desires. And there is a key to governing. Governing is not political, governing is taking care of people, promoting the growth of the people. There is no way to do it to satisfy all the many different kinds of people, and different requirements of people. People who live in California have different considerations from people who live in Iowa.

GE: I want to try and get at the essence of what you are expressing.

Candace: The essence is that what we need is to raise the collective consciousness and have a wing of the government that is focused on creating coherence, to making the country invincible.

GE: That is beautiful—it may be difficult for many people to understand. But in reality it is simple and basic. You are discussing a very powerful issue that has put our country in a deadlock. The political parties are created by the present collective consciousness. You appear to be suggesting that the creation of a coherence-creating group working, if you will, from the "inside out," will raise the collective consciousness, providing more integrity within the structure of the government—so the deadlock is broken. Yes?

Candace: Not only is the deadlock broken, but the desire from the government is focused on the growth of the people, regardless of party, doing what is best for the people.

GE: Rather than the divisiveness we see, right?

Candace: Yes, and then the decisions are not made with relationship to majority votes, because that way a large percentage of the population remains unsatisfied and unfulfilled.

GE: What you are suggesting has been validated by scientific research on developing individual and collective consciousness. Can you elaborate?

Candace: What research has shown is that when you have the square root of one percent of a country's population practicing the TM-Sidhi program (advanced TM practice, generating even more coherence) in a group, more unity and coherence is enlivened in the nation. This is not fanciful thinking. It has its basis in science.

GE: What thoughts or reflections would you like to share with the readers?

Candace: The most important insight I have gained from my journey is that life is bliss—and that I am pure unbounded consciousness and everyone else is, too. Our true nature is bliss. And, therefore, there is no use, and no requirement, for suffering anymore. The TM technique has been shown to have been effectively applied in almost every area of life. Particularly, areas with populations of African descent, in the U.S. and around the world, have a lot of issues and challenges. These challenges exist in the areas of health—especially cardiovascular disease, diabetes, learning disabilities and crime. On an individual level, our children and adults who are in prison are caught up in the recidivism cycle. TM not only reduces the recidivism rate but the individuals can grow regardless of what setting they are in. No matter what challenges they are facing, growth is still possible, when they have the right inner environment, and practicing TM gives them just that.

The urgent need is to get this knowledge to all the children. They need to know what their full potential really is. I was told by my parents that my full potential was that I could be whatever I wanted to be, that I could have any profession I wanted to have. But full potential is so far beyond that. We have infinite potential—more than we could ever dream of. The children need to know that. If my parents had had this knowledge they certainly would have given it to me. I have had long experiences of exploring the inner space of transcending, and exploring, then experiencing, in the transcendent, that I am unbounded awareness. And I have experienced that I am one with everybody, and every aspect of creation. I have experienced unbounded love, flowing not in anyone's direction, or directed at anything, but just pure love. Then I find that I am connecting on this level of pure love—and this is everyone's reality. Everyone has the ability to experience that frictionless flow of love.

Maharishi said the only business of life is the pursuit of happiness. And it does not even have to be pursued, because it is our birthright, our nature, and it is so simple. Where is happiness located? It is just a matter of transcending to where you experience that field of bliss and happiness. It is simple. Every child needs to know, and have this tool.

I recently taught a child who was about 5 years old, and she had been asking her parents to arrange for her to learn TM. The child said she had trouble sleeping, that she was waking up during the night afraid, and she thought TM would help her. I taught her, and she began sleeping at night right away. She continued to use her TM technique for children, called the "Word of Wisdom," and she wanted to tell other children that this was something they could do, too, so they wouldn't be afraid. So even children have some instinctual knowingness about the way they are supposed to feel. And when they do not feel happy, they know they want to do something about it. She was fortunate to have parents who meditated, because the parents need to bring it to their children.

GE: Each person has her, or his, own cultural history. How has your world view changed?

Candace: What I have found is—my own invincibility. Every day, twice a day, I am experiencing the transcendent, and this is a field which is untouchable, a field of non-change. As I become more established in that field of non-change, I am not influenced by the environment—not influenced by what someone is thinking or saying. Also, through this period of identification with myself that I spoke about earlier, it was a cultural identification, being my self, being an African-American woman. Over the years, my self-identity has expanded and my family has expanded. There is the experience of feeling "the world is my family." I feel connected to everyone. I do not feel bound by any laws or opinions. I do not feel bound by my body, or the environment.

GE: You have become a universal citizen who has transcended culture. How do you juxtapose that freedom with the issues facing African-Americans?

Candace: Although I have evolved beyond the boundaries of any culture, the uniqueness of me, my expression is that I am an African-American.

GE: How do you understand this evolution of your consciousness in the context of African-American culture—as an instrument to breaking the boundaries and issues faced by African-Americans? What is your perspective?

Candace: There is beauty in difference; there is beauty in all the different flowers.

Chapter XXII

Sun-beaconed with Hope

Ayida Mthembu

Ayida Mthembu is an Associate Dean for Student Support Services at the Massachusetts Institute of Technology (MIT) undergraduate education. In 1997, she was selected as the 1997 winner of the YMCA Black Achiever Award at MIT, which recognizes African-Americans for their professional accomplishments and volunteer community service. Ms. Mthembu has demonstrated a long-standing commitment to scholarship in the field of comparative studies and developing a better understanding of multiculturalism. Ms. Mthembu received her BA in Political Science from the University of California at Los Angeles (1970), the M.F.A. in Screenwriting (1982) from the American Film Institute, and the M.A. and A.B.D. in Comparative Culture (1985) from the University of California at Irvine. Ayida Mthembu, co-founder of the Freedom from Stress Project, *oversaw the first federally funded community resource development project in the United States employing the Transcendental Meditation program. Ayida is a proud African-American woman who is also a teacher of the TM program. Ayida has been committed to developing her culture. She is an educator, musician, and author of* Ambrosia: A Montage of Inner Recordings. *Her vision is not limited to one race or one nation, but extends far beyond, to touch the heart of any human being striving for freedom and justice. Ayida speaks from her heart.*

I look from my window as I have for centuries
looked from windows
to see my life's trials leaving me.
to see my dreams once so full, laughing,
rhythmically bouncing, berry-red and blinking,
sun-beaconed with hope.

Yes, my dreams of mended fences
fields of our grains

cows with nectar for milk.
trees and churches where our voice would lift
up to the clouds because our lives are bountiful.

Yes, my dreams of my children leading marches of hope
learned doctors and scientists, caretakers
of the world's right to be free
raising their own ad infinitum generations.
while I, my hands so full of blessings,
my heart so pierced with arrows of peace
rejoin those from whom I was born
the counsel of elders who will oversee
the sacred traditions . . .

— Ayida Mthembu

A sane person allows all aspects of feeling to exist, each in its own right. I lament at times, because I am historically a black woman, realizing the centuries of despair my people have experienced. So I lament to cathart, to clear the debris, to make way for clarity of thought and perception. So I lament acknowledging the pain I have felt watching black people go around in circles seeking a way to stop the torment and hopelessness. What are the circles I speak of? We alternate between clarity of direction and purpose, and for a while we seem to make great progress; then before our eyes, the forward direction disappears, and we are directionless, confused, and disillusioned once again. Great black leaders—men and women—emerge and then, when the society at large clamps down, we flounder. Great ideas for reform and upliftment emerge, and we do not seem to be able to actualize our desires, our dreams. To paraphrase Langston Hughes: our dreams seem to shrivel like raisins in the sun, but yet growth begins with a dream—with a desire that must be nurtured, cultivated, protected and allowed to mature.

We are necessarily wary of anyone who comes to us with solutions, of anyone who says, "Hey, I have found something that may be part of the solution." As a teacher of the TM program I have often been accused of pushing utopian ideas—of being simplistic and naïve. I am asked: What about the power of the gun? What about the racism? Why am I pushing something that could make people passive? In the beginning, I had to understand and resolve these questions for myself. I admit very freely now of being an idealist who is helping to push utopian ideals. The TM and TM-Sidhi programs are filled with the light of a dream, but that dream is coupled hand in hand with a way to accomplish it.

Black people in America are fighting for their lives. So many panaceas have been shoved at us. So many promises have failed. Yet it is foolish to give up seeking, to ignore new concepts and ideas that emerge, on the grounds that we have tried everything. His Holiness Maharishi Mahesh Yogi introduced to the Western world a program that integrates the finest knowledge of the East with the progressive, innovative, explorative attitudes of the West. At the core of this program rests a revolutionary (although ancient) concept: it is possible to solve the age-old problems of the world by developing the consciousness of each individual.

A recurring theme of black speakers from all walks of life, historians, politicians, artists, scientists, preachers, educators, has been that we are involved in a battle for our minds. All too often our geniuses, our creative essences are found either behind prison walls or suffering from the stunning effects of drugs, TV, or school systems that do not reflect the positive potential of the black students. The battle of the black minds is intricately tied to the battle for the reaffirmation of the integrity of black culture. Culture is education; it is the way any people learn to look at the world—it is the way people express what they have perceived; it is the face they show the world. I paraphrase Maharishi: in every land, cultural values show how to live life in accord with the laws of nature as they operate in a particular region or climate. Every nation has ancient traditions that have passed the test of time and that allow each individual and family to flourish in ways of life suitable to their region. Customs of working, diet, family life, and social order allow life to progress smoothly in a condition of maximum harmony and health. Every nation, from the civilizations of Asia, America, Australia, and Polynesia, show evidence of highly integrated cultural systems for maintaining life in harmony with nature. In every case performance of sidhis are recorded as central to this adaptation.

With the rise of rapid progress and intense mixing of cultures in the world, it has become necessary to strengthen every culture at its base. The culture of a nation is its life, its ability to grow. Far from being static, a healthy, living culture is in a continuous process of evolution toward higher patterns of orderliness. The fundamentals of culture are those features that make it possible for life to progress. An analysis of the process of growth leads to the discovery of six fundamentals of culture: creativity, stability, adaptability, integration, purification, and growth. These are fundamentals common to any homeostatic or homeokinetic system that is capable of growth. The basis of culture is creativity, which allows continuous adaption to change, both within and without. At the same time a healthy culture remains stable, keeping its character and identity by integrating useful new values into its structure and purifying itself of elements unsuitable for its further growth.

Without a culture that can withstand the test of time and remain strong and intact, how can a people survive? How can people survive without knowing they have a culture, or believing more in the culture of others than in their own culture? The integrity and strength of every culture is tied to the integrity of each individual within that cultural context. There can be no glorification of culture without the glorification of the individual consciousness of the members of that culture. So seemingly simplistic, the TM and TM-Sidhi programs are scientifically verifying that those six fundamentals of culture are being enhanced in individuals practicing the TM and TM-Sidhi programs.

What we are speaking of is the possibility of rebuilding and re-strengthening the foundation of life itself. I could march a frightening log of statistics at this point, statistics that show how many black men and women are in prison, how many are on drugs, how many are in mental institutions, but that is not necessary. All that is important is that we must stop the cycle of negativity for ourselves and for the world. As a result of the TM and TM-Sidhi programs, the individual grows in appreciation and acceptance of his or her own essential nature. We have seen that even those who are confined in prison begin to realize that they are, in fact, free—that no one can contain or enslave who they really are. With the blinders removed each individual gains in self-worth and knowledge and begins to reflect that inner reality. The light of consciousness shines through the channels that culture provides. As we all grow in cultural strength and integrity, who has the desire or need to threaten or destroy anyone if they are themselves indestructible?

There is no way to overestimate the need for the TM and TM-Sidhi programs among black people, wherever we are, and in whatever situation we find ourselves. It is a popular misconception that those who support and advocate utopian ideals think it would be easy to achieve them. In my case that could not be further from the truth. I am conscious of the feeling that I am pushing upstream, but then evolution is like that; changing minds is like that—at first no one seems to hear you; then, if keep on speaking the same thing over and over again, everyone hears you, although they may not act. Getting them to act is another matter. But it begins with a logical and clear perception of the direction, and a way to achieve it. Both ingredients can be found within the TM and TM-Sidhi programs. The rest is up to us. Maharishi's idea of cultivating invincibility for all nations while maintaining the integrity of each culture, and the idea of transforming criminals into enlightened human beings, may appear utopian. However, anyone who has had the experience of the TM and the TM-Sidhi programs and intellectually understood their mechanics, or who has reviewed the distinguished research and recent discoveries of consciousness at MERU and MUM, finds that such dreams are being structured for the entire world, one individual at a time.

All fields of science, sociology, and criminal rehabilitation inspired by this research are now directed toward a full understanding of natural laws. Now that physics and the TM and TM-Sidhi programs have brought such intimate parallels between the various scientific disciplines and consciousness, a true inspiration for the ending of suffering in society can be seen on the horizon. Maharishi expressed that invincibility results from perfect order in individual and collective consciousness. When any nation's collective consciousness is fully integrated and perfectly orderly, then invincibility will be its status.

The objective and fulfillment of life is to bring this state of perfect order in society. The necessity of life is to ensure that every individual is trained to be orderly in his or her thoughts and action. People are trained to act in accord with natural law and thereby not create problems, disorder, sickness, and suffering for themselves and their nation. When an individual is weak the unit of the nation is weak. For the nation to be strong and invincible the individual has to be trained to use his or her full potential—action in perfect orderliness, action spontaneously right and in accord with natural law. The prevention of lawlessness, and the growth of freedom to act in accord with natural law, are available through the TM and TM-Sidhi programs. The TM and TM-Sidhi programs establish the mind in the state of least excitation of consciousness, the simplest form of awareness, a field of perfect order, and the home of all the laws of nature.

Chapter XXIII

Cosmic Inner Stillness
for All Cultures

David Orme-Johnson, Ph.D.

Dr. David Orme-Johnson is an artist and a scientist with a profound compassion for humanity. As a scientist he understands that the process of discovery and the validation of research requires that the researcher not be influenced by positionality, and his Truth About TM website documents that commitment. Furthermore, his years of traveling and conducting scientific research throughout the world have provided him a unique perspective and keen understanding of multicultural society, and the underlying connections that exist independent of cultural differences. In the following exposition he highlights research specifically in the African–American community.

It has been my great good fortune to be a participant and witness to the scientific quantification of the growth of cosmic stillness in the lives of people from all parts of the world. There have been over 600 studies conducted in more than 250 universities and research institutions in 30 countries showing that all areas of life improve holistically through TM practice. In one of my own studies of health insurance statistics of 2,000 meditators over a five-year period, I found that TM practice reduced both inpatient and outpatient medical care by an astounding 50% on average. I sent it in to a journal and one of the reviewers said he wanted to see what the effect of the TM technique might be on different categories of disease. I suspect he thought that TM practice only influenced minor diseases, not major ones like heart disease and cancer. In any event, I dug into the data, and to my amazement medical utilization decreased in *all* categories of disease, with reductions up to 87% for heart disease and diseases of the nervous system and 55% less for cancer (1). I have to credit this discovery to that reviewer.

I wondered: how could this one simple thing have such wide-ranging effects? One level of explanation was that the TM technique produces deep rest, and we know that the body goes into a healing mode when we rest.

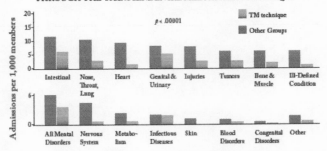

Fewer Hospital Admissions for All Disease Categories
THROUGH THE *TRANSCENDENTAL MEDITATION* TECHNIQUE

A five-year study of health insurance statistics of 2,000 people practicing the Transcendental Meditation program found that they had reduced medical care utilization in every category of disease, including 87% less for heart disease, 55% less for cancer, 65% lower for metabolic disease, including diabetes, and 87% less for diseases of the nervous system.

Reference: Orme-Johnson DW. Medical care utilization and the Transcendental Meditation program. *Psychosomatic Medicine*. 1987;49:493-507.

That is why doctors universally prescribe getting extra rest as part of their prescription for virtually any disease. But the effects of TM practice appear to go far beyond ordinary rest. After all, both the control group and the meditator group slept and dreamed every night. There must be something special about the rest provided by TM practice that gives it such broad healing ability.

In addition to that, the holistic effects of the TM program extend far beyond just health. Any explanation of the TM mechanism must include these studies also. For example, one of my graduate students, now Dr. So Kam Tim, did a study of the TM technique's effects on cognitive variables in Chinese secondary students 14 to 17 years old in three different schools in Taiwan, 362 students in all. In all three schools we found that TM practice improved creativity, practical intelligence, the ability to quickly identify a hidden target (field independence), the ability to make quick decisions (inspection time), and the kind of intelligence that allows you to figure things out in a novel situation in which you do not have any book learning to help you out (fluid general intelligence). And we also found it decreased anxiety in the moment (state anxiety) and how anxious one is in general (trait anxiety) (2). How can TM practice improve all areas of health and all areas of thinking and emotions? To start with, how does it differ from ordinary forms of rest?

One difference from sleep and dreaming is that during TM practice the mind is quietly aware while the body is gaining deep rest, whereas during sleep there is no awareness and during dreaming there is illusory awareness. That inner awareness during TM can sometimes be sublime unbounded awareness and bliss. At Maharishi European Research University (MERU) in Switzerland in the early 1970s we undertook to study what was happening in the physiology during deep meditation. We asked subjects to press a button to signal us when they had just had an experience of that cosmic inner stillness or Transcendental Consciousness. The button press had to be right after the experience because during it the person is completely absorbed in the experience. What we found was that during those experiences of Transcendental Consciousness, the respiration slowed to almost a standstill, and the EEG became highly coherent (3-6).

There were people from every part of the world and culture around Maharishi. You heard every kind of English accent spoken at MERU— English, Irish, Scottish, Australian—as well as Scandinavian, French, Dutch, Swiss, German, Russian, Romanian, Indian, Pakistani, Nepali, Chinese, Japanese, Korean, West Indian, Mexican, Brazilian, Argentinean, Ethiopian, South African, Sudanese, and every variety of North American accent from British Columbia and Quebec to New York, Mississippi, and west Texas. People from all over the world were having these same experiences of cosmic inner awareness. Our findings in the lab were universal, describing a law of nature. A law of nature means that the law applies for all times and place. Gravity did not come into being when the apple fell on Newton's head. It was always there and always will be there, everywhere in the universe. Newton only described it scientifically. EEG coherence and respiratory suspension during Transcendental Consciousness were not invented when we first observed them in the MERU lab. They always occur in the physiology whenever anyone experiences Transcendental Consciousness, wherever they are in the world, whatever language they speak, whatever culture they belong to, whatever their DNA X and Y haplogroups are, whether they are sitting around a campfire or meditating in a palace, and whatever epoch of time they live in, present, past, or future. I often look out for and read the beautiful descriptions of Transcendental Consciousness that are expressed in the literature, songs, and philosophies of so many different cultures around the world, and a wave of love and feeling of a common bound swells in my heart. I think, "I know what these guys are talking about." I feel close to them. They are my brothers and sisters because we have a profound common bond. There is a cosmic stillness at the basis of our minds and we have dipped into it, and we are one on that level. *And I know what was happening in their brain when they experienced that!*

I think the reason that TM has enhanced healing powers, has broad holistic effects on thinking and emotions, is because of the increased EEG coherence it produces. EEG coherence enhances information flow in the brain. This has been proven over the last few decades by dozens of experiments in laboratories all over the world. They have shown that high EEG coherence creates an environment in which neurons communicate with each other with less interfering noise in the system. The brain is more wide awake, functioning at a more optimal level. It is our everyday experience that when you are rested and very awake, the brain is very coherent and your thinking is clear. When you are drowsy, brain coherence decreases and thinking becomes sketchy. When you fall asleep, coherence decreases even further and the ability to think disappears altogether. The body does heal during sleep and there is communication going on among deep brain areas, but it is on the unconscious level. The unusual thing about the rest during TM is that the deep rest it provides also produces that unconscious communication in subcortical areas that you get with sleep *plus* there is also that kind of communication going on in the cerebral cortex that produces conscious awareness. When you transcend thoughts to experience unbounded awareness, all the specific allocation of cortical resources the brain uses to produce specific thoughts quiets down and the brain goes into a state of pure consciousness and infinite correlation. The mind is attracted towards that state, without any thinking about it, because it is a more charming state. On the way to automatically settling into that state, any abnormalities along the way are detected and normalized. It is all automatic. The person is not aware of any of this. He is only aware that there is a bubbling up of different thoughts and feelings as the mind settles in the direction of the transcendent. Those thoughts and feelings are created by the physiological activity of stresses normalizing. It is like a wrinkled balloon inflating. The fully inflated balloon is smooth and perfect, but the starting point, the deflated balloon, is all full of wrinkles and misshaped. As the balloon begins to inflate, the wrinkles begin to stretch out and disappear, first the superficial ones and later the deep-seated ones, until finally all the wrinkles are gone and the balloon is perfectly smooth. The little snapping and crackling sounds the balloon makes as the wrinkles are straightening out is analogous to the thoughts generated by the physiological activity of stress normalization during TM practice. Thoughts during the TM technique are just a by-product of the normalizing process.

In order for the body to heal, all the different physiological systems need to communicate with each other. For example, there are pressure receptors in the arteries that tell the central control centers in the brain if blood pressure is too high or too low, and the control centers send out signals to constrict or dilate the vessels to increase or decrease the pressure, as required. EEG coherence sets up an optimal internal milieu that allows all the homeostatic feedback systems, which are trying to restore balance and health in the body, to talk to each other and do their job. The whole system becomes wide awake, with each area talking to the other centers it needs to talk to, and doing its job. The etymology of "health" is "wholeness, a being whole, sound, or well." What restores wholeness, holistic coherence, is integration of brain function- ing. TM provides that. All areas of the body are in communication with each other via the body's great communicator, the brain. The combination of deep rest and increased communication among brain areas identifies structural and functional abnormalities in the system and repairs them. These abnormalities are stresses in the body. Their normalization happens progressively through TM practice. Each meditation chips away at the stresses, eliminating them more and more, and the person increasingly becomes healthier and smarter on many dimensions.

By far the best-controlled research on TM has been on cardiovascular disease within the African-American community, because NIH grant fund- ing has been available for doing research in this area (Appendix B). But the results apply to every ethnicity. Universally, for all ethnicities and cultures, the causes and progression of cardiovascular diseases are intensified by stress. Randomized controlled studies on African-American adolescents at risk for hypertension have found that TM practice reduces resting and ambulatory blood pressure (7, 8). It also decreases left ventricular mass, lowers cardiovas- cular reactivity to stressors, helps with weight control, and improves school behavior in African-American youth (9-13).

Research on adult African-Americans with mild or moderate essential hypertension has shown that TM practice decreases blood pressure, reduces use of anti-hypertensive medication, prevents the development of left ventricular hypertrophy, and decreases carotid atherosclerosis (14-19). It also significantly decreases cardiovascular and all-cause morbidity and mortality (20, 21). Studies of subjects of many ethnicities have also shown that the TM technique decreases symptoms of angina pectoris (22) and reduces cardiovascular risk factors, including alcohol and tobacco use (23).

On a deeper level of explanation, the global benefits from transcending occur because the transcendent, pure consciousness, is the unified field of natural law that governs all forms and functions in the universe. What gives structure from that undifferentiated wholeness is vibration, generated from its own self-referral interaction. The transcendental field is the first cause, so there is nothing outside of itself to cause creation. It creates from within itself, and the first, most fundamental levels of natural law to emerge from the undifferentiated wholeness of the transcendent are vibrational modes of the universal field of consciousness, and the resonances and harmonies created by their interactions create the hierarchical structure of the universe from unmanifest to subtle to gross levels of creation. The great physicists of the 20th century—Einstein, Planck, Schrodinger—deduced that a universal field of consciousness was the primary reality. But it took quantum field theorist Dr. John Hagelin, formerly of CERN, to posit that the vibrational modes of the field are expressed in the vibrations of the Veda and Vedic literature. Dr. Hagelin was able to do this because he is in a unique position of having deep knowledge of both quantum field theory and Vedic literature, having spent hundreds of hours with Maharishi discussing these connections. Hagelin has shown that the fundamental level of natural law described by modern physics corresponds exactly with the fundamental levels of the Veda (24, 25). Like any true law of nature, this has applied technologies, made even more powerful because the knowledge is fundamental. Knowledge of the elementary vibrational modes of the universe allows one to create holistic effects in the individual and society. The TM and TM-Sidhi programs and other Vedic technologies are this technology, as we saw in the examples of medical care utilization and cognitive functions; they have an unprecedented holistic integration of those levels. And this is true in every area of human physiology and psychology. Beyond that, over 50 research studies have shown that these Vedic techniques have the ability to integrate society, seen as decreased negative trends and improved positive trends on the levels of cities, states, nations, and the world (26-32).

Dr. Tony Nader has shown that the vibrational modes, expressed in the Veda and Vedic literature, give rise to structures and functions of the human brain (33). The brain is the perfect image of the fundamental vibrations, harmonies, and interactions of the transcendental field, and the TM program makes use of these special vibrations to create its holistic effects on optimizing brain functioning. Other vibrational modes will not do the same job of setting up global wakeful communication throughout the brain by enlivening the most basic levels of integration and communication among brain areas because they are not those fundamental vibrational modes. These vibrations are universal, and do not belong to any one culture. They are fundamental to nature and work the same way for different brains from all different cultures and all times. The differences among people and cultures are on a more superficial level. The sameness among us is universal.

All of these highly specific repair processes in the mind and body happen completely automatically through TM practice. All the individual is aware of is that he or she is quietly settling into a very enjoyable experience of inner cosmic stillness, routinely, twice every day— that same sublime experience that previous generations have only been able to glimpse sporadically, but which is now available to everyone in the world, thanks to Maharishi.

References

1. Orme-Johnson DW. Medical care utilization and the Transcendental Meditation program. Psychosomatic Medicine. 1987;49:493-507.

2. So KT, Orme-Johnson DW. Three randomized experiments on the holistic longitudinal effects of the Transcendental Meditation technique on cognition. Intelligence. 2001;29(5):419-40.

3. Farrow JT, Hebert JR. Breath suspension during the Transcendental Meditation technique. Psychosomatic Medicine. 1982;44(2):133-53.

4. Badawi K, Wallace RK, Orme-Johnson DW, Rouzeré A-M. Electrophysiologic characteristics of respiratory suspension periods occurring during the practice of the Transcendental Meditation program. Psychosomatic Medicine. 1984;46(3):267-76.

5. Orme-Johnson DW, Haynes CT. EEG phase coherence, pure consciousness, creativity and TM-Sidhi experiences. International Journal of Neuroscience. 1981;13:211-7.

6. Orme-Johnson DW. Coherence during Transcendental Consciousness. Electroencephalography & Clinical Neurophysiology. 1977;43(4):581-2 (Abstract).

7. Barnes VA. Impact of Meditation on Resting and Ambulatory Blood Pressure and Heart Rate in Youth. Psychosomatic Medicine. 2004;66(6):909-14.

8. Barnes VA, Johnson MH, Dekkers JC, Treiber FA. Reproducibility of ambulatory blood pressure measures in African-American adolescents. Ethnicity and Disease. 2002;12(4):S3-101-6.

9. Barnes VA, Kapuku G, Treiber FA. Impact of Transcendental Meditation on Left Ventricular Mass in African-American Adolescents. eCAM 2012. 2012;2012:1-6.

10. Barnes VA, Treiber FA, Turner JR, Davis H, Strong WB. Acute effects of transcendental meditation on hemodynamic functioning in middle-aged adults. Psychosomatic Medicine. 1999;61(4):525-31.

11. Barnes VA, Johnson MH, Treiber FA, editors. Transcendental Meditation Lowers Body Mass Index in African-American Adolescents. Childhood Obesity Research Conference; 2009 Nov 19-20; Atlanta, GA.

12. Barnes VA, Treiber FA, Davis H. Impact of Transcendental Meditation on cardiovascular function at rest and during acute stress in adolescents with high normal blood pressure. Journal of Psychosomatic Research. 2001;51(4):597-605.

13. Barnes VA, Bauza LB, Treiber FA. Impact of stress reduction on negative school behavior in adolescents. Health Quality of Life Outcomes. 2003 Apr 23;1(1):10.

14. Schneider RH, Alexander CN, Staggers F, Orme-Johnson DW, Rainforth MV, Salerno JW, et al. A randomized controlled trial of stress reduction in African-Americans treated for hypertension for over one year. American Journal of Hypertension. 2005 Jan;18(1):88-98.

15. Anderson JW, Liu CH, Kryscio RJ. Blood pressure response to Transcendental Meditation: A meta-analysis. American Journal of Hypertension. 2008;21(3):310-6.

16. Rainforth MV, Schneider RH, Nidich SI, Gaylord-King C, Salerno JW, Anderson JW. Stress reduction programs in patients with elevated blood pressure: A systematic review and meta-analysis. Current Hypertension Reports. 2007;9(6):520-8.

17. Castillo-Richmond A, Schneider RH, Alexander CN, Cook R, Myers H, Nidich SI, et al. Effects of stress reduction on carotid atherosclerosis in hypertensive African-Americans. Stroke. 2000;31:568-73.

18. Salerno JW, Schneider RH, Alexander CN, Orme-Johnson DW, Castillo-Richmond A, Rainforth M, et al. A controlled trial of effects of stress reduction on left ventricular mass in hypertensive African Americans. Ethnicity & Disease. 2004(M(SuppL)):S2-S54.

19. Kondwani K, Schneider RH, Alexander CN, Sledge C, Staggers F, Clayborne BM, et al. Left ventricular mass regression with the Transcendental Meditation technique and a health education program in hypertensive African-Americans. Journal of Social Behavior and Personality. 2005;17(1):181-200.

20. Schneider RH, Alexander CN, Staggers F, Rainforth MV, Salerno JW, Hartz A, et al. Long-term effects of stress reduction on mortality in persons ≥ 55 years of age with systemic hypertension. American Journal of Cardiology. 2005;95(9):1060-4.

21. Schneider RH, Grim CE, Rainforth MA, Kotchen TA, Nidich SI, Gaylord-King C, et al. Stress reduction in the secondary prevention of cardiovascular disease: a randomized controlled trial of Transcendental Meditation and health education in African-Americans. Archives of Internal Medicine. 2011:in review.

22. Zamarra JW, Schneider RH, Besseghini I, Robinson DK, Salerno JW. Usefulness of the Transcendental Meditation program in the treatment of patients with coronary artery disease. American Journal of Cardiology. 1996;78:77-80.

23. Alexander CN, Robinson P, Rainforth MV. Treating alcohol, nicotine and drug abuse through Transcendental Meditation: A review and statistical meta-analysis. Alcohol Treatment Quarterly. 1994;11:13-87.

24. Hagelin JS. Restructuring Physics From its Foundation in Light of Maharishi's Vedic Science. Modern Science and Vedic Science. 1989;3(1):3-72.

25. Hagelin JS. Is Consciousness the Unified Field? A Field Theorist's Perspective. Modern Science and Vedic Science. 1987;1(1):29-88.

26. Orme-Johnson DW. Preventing crime through the Maharishi Effect. Journal of Offender Rehabiliation. 2003;36(1/2/3/4):257-82.

27. Orme-Johnson DW, Alexander CN, Davies JL, Chander HM, Larimore WE. International Peace Project: The Effects of the Maharishi Technology of the Unified Field. Journal of Conflict Resolution. 1988;32(4):776-812.

28. Dillbeck MC. Test of a field theory of consciousness and social change: Time series analysis of participation in the TM-Sidhi program and reduction of violent death in the U.S. Social Indicators Research. 1990;22:399-418.

29. Dillbeck MC, Banus CB, Polanzi C, Landrith III GS. Test of a field model of consciousness and social change: Transcendental Meditation and TM-Sidhi program and decreased urban crime. The Journal of Mind and Behavior. 1988; 9(4):457-86

30. Dillbeck MC, Cavanaugh KL, Glenn T, Orme-Johnson DW, Mittlefehldt V. Consciousness as a Field: The Transcendental Meditation and TM-Sidhi Program and Changes in Social Indicators. The Journal of Mind and Behavior. 1987;8(1):67-104.

31. Hagelin JS, Rainforth MV, Orme-Johnson DW, Cavanaugh KL, Alexander CN, Shatkin SF, et al. Effects of group practice of the Transcendental Meditation program on preventing violent crime in Washington D.C.: Results of the National Demonstration Project, June-July, 1993. Social Indicators Research. 1999; 47(2):153-201.

32. Orme-Johnson DW, Dillbeck MC, Alexander CN. Preventing terrorism and international conflict: Effects of large assemblies of participants in the Transcendental Meditation and TM-Sidhi programs. Journal of Offender Rehabilitation. 2003;36:283-302.

33. Nader T. Human Physiology—Expression of Veda and the Vedic Literature. Vlodrop, Holland: Maharishi University Press; 1995.

GE Commentary: As I reflect on the words of Candace Martin, Ayida Mthembu, and David Orme-Johnson I reminisce on the intentions of Maharishi to eliminate human suffering, and cultivate in the collective consciousness a sense of justice, integrity, and compassion. As I was editing the book in preparation for publication, there was a replay on television of the 1962 film *To Kill a Mockingbird*, starring Gregory Peck, and the young protagonist played by Mary Badham. The replay was celebrating the 50th anniversary of the historic film. In fact, there are two additional films that came to mind: *Inherit the Wind*, starring Spencer Tracy, and *Brubaker*, starring Robert Redford, which articulated my quest for justice, integrity, and the development of consciousness. These films connected to experiences in my life; the films presented themes and characters who reflected courage and a commitment to what is right and just, and concluded with events that pave the way, and point to a direction that highlighted the journey's end is an open book to be discovered.

To Kill a Mockingbird reminded me of my initial work in the criminal justice system, where injustice and fear because of race and poverty has resulted in a system that rejected the idea that rehabilitation was possible. The verdict of the jury in the film *To Kill a Mockingbird* reflected what great leaders such as Martin Luther King, Jr. struggled to correct. The films *Brubaker* and *Inherit the Wind* are reminiscent of my time in a southern state, where because of limited thinking and political expediency, an opportunity for social transformation was diverted. However, evolution is inevitable and unstoppable, similar to the power of water continuously flowing and dissolving hardened rocks and obstacles in its path. Moreover, in a beautiful film entitled *The Main Purpose*, Maharishi remarked that life grows toward truth and anything less than truth tends to fall away. Movies and art reflect the images of our human history, like an impressionistic painting capturing a moment in time in a certain light. Human beings of good character and sincere intentions make history, and are pushed by the force of nature to seek avenues to raise the collective consciousness. They integrate its diversity to facilitate a world beyond the illusions created by stereotyping individuals because of gender, race, or politics.

Part VII

Whisperings of Inner Beauty

Chapter XXIV

A Sense of Wholeness

Jennifer Hawthorne

I have known Jennifer for over 25 years. She is a teacher of TM, and I was pleasantly amazed at her success as one of the authors in the Chicken Soup of the Soul *series, and as a public speaker. Jennifer has sold more than 12 million books. We worked together many years ago in the area of human development. Jennifer has a precise mind complemented by an inner depth and compassion for humanity, which shines through her personality. I am grateful to have her thoughts and reflections in this excursion through* A Symphony of Silence.

TM is my time to take a break from the business, the noise of the world, and settle into the field of silence underlying all that noise and activity. If it weren't for my meditation practice of 36 years, I wouldn't even realize that such a field exists! The gifts of my practice of TM are two-fold. First, it offers deep rest and relief from the activity of daily living, and brings a sense of comfort, ease, and balance. Second, it has shown me what the Self is, the desire of all spiritual seekers, the only thing that doesn't change, the only thing that's real.

I tried to exercise for many years, knowing that it would be "good for me." I tried working with a trainer at the gym (at least three times). I tried aerobics. I tried Pilates. I walked. I bought an ab-roller advertised on television (now in my closet). I also bought a Swiss ball, rebounder, and hula-hoop (also in my closet). Then I discovered yoga. I studied with many teachers and ultimately developed my own style, so that I no longer need to go to a class to do it. My style is slow, gentle, and comes from a place of nourishing my body rather than *having* to do it.

I have had many profound experiences of inner silence in nature, but my top two were seeing Mt. Everest (Nepal) and the Ganges River (India) for the first time. I was traveling in a Nepalese taxi when suddenly the hair stood up on the back of my neck; something made me turn around, and I found myself looking at Mt. Everest for the first time. My mind and breath stopped for a moment as the beauty and grandeur before my eyes made me feel as if I were touching the feet of God. Upon leaving Nepal, I rode a bus all night to Benares, India's holiest city. In the wee hours of the morning, I found my way to one of the *ghats* by the river and sat on stone stairs waiting for the sun to come up. I could hear the water lapping against its banks, and a man performing his morning bath and ablutions in the water. Then the sun rose to reveal the river. As I took in the beauty and the energy of sacred ritual, everything became perfectly still. Time stopped in a moment of grace, and holiness was the quality of that grace. Another time, I was on an island in the Indian Ocean. It was sunset, and the water from the shore to the line where the waves broke on the coral reef was still, like glass. A golden light spread across the horizon and high into the sky, reflected in the water as a soft brilliance. At the water's edge, two small island boys played quietly, joyfully at their evening bath. I was overcome with a sense of wholeness, the recognition that this event was complete and full, and nothing more could be added to it—this was life in its fullness. It was a moment of complete presence that showed me there is nothing other than the now.

In the context of spirituality, one understanding of enlightenment is that it is the ability to accept "what is," to feel comfortable with yourself and others. I feel my mother embodied this wisdom in her ability to accept everything about all three of her children. For me, looking at almost any work of the Impressionist artists or listening to the great classical music masters evokes expanded awareness. I can sit for an extended period before a van Gogh, for example, because his art must have arisen out of his own experience of timelessness. At the end of a piece of music such as Beethoven's *Moonlight Sonata*, something happens after the last note; I seem to "come back" from some place I have "gone." This, of course, is Transcendental Consciousness, and most great works of art are capable of carrying me into this place.

Long-distance drives on the highway provide some of my most expanded and creative moments. In fact, the entire structure of my last book burst forth while I was driving from home to the airport, 80 miles away. I could hardly wait to arrive so that I could write down the ideas that seemed to be spilling out of my consciousness. I think this happens because the mind has to be fully awake in order for a person to be behind the wheel, yet the physical act of driving is itself automatic, allowing the mind to drop into an alpha state that promotes insights, and heightened states of awareness and creativity. Time also feels altered in this state, which I always identify as a quality of Transcendental Consciousness. Sometimes, for example, on long trips I will listen to a book on CD. With my body engaged in driving and my mind captivated by the story, I often experience that time is suspended, and a span of six hours can feel like a few minutes.

I have experienced a profound shift and maturing of emotional intelligence that correlates precisely with one cultural model of aging. This model describes youth as the years from birth to 35, mid-youth from 35 to 50, and the fifties as a time of integration between youth and mid-youth. Sixties are the youth of the elder years, seventies the mid-youth of the elder years, and eighties and older the years of true eldership. Shortly after I turned 60, a friend approached me for advice. We were both amazed at what seemed like true and deep wisdom coming through me. This wisdom continues to grow and express itself in my work and daily relationships. I am often asked for advice, feedback, and input. I often experience life "going by itself." This is especially true when I am in front of an audience delivering an inspirational keynote address—my passion and dharma. I will suddenly realize that I am almost at the end of my talk and think to myself, how could I be here already? Where did the time go? Did I miss something? This experiencing of witnessing always reminds me of what I believe to be the highest spiritual understanding: I am not the doer.

I also remember walking home from the bus stop one day when I was in the first grade. It was winter, and I was freezing cold. I remember vowing to myself that I would never forget this day. Now, years later, I call upon that experience as a reminder of the part of me that does not change—my awareness. My understanding is that praise and gratitude are the truest or highest form of prayer. Praying of this nature brings me into the present; I find myself giving thanks for the warmth of the air, the clothes on my body, beautiful, comfortable shelter, good, organic food to eat, the sunshine and the breeze, the ocean nearby. Settling into silence is what allows me to come into the present. When I experience deep silence, there is a quality of love to it. It often manifests as physical bliss, especially concentrated around my heart and eyes. My mother modeled unconditional love to me. Present in my life for 60 years, she accepted every fad, phase, craze and weirdness I attempted to perpetrate on her or anyone. She supported me with every school project, homework assignment, athletic event, prom dress, divorce, illness, financial need—the list goes on. It didn't matter to her whether I was successful or not, married or not, wealthy or not—she just cared that I was happy. No strings attached.

I had the privilege of being present at my father's death. As was the case with two births I attended, I found the inner silence to be palpable at the moment of the body's leaving or arriving. In one case the body arrives; in the other the soul departs. In every instance, a continuity of consciousness could be felt before and after the celestial passage, showing an underlying continuum of life whether expressed in a physical form or not. In the case of death, despite my deep sorrow at the loss of my father, the experience was one of ecstasy.

Chapter XXV

The Ineffable Embrace

Each contributor in this chapter has experienced the embrace of the inner stillness of transcendental pure consciousness during their life in various situations, and enhanced its integration through the knowledge and technique of TM. They share with the reader unique perspectives and moments that highlight how human evolution is similar to swimming in a river, which is in constant motion, never ending, and one must learn to flow with the current. Each human being in the natural process of their evolution is slowly awakening to this mysterious, but accessible, and infinite inner beauty. It is the essence of their own nature. Communicating these deep, and at times inexpressible, experiences, affirms that each person has the power within them to become enlightened, and free from limitations, but it depends on the choices that each individual makes.

The Quest

I met Maria in Latin America, a sweet and gentle soul with an excellent intellect. She dedicated her life to teaching the TM program throughout the world. I arranged for her to travel to India in 1986 with a group of TM teachers from Guatemala, to attend a special course conducted by Maharishi. Maria would spend many years based in Europe working on TM projects. She shares her insights and experience related to Transcendental Consciousness.

Maria

As a child I was seeking the direct experience of spirituality, and I would pray and cry to have a glimpse of that experience. I did not know how to realize my aspiration until the day I learned the TM technique; the experience was peaceful, like landing on a cloud—this is what I was looking for. Throughout the years because of my regular practice of TM, the experience has changed, in that the contrast is less when I come out of TM. It is as if the silence is always surrounding me during the day. Through physical activity the experience seems to be integrating and a growing sense of happiness and being alive is present.

I was fortunate to spend many years on staff at the international TM headquarters in Vlodrop, Holland working closely with Maharishi on numerous projects. The development of my consciousness during those years removed many fears, and provided a new clarity in life—a feeling that I am not alone, but rather united with everything. My intuition and human sense of connectedness have grown. My heart has expanded, and after the experience of transcendence my empathy and intuition have been enlivened. I can feel what others are feeling, as a growing sense of oneness with everything grows. I have had this experience triggered by the beauty of nature, some beautiful music, the presence of a saint, or after a quiet experience during TM. When I walk in nature, it is like a continuous meditation in action. When I was living in Switzerland and would walk in the forest, the beauty of nature was so overwhelming that I would fall into a state of inner silence, and felt the unity of all in nature—it was beautiful.

One lovely memory was when I visited the church of St. Francis in Assisi. Inside the church, I closed my eyes for a few moments, and because of the habit of my nervous system being familiar with transcending through TM, I immediately began to experience a deep diving into transcendental silence, which stayed with me for the entire day. I have had this experience in several churches in different countries. The first time I experienced it was as a young child when I received the confirmation in the Catholic faith, in which the bishop anoints you on the forehead with special oil. It was a precious moment. I immediately transcended and felt my heart expand. Furthermore, a very cosmic feeling came to me recently, as we were signing a business contract. It felt as if this had been planned before, and was like a reunion, even though we had just met the other person. It had a surreal feeling as if I was witnessing my own actions.

One particular incident that remains with me was when I was walking in New Delhi, India. I was in a busy marketplace, and crossed the path of a *sadhu*, and I looked into his eyes. They were beautiful and clear—I saw so much depth and bliss, and this brought an incredible peace in my heart. It felt like time stood still while we passed each other, a big silence in the midst of the exterior chaos, a nod of acknowledgment, and then we continued on our respective ways.

My experience with prayer, to be effective, has to emerge within a state of surrender, inner peace, and unconditional love. I have experienced love in different ways, but the most beautiful is when it triggers silence and transcendence. When this happens, everything is all right in life, one floats in bliss, and all the mundane aspects of life sort out easily. I had a very clear experience of this unconditional love many years ago on a TM course where my heart expanded and gave me a constant feeling of silence during the day. One evening, as I was walking home after a celebration, I felt enraptured in bliss and understood the meaning of the flow of soma that is mentioned in the Vedas. It was like being inebriated without the negative side effects, just pure bubbling bliss—it was fantastic!

Another experience I had was a few years later in the U.S., during another TM course, which also was activated by the experience of love. It happened one night as I was about to fall asleep. I felt a surge of energy rising from the base of my spine. It was like a river of light, very powerful, pushing upwards. There was a blockage in the middle of the spine, but this energy kept pushing until I heard a "boom" sound, like an explosion, and my whole body was filled with bliss. I experienced a river of energy going up my spine at an incredible speed, which went on for the rest of the night. I felt completely at peace and silent inside. At some point in the morning it subsided, and I got up and practiced TM. I experienced heightened energy, as if I had a full night's sleep, and this feeling lasted for a month; the experience facilitated events and decisions that again changed the course of my life.

In terms of unconditional love, I have loved a person so much that I only wanted what was best for his evolution, in spite of my individual preferences. You do not want to use the individual for your personal happiness because you feel happy independently of the person, and you just want him to feel the same happiness. The experience of transcendence has many dimensions: for example, I had that experience while studying advanced mathematics at a university, and also while appreciating a masterpiece of art. I do not remember the exact instances, just the general feeling of peace and unity with everything. It is also a feeling of expansion at the level of the heart.

I used to witness my sleep as a child regularly. I did not know that it was called witnessing, and thought it was the normal thing. I would lie on my back in bed, and be very awake inside while the body was fully asleep. I also experienced witnessing my dreams, and used to have very vivid dreams that would come true in the future. I would forget those dreams, but then some time later found myself in that specific situation as in the dream, and would remember it. In the beginning, I was a bit shocked and would just witness the events unfold before me. One day at a TM center, I heard a lecture about witnessing as an indication of the development of Cosmic Consciousness, and learned that this was what I had been experiencing all along. Probably, due to the loss of innocence, the experience became less frequent, but left a very deep impact on me, and made me focus my whole life into a spiritual search.

I once had a near-death experience. I was living at the time in the north of Mexico, in the winter, and there was a leak in the gas heater. When this happens, as the gas has no smell, one goes to sleep and never wakes up. I started to dream that I was dying from asphyxia, and this woke me up, but I was so weak that I could hardly move. After some struggle, I managed to crawl out of bed toward the window and tried to open it, but I was so weak already that I did not reach the window, and just passed out. I went out of the body and saw my own body lying there on the floor, and felt very free and relieved. My husband heard the noise I made when I fell, and he woke up and was able to open the window. I saw how he tried to bring me back to life, but I felt perfectly calm, at peace, and did not want to go back into that body. Then I saw some light and went toward it—into a kind of tunnel. The light at the end of the tunnel was very bright, and I felt attracted to it. As I proceeded, I "saw" my life pass in front of my eyes in a kind of slide show—very fast. Some images kept repeating themselves; as if these were issues I still had to sort out. I wanted to proceed toward the light, but an internal voice—not a sound but more a feeling—kept saying that I have to go back, it is not my time because I still have things to do here. Then I felt as if I was being pulled by a rubber band back into my body, and did not want to return; the experience was like being in a very tight suit.

My husband, of course, was very happy and relieved, but I felt resigned to be back. One realization which I derived from this experience is that I lost the fear of death; it also took away the fear of life, as the worst thing that can happen in life is to die, and it is not really a bad thing at all. However, the experience changed the way I perceived the passing of other people. I could not feel really sad, but only that I missed their physical presence. Another insight, at least in my case, was that I came back because I still had unresolved issues with relationships. At that time, the relationship with my mother was not very good, and we had not spoken with each other for four years.

After this experience, I believed I had to correct this, and today I have a very good relationship with her, and we enjoy spending the holidays together.

I considered that it was important to set all my relationships straight, and not to let things be unspoken with close relations. This experience also taught me not to take life so seriously because it is just a bundle of experiences in the process of our evolution. I still become entangled in the experience, as it can be overwhelming to be in this 3-D reality, but it's not for long, and this gives a different perspective to my life. I'm very grateful for having had these experiences of inner stillness and expansion of consciousness.

Waves of Love

Julia was born in Romania in the area that is Hungarian (called Transylvania, formerly part of Hungary before WWI). At 12, she emigrated to Australia, eventually traveling to Holland and then Switzerland.

Julia Benczedi

When I practice TM and yoga, my awareness becomes permeated by a wholeness and experience of unconditional love. In fact, when practicing yoga exercises as complement to my TM practice, I move through the motions or postures, and I experience enlivening this quality of wholeness with each movement. The process of transcending has cultivated my intellect and intuition. I often have strong intuitive thoughts about what action to take, but have no idea how I came to the particular conclusion. I recognized that it unfolded from a quiet region of stillness, and silence within my consciousness.

Once during the practice of TM I transcended the finest impulse of thought—I became aware that I was infinite, and nothing else existed except the Self. There was a flow of bliss throughout my consciousness and physiology and a great sense of freedom. When my mind becomes silent, and I have a thought of someone, my heart automatically fills with love toward that person; this love gradually becomes unbounded, filling my entire physiology. This reality is continuous with each passing day. The love that emerges from the field of silence is linked to the experience of wholeness that occurs along with it, although the intensity of the love can depend on the recipient. I can experience this emotion on its own without any object to direct it to. I believe the inner bliss consciousness within me becomes a transmitter, much like a telephone line, embracing me in waves of love; then whomever I choose to think about becomes the recipient. Sometimes the love I experience flowing from the inner stillness of pure consciousness becomes so intense that it stirs waves of bliss or ecstasy in my physiology.

It is my intellectual understanding that the unconditional, infinite love I experience in and out of the practice of TM is nothing other than love directed toward and from my higher Self. I perceived that the fabric of love I experience is completely self-referral, and unfolding from Transcendental Consciousness. Maharishi said that in enlightenment all love is directed toward the Self—it is the infinite Self within us recognizing the infinite Self in another, and therefore, the Self is loving the Self. Sometimes I experience other emotions becoming unbounded, like gratitude and devotion, which is connected to prayer and fulfillment of desires. Whenever I put my attention back on the Self, I would perceive myself as being embraced by the Divine, and then I would start feeling unbounded waves of love from outside of myself, which would come crashing into me. I think as a result of these experiences my physiology is experiencing more of the consciousness value.

Empathy and Unconditional Love

Stephen Ulicny studied and received his master's degree in Vedic Science from MERU in Seelisberg, Switzerland, and presently resides in Fairfield, Iowa.

Stephen Ulicny

I practice TM and often the solution to problems comes to me without any intent from my side. The problems may be mundane, but the creative solution seems to turn every problem into a situation, and what was once a challenge suddenly disappears. My experience with regularly pursuing the development of inner silence has influenced my emotional intelligence, and has impacted my life experiences. My nervous system seems to take the stress like a line on water rather than an etching in concrete that lingers. Memories of yesterday's sorrows and human abuse tend to fade as a gradual awakening is taking place.

Before learning the TM technique my empathy and compassion regarding the suffering of others would overshadow my emotions and pull me into their suffering. Since I began TM the inner silence or stillness has grown and integrated into my consciousness. I feel human suffering more deeply, but I am not swallowed up by it. There have been incidents in my life that seem to have been pure coincidence, but as I reflect upon them, they amaze me. It seems when we are living our life, we take so many moments for granted, such as the universal experience of love. Love is a strong emotion that emanates from the region of my heart, often during TM. Sometimes it is overpowering and fills every part of my body. It is generally directed at another person, for example one of my daughters or my partner. The feeling grows as thoughts of the individual flow into my awareness, and sometimes leaves me tearful and aching, but with a beautiful exhilarating ache, not a hurtful pain. These feelings of love sometimes continue outside of TM, but not with the strength and power that they have during the silence of TM. I want to hold onto the feeling, but it dissipates as the mundane takes over, and activities must be attended to. I experienced unconditional love when I became a parent. Children come with blank slates, no emotional baggage, and no motives or agenda other than to be cared for, and show love and affection for their family. Unconditional love has grown over the years, and I have experienced it with others as consciousness grows in my life.

My brother left his body a few years ago. He was severely emotionally disturbed all his life, and died with major medical illnesses and unresolved emotional issues. Over the course of his lifetime, he was institutionalized at mental hospitals four times; he was a borderline personality with bipolar disease and experienced mild paranoia. He saw himself as a "victim" and in his mind, it was others who created his situation and prevented him from succeeding. I often thought if I had not started TM when I did, I might have followed in his footsteps. I was unable to concentrate in college, was always anxious, and suffered from bouts of depression when I was in high school and college. I could complete college by taking "gut" courses—those that were known to be easy A's. I had wanted to go to medical school, but could not concentrate enough to get good grades in math and science. One morning, after learning TM, I looked at myself in the mirror, and I realized that my facial muscles had relaxed for the first time in many years. The tension was gone, and my face looked different. The lines from muscle strain were gone.

I have had a good life, and I progressed in my career until a shift a few years back. Even that challenging experience, I considered a good thing. My job at the time was extremely stressful, and emotionally draining and unfulfilling. It paid well, so I stayed and put up with it. In my present position, although I am earning less, I enjoy life more and the growth of consciousness in my life has been enhanced. I anticipate this will be a bridge to something better in my life. Setbacks over the years have always led to "more" and there is no reason to expect this situation to be different. I recognize in silence there is a value and beauty, which all human beings share. Stress impacts us, and as time goes by we simply forget the power that is residing within us. We need to find a method or technique such as TM, to experientially re-awaken the wonderful secrets that have been hidden within us all the time.

Dancing on a Point

Marty Howe lives in Nanaimo on Vancouver Island. The growth of consciousness through the TM program expands our view of the challenges and changes that take place in life. As a jazz musician Marty echoes the sentiments expressed by Paul Horn in terms of letting go. He shares a tender and personal moment and the perspective of an individual with a developed consciousness.

Marty Howe

When my mother passed, I was sitting alongside her, holding her hand, and immediately a wonderful bliss started resonating in my heart. It was a gentle silence, golden, permeating every extension of my awareness and Being, but concentrated in the area around my heart. This experience saturated every aspect of my intellect, emotions, and senses. Along with this glowing and almost pulsating bliss was a knowingness that went beyond the need of the intellect to understand in terms of boundaries. This experience lasted for three months, and my physiology was transformed forever. This subtle inner joy and bliss is still with me at this very moment. No matter what is happening in my life, even amidst challenging situations, this inner silence, happiness, joy, knowingness, is always awake in me.

I am also a jazz musician. The experience I have when I play, especially when I improvise, is that I am dancing on a point, where I experience profound inner silence, unbounded on one side, keenly focused and playfully dynamic at the same time. In my life there is a similar experience of being very wakeful and purposefully surrendering or letting go; at the same time my attention is also riding on a playful melodic idea that requires a very intense focus, which is willing to follow and explore any subtle intention. I love that space where I am so awake and silent simultaneously, yet so engaged and dynamic. This experience validates me as a human being—a dance of joyfulness flows through me.

Intentions and Expectations

Elizabeth Cline is a woman of keen intelligence and sensitivity. She is a teacher of TM and a professional book indexer living with her husband and sister in Woodstock, New York.

Elizabeth Cline

After years of experiencing transcending through TM, an inward process of unfolding silence, I have begun to enjoy stillness, expansiveness, and the presence of fullness. Just having the intention will enliven the silence within me even in the middle of activity. Transcending our opinions of being right or wrong, which often takes place in relationships, is the evolution of unconditional love. My husband and I, in the beginning of our relationship, had regular conflicts, and yet my love for him eventually resulted in the transcendence of right or wrong—a suspension of judgment. I thought it was strange in relationships when someone wanted their partner to change certain things about themselves. It always seemed so arbitrary. One boyfriend might prefer I was this way, and the next prefer me to be different. It is silly when you think about it. I think true love—unconditional love—does not require the object of love to be anything different from who they are. I realize any judgmental thought that I have, I could just as easily have the opposite thought, and it is usually just as true as my original thought. The realization that I am not my thoughts has had the biggest impact on my life. It certainly saved my marriage.

The experience of transcendent silence can appear unexpectedly. I remember Maharishi talking about how an individual could experience enlightenment standing behind a bus smelling the fumes. I spent years standing, metaphorically, behind buses until I realized that we are destined to be our own surprise. There have been many moments of simple, sweet experiences of Self. They are not dramatic, but are beautiful in their genuine simplicity. Love includes utter silence. I may not speak to someone for years, and still love them completely. Words can be sweet, but are not necessary. Love is love—it is beyond words. Having a child taught me unconditional love. I never expected him to be anything other than exactly who he was. I have always loved him, just as he is.

My experience as a result of TM, and my commitment to the development of my consciousness, has resulted in a contentment in which I am less invested in my opinions and letting go of expectations. I remember a moment in Switzerland with Maharishi that reflects the sweet connectedness that flows from our intentions. My sister Tricia and I were each waiting to give Maharishi a flower after a lecture. When he was leaving the lecture hall, we tried to push our way closer to him to give him our flowers, but there was a crowd, and we could not get through as he walked past us. So we just looked at each other, and resigned ourselves that we may not be able to give him our flowers. Then, he stopped, turned around, and walked directly to where we were standing, behind some people, and gestured for us to give our flowers, which we did.

Sweet Relaxation

Claudia Cline is an executive in a multinational company, working and living in Cincinnati, Ohio. Claudia's career began in supporting the rights of Native American Indians in Sacramento, California, and as a corporate lawyer.

Claudia Cline

I have been a long-time practitioner and instructor of TM and for many years cultivated a familiarity with the process of transcending. After 35 years, it has become an experience so intimate to my attention that I can experience inner silence and transcending with just the shift of my attention. I love to sit quietly during TM and enjoy its sweet relaxation. Last week I walked through the woods after an ice storm. The sun was out, and the icicles on the trees were lit up with the colors of the rainbow. I had never seen this before in my life, and the true beauty was not in what I saw, but that I did not feel separate from it. Any moment I may feel joy or bliss for no reason other than that I am. I feel it in the center of my chest, and it radiates to my fingers and toes. Every part of me is as alive as any other. I always smile with my whole body when this happens. The great gift Maharishi gave the world was the knowledge that unbounded love and silence are accessible to everyone, and he provided a technique, which effortlessly can be used by anyone to enliven the wonders of consciousness.

As we expand our consciousness through transcending we develop our capacity to love. Love is transformational and visits us in strange situations. I have begun to have trust and confidence in the inner feelings that emerge from the quiet regions of awareness. Feelings, silence, and presence happen at the moment before my brain is engaged, or before I have named what is happening. It is necessary to turn within and experience the silence because love is the feeling of silence, and there is no other kind of love in the context of spirituality. Conditional love is given by the small self; the large Self only loves purely.

The Silence in Me

Patricia is a teacher of TM. She is a full-time artist and an instructor at the Woodstock School of Art, and lives with her husband and sister in Woodstock, New York.

Patricia Cline

My knowledge of transcending has come to me from many angles. In my practice of TM, as my mental activity settles, there is an energetic aliveness in my body. During TM, I experience an effortless acceptance of whatever I am experiencing in the moment, resulting in a letting go of the heaviness that comes with being human. My walks through the woods, although beginning with multiple reflections of the past and the future, can often result in being lost in thought and then witnessing thoughts, allowing and accepting them. This experience creates a space between me and the thoughts. I am that space—it is a total high. I love the woods because I am amazed at the silence and stillness that emanate from trees and animals. The silence in me recognizes the silence in them—it is the same silence.

I experience love uniquely when I realize there is only the present moment, which I see as my Self, not in the form of a phenomenon that is happening, but the space in which activity takes place—then I am love. Transcendence can come as a surprise creating insight, in any situation. I experience thought as a concept created by the mind to maintain the illusion of separation. I am not my thoughts: I "am." It was a moment of cosmic significance for me, when I realized I was not my thoughts or emotions, but the space in which the thoughts occur. Sometimes we all lose ourselves in thoughts, but I find I am always returning to the awareness of my Self. Silence and stillness are who we are. In silence, we are love. Conditional love is partial love—it is only an idea of what love is because real love is unconditional.

I am a sculptor, and as I create a form, thoughts and images come in and out of my consciousness. As I sculpt, I treat thoughts the same way you would during TM: I do not mind them; I do not let them guide me, I just effortlessly return to sculpting the form. In sculpting, my awareness usually goes into my body, and the mind becomes still. There is a witnessing that is cultivated from the combination of developing consciousness through TM, and the activity of the creative process. I move back and forth throughout the day, where I become immersed and identified with thoughts, and then I completely accept whatever sensations are occurring in that moment and in that letting go. I become aware that I have been observing during the creation of my sculptures.

My experience of letting go during the creative process resulted in a personal revelation that the fear of death is the fear of the death of the small self—the ego. I came to realize that my true nature did not exist in the boundaries we experience through our perception of the objective world. I remember a special moment sitting on a couch with my husband visiting with a dear friend. It was a very quiet and calm experience, and I experienced incredible bliss. I suddenly realized the bliss was the absence of thoughts, the absence of mental noise, and feeling bliss was simply what I was and who I am. Any thought, belief, emotion, or memory is a form. All forms are temporary. Once you know that you are the formless, you can enjoy or simply allow all forms to arise and pass through. This is the play of the Absolute, which is you and creates endless forms, to witness its Self in them all.

The inspiration for my sculpture is life or the images around me, and then they form by me stepping out of the way. The image emerges and the story I tell through the sculptures comes afterwards. The meaning is a synthesis of my reflection and the perceiver of the work. It is the feeling of the formless, consciousness, or the awareness that we are, and which is always seeking to emerge. The sculpture entitled *The Bottom of the World Passes by Unseen* presents an image of a lion, which symbolizes the force of life that is moving by unnoticed. The entire essence of the world passes by unseen; the female figure senses it, she is looking for it. Her clothing is moved by the wind as the unseen passes by, but she is looking the other way. It is the quest for understanding the source of the mystery of life, but we are often looking in the wrong direction.

The Bottom of the World Passes by Unseen©

I tend to use animals to represent pure consciousness because I live on the edge of the woods. Whenever I have had the opportunity to look at a wild animal, I noticed that they have a presence in harmony with nature. The innocent harmony with nature provided me the impression that it was just pure awareness looking back at you, so I use animals as a metaphor for pure awareness. It is a metaphor on the movement of seeking self-awareness. We seek that awareness or presence that we are. Many of us practice a form of meditation, or participate in a group where we are seekers. We realize as we meditate, or take a walk in the woods, that what we are seeking is what we are; it has always been there. *The Bottom of the World Passes by Unseen* is like the thinker pointing at the moon. The seeking is what we do; there is a poetry and beauty in that seeking, but in the end what we discover is that it was always what we are—we were that all along. In some ways, it is highlighting the dance of playing in a human condition to discover our Self.

There is a second version of the *Papa Wolf Sings to the Acolytes* sculpture, in which I replace *Papa Wolf* with a small cat. It is the same story, but the Acolytes have the similar expressions with an ordinary cat. The idea is there is the same awe because the infinite consciousness is disguised in many forms, but when it is recognized behind the images and forms, the majestic unboundedness is appreciated. The acolytes are mystified in wonder regarding *Papa Wolf* because it embodies what they seek. The Acolytes are symbolic of seekers of enlightenment and pure consciousness represented by *Papa Wolf*, which with all its strength illuminates infinite consciousness. My inner feeling when I created this piece was nonverbal. The process is simple, and if I am going in the right direction my heart is literally expanding. If I attempt to be clever, and allow the mind to step in, my heart contracts. I teach at the Woodstock School of Art, and I tell my students this is a language that we learn as a human being and as an artist. It sounds very simple, and yet in real life if our hearts contract we will overanalyze, or rationalize instead of just moving in a different direction back toward the expansion. So when I work the heart is an aperture: it is either opening or closing, and it does not matter because the closing moves me in diverse directions just as the opening does. Often when an artist expresses this invisible force within them, they use the words "it pushed me in a dissimilar direction," as if it were something independent from them. However, it is their Self-referral consciousness, the inner stillness of unbounded awareness that moved them in a different direction; it is only different when we view it from the perspective of the seeker. If I become stuck, and I cannot move forward in my art because I try to think my way through an aesthetic problem, I cannot resolve it, but when I let go, allow it to be, and get out of the way, I am astonished how things just start to form; it is an amazing process.

To paraphrase Albert Camus (Nobelprize.org, 2012), an artist is just a person going through life, and recreating one or two images in whose presence their heart first opened. So I believe in my sculptures. I have five unique characters, which are performing different actions, and the awe is an expression within me of when my heart first opened and I keep returning to that experience.

Papa Wolf Sings to the Acolytes©

I am drawn to that inner beauty. The wonder, awe, and innocence are like walking behind a little child, and he or she sees a rock, and everything on the ground is a miracle and curiosity to that child. Everything is fascinating and incredible, and I remember what they felt like, and I try to express the quality of innocent awe in my work. Because I have focused on the development of my consciousness, the inner silence has grown. Additionally, I am self-taught and I experienced making art on my own. What I cultivated during the creative process was similar to transcending during TM. The opening of the heart is like transcending, and then thoughts may come and go, and you go back to the opening or source of thought, or Transcendental Consciousness. My making art in my studio, in contrast to people who have gone to art schools and obtained intellectual ideas of what art is, may be more a spontaneous expression from inner silence. My creative process is an experience of opening the heart, expanding awareness, and beauty. Just as a thought can have form, content, or no content, and emerges from the inner stillness of pure consciousness.

The forms I create emerge from the quiet levels of my experience of consciousness, or Being, and then they flow within me and manifest through my skill into an objective form. The mythologies that I work from are Native American, Eastern philosophy, Vedanta, and so forth. I combine them all into my own mythology. In the sculpture entitled *Pope Joey Leads Loud-Neigh Carrying the Wife of Eternity*, the wife of eternity represents a Goddess. The deeper point beyond the mythology is that her head represents her mind or thoughts, and generally is how most people identify themselves, as their thoughts. There is an individual identification from the neck up, and people believe that is who they are, and live within a very limited and separate perspective. Pope Joey is carrying away that imperfect perspective, which would be ignorance and misidentification of the Self. I have been practicing TM for many years, and transcending has become almost automatic when I close my eyes or shift the attention to something quieter or more subtle. I have cultivated my nervous system and consciousness, which allows me to move into the stillness of self-referral consciousness. I would say that this is also a good definition of the creative process, a shift into stillness. It is from where all of my work emerges—a quiet,

Pope Joey Leads Loud-Neigh Carrying the Wife of Eternity©

still place. It is the recognition of my Self. When I say my heart expands or contracts, all of that is recognition of the still, quiet place that is the inspirational source within me that is based in truth. The experience of the process of transcending is the same experience that produces art. Just as in TM you go in and there is an expansive feeling, in art you also create from that deeper level of consciousness.

In terms of art and life, I take into account imagery that thrills me. When I start on an image that has inspired me, it will utterly transform from within me and it becomes authentically my own. I compare it to Pablo Neruda, who wrote the Ode to Salt (Levine, 2005). He describes looking at a common salt shaker. The beauty of art is that although we are all looking at the same objective reality, it travels and filters through an interpretive process. It filters through an individual consciousness, which gives it a special flavor, and that is thrilling—it is the excitement of diversity. In our limited perceptions we begin to understand how the whole show works. The infinite is being expressed through the eyes of the restricted individual diversity, and the result is an exquisite and sublime beauty—it is that process in art, which is so breathtaking. When you read Pablo's poem, you travel from observing this common item—salt—to infinity and back. I believe infinity is where you arrive at the realm of art and you are shaping infinity into the finite, which of course is impossible, sublime, and beautiful.

In terms of my work, I have met some of the individuals who have purchased my sculptures. There is a beautiful transference because of their love for the piece; they have their personal interpretation and relationship to it—it becomes their work. As Maharishi explains, when you reach a higher state of consciousness, the difference between the inner experience of pure consciousness and perception of it in the world becomes minimized. I have experienced that reality most clearly in my art. There is a confidence in returning to stillness when I am creating my art. When I teach my art students, I share with them to not be concerned about doubt or failure in the process. Just move in the direction of fluidity. I try to share that light, and darkness, and the various contrasts we experience are part of life; however, it is not who we are. I identify with this inner stillness of pure consciousness in the studio, and even if I do not understand how to reach my artistic goal, it never bothers me in my work.

During my creative process, it is a dance, I know how to transcend within the dance, and I hope that it can gradually be applied more in my daily life.

Creativity is the formless appearing in form. It is the entire universe participating in that play, or that dance. When I am in my studio, I am participating in bringing the formless to form, and it is a natural, spontaneous, and incredibly delightful process.

> People have forgotten the transcendent power of art. Here in the West art has been glorified as a product of the ego, as personal revelation—this couldn't be less true. Art comes from beyond the personal, from the transcendent whisper that is ever present to everyone, and therefore, there is . . . nothing personal about it. So the images that come to us are not based on ideas out of the mind, the images that come are transcendent guests—friends—that we develop ongoing relationships with. The image is a friend that has come to teach you its life through the direct (non-interpretive) observation of it . . . It is through respect that the relationships open outward into beauty, respect that allows the image to be who it is and not just a thing in relation to us. (Tricia Cline Sculptures, 2012)

Part VIII

Closing Reflections

Chapter XXVI

Vision for a Better World

The myriad of voices within *A Symphony of Silence* provide a glimpse of Maharishi's knowledge. The capability to experience transcendence is within the grasp of every human being in every country from luxurious mansions to the tin-roofed huts of the Mayan Indians of Central America. *A Symphony of Silence* highlights the inner enlightenment that Maharishi enlivened in the world through the experiences of a broad spectrum of individuals in the humanities and sciences. The voices in this book included legendary musicians, artists, scientists, philosophers, religious leaders, mothers raising their children, and people from every sector of society.

The purpose of *A Symphony of Silence* is to communicate a simple message: If we take the time to shift our attention with an effective technique to experience the inner stillness of transcendental pure consciousness, morning and evening, for just a few moments, the individual and collective consciousness of the world will be transformed. The true power of an individual or a nation is not located in military might or economic wealth; it is within the silent region of our consciousness.

This book emphasizes that Transcendental Consciousness is within everyone, and the inner stillness of unbounded pure consciousness is constantly emerging to embrace our life—the experience whispers that the inner beauty is our birthright. *A Symphony of Silence* is offering an insight, an inspiration, a reminder of who we are, and a simple method to enhance the natural evolution of life toward enlightenment. It is not enough intellectually to just discuss living in the present moment. We must inhabit and develop the consciousness which makes living in the now an effortless and automatic consequence of experiencing the inner stillness through a technique for transcending the duality of thought.

The experience of teaching TM is unique. I remember a comment that Maharishi made to me in Estes Park, Colorado (1970), regarding the responsibility of a TM teacher: "When a TM teacher guides a person to transcend,

467

he has the responsibility for their spiritual evolution for the rest of their life." I took that seriously, and although each person is responsible for his or her own decisions, giving a seeker the right start is important. My commitment to the integrity of Maharishi's knowledge, and my desire to eliminate human suffering in myself and then in the world in which I lived, was all that mattered. I believe our word is a binding contract. Maharishi entrusted me with a great gift, and I will continue to cherish it, to respect the purity of his teaching, and will never violate that trust.

I am constantly surprised at how experiences would come into my life without asking or seeking. One evening, after teaching about 40 individuals to transcend, the light of the day was blending into the darkness of the night. I began to hear a perpetual music—it was there and not there at the same time. I placed my hand on the tree in front of the house, and I could feel a divine intelligence flowing through the tree and beneath my feet like pulsating energy. In that moment, there was nothing but infinite intelligence vibrating in every fabric of existence; there existed nothing without life energy at its core. The experience seemed to be the residue of the silence awakened in my consciousness and perception after I spent the day teaching people to meditate. The silence produced bliss and unconditional love flowing throughout my physiology.

These experiences have come and gone during the passing years as part of a lifetime journey exploring the Self and seeking truth. As an undergraduate student at California State University in Sacramento, I had a similar experience. In the early afternoon, I arrived at the campus and had time in between classes to sit and meditate in my car. I believed I had been meditating just a few moments, but when I opened my eyes, I noticed I had been meditating an hour. When I stepped out of the car, I perceived the world with an exquisite clarity, and I experienced a profound inner silence. Before my eyes, nothing felt solid: it had a liquid feel to it—everything was made of consciousness, and everyone was reflecting back my own Self, a shared experience of Being, like different waves on the same ocean of consciousness. The Self of everyone walking toward me, and my inner Self, were essentially the same. I experienced an unbroken state of unity. It was clean and peaceful. The experience lingered for some time and then melted back behind the veil. Nevertheless, in that moment, I recognized that if this experience could be enlivened and made permanent, life would be majestic, and human suffering would vanish from our little blue planet, floating in space.

Light Removing Darkness

One Saturday evening, I was watching a television program, and the singer Paul Simon called his friend Art Garfunkel up to the stage, and they sang beautiful melodies together. I was especially moved by *Bridge Over Troubled Waters.* I wondered why they had ever broken up, because their union touched the soul of a generation and added softness to an uncivilized world. As I listened to their beautiful songs that night, I reflected that I wanted to do something in my life that touched the hearts of humanity and helped make a better world. Destiny has a way of becoming reality through our persistence. As time passed, I had forgotten about a job application that I had submitted to a local college. I had previously applied to various colleges, and never imagined it would become an instrument to enliven a dream. One afternoon the phone rang, and it was the Dean of Fine Arts at Sacramento City College. The Dean said: "I read your application and we cannot find anyone to go to Folsom Prison and teach Philosophy, and you are our last hope." I thought this was not the most gracious job offer; however, it was an opportunity for employment, so I said yes, I would do it. I never realized it was going to transform my life and touch the hearts of people around the world.

I drove to Folsom Prison for my orientation meeting. As I pulled up, I saw the old gray thick 40-foot-high walls, gun towers, and iron gates. I experienced the history of the prison and its memories of human despair. As I passed through the gates and began to walk to my meeting, I had an intuition that a special moment in my life was about to happen. The head of the Education Department took me on a tour. He showed me the old hanging room and the adjacent honor block. The doorways had dense black iron doors, decades old, with holes in the doors to allow small currents of air to pass through. I noticed as we walked to the Education Department that everything was metal, iron, and cement. I also became aware of a unique odor that I have found in almost every prison I have visited—the smell of toxic human suffering. I entered the Education Department and saw partitioned rooms with no ceilings where one classroom lecture would interrupt another. In this setting, I taught my first class in philosophy. The prison students were members of the Hell's Angels, Nazi Aryan Brotherhood, Mexican Mafia, Black Guerrilla Family, and a smattering of unaffiliated independents.

At this point, I was only thinking about helping one man at a time reduce his suffering. On my own time, I came to the prison and taught TM to Pat Corum. After practicing the technique for a few moments, he turned to me and said, "This is the first time in 13 and a half years I have felt relaxation and peace." I realized at that moment that there existed an enormous potential to make a statement regarding the value of TM, and reduce institutional violence and human suffering in prisons throughout the world. After Pat had been meditating a couple of weeks, other inmates and staff observed changes in him. They questioned him on how they could learn more about what he was doing.

I had Pat bring me 10 leaders from throughout the prison, and said to him, "We will see what happens!" Pat brought them, and I taught them all TM with the same results.

Maharishi heard about the results and sent me a message through his national leader, Jerry Jarvis. Maharishi said: "Let Folsom Prison be a glass house, a window through which the potential for human transformation can be observed and realized." These words opened a door in which the TM program would eliminate enormous human suffering through the expansion of consciousness. I would then teach the TM program for the next 25 years, throughout the world, from prisons in North America to the Mayan Indian villages of Guatemala. Although much of my work was in the darker corners of society, I could only see beauty because I was walking in harmony with an enlightened vision, provided by an enlightened visionary. Maharishi brought a knowledge that was a gift of light in which darkness could not prevail, or even exist.

A Symphony of Silence contains voices from different dimensions of society, and echoes an opportunity to overcome the challenges facing humanity in any generation. Maharishi (1966) remarks:

> It may be stated emphatically, that unless a man achieves permanent happiness, he will not be contented and satisfied with life. To bring about permanent contentment is the final aim of economics. It therefore appears that the field of economics should not be restricted to material production and consumption alone, but should be extended to bring the greatest happiness of a permanent nature within the reach of mankind. Industry

and business are the foundation of economics, and man is the basis of the industrial success or failure.

As an individual practices the TM technique, his mind and body become stronger and more coordinated. The result is more skillful action. From experiencing greater skill in action, one orients his or her attitude to achievement, rather than failure. Furthermore, the assimilation of new knowledge is fundamental to meeting the challenges of the changing competitive global environment. The TM program improves learning capacity and cognitive capability. Additionally, stress is the greatest challenge to individual and societal success, and meaningful work is essential to a person's enjoyment in life. Equally important is rest. Skill in action depends upon skill in resting, which results in creative thinking and sound health. The unique psycho-physiological state of restful alertness produced during the practice of the TM technique allows a person to remain refreshed and will enhance his ability to fulfill desires.

Timeless Journey

From the housing projects and poverty of Pennsylvania to the luxury of Hollywood, and the boardrooms of the private sector, I have had the good luck of receiving support from volunteers, entertainers, and the founders and family members of W.L. Gore & Associates. I have recognized one simple truth—love is the underlying reality that drives humanity forward. We must recognize that regardless of gender or culture, everyone is interconnected. My personal journey has taken many different roads. The journey has included introducing TM into the California and Vermont prison systems, residential treatment facilities, and jails. Furthermore, I developed several private enterprises to support the TM program in Central America for prisoners, Mayan Indians, and a public trying to emerge from oppressive dictatorships—where a second job might include kidnapping. My personal quest has been to be an instrument to eliminate human suffering for those without the means to help themselves.

From the moment I learned TM, I realized that I had found a path to inner peace that I had been looking for all my life. I recognized I had an obligation to share it with those around me. In 1970, I was preparing to travel to India to become a teacher of TM, and Maharishi's secretary at the time, Davindra, sent me a message that Maharishi was going to be in Humboldt,

California, and I should come there instead, which I did. As I sat in the middle of 1,500 people, I watched Maharishi walk on stage, sit down, and begin to speak. At that moment, I recognized that in Maharishi, I had discovered a living embodiment of knowledge, enlightenment, and truth beyond books. Maharishi opened the evening with a simple gesture, saying: "Let's remove all doubt," and he took questions and provided wisdom for about 12 hours a day for an entire month.

I traveled to the only Teacher Training Course conducted by Maharishi held in the United States, in Estes Park, Colorado. It was held in the middle of winter, and during the course we meditated all day and most of the evening, and spent four hours every night with Maharishi, and eventually I became a teacher. Maharishi had come out of the sublime silence of the Himalayas into the mud of the world with a simple message: "Life is to enjoy, not to suffer." Whenever people tried to ask Maharishi to discuss his life, he would often remark that the story of his life was the story of the Absolute and the relative—the two sides of life in unity. Maharishi would state: "I have no followers, just followers of the truth." In that spirit when about 300 of us became teachers in Estes Park, I understood in my heart that Maharishi was trying to bring happiness to the entire world, and I had an opportunity to play a part.

One evening, near the end of the course, in the middle of winter, I had located a rose that I wanted to give to Maharishi in appreciation for his efforts to bring happiness to the world. I smelled the rose and a person next to me said: "You can't give that to Maharishi; it is like taking a bite out of an apple." I reflected—this was all I had, so I gave the rose to Maharishi without any expectations, and instantly there was an experience of bliss and love that flowed between us, and jolted my skeptical and pragmatic understanding. In that moment, I understood that his reality was beyond my vision, and his actions were an exquisite gift for humanity. The first impulses were silent and wordless, and I found them turning into action with the universal motivation to eliminate human suffering. Thus, it was the force of love that nurtured my motivation to help others.

The beautiful expressions of truth presented by the various contributors to *A Symphony of Silence* are glimpses of individuals fulfilling a promise to a majestic and enlightened man. Maharishi often stated that his duty in the world was the result of fulfilling the desire of his spiritual teacher Guru Dev: to eliminate human suffering and awaken humanity to their potential. Maharishi's infinite vision was hidden in a human nervous system that emanated unconditional love. I spent decades teaching individuals to transcend in the dark corners of the world. I was often asked how I could handle dealing with the stress. As I reflect back, I can honestly say it was bliss, because I believe the unconditional love and gratitude I had for Maharishi left no room in my heart for anything but bliss in this act of service to humanity. Because in truth, I was also serving humanity, one person at a time, and simultaneously awakening to my inner Self, all the while observing that unbounded love reflecting back through others, regardless of the external environment.

Vision for a Better World

Every generation has aspired to enrich life and to prepare a bright and fulfilling future for its children. Because of Maharishi's wisdom and insights, we have an opportunity to facilitate the creation of a peaceful world free from suffering. As we watch the daily news, we observe exploding violence around the globe, as new generations cry out for freedom. The destiny of mankind is in the hands of the leaders of society, and yet governmental leadership is also in the hands of the collective consciousness. The human environment is essentially social. Elimination of negative influences such as crime, war, disease, and poverty will be accomplished by nourishing the creativity and intelligence within the individual.

Nations remain operating under the illusion that force and overt power will correct the wrongs in the world. Life-supporting behavior within the individual and society can only be created by raising individual and collective consciousness. The common aim of any evolved and civilized legal system is justice for all members of society. To obtain justice requires clarity of mind, cognitive acuity, and sensitivity to the essential nature of a compassionate society.

One of the most valuable features of the TM program is in its appeal to global cultural diversity. As long as large numbers of its citizens are alienated, apathetic, impoverished, or preoccupied with a fragmented or overspecialized view of national goals, no coherent plan of action will ever be found that will create a satisfied population. The individual is the basis of the social order and his or her capacity to function can easily be improved on all levels simultaneously. Maharishi in Lucerne, Switzerland on January 12, 1975 offered the following vision:

> On the basis of scientific verification, we are recognizing the objective validation of our teaching in the world. Experience of consciousness has been our field of specialization. It is ignorance that is the basis of all suffering, all weakness. Once we are in the light of life, life will not be lived in suffering. Life will not have to move through problems. We are not unmindful of the situation in the world. We know that the world is sunk in the deep darkness of ignorance. What we see through the window of science is the coming of the dawn. When only a small area of the whole room is lighted, the whole room is lighted. And what is a bulb? It is a very small filament. How much is that in relation to the whole volume of the room? A very insignificant area—we might not see at all were it not lighted. Yet it does light. And in that way one person, one slightly enlightened person, may illuminate a whole society.

As was highlighted throughout this book, Maharishi was a man of humble simplicity, and when he was asked by a scientist in an interview what he wanted to be remembered for, he responded with a modest response: "Nothing." Nevertheless I, along with millions of others, choose not only to remember Maharishi, but to carry forward his vision of a better world, free from suffering and embraced by love.

Acknowledgments

My greatest debt is to His Holiness Maharishi Mahesh Yogi. His wisdom and unconditional love have been a guiding light throughout my life. I want to express my gratitude and respect to Dominique Ellis, not only for her contribution to the book but for her attention to detail, without which this book would not have been completed. My appreciation also goes to Gustavo Martinez, for translating, editing, and formatting into Spanish *A Symphony of Silence: An Enlightened Vision (Sinfonía del Silencio: Una Visión Iluminada)*. Additionally, I want to recognize George Foster of FosterCovers.com for his brilliant cover design; he captured visually the essence of the book. I am grateful to Fran Clark for her excellent proofreading and editing, along with Elisa Maria Argiro and Cynthia Johnson for their additional editorial suggestions, and Elizabeth Cline for indexing the book, and for her Photoshop contributions.

I am indebted to the contributors to the book, for their creativity, vision, artwork, and generous service to society and culture throughout the years: Paul Horn, Rhoda Orme-Johnson, Ph.D., Debbie Arnold, Jonathan Shear, Ph.D., Jerry W. Jarvis, Rev. Roger Wm. Johnson, Ph.D., Cynthia Johnson, Brother Elias Marechal, Michael Willbanks, Evan Finkelstein, Ph.D., David W. Orme-Johnson, Ph.D., Arthur John Anderson, J.D., LL.M., Susan W. Gore, Ann Mortifee, Helen Boyce, Ayida Mthembu, Candace Martin, J.D., Jennifer Hawthorne, Marisa Carbonnel, Claudia Cline, Elizabeth Cline, Patricia Cline, Stephen Ulicny, Marty Howe, and Julia Benczedi.

I wish to acknowledge the following professionals in government, law, corrections, and entertainment who supported TM correctional and substance abuse projects throughout the years: Rudy Deleon, Kurleigh King, Ph.D., The Honorable David Mason, Richard Wright, John Carpenter, Claude Melanson, Lynn Walthers, Karen Ross-Sheldon, C. Blakely, Nancy Watkins, founding president of the American Correctional Association Don Hutto, Mike Love, Doug Henning, Steven Collins, Charlie Lutes, and Andy Kaufman. I am grateful to the other scientists and educators who have provided the empirical research and intellectual understanding to validate the benefits of the TM program in society: Keith Wallace, Ph.D., John Hagelin, Ph.D., Bevan Morris, Ph.D., Bob Roth, Catherine R. Bleick, Ph.D., Allan Abrams, Ph.D., and Charles Alexander, Ph.D.

I want to extend a special thanks to the incarcerated men and women who learned the TM program, for their commitment to their personal transformation, including the pioneers of freedom behind bars: Pat Corum, Frank Billingsley, Charles Hamilton, and Rex Spross. I want to express my deepest appreciation and respect to David Lynch for creating his foundation to carry the message of Maharishi to help and develop consciousness in those sectors of society most in need.

About the Author

The professional career of George A. Ellis has been eclectic, embracing the private, nonprofit, human development, and educational sectors. He introduced, developed, and taught the first course on the Science of Creative Intelligence for general-education credit in the Interdisciplinary Studies Department at California State University, Sacramento. Ellis received international recognition as a Director for the Institute for Social Rehabilitation, and for his pioneering research introducing the Transcendental Meditation program into the California Youth and Adult Correctional Agency, including Folsom and San Quentin Prisons. In partnership with the private sector Ellis introduced stress reduction research projects on the TM program for staff and inmate development in the Vermont Department of Corrections. At the request of Maharishi Mahesh Yogi, Ellis created educational teaching manuals and videotapes for global rehabilitation projects, published scientific papers, and authored numerous articles about the TM program and human development. Additionally, in collaboration with various philanthropists, he co-financed, produced, and hosted national educational documentary productions on Leadership and the Science of Creative Intelligence. His first book, *Inside Folsom Prison*, was translated into Spanish as *Hacia La Libertad*, and in French as *Reappendre La Liberte*.

Ellis developed entrepreneurial private-sector companies, projects, and profit centers in various countries including the United States, Canada, Guatemala, Argentina, Brazil, and Mexico. He also was involved with development projects for the Mayan Indians in Guatemala, which included building and expanding educational institutions from elementary through high school, agricultural training, and other programs for human development.

Ellis has lectured internationally, including conferences in Spain, France, Germany, and Italy with members of the International Court. He has worked with corporate directors, government officials, and the entertainment industry to financially support the TM program in facilitating the elimination of human suffering.

Academically, Ellis obtained an A.S. in Biology from Mercer County Community College, Trenton, New Jersey; Bachelor's in Philosophy and Master's in Art History from California State University, Sacramento; an M.B.A. and doctoral studies in Management and Organizational Leadership, University of Phoenix. He has received various honors and academic certifications in Public Administration and Criminology based on his work in the fields of law, justice, and rehabilitation.

Ellis considers his meeting Maharishi and becoming a teacher of the Transcendental Meditation program to be a great honor and his most important professional and personal accomplishment. Maharishi's wisdom and programs enrich the author's work in business and education, and provide tools to improve the quality of life. The book, *A Symphony of Silence: An Enlightened Vision*, is a tribute to this wisdom, and encourages humanity to look within and locate a foundation for living a fulfilled life.

Seelisberg, Switzerland 1978, His Holiness Maharishi Mahesh Yogi and George A. Ellis©

References

A Jossey-Bass Reader (2003). *Business leadership* (1st ed.). San Francisco, California: Jossey-Bass

Alexander, C. N. (1989). Seven states of consciousness: Unfolding the full potential of the cosmic psyche in individual life through Maharishi's Vedic Psychology. *Modern Science and Vedic Science, 2*(4), 325-371.

Alexander, C. N., Barnes, V. A., Schneider, R. H., Langer, E. J., Newman, R. I., Chandler, H. M., Rainforth, M. (1996). A randomized controlled trial of stress reduction on cardiovascular and all-cause mortality in the elderly: Results of 8 and 15 year follow-ups. *Circulation, 93*(3), P19.

Alexander, C. N., Davies, J. L., Dixon, C. A., Dillbeck, M. C., Druker, S. M., Oetzel, R. M., . . . Orme-Johnson, D. W. (1990). *Growth of higher states of consciousness: Maharishi's Vedic Psychology of human development.* New York: Oxford University Press.

Alexander, C. N., Druker, S. M., & Langer, E. J. (1990). Major issues in the exploration of adult growth. In C. N. Alexander & E. J. Langer (Eds.), *Higher stages of human development: perspectives on adult growth.* New York: Oxford University Press.

Alexander, C. N., Langer, E. J., Newman, R. I., Chandler, H. M., & Davies, J. L. (1989). Transcendental Meditation, mindfulness, and longevity: An experimental study with the elderly. *Journal of Personality and Social Psychology, 57*(6), 950-964.

Alexander, C. N., & Orme-Johnson, D. W. (2003). Walpole study of the TM program in maximum security prisoners II: Longitudinal study of development and psychopathology. *Journal of Offender Rehabilitation, 36*(1-4), 127-160.

Alexander, C. N., Rainforth, M. V., Frank, P. R., Grant, J. D., Von Stade, C., & Walton, K. G. (2003). Walpole study of the Transcendental Meditation program in maximum security prisoners III: Reduced recidivism. *Journal of Offender Rehabilitation, 36*(3), 161-180.

Alexander, C. N., Walton, K. G., & Goodman, R. S. (2003). Walpole study of the TM program in maximum security prisoners I: Cross-sectional differences in development and psychopathology. *Journal of Offender Rehabilitation, 36*(1), 97-125.

Alexander, C. N., Walton, K. G., Orme-Johnson, D. W., & Goodman, R. S. (2003). Transcendental Meditation in criminal rehabilitation and crime prevention. *Journal of Offender Rehabilitation, 36*(1/2/3/4), 1-383.

Assimakis, P., & Dillbeck, M. C. (1995). Time series analysis of improved quality of life in Canada: Social change, collective consciousness, and the TM-Sidhi program. *Psychological Report, 76*, 1171-1193.

Babcock, M. D. (1996). *This is my Father's world* [Hymn]. In Hawkinson, J.R., Phelan, J.E., & Wiburg, G.V. (Eds.), *The covenant hymnal: A worshipbook.* Chicago, IL: Covenant Publications.

Badawi, K., Wallace, R. K., Orme-Johnson, D. W., & Rouzeré, A.-M. (1984). Electrophysiologic characteristics of respiratory suspension periods occurring during the practice of the Transcendental Meditation program. *Psychosomatic Medicine, 46*(3), 267-276.

Ballou, D. (1977). The Transcendental Meditation program at Stillwater Prison. In D. W. Orme-Johnson & J. T. Farrow (Eds.), *Scientific research on Maharishi's Transcendental Meditation programme: Collected papers* (Vol. 1, pp. 713-718). Rheinweiler, West Germany: MERU Press.

Banquet, J. P. (1972). EEG and meditation [Journal]. *Electroencephalography and Clinical Neurophysiology, 33*, 449-458.

Banquet J. P. (1973). Spectral analysis of the EEG in meditation [Journal]. *Electroencephalography and Clinical Neurophysiology, 35*, 143-151.

Barnes, V., Schneider, R., Alexander, C., Rainforth, M., Salerno, J., Kondwani, K., & Staggers, F. (2005). Impact of Transcendental Meditation on mortality in older African-Americans with hypertension—Eight-year follow-up. *Journal of Social Behavior and Personality, 17*(1), 201-216.

Barnes V.A., Kapuku G., Treiber F.A. Impact of Transcendental Meditation on Left Ventricular Mass in African-American Adolescents. eCAM 2012. 2012;2012:1-6. Retrieved from http://www.truthabouttm.org/truth/TMResearch/NewStudies/HeartHealth/index.cfm

Baxter, R. (1996). *O holy angels bright* [Hymn]. In Hawkinson, J.R., Phelan, J.E., & Wiburg, G.V. (Eds.), *The covenant hymnal: A worshipbook.* Chicago, IL: Covenant Publications.

Bleick, C. R., & Abrams, A. I. (1987). The Transcendental Meditation program and criminal recidivism in California. *Journal of Criminal Justice, 15(3),* 211-230.

Brooks, J., & Scarano, T. (1985). Transcendental Meditation and the treatment of post-Vietnam adjustment. *Journal of Counseling and Development, 64,* 212-215.

Campbell, A. (1973) *Seven states of consciousness.* London, Victor Gollancz Ltd.

CBEA. (2002). Highlights by conference speakers. http://www.cbeprograms. org/conference/highlights.html.

Chalmers, R., Clements, G., Schenkluhn, H., & Weinless, M. (Eds.). (1988a). *Scientific research on Maharishi's Transcendental Meditation and TM-Sidhi programme: Collected papers (Vol. 2-4).* Vlodrop, The Netherlands: MVU Press.

Chalmers, R., Clements, G., Schenkluhn, H., & Weinless, M. (Eds.). (1988b). *Scientific research on Maharishi's Transcendental Meditation and TM-Sidhi programme: Collected papers (Vol. 2-4).* Vlodrop, The Netherlands: MVU Press.

Chan, Wing-tsit. (1963). *A source book in Chinese philosophy.* Princeton, N.J.: Princeton University Press.

Crowe, K. (2005). *Speaking in the silence* [Sermon]. Retrieved from: http://www. firstpres-charlotte.org/sermons/20051026-1200.pdf

David Lynch Foundation for Consciousness-Based Education and World Peace. (2011). www.davidlynchfoundation.org

Davies, J. L., & Alexander, C. N. (2005). Alleviating political violence through reducing collective tension: Impact assessment analysis of the Lebanon war. *Journal of Social Behavior and Personality, 17(1),* 285-338.

Dillbeck, M. C. (1990). Test of a field theory of consciousness and social change: Time series analysis of participation in the TM-Sidhi program and reduction of violent death in the U.S. *Social Indicators Research, 22,* 399-418.

Dillbeck, M. C. (Ed.). (2011). *Scientific research on Maharishi's Transcendental Meditation and TM-Sidhi programme: Collected Papers (Vol. 6).* Vlodrop, The Netherlands: Maharishi Vedic University Press.

Dillbeck, M. C., & Abrams, A. I. (1987). The application of the Transcendental Meditation program to corrections: Meta-analysis. *International Journal of Comparative and Applied Criminal Justice, 11*(1), 111-132.

Dillbeck, M. C., Banus, C. B., Polanzi, C., & Landrith III, G. S. (1988). Test of a field model of consciousness and social change: Transcendental Meditation and TM-Sidhi program and decreased urban crime. *The Journal of Mind and Behavior, 9*(4), 457-486.

Dillbeck, M. C., Cavanaugh, K. L., Glenn, T., Orme-Johnson, D. W., & Mittlefehldt, V. (1987). Consciousness as a field: The Transcendental Meditation and TM-Sidhi program and changes in social indicators. *The Journal of Mind and Behavior, 8*(1), 67-104.

Dillbeck, M. C., Landrith III, G., & Orme-Johnson, D. W. (1981). The Transcendental Meditation program and crime rate changes in a sample of forty-eight cities. *Journal of Crime and Justice, 4,* 25-45.

Dillbeck, M. C., Orme-Johnson, D. W., & Wallace, R. K. (1981). Frontal EEG coherence, H-reflex recovery, concept learning, and the TM-Sidhi program. *International Journal of Neuroscience, 15*(3), 151-157.

Dillbeck, M. C., & Rainforth, M. V. (1996). *Impact assessment analysis of behavioral quality of life indices: Effects of group practice of the Transcendental Meditation and TM-Sidhi program.* Paper presented at the American Statistical Association. Proceedings of the social statistics section, Alexandria, VA.

Ellis, G.A., & Corum, P. (1994). Removing the motivator: A holistic solution to substance abuse. In D. F. O'Connell and C. N. Alexander (Eds.), *Self recovery: Treating addictions using Transcendental Meditation and Maharishi Ayur-veda* (1st ed., pp. 271-296). New York: The Haworth Press, Inc.

Ellis, G.A. (1983). *Inside folsom prison: Unified Field based rehabilitation* (2nd ed.). Burlington, Vermont: Accord Publications

Ellis, G. J. (1974). *Analysis of the creative process of Vincent van Gogh in terms of internal necessity and creative intelligence* (Unpublished master's dissertation). California State University, Sacramento, California.

Emerson, R. W. (1841). The oversoul. Retrieved from http://moonchalice. com/emerson_oversoul.htm

Finkelstein, E.I. (2005). *Universal principles of life expressed in Maharishi Vedic Science and in the scriptures and writings of Judaism, Christianity, and Islam* (Unpublished doctoral dissertation). MUM, Fairfield, Iowa

Finkelstein, E. (2011, June). Speech given at the golden flag ceremony. In J. Hagelin, *Speech*. Symposium conducted at the Flag Day, Fairfield, Iowa.

Forem, J. (1973). *Transcendental Meditation: Maharishi Mahesh Yogi and the Science of Creative Intelligence*. New York, N.Y., E.P. Dutton & Company, Inc.

Fromm, E. (1956). *The art of loving* (1st ed.). New York, NY: Harper and Row.

Gelderloos, P., Goddard, P. H. I., Ahlstrom, H. H., & Jacoby, R. (1987). Cognitive orientation towards positive values in advanced participants of the TM and TM-Sidhi program. *Perceptual Motor Skills, 64,* 1003-1012

Glaser, J. L., Brind, J. L., Vogelman, J. H., Eisner, M. J., Dillbeck, M. C., Wallace, R. K., . . . Orentreich, N. (1992). Elevated serum dehydroepiandrosterone sulfate levels in practitioners of Transcendental Meditation (TM) and TM-Sidhi programs. *Journal of Behavioral Medicine, 15*(4), 327-341.

Graetz, H. R. (1963). *The symbolic language of Vincent van Gogh* (1st ed.). New York, NY: McGraw-Hill Book Company, Inc.

Grof, S. (1988). *Human survival and consciousness evolution*. Albany, N.Y.: State University of New York Press

Hagelin, J. S. (1987). Is consciousness the Unified Field? A field theorist's perspective. *Modern Science and Vedic Science, 1*(1), 29-88.

Hagelin, J. S. (1989). Restructuring Physics from its foundation in light of Maharishi's Vedic Science. *Modern Science and Vedic Science, 3*(1), 3-72.

Hagelin, J. S., Rainforth, M. V., Orme-Johnson, D. W., Cavanaugh, K. L., Alexander, C. N., Shatkin, S. F., . . . Ross, E. (1999). Effects of group practice of the Transcendental Meditation program on preventing violent crime in Washington D.C.: Results of the national demonstration project, June-July, 1993. *Social Indicators Research, 47*(2), 153-201.

Harung, H. S., Travis, F., Pensgaard, A. M., Boes, R., Cook-Greuter, S., & Daley, K. (2011). Higher psycho-physiological refinement in world-class Norwegian athletes: brain measures of performance capacity. *Scandinavian Journal of Medicine & Science in Sports, 21*(1), 32-41. doi: 10.1111/j.1600-0838.2009.01007.x

Harvey, A. (1998) *Teachings of the Christian mystics*. Boston: Shambhala Publications.

Hatchard, G. D., Deans, A. J., Cavanaugh, K. L., & Orme-Johnson, D. W. (1996). The Maharishi Effect: A model for social improvement: Time series analysis of a phase transition to reduced crime in Merseyside metropolitan area. *Psychology, Crime, & Law, 2*(3), 165-175.

Herron, R., & Cavanaugh, K. (2005). Can the Transcendental Meditation program reduce the medical expenditures of older people? A longitudinal cost reduction study in Canada. *Journal of Social Behavior and Personality, 17,* 415-442.

Herron, R., & Hillis, S. (2000). The impact of the Transcendental Meditation program on government payments to physicians in Quebec: An update. *American Journal of Health Promotion, 14*(5), 284-293.

Herron, R. E. (2011). Changes in physician costs among high-cost Transcendental Meditation practitioners compared with high-cost non-practitioners over 5 years. *American Journal of Health Promotion, 26*(1), 56-60. doi: 10.4278/ajhp.100729-ARB-25.

Hesse, H. (1968). *Narcissus and Goldmund.* New York, N.Y.: Bantam Books.

Hesse, H. (1951). *Siddhartha.* New York, N.Y.: Random House.

James, W. (1958). *The varieties of religious experience.* New York: Mentor-NAL.

Jex, S.M., & Britt, T.W. (2008). *Organizational psychology: A scientist-practitioner approach* (2nd ed.). Retrieved from https://ecampus.phoenix.edu/content/eBookLibrary2/content?eReader.aspx

Johnson, C.E. (1987). *An exegesis of John 8:31-32: Knowing the truth as union with the divine.* (Unpublished paper). Harvard Divinity School, Cambridge, MA.

Johnson, R.J. (1964). *The concept of responsible trust in the theology of John Baillie.* (Unpublished doctoral dissertation). Harvard University, Cambridge, MA. Dissertation summary in *Harvard Theological Review,* Vol. 57, No. 4, Oct., 1964. Retrieved from http://www.jstor.org/stable/i267043

Kandinsky, W. (1947). *Concerning the spiritual in art* (9th ed.). New York, N. Y.: Wittenborn Schultz

Kaplan, A. (1982). *Meditation and Kabbalah.* New York: Samuel Weiser, Inc.

Katz, V. (2011). *Conversations with Maharishi: Maharishi Mahesh Yogi speaks about the full development of human consciousness* (Vol. 1). Fairfield, Iowa, USA: Maharishi University of Management Press.

Kimble, C. J. (1975, Spring). Transcendental Meditation in the youth authority [Journal]. *California Youth Authority Quarterly, 28*(1).

Lipsett, S., & Miller, S. (1998). *After death: How people around the world map the journey after life* (1st ed.). New York, NY: Touchstone.

Lynch, David. (2006). *Catching the big fish: Meditation, consciousness, and creativity.* New York, N.Y.: Jeremy P. Tarcher/Penguin.

Maharishi Academy of Total Knowledge. (2012). Message from founder. http://www.maharishiacademy.org/about/founder.html

Maharishi Ayurveda Health Center. (2011). http://www.ayurvedalancaster.com

Maharishi Mahesh Yogi. (1973). *The science of being and art of living* (3rd ed.). Fairfield, Iowa: Maharishi International University Press.

Maharishi Mahesh Yogi. (1967). *Maharishi Mahesh Yogi on the Bhagavad-Gita: A new translation and commentary, chapters 1-6.* New York, N.Y.: Penguin Book, Inc.

Maharishi Mahesh Yogi. (1977). *Creating an ideal society.* West Germany: Maharishi European Research University Press.

Maharishi Mahesh Yogi. (1986). *Life supported by natural law.* Washington, D.C.: Age of Enlightenment Press.

Maharishi Mahesh Yogi. (1994). *Vedic knowledge for everyone.* Vlodrop, Netherlands: Maharishi Vedic University Press.

Maharishi Mahesh Yogi. (1995a). *Maharishi's Vedic approach to health.* Vlodrop, Holland: Maharishi Vedic University Press.

Maharishi Mahesh Yogi. (1995b). *Maharishi forum of natural law and national law for doctors.* India: Age of Enlightenment Publications.

Maharishi Mahesh Yogi. (1996). *Maharishi's absolute theory of defence.* New Delhi: Age of Enlightenment Publications.

Mason, L. I., Alexander, C. N., Travis, F. T., Marsh, G., Orme-Johnson, D. W., Gackenbach, J., . . . Walton, K. G. (1997). Electrophysiological correlates of higher states of consciousness during sleep in long-term practitioners of the Transcendental Meditation program. *Sleep, 20*(2), 102-110.

Mason, L. I., & Orme-Johnson, D. W. (2010). Transcendental Consciousness wakes up in dreaming and deep sleep. *International Journal of Dream Research, 3*(1), 28-32.

Menninger, MD, K. (1969). *The crime of punishment* (1st ed.). New York, N.Y.: The Viking Press.

Mortifee, A. (2010). *In love with the mystery* (1st ed.). Vancouver, BC, Canada: Eskova Enterprises Ltd.

Nader, T. (1995). *Human physiology—Expression of Veda and the Vedic literature.* Vlodrop, Holland: Maharishi University Press.

Nidich, S. I., Ryncarz, R. A., Abrams, A. I., Orme-Johnson, D. W., & Wallace, R. K. (1983). Kohlbergian moral perspective responses, EEG coherence, and the Transcendental Meditation and TM-Sidhi program. *Journal of Moral Education, 12*(3), 166-173.

O'Connell, D. F., & Alexander, C. N. (1994a). Introduction: Recovery from addictions using Transcendental Meditation and Maharishi Ayur-Veda. In D. F. O'Connell & C. N. Alexander (Eds.), *Self recovery—Treating addictions using Transcendental Meditation and Maharishi Ayur-Veda* (pp. 1-10). Binghamton, NY: Harrington Park Press.

O'Connell, D. F., & Alexander, C. N. (Eds.). (1994b). *Self Recovery—Treating addictions using Transcendental Meditation and Maharishi Ayur-Veda*. Binghamton, NY: Harrington Park Press.

Orme-Johnson, D. W. (1973). Autonomic stability and Transcendental Meditation. *Psychosomatic Medicine, 35*, 341-349.

Orme-Johnson, D. W. (1987). Medical care utilization and the Transcendental Meditation program. *Psychosomatic Medicine, 49*, 493-507.

Orme-Johnson, D. W. (2003). Preventing crime through the Maharishi Effect. *Journal of Offender Rehabiliation, 36*(1/2/3/4), 257-282.

Orme-Johnson, D. W. (2011). Commentary: The use of Meditation in corrections. *International Journal of Offender Therapy and Comparative Criminology, 55*(4), 662-664.

Orme-Johnson, D. W., Alexander, C. N., & Davies, J. L. (1990). The effects of the Maharishi Technology of the Unified Field: Reply to a methodological critique. *Journal of Conflict Resolution, 34*, 756–768.

Orme-Johnson, D. W., Alexander, C. N., Davies, J. L., Chander, H. M., & Larimore, W. E. (1988). International peace project: The effects of the Maharishi Technology of the Unified Field. *Journal of Conflict Resolution, 32*(4), 776-812.

Orme-Johnson, D. W., Clements, G., Haynes, C. T., & Badawi, K. (1977). Higher states of consciousness: EEG coherence, creativity, and experiences of the sidhis. In D. W. Orme-Johnson, & Farrow, J. (Ed.), *Scientific research on Maharishi's Transcendental Meditation programme: Collected papers (Vol. 1)*. Rheinweiler, Germany: MERU Press.

Orme-Johnson, D. W., Dillbeck, M. C., & Alexander, C. N. (2003). Preventing terrorism and international conflict: Effects of large assemblies of participants in the Transcendental Meditation and TM-Sidhi programs. *Journal of Offender Rehabilitation, 36,* 283-302.

Orme-Johnson, D. W., & Farrow, J. T. (1977). *Scientific research on Maharishi's Transcendental Meditation programme: Collected papers* (2nd ed.). Weggis, Switzerland: Maharishi European Research University Press.

Orme-Johnson, D. W., & Gelderloos, P. (1988a). The long-term effects of the Maharishi Technology of the Unified Field on the quality of life in the United States (1960 to 1983). *Social Science Perspectives Journal, 2*(4), 127-146.

Orme-Johnson, D. W., & Gelderloos, P. (1988b). Topographic EEG brain mapping during Yogic Flying. *International Journal of Neuroscience, 38*(3-4), 427-434.

Orme-Johnson, D. W., & Haynes, C. T. (1981). EEG phase coherence, pure consciousness, creativity and TM-Sidhi experiences. *International Journal of Neuroscience, 13,* 211-217.

Orme-Johnson, D. W., & Oates, R. M. (2009). A field-theoretic view of consciousness: Reply to critics. *Journal of Scientific Exploration, 32*(2), 139-166.

Orme-Johnson, D. W., Schneider, R. H., Son, Y. D., Nidich, S., & Cho, Z. H. (2006). Neuroimaging of meditation's effect on brain reactivity to pain. *Neuroreport, 17*(12), 1359-1363. doi: 10.1097/01.wnr.0000233094.67289.a800001756-200608210-00026 [pii]

Otto, R. (1958). *The idea of the holy* (2nd ed.). New York, N.Y.: Oxford University Press, USA

Prince II, HT. (1995). Moral development in individuals. In J.T. Wren (Ed.), *The leader's companion: Insights on leadership through the ages* (pp. 484-491). New York, NY: The Free Press.

Rainforth, M. V., Bleick, C., Alexander, C. N., & Cavanaugh, K. L. (2003). The Transcendental Meditation program and criminal recidivism in Folsom State prisoners: A 15-year follow-up study. *Journal of Offender Rehabilitation, 36,* 181-204.

Rosenthal, J., Grosswald, S., Ross, R., & Rosenthal, N. (2011). Effects of Transcendental Meditation (TM) in Veterans of Operation Enduring Freedom (OEF) and Operation Iraqi Freedom (OIF) with Posttraumatic Stress Disorder (PTSD): A Pilot Study. *Military Medicine, 176*(6), 626.

Russell, B. (2000). *The autobiography of Bertrand Russell.* London: Routledge

Sartre, J.P. (1964). *Nausea.* New York, N.Y.: New Directions.

Schneerson, M. M. (2011). The ten days of Teshuvah. Retrieved from http://www.chabad.org/library/article_cdo/aid/149008/jewish/The-Ten-Days-of-Teshuvah.htm.%202011

Schneider, R. H., Alexander, C. N., Staggers, F., Rainforth, M. V., Salerno, J. W., Hartz, A., . . . Nidich, S. I. (2005). Long-term effects of stress reduction on mortality in persons ≥ 55 years of age with systemic hypertension. *American Journal of Cardiology, 95*(9), 1060-1064.

Smith, M. (1994). *Readings from the mystics of Islam.* Westport: Pir Publications.

So, K. T., & Orme-Johnson, D. W. (2001). Three randomized experiments on the holistic longitudinal effects of the Transcendental Meditation technique on cognition. *Intelligence, 29*(5), 419-440

Thomas, V., &Lamb, C. (1964). *Creativity in the arts* (1st ed.). Englewood Cliffs, N.J., Prentice Hall, Inc.

Thompson, R. (1936). *The peaceable kingdom* [Choral Work]. Retrieved from http://harvardmagazine.com/2001/07/randall-thompson.html

Thoreau, H. D. (1985). *Henry David Thoreau: A week on the Concord and Merrimack Rivers / Walden; Or, Life in the Woods / The Maine Woods / Cape Cod.* New York, N.Y.: Library of America

Thurman, H. (1953). *Meditations of the heart* (1st ed.). New York, N.Y.: Harper and Row.

Thurman, H. (1971). *The search for common ground* (1st ed.). Richmond, Virginia: Friends United Press.

Thurman, H. (1978). *Deep is the hunger.* Richmond, Virginia: Friends United Press.

Thurman, H. (1981). *With head and heart: The autobiography of Howard Thurman.* Mariner Books.

Thurman, H. (1984). *For the inward journey.* Richmond, Virginia: Friends United Press.

Tillich, P.J. (1948). *The shaking of the foundations.* New York, N.Y.: Charles Scribner's Sons.

Tillich, P.J. (1951). *Systematic theology: Volume one.* Chicago: University of Chicago Press.

Tillich, P. J. (1955). *The new being* (1st ed.). New York, N.Y.: Charles Scribner's Sons.

Tillich, P. J. (1963). *The eternal now.* New York, N.Y.: Charles Scribner's Sons.

Torrey, B. (1906). *The writings of Henry David Thoreau: Journal, ed.* (1st ed). Retrieved from http://books.google.com/books/about/The_Writings_ of_Henry_David_Thoreau_Jour.html?id=X_YRAAAAYAAJ

Travis, F., Haaga, D. A., Hagelin, J., Tanner, M., Nidich, S., Gaylord-King, C., . . . Schneider, R. H. (2009). Effects of Transcendental Meditation practice on brain functioning and stress reactivity in college students. *International Journal of Psychophysiology, 71*(2), 170-176. doi: S0167-8760(08)00808-8 [pii]10.1016/j.ijpsycho.2008.09.007

Travis, F. T., & Arenander, A. (2006). Cross-sectional and longitudinal study of effects of Transcendental Meditation practice on interhemispheric frontal asymmetry and frontal coherence. *International Journal of Neuroscience, 116*(12), 1519-1538. doi: 10.1080/00207450600575482

Travis, F. T., & Orme-Johnson, D. W. (1990). EEG coherence and power during Yogic Flying. *International Journal of Neuroscience, 54*(1-2), 1-12.

Wallace, R. K. (1970). The physiological effects of Trancendental Meditation: A proposed fourth major state of consciousness. In D. W. Orme-Johnson & J. T. Farrow (Eds.), *Scientific research on Maharishi's Transcendental Meditation Programme: Collected papers* (2 ed., Vol. 1, pp. 43-78). Livingston Manor, New York: MERU.

Wallace, R. K. (1970). Physiological effects of Transcendental Meditation. *Science, 167,* 1751–1754.

Wallace, R. K. (1972). The physiology of Meditation. *Scientific American, 226,* 84-90.

Wallace, R. K., Benson, H., & Wilson, A. F. (1971). A wakeful hypometabolic physiologic state. *American Journal of Physiology, 221,* 795-799.

Wallace, R. K., Dillbeck, M., Jacobe, E., & Harrington, B. (1982). The effects of the Transcendental Meditation and TM-Sidhi program on the aging process. *International Journal of Neuroscience, 16,* 53-58.

Wallace, R. K., Orme-Johnson, D. W., & Dillbeck, M. C. (Eds.), (1990). *Scientific research on Maharishi's Transcendental Meditation and TM-Sidhi Program: Collected Papers, Vol. 5.* Fairfield, Iowa: MIU Press.

Washington University Law. (2011). Honorable David C. Mason. http://law.wustl.edu/alumni/pages.aspx?id=161

Wesley, C. (1996). *Love divine, all loves excelling* [Hymn]. In Hawkinson, J.R., Phelan, J.E., & Wiburg, G.V. (Eds.), *The Covenant hymnal: A worshipbook.* Chicago, IL: Covenant Publications.

Whittier, J.G. (1996). *Dear Father of all humankind* [Hymn]. In Hawkinson, J.R., Phelan, J.E., & Wiburg, G.V. (Eds.), *The Covenant hymnal: A worshipbook.* Chicago, IL: Covenant Publications.

Appendix A

Commentary by Maharishi on education, and excerpts from the documentary: *Leadership and Unified Field Based Rehabilitation.*

Maharishi

The potential of every student is infinite. The time of student life should serve to unfold that infinite potential so that every individual becomes a vibrant center of Total Knowledge. We are happy to present to the world an ideal system of education, where not only will the intellect be fed and satisfied, but the basis of the intellect, the field of pure intelligence, the source and basis of life, will be realized by everyone. The result will be a life that is not baseless, but that has a profound basis in the lively field of all possibilities.

Developing the full creative potential of consciousness makes the student a master of his life—he spontaneously commands situations and circumstances. His behavior is always nourishing to himself and everyone around him. He has the natural ability to fulfill his own interests without jeopardizing the interests of others. Such an ideal, enlightened individual is the result of ideal education—my Consciousness-Based education (Maharishi Academy of Total Knowledge, 2012).

Bevan Morris, Ph.D.

Dr. Bevan Morris, President, MUM; President, Global Country of World Peace; President, Maharishi World Peace Fund

What we have with TM at MUM is a way of not only eliminating existing stresses in the nervous system of students, inmates, correctional institutions, and people in any sphere of life, but giving an education that trains them not to perform those actions which create stress in their life.

Keith Wallace, Ph.D.

Dr. Keith Wallace was the first president of MIU, now MUM, and a pioneering researcher on the TM technique.

After the person meditates, he feels better—his physiology is more expanded. Instead of a physiology that is cramped, and his mind saying: there are so many problems, so many difficulties, anger is expressed—now he has a physiology of all possibilities. The mind flows smoothly, there is a lot of creativity in terms of the individual, and he just sees things clearly.

This is not just a mood, it is not just an idea; it is clearly demonstrated in terms of biochemical studies that as a result of TM there are definite changes, such as neurotransmitters in the brain, in the hormone system, and metabolism. At almost every level there are profound changes, which can be directly associated with a more creative and positive style of behavior.

TM is a technique that allows the individual to balance the different aspects of the physiology. It is impossible to stop bad habits because if the individual is unsatisfied and if there is some deep lack in him, he will never stop these bad habits. The only way to strengthen the individual on a physiological level is from inside and spontaneously the individual finds he does not want to do these things anymore. Several hundred studies have verified the holistic effect of the benefits of the practice of the TM technique, and the more advanced TM-Sidhi program. A number of these programs have shown clearly that there is a marked physiological improvement in the individual's response to stress. In a correctional environment there is obviously an enormous amount of stress. It is well known that stress speeds up the aging process.

Recent research on the TM and TM-Sidhi programs has shown that these techniques can reverse the whole process of biological aging. When we talk about aging, we can distinguish between chronological aging, which is measured in terms of the number of years, and biological aging, which is measured quite differently—it is measured in certain physiological functions. We know that chronological and biological aging generally proceed together. We anticipate as the person grows older there are certain changes: blood pressure goes up, cholesterol levels increase, along with a loss of memory and an increase in various sleep disturbances. With the regular practice of the TM program these problems have been shown to decrease. In fact there are about 30 or more different measures of the whole process of aging that have been shown to improve with the TM and TM-Sidhi programs.

One study that summarizes all of these results showed specifically through a measure of biological aging that people who have been practicing the TM program for over five years had an average biological age of 12 years younger than their chronological age. This is clear evidence that the aging process is either slowed down or reversed through the TM technique. I would expect that it would be a great relief to anyone who is in the situation of high stress in a prison setting, where the whole process of aging is obviously being accelerated, to start practicing the TM program.

David Orme-Johnson, Ph.D.

Dr. David Orme-Johnson is one of the leading researchers in the world on TM, and for several years in Switzerland was Maharishi's instrument for translating the scientific data to society.

Psychological studies of great leaders have shown that they are people who are more in tune with the silent strata of their own inner consciousness. This attunement with this inner silent level of consciousness is developed through the TM program. I think that Maharishi's great genius has been to bring out the knowledge that this total potential of Natural Law, the Unified Field discovered by modern physics, is identical with the silent inner nature of human nature—that human nature and nature in general are not two different things but are the same thing.

Charles Alexander, Ph.D.

Dr. Charles Alexander, Harvard University graduate, and expert on Moral Reasoning and Ego Development

When we taught and applied TM in Walpole State Prison as an adult developmental technology, it proved even beyond our wildest expectations to be an extremely powerful mechanism for releasing human development in the prison.

We found that with prisoners, half of the group was in for murder, and the other half were heroin addicts; their education ended in the ninth grade. They were not a group that was ripe for unfreezing human development. What we found in one year is the prisoners went up more on a measure of cognitive and social development—the best measure available in psychology—in one year than college students do in four years, and they did it at an age when development does not change.

John Hagelin, Ph.D.

Dr. John Hagelin is an American particle physicist, three-time candidate of the Natural Law Party for President of the United States, and the director of the TM movement for the United States. Dr. Hagelin was a researcher at CERN and the Stanford Linear Accelerator Center (SLAC) and is Director of the Board of Advisors for the David Lynch Foundation.

Since the fundamental properties of the Unified Field are identical to those of consciousness in its self-referral state, it is natural to conclude that the Unified Field of Natural Law and the field of pure consciousness are equivalent. This is easily verified through the TM technique, which opens human awareness to the direct experience of pure consciousness, where consciousness is found identified with the Unified Field of all the Laws of Nature.

Kurleigh King, Ph.D.

Dr. Kurleigh King was former Director General of the Institute of World Leadership, and former Secretary General of the Caribbean Economic Community.

There is not a single leader in this world who does not need rest—every single one. Most of them work 15 to 16 hours a day. By allowing them to have this deep rest without doing anything else, it improves their effectiveness. Being more rested results in clarity of thought, greater imagination, and better performance.

The TM program works for leaders at any level; the supervisor of a dozen or fifteen people in a single institution is a leader, and the principles of leadership will apply also to him or her.

Vermont Correctional Professionals

Richard Wright, Assistant Superintendent, Rutland CCC

Feelings run high in the community correctional centers, and you cannot really put your finger on it. Little and big incidents happen, and they all seem to run together. During that time when TM was introduced, I just felt in this facility those things were not happening, and people were going around saying—it is awfully quiet in here, what is going on? I would like to see all the staff and inmates meditate; I would like to see everyone do it.

John Carpenter, Correctional Officer, Rutland CCC, Vermont

Everyone who has worked in corrections knows that high security is very stressful at times. If all the staff and all the residents could have a certain time to meditate, I think the calming effects would be beneficial to the institution. I believe that the disciplinary reports would go down and the high risk that is involved toward the officers would be nil. The residence course on TM offered for staff was very relaxing, and the participants were members from probation and parole, other correctional officers, and a captain from the New York City police department. Monday morning when I came back from the residence course I was scheduled to work in the security housing unit. Work in high security, everyone knows, is very stressful at times. I was mellow and calm about the situation. I did not lose my temper and I had calming effects on the inmates. Residence courses provide time for deeper rest, to accelerate release of stress and expansion of consciousness under the supervision of a certified instructor of the TM program.

Claude Melanson, Probation Officer, Rutland CCC, Vermont

There are a lot of heated situations in my position as a Probation Officer. I am put on the spot to relate my facts clearly and in an orderly way, and I found a much greater ability to do that through meditation.

Karen Ross-Sheldon, Director of Volunteers, Rutland CCC, Vermont

When I first began practicing the TM technique, I found I could remember things that I never thought I would ever be able to remember all at one time. Everything became clearer, easier to do, and I am not as excitable as I might have been otherwise. Initially, I decided to learn the technique because my position is very stressful and well known for burnout—I did not want to burn out. I wanted to continue in the position, and be able to do a good job at it.

Appendix B

The Heart Lighter than a Feather

The left ventricle of the heart is the quadrant of the heart that is responsible for pumping blood throughout the body. When the heart contracts, blood is forced out of the left ventricle into the aorta, as the blood is distributed to every cell in the body. There are numerous anatomical and physiological problems associated with a thick or heavier left ventricle. The pressure of the blood increases as the walls become thicker. Just like a balloon, the thicker the wall of the balloon, the more pressure you need to blow it up. As the left ventricle wall increases in thickness and weight, the more pressure is needed to fill the ventricle and eject the blood from the ventricle throughout the body (Barnes, Treiber & Kapuku, 2012).

Research has been conducted in a randomized clinical trial with African-American participants which evaluated potential changes in the left ventricle mass after a year of practicing TM as compared to a health education control group. After a three-year study there was a clinically significant reduction in left ventricular mass in the TM and control groups. In addition to improved left ventricular mass, the TM group had psychological improvements such as reduced anxiety, depression, and trait anger, with increased energy levels and improved sleep, whereas the control group did not show improvements in these areas.

An MUM graduate shared with me a poetic and philosophical way of understanding the significance of this research on many levels, including the spiritual evolution of a human being. *In the spiritual tradition of ancient Egypt concerning the journey after dying, a person's heart—understood as the seat of consciousness and symbol of the soul—would be weighed against the feather of truth, justice and righteousness.* If the heart was lighter than the feather, that person could move forward to meet the Creator. If, however, the heart was heavier than the feather, that person needed to continue his or her journey until their heart became lighter than a feather. Even in modern times, a light heart is associated with less stress and right action, and a heavy heart is associated with stress and mistakes. The more your left ventricle weighs, the more likely it is that you will have a negative cardiac event in the future. When the heart is heavy, the left ventricle is not as elastic as it needs to be to absorb a sufficient volume of blood before it constricts again, distributing the blood from the heart throughout the body. If the heart muscle is thick, all the cells cannot be supplied with proper nutrition because there is not enough vasculature to handle the extra cardiac cell growth. Additionally, the electrical conductivity of the heart is impeded due to an increased resistance in the cardiac wall. Irregular electrical conductivity can cause fibrillations and arrhythmias in the heart. There are numerous other life-threatening events associated with an enlarged heart, or what is called left-ventricular hypertrophy.

The improved psychological wellbeing in the TM group was a side benefit. The control group did not mirror the psychological findings. The results of these research findings were published in the *Journal of Social and Behavioral Studies*, in the issue dedicated to the late Dr. Charles "Skip" Alexander. It is titled: Left ventricular mass regression with the TM technique and a health education program in hypertensive African-Americans.

The African-American community has a special sensitivity to these types of heart problems. There are disparities between African-Americans, who suffer disproportionately from hypertension, which can lead to left-ventricular hypertrophy if it remains unaddressed, and other groups. A study was conducted in Oakland, California at the West Oakland Health Center, which provided profound insight into African-American health (Barnes, Treiber & Kapuku, 2012).

Cross-cultural communications in health

In my conversations with African-American healthcare trainers, they postulated that just as an individual can influence his or her health with behaviors such as choosing healthy foods, exercising, meditating regularly and so on, the behavior of the health care providers when interacting with a client is also critical. People from different cultures have different expectations when it comes to health care. Culture counts in health and wellness, as well as death and dying. A patient who is not treated with respect by their health care provider may not comply with recommendations that could ease their pain or save their life. There are skills in assessing and affirming cultural differences. These differences are not deviant or deficient compared to some perceived superior culture—this is a learned cross-cultural skill. For example, a patient may intentionally not look the health care provider in the eyes out of respect according to the patient's culture. The health care provider may feel culturally disrespected if they are not looked in the eye. The health care professional may assume the patient is dishonest, shy, lying, or trying to hide something. The health care service personnel may treat the patient differently due to their own discomforts. This behavior impacts patient outcomes and contributes to health disparities found among various ethnic groups and cultures now living in America.

We have observed a societal evolution from Martin Luther King, Jr. to President Barack Obama. The interesting issue with President Obama is that he is a biological merger of the African and the white culture, and in a way he represents a transcendence of the divisiveness among cultures. The collective consciousness has changed. This is a reality beyond black and white, and the evolution of the collective consciousness is wisdom coming to light. Wisdom can rise to the top when ignorance is removed. Eventually, wisdom will manifest itself. The blockages of ignorance will fall to the side and allow wisdom and knowledge to prevail. As long as that can happen, we will be moving in the direction of enlightenment. I hope the coming years reflect positive changes that indicate we are shifting from an age of ignorance to an age of enlightenment. The transcendental stillness of pure consciousness is colorless, shapeless, and ageless—it is formless. You cannot hold onto hate while transcending; TM takes all of that away.

One of the threads that pervade this book is the recognition that people in their life have experiences that allows them to have a glimpse behind the veil of ignorance into cosmic life. Every human being possesses the cosmic inner stillness; if people did not have the ability to experience Transcendental Consciousness within them, these illuminating moments of insight and wisdom could not take place. It is not mood-making because it is a common experience in all the philosophical and spiritual traditions through human history, and in contemporary society. What has been highlighted through the book is the shared and universal story of the emergence of enlightenment.

Every time someone transcends through TM, they settle down and experience pure consciousness. If they can experience consciousness in its purest form, then when a person has a thought, impulse, or a desire, it will be more powerful and facilitate achievement and fulfillment. For example, the TM-Sidhi program helps an individual to experience thinking at more subtle and powerful levels of the mind. The TM-Sidhi training permits a person to think softly at a level where thought originates.

To have the skill of transcending is valuable for not only the African-American community, but for every community. To be able to sit quietly and experience that quiet inner stillness will strengthen the individual, the family, and society. If a person has the experience of peace daily, they will influence their external environment with peace, and live a life that is larger than the universe that we can see with our eyes. Most people are responding from trouble, pain, or some unfulfilled desires. The more we cultivate and integrate higher consciousness, the less bound we are by life's challenges. We can transcend problems, and operate from the deeper laws of nature within our own consciousness. Every culture needs this skill to be abundant. We need to continue to scientifically demonstrate that pure consciousness exists, and that it influences the body, mind, and behavior. This knowledge could change the world. We are ordinary people who have had the experience of transcending over the years, which has influenced our thinking and behavior. As a result of our experience, we are sharing what we know to contribute toward creating a better world.

Index

31733855R00315

Made in the USA
Lexington, KY
23 April 2014